AVENGING BATAAN

The Battle of ZigZag Pass

AVENGING BATAAN

THE BATTLE OF ZIGZAG PASS

For Bryant James.
Best of success at ECU. Hope you
enjoy this book.

B. David Mann may 22, 2003

B. DAVID MANN

Pentland Press, Inc.
www.pentlandpress.com

Oil painting on back cover entitled "Avengers of Bataan,"
by Rick Reeves. Courtesy of Americana Historical Art,
Willow Street, Pennsylvania.

PUBLISHED BY PENTLAND PRESS, INC.
5122 Bur Oak Circle, Raleigh, North Carolina 27612
United States of America
919-782-0281

ISBN 1-57197-302-8
Library of Congress Control Number: 2001 132679

Printed in the United States of America

This book is dedicated to all the men
who fought in the battle for ZigZag Pass.

TABLE OF CONTENTS

ILLUSTRATIONS

MAPS

PHOTOS

FOREWORD

America's military future looked bleak in May 1942. After nearly six months of war, its only army fighting the Axis had surrendered on Bataan and Corregidor. The Navy was beginning to flex its muscles, but nearly six more months would elapse before the Army took the offensive. MacArthur's vow to return to the Philippines had a hollow ring. How long would it take America to build a military machine capable of challenging the Japanese in the Philippines?

Surprisingly, the time came sooner than anyone had expected. First, on the island of Leyte in October 1944, then at Lingayen Gulf on Luzon in January 1945, the Americans landed in the Philippines and relentlessly pursued the Japanese. A third landing in late January 1945 would result in the capture of Bataan and Corregidor. Finally, the humiliating defeat of 1942 would be avenged.

Avenging Bataan: The Battle of ZigZag Pass tells the story of this first and most significant phase in the campaign to reconquer Bataan and Corregidor. Fought in Zambales Province north of the Bataan Province/Peninsula, this battle had to be won before Bataan could be liberated. Only then could Corregidor and three smaller islands at the entrance to Manila Bay be assaulted. Recapture of Corregidor would open the great port of Manila, sorely needed by MacArthur to complete his conquest of the Philippines.

By the end of January 1945, the Sixth Army had driven south from Lingayen Gulf and was poised to strike for Manila. General MacArthur assigned the Bataan phase of his campaign to liberate Manila to XI Corps. This corps, stationed on Leyte, would board transports and land on the west coast of Luzon 25 miles northwest of ZigZag Pass and 50 airline miles from Manila.

Hovering over Bataan was the ghost of the last American army to fight there, MacArthur's doomed Filipino-American force of 78,000 men. From January until April 1942, MacArthur's Philippine Army had fought with poorly armed infantrymen, antiquated artillery and one of the most miserable supply situations ever to befall an American armed force. When the army finally surrendered to the Japanese, its men were starving on one-quarter rations, and one day's supply of food remained in supply dumps.

MacArthur's new army, although well-fed, equipped, armed and manned to a level that would make the Japanese defenders gasp in admiration, would find the return to Bataan a hard task.

On 31 January 1945, XI Corps began a painful crawl through ZigZag Pass, a position defended by slightly more than 2000 Japanese. The corps's principal component, the untested 38th Infantry Division (National Guard), found that the dense jungle, rugged draws and razorback ridges negated U.S. matériel superiority. Putting an emphasis on speed versus fire support, the first American attacks barely dented the well dug-in and concealed Japanese positions. After repeated failures and only with the weight of American artillery, saturation of rear areas with bombs and napalm, and the determined efforts of individual riflemen could American lines advance. They did advance, but always at a cost.

One constant between the first and second campaigns for possession of Bataan was the determined professionalism and fanatical fighting qualities of the common Japanese soldier. Of great interest in the book is the detailed look into Japanese deployments and operations in ZigZag Pass, seen through Japanese eyes and reports. Seldom has the Japanese side of an action been so well portrayed.

For XI Corps and their Japanese opponents, the campaign's outcome was as predetermined as had been the first Bataan campaign. Only this time, the Japanese were the ones to be ground down and destroyed.

John W. Whitman
Alexandria, VA
Author of *Bataan: Our Last Ditch*

PREFACE

In April and May 1942, the American Army suffered the worst defeat in its history on the Bataan Peninsula and the island of Corregidor at the hands of the Japanese. After arriving in Australia, General MacArthur electrified both Filipinos and Americans with his promise, "I shall return." Bataan and Corregidor became household words in America, signifying a humiliating defeat that must be avenged. The Philippines would be a major battleground as soon as the Americans could mount an offensive.

The battle to recapture Corregidor in the latter half of February 1945 has been expertly covered in several publications. Before Bataan could be overrun and Corregidor conquered, however, ZigZag Pass, on the road connecting Subic Bay and Manila, had to be seized. The battle for this strategic pass occurred during the first two weeks of February 1945 when the world's attention was focused on the recapture of Manila and the freeing of American and Filipino internees. As a result, The Battle of ZigZag Pass received scant notice in American newspapers or later publications.

Avenging Bataan: The Battle of ZigZag Pass tells the story of America's re-entry to Bataan in 1945 after a three-year absence. It is told through the official U.S. Army records, published Japanese unit histories, interviews with both American and Japanese survivors of the battle and letters and monographs written by the participants. The Japanese sources provide an insight into Japanese methods and reactions in combat seldom found in other books about the War in the Pacific.

The seed that produced this book took root in 1984 when I resolved to record, for my children, my reminiscences of World War II in the Philippines. I first wrote from a personal viewpoint of the operations in which I participated on the islands of Luzon, Mindoro and Mindanao. The action at ZigZag Pass riveted my attention and seemed to demand more than a cursory, personal treatment. I had always had a gnawing curiosity to know the full story after my regiment, the 34th Infantry, retired under duress early in the battle. Attendance at reunions of both my own 24th Division and the 38th Division, to which my regiment was attached, revealed that I was not the only one consumed with curiosity. This book is an attempt to tell the story of the battle accurately and impartially from the point of view of both the Japanese and Americans.

BDM
Richmond, VA
February 2002

ACKNOWLEDGMENTS

I am indebted to many for assistance in writing this book, foremost to Robert Ross Smith of Lewisburg, WV, the United States Army historian who authored *Approach to the Philippines* and *Triumph in the Philippines*. He guided me toward the focus of the book by insisting that description of a battle would be more readily accepted than an account of personal experiences.

David E. Evans (now deceased), Professor of Japanese and Far Eastern History at the University of Richmond, provided unique help. From his military contacts in Japan, he initiated correspondence that led to meetings on the battlefield with Japanese participants in the battle. Their knowledge of the battle and access to Japanese records enabled me to give a picture of both sides of the story. Dr. Evans also taught me the truism that anyone who attempts to write history "must write a lot of letters."

Every manuscript must have a "devil's advocate" to have any chance of success. I am blessed in having two. The first was Lieutenant Colonel John W. Whitman, U.S. Army (Ret.), author of *Bataan: Our Last Ditch*, the definitive history of the First Battle for Bataan. An accomplished infantry officer, Colonel Whitman corrected errors in logistics and infantry tactics and recommended describing in greater detail weapons and equipment to give the manuscript more body. An excellent writer himself, he gave me many suggestions that have hopefully given my writing some measure of acceptability.

The second was Dr. Stanley L. Falk, noted historian of the Pacific War, author of *Bataan: The March of Death, Decision at Leyte, Liberation of the Philippines, Bloodiest Victory: Palaus* and *Seventy Days to Singapore*. Dr. Falk made several helpful suggestions, the most important of which was careful, complete footnoting. He pointed out many errors in the original manuscript and voided much extraneous material to streamline the final version.

Dr. Edward J. Drea, Chief, Research and Analysis Division for the Center of Military History, provided much information about the Japanese Army and submarine activity against Japanese shipping. He also kindly critiqued the portion of the book that deals with elements of the Japanese regiment, which defended ZigZag Pass.

Three former commanders of my regiment, the 34th Infantry, were a source of inspiration. They are: Major General Aubrey S. Newman, commander of the 34th on Leyte; Major General Chester A. Dahlen, Leyte and Mindanao; and Brigadier General Lester L. Wheeler, Mindanao and Occupation of Japan.

Interpreters and translators have been so essential to the completion of this work that I cannot give too much credit for their vital task. Dr. Evans took valuable time from his writing and teaching to correspond with his military contacts in Japan and translate two important documents. Ikuko Matsumoto Arche, professor of Japanese first at Randolph-Macon College, Ashland, VA, then at Emory University, Atlanta, GA, translated many letters, a considerable portion of a Japanese unit's reminiscences of the battle, and a section of the history of the 39th Japanese Infantry. Dr. Fumiko Radile, Professor of Japanese at Randolph-Macon Woman's College, Lynchburg, VA, translated major portions of the 39th's lengthy history. Takehiko Yoshikawa of Richmond translated many letters and the 100-page portion of the 39th Infantry's history covering the Battle of ZigZag Pass.

Teresita L. Fujita of Manila, a Filipina, interpreted during four visits by the author to the battlefield with former Japanese soldiers who fought in the battle. Tomi Takakuwa of Kobe, Japan, and Michiko Fukuda of Houston, TX, were most helpful in translating a battalion commander's memoirs of the battle. Throughout the book, I have taken the liberty of following the Western tradition of giving the first name and then the surname of the Japanese.

I am grateful to the American soldiers who kept diaries or wrote extensively about the battle. Their interest and scholarship inject a personal flavor and help interpret the action. These are: Paul Austin, Fort Worth, TX; Kenneth W. Brewer, New Albany, IN; Arthur Brinson; Donald B. Cameron, Mayfield Heights, OH; Chester A. Dahlen, San Antonio, TX; Weldon B. Hester, Riverview, FL; William J. McKenna, Albany, CA; George E. Morrissey; Hanford Rants, Downey, CA; James F. Schoonover, The Infantry School, Fort Benning, GA; Douglas W. Thornton Jr., Riverdale, GA; Stephen M. Walker, The Infantry School, Fort Benning, GA; and Edward E. Walters, The Infantry School, Fort Benning, GA.

Many others shared their reminiscences with me or provided information: Jean P. Ancelet, Indianapolis, IN; Lieutenant Commander Gerald R. Anderson, U.S. Navy; Bronco Atkinson, Las Vegas, NV; Donald M. Bayles, Southold, NY; David H. Bibby, Verona, NJ; R. S. "Buck" Bowen, Little Rock, AR; Jack E. Brown, Gallatin, MO; Robert S. Bruce,

Richmond, VA; Paul J. Cain, Urbana, IL; Charles W. Card, Houston, TX; Willis L. Chilcote, St. Louis, MO; Cecil O. Cox, Cayce, SC; W. John Cowart, Radnor, PA; Danny Cuomo, West Orange, NJ; Eric Diller, Redondo Beach, CA; Edwin A. Ellinghausen, New Orleans, LA; John J. Evert, Proctor, WV; J. Gordon Fairbrother, Pascoag, RI; Colonel and Mrs. Marc Fisher, U.S. Marine Corps; Clarence Fowler, Muncie, IN; George H. Franklin, Clarksville, IN; Jim Frederick, Arlington, TX; Max Garland, Pinehurst, NC; Edmund F. Henry, Attleboro, MA; Leon F. Hesser, Arlington, VA; Yoshikazu Higashi, Monterey, CA; Joseph H. Hodges, Jr., Hilton Head Island, SC; Peyton Hoge, III, Anchorage, KY; Sue Hopkins, Richmond, VA; Jessie T. Huberty, Wilton, CT; Kyujiro Iga, Kinosaki, Japan; Raymond Johnson, Jonancy, KY; George M. Jones, Tucson, AZ; Kiyotaka Kato, Shimoina, Japan; Don Kreis, Milford, IN; Wally Kuhner, Charleston, SC.

Also Robert P. Lavender, Hurst, TX; Robert W. Maraman, New Albany, IN; Kazunobu Miyazaki, Aioi City, Japan; Kiyoshi Morimoto, Hyogo Prefecture, Japan; Heiichi Nakamura, Hyogo Prefecture, Japan; Philip H. Nast, Northville, NY; Samuel J. Needham, Terre Haute, IN; Robert A. Newkirk, Franklin, IN; Tamotsu Nagai, Kyoto, Japan; Yuichiro Nagata, Tokyo, Japan; Takako Nagayoshi, Kagoshima, Japan; Donald R. Peach, Huntingburg, IN; James F. Pearsall, Lancaster, VA; Dorothy Rapp, West Point, NY; Edward J. Reese, National Archives, Washington, D.C.; Kenwood Ross, Springfield, MA; Wayne L. Sanford, Indianapolis, IN; Carl Schaad, McLean, VA; George R. Scott, Waco, TX; R. Gary Shields, Lake City, FL; Rudolph Sillato, Rochester, NY; John J. Slonaker and Richard J. Sommers, U.S. Army Military History Institute, Carlisle Barracks, PA; Mrs. Harry L. Snavely, Stuart, FL; Leroy Soden, Rochester, NY; Alan Stephens, New Albany, IN; Stuart W. Stillwell, Williamston, MI; Dennis Symanski, Pittsfield, MA; Atsumi Takakura, Kakogawa, Japan; William P. Todd, Tallahassee, FL; Clyde Townsend, New Albany, IN; Daniel Valles, Peoria, AZ; Ben H. Wahle, Burlingame, CA; Les Westfall, Evansville, IN; Jack Wheat, Louisville, KY; Toshio Yoda, Kinosaki, Japan and Hannah M. Zeidlik, Center of Military History, Washington, D.C.

Last, but far from least, I acknowledge the contribution of the many writers of the messages, daily reports, and unit journals written in 1945 and still extant in the National Records Center, College Park, MD. Sometimes writing in the heat of battle and usually at the end of the day, they described the action as it took place. I have used their voluminous papers to try to reconstruct the course of the battle and tell the American side of the story, whenever possible, in their own vernacular.

My daughter, Cathy Johnson, provided valuable help in revising the first chapter and in the typing of the final manuscript. I am especially grateful to my wife, Helen, for her proofreading as well as her companionship during division reunions. Her patience, support and encouragement during the many years of preparation of this volume are much appreciated. Only the writer commits errors or overlooks inaccuracies, and for either of these transgressions, I take full responsibility and blame.

BDM
Richmond, VA
February 2002

PART I
Preliminaries

FALL OF BATAAN

In the first four months of its war with Japan, America and the free world could show nothing but a grim list of reverses in the Pacific—Pearl Harbor, Hong Kong, Malaya, Singapore, Thailand, Java, Sumatra and Borneo. Buried in the constantly worsening war news of the day had been one still glimmering light—the hold-out of the "battlin' bastards of Bataan." Now this one light too was extinguished with the announcement by Secretary of War Henry L. Stimson on 10 April 1942 that the Filipino-American Army on Bataan had finally succumbed to overpowering Japanese forces the previous day.[1]

Anticipated and expected for months, the surrender was still a shock and embarrassment to a nation always victorious in the past. Military historians were quick to point out that the defeat and surrender of the Filipino-American force of 36,853 men the *New York Times* reported "as counted officially" was the worst in American history. But the number of prisoners must have been much larger. When the full story was known, it was difficult to reconcile this figure with the 75,100 established by later historians (after 3,000 men escaped to Corregidor) listed on the rolls of Luzon Force on 3 April.[2]

America had tried to provision the Bataan garrison during the four months it held off the Japanese. Secretary of War Henry L. Stimson said, "Several shiploads of supplies" were sent into the Philippines, "but for every ship that arrived safely, we lost nearly two. I am glad to say the men were never short of ammunition." Lack of food was the primary reason for the collapse of the defenses. Secretary Stimson, a former Governor General of the Philippines, echoing both Generals Douglas MacArthur, the initial commander of the forces on Bataan, and his successor, Jonathan Wainwright, had nothing but praise for the Filipinos fighting side by side with the Americans. "I believe it [the Philippines] to be a temporary loss. This country, in fulfillment of its pledge, will ultimately drive out the invaders."[3]

The entire nation took up the battle cry. Senator Tom Connolly, chairman of the Foreign Relations Committee, summed up the feelings of Congress, "Eventually, all lost ground will be recaptured." Chairman

Andrew J. May of the House Military Affairs Committee said, "It's tough to lose the Philippines, but, damn them, we'll be back." The British, no strangers to bravery and suffering, joined the chorus. The *London Daily Mail*, speaking of the American and Filipino troops said, "They have written a chapter of stubborn heroism which will never be forgotten."[4]

After the surrender of the surviving forces on Corregidor on 6 May, a curtain of silence descended upon the captives. Americans knew at the time of the surrender that they were starving on rations of scarcely 1,000 calories a day and that many were wounded or racked with dysentery, beriberi and malaria. Imprisonment would almost be a blessing. At least the captives' rations would be increased, the sick and wounded would receive attention and there would be no more fighting and killing. How wrong and naive was the American public during the first months of the war.

The fate of the prisoners was thrust abruptly on the world on the morning of 28 January 1944 when the newspapers told of the Bataan Death March—tales of atrocities so hideous as to be unbelievable. To a nation whose resolve for revenge was already hardened by 26 months of war, fresh stories of the brutal treatment directed toward the brave defenders of Bataan further fueled its hatred of the enemy and gave further reason to demand unconditional surrender of the perpetrators. *The New York Times* described the Japanese atrocities in remarkably accurate and comprehensive detail for breaking news reporting. Three officers, Commander Melvyn H. McCoy, USN, Indianapolis, IN; Lieutenant Colonel S. M. Mellnik, Coast Artillery Corps, Dunmore, PA; and Lieutenant Colonel (then Captain) William E. Dyess, Air Corps, Albany, TX, initially imprisoned on Luzon, were later transferred to Davao Penal Colony on Mindanao. They escaped, made their way to Australia and reported their experiences, relating only what they had endured or actually seen. Their reports were later verified in spades after the war when other prisoners returned.[5]

The prisoners were merely surviving at the time of the surrender and certainly in no condition to continue the fight. They had given their all only to begin a three-year nightmare of unimaginably brutal treatment, malnutrition and inattention to their diseases in camps in the Philippines, aboard ships to Japan and in Japan itself. Nearly half the approximately 10,000 Americans and an unknown, but certainly much greater number of Filipinos, would never return home alive.

The thousands of captives on Bataan had been herded the day after the surrender into a long procession of tired and bedraggled troops for a march of 65 miles to San Fernando, then a train ride to Capas and then a nine-mile march to Camp O'Donnell. The Japanese did not permit the Americans and Filipinos to eat any food they brought with them. They were searched immediately upon surrender. Food and personal belongings, especially rings and watches, were taken from them during the search. Prisoners with Japanese tokens or money in their possession were beheaded.

The trip by train was as terrifying as the march. The Japanese packed 115 men into small, narrow gauge boxcars for the trip from San Fernando to Capas. The doors were closed and locked; movement was impossible. Most of the prisoners were suffering from diarrhea and dysentery. The heat and stench were unbearable.

The march was an indescribable ordeal. Some men were bayoneted to death, others beheaded by the fiendish, saber-wielding Japanese. Leaving the march only temporarily for any reason brought swift retaliation, if not by a bayonet thrust, then by a rifle butt to the jaw. Faces were slapped because neither the Americans nor the Filipinos understood Japanese. Sun helmets were a priceless commodity against the relentless tropical sun. They were confiscated from the hapless prisoners even though the Japanese soldiers wore caps with long flaps of cloth over the neck to ward off the sun.

As they marched, prisoners observed ghastly sights along the road, some prisoners bayoneted, others run over and flattened by Japanese trucks. An officer asked permission to get water for his men and a guard beat him with a rifle butt. A Japanese officer finally allowed the prisoners to drink water from a carabao wallow. The Japanese inflicted a form of torture, which came to be known as the "sun treatment." Prisoners were made to sit in the broiling sun all day without cover. Half-crazed with thirst, six Filipino soldiers made a dash for a well for fresh water. All six were killed.

The individual Japanese soldier seemed to have a passion for barbaric behavior that could only be classed as callous, inhumane and sadistic. On two occasions, Filipino 2nd Lieutenant Mariano Villarin saw the enemy drive a truck deliberately into the marching column, killing one or two POWs and injuring several others. Other Japanese riding in trucks would jab men in the column with their bayonets, laughing uproariously as they sped away.

In one instance, 12,000 men were jammed into a space 100 yards square and compelled to stand on a concrete floor for seven days without food and with a single spigot as the only source of water. This kind of torture was repeated later in the war for longer periods of time as the

Japanese packed men like sardines aboard ships transporting prisoners among Japanese camps in the South Pacific and to Japan.

Hospital patients received no mercy. Hundreds still wearing their pajamas and covered with bandages were ordered out of the hospitals to join the march. The pitiful amputees hobbled along as best they could. The Americans and Filipinos had fought together to defend Bataan. Now they marched together out of Bataan in captivity, all suffering the same cruel treatment.

After the prisoners had been at Camp O'Donnell for one week, American soldiers were dying at the rate of 20 a day, Filipinos at 150 a day. After two weeks, the death rate for Americans had increased to 50 a day and for Filipinos, 500 a day. To find men strong enough to dig graves was a problem. Men shrank from 200 pounds to 90. They had no buttocks; they were human skeletons. Around 1 June, the American prisoners at O'Donnell were transferred to Cabanatuan.

Two American Army officers and a Navy officer attempted to escape from Cabanatuan. Their Japanese captors beat them about the feet and legs until they could no longer stand and then took them clad only in their shorts to the road in full view of the camp with their hands tied behind them. They were pulled up by ropes from an overhead beam, so they had to remain standing, but bent forward to ease the pressure on their arms. Here they stood for two days in the blazing sun. Periodically, the Japanese beat them with a two-by-four. Any Filipino unlucky enough to pass by was required to beat them and he himself was beaten if he didn't beat the prisoners hard enough. After two days of this, one of the officers was beheaded and the other two were shot.

Of the total force of 75,100 on 3 April, there were only 54,300 on the rolls at Camp O'Donnell on 4 June. The near 21,000 discrepancy was due to fighting, the Death March and the disease and starvation so prevalent at O'Donnell in the first two months of captivity. Most of the prisoners died of starvation, forced hard labor and general Japanese brutality.

These stories and those of other prisoners after the war seem to go on endlessly. Some former prisoners broke down when telling of the events and were unable to continue. They said that some Japanese actions were so fiendish that the interviewers would not believe the stories they could tell.[6]

Hatred became even greater after the barbarity and cruelty of the Japanese had been fully disclosed in January 1944. War Bond sales soared nationwide. The slogan for the remainder of the War Loan drive was changed to "Bonds for Bataan." "Ruin Japan" was the cry. Refusal of the Japanese Government to allow neutral inspections of the camps in the

Philippines or to permit the International Red Cross to visit the prison camps further inflamed and infuriated Americans.[7]

❧ ❧ ❧

The odyssey on Bataan had begun 23 December, the day after the Japanese landing at Lingayen Gulf, when General Douglas MacArthur decided to withdraw his forces to the Bataan Peninsula. All American and Filipino troops from northwest and southeast of Manila passed through two bottlenecks, first San Fernando and later Layac Junction and Dinalupihan, and reached the relative safety of Bataan in early January 1942.

MacArthur, commander of U.S. Army Forces Far East, could muster on Bataan 19,000 Americans of all branches of the service and 12,000 well-trained Philippine Scouts of the Philippine Division. To this nucleus could be added seven poorly-trained and ill-equipped—but loyal and valiant—Philippine Army divisions with some American officers, totaling approximately 60,000 men. These 91,000 swelled to beyond 100,000 when Philippine Constabulary and other supporting units were added. But there was only one regiment of regular United States infantry—the 31st Infantry of the Philippine Division.

It was essential that the Americans hold ZigZag Pass and Olongapo if the withdrawal into Bataan was to succeed. If the Japanese landed at Subic Bay and moved the 14 miles east through the pass to Dinalupihan, they could close the door to the only road into the peninsula from the east.

As early as 11 December, most of the 45th Infantry of the Philippine Division was in an assembly area on the Dinalupihan-Olongapo highway near the "zigzag" prepared to resist a hostile landing in Subic Bay and prevent any Japanese advance from Olongapo. On 19 December, when enemy vessels were reported to be in the vicinity of Subic Bay, the 57th Infantry of the same division occupied Olongapo to resist an expected invasion. Headquarters Bataan Defense Force G-2 summarized the situation bluntly on 28 December 1941: "The road junction at . . . Dinalupihan is vital to our forces and must be held at all costs until all of our troops have cleared the point."[8]

On that same day, Major General George M. Parker, Jr., commanding Bataan Defense Force, ordered probably his most reliable element, the United States 31st Infantry, to cover the withdrawal of troops through Layac Junction and then ". . . move without delay, via the Dinalupihan-Olongapo road, to the vicinity of the ZigZag . . ."[9] This movement was completed "5:45 P.M., 30 Dec. '41" when two battalions of the 31st American Infantry Regiment joined one battalion of the 31st Philippine

Division to set up a defensive line in ZigZag Pass at approximately the same positions the Japanese were to hold in 1945.

By 4 January 1942, most of the Filipino-American troops had moved into the Bataan Peninsula. Major General Jonathan M. Wainwright, commander of the North Luzon Force, ordered the units in ZigZag Pass to move to Layac Junction, destroy bridges as they withdrew and block the highway as much as possible.

Early in January 1942, General Count Hisaichi Terauchi, commander of the Japanese Southern Army, received the approval of Imperial General Headquarters (IGH) to remove the 48th Division from General

ZigZag Pass in the 1930s

Homma, the Japanese commander in the Philippines. The division had been earmarked for the invasion of Java after its mission on Luzon was completed. IGH replaced it with the untried 65th Brigade, called by its commander, "absolutely unfit for combat duty."[10] Gallant efforts by the Filipinos, fighting side by side with the Americans, successfully repulsed Japanese attacks during January, February and March.

In late March, the same IGH, which had taken the 48th Division prematurely, reinforced Homma with the 4th Division and additional artillery and air power. His renewed massive onslaught overwhelmed the Filipino-American troops and forced their surrender on Bataan on 9 April (the 77th anniversary of Lee's surrender to Grant) and on Corregidor on 6 May. IGH originally gave General Homma 50 days to conquer the Philippines. He was relieved after the final capitulation of the remaining American forces in the Philippines on 9 June and was returned to Japan to serve the rest of the war as a reserve officer.

The Japanese penchant for cruel and inhuman treatment of conquered peoples cost them dearly. Their goal was to replace the Western powers as the dominant force in Southeast Asia. They would be the leader of the Greater East Asia Co-Prosperity Sphere they envisioned for the countries of the Far East.

The timing was perfect for such a move. The Javanese were ready to throw out the Dutch and claim the Netherlands East Indies as their own. Millions in India, Burma and Malaya were tired of British rule and eager to rid themselves of the yoke of colonialism. By their arrogance, brutal treatment and ruthless exploitation of these fellow Orientals, the Japanese squandered a huge opportunity to create a true "Asia for the Asiatics."

Colonel Carlos P. Romulo, a Filipino on MacArthur's staff, placed the Japanese invasion of the Philippines in perspective. "In this battle, Filipinos were the first people in all history to fight by the side of the people who had been their conquerors. The fact that the Philippines had sided against all Asia on behalf of democracy was final proof of the pragmatic and Christian advantages of the American way."[11]

The surrender of Bataan and the revelation of the atrocities solidified the unity of the nation begun at Pearl Harbor. Just as the Navy was relentless and merciless in its pursuit and destruction of the Japanese fleet to avenge Pearl Harbor, the Army, personified by General MacArthur, was relentless in its determination to avenge Bataan. Almost three years would elapse before American forces would be strong enough to return to Bataan. There was no competition among Army units as to who would be the liberators of Bataan and Corregidor, but those selected, entirely by chance, would always take pride and satisfaction in their accomplishment.

The Japanese defenders in 1945 were the 39th Infantry Regiment of the 10th Division, a regiment with a long history of service to the Empire, two years fighting in China and four years training in Manchuria preparing to defend against an attack by the Soviet Union. ZigZag Pass would be its first engagement in the South Pacific. For the Americans, it would be the XI Corps composed of the untried National Guard 38th Division from Indiana and Kentucky and the regular Army 34th Infantry Regiment of the 24th Division, experienced, but heavily laden with replacements.

The mission of the Americans was hazy to the individual soldier at the outset of the campaign. Many thought they were to join Sixth Army's attack toward Manila, but the liberation of Bataan and Corregidor was to be their goal. Revenge for the surrender of Bataan and shameful treatment by the Japanese of U.S. soldiers was a seldom discussed but ever present motive for making this operation successful. Some of the stories the men had heard about the Death March defied logic and the actions of sane men. "Remember the Alamo" and "Remember Pearl Harbor" had been rallying cries in the past. For the men of XI Corps, the rallying cry could have been "Remember Bataan!"

Despite differences in race, history, culture and education, the soldiers of the American corps shared one attribute in common with their counterparts in the Japanese regiment on Bataan. Both the Americans and the Japanese came from warlike nations with centuries of military tradition handed down from generation to generation. Both drew on romantic pasts to fill their cup of courage. Both had ancient heroes: the Samurai for the Japanese and the Knights of the Round Table for the Americans. Both had battle creeds—*Bushido* (the way of the warrior) for the Japanese and Chivalry for the Americans. As the ruling class, the samurai had set the Japanese standards for waging war; the military art of their American opponents had been honed for centuries on battlefields across North America and Europe.

Recent history provided both Americans and Japanese with stirring military performances to emulate. From the Meiji Restoration of 1868 to the early successes of World War II, the Russo-Japanese War of 1904-05 was the crowning achievement of Japanese arms. To the Japanese soldier this was *the* war that his family referred to just as the Civil War and in turn World War I was *the* war to successive generations of Americans.

Many Japanese soldiers could name a father or grandfather who had fought in 1904-05 just as many of the Americans' fathers had fought in World War I and grandfathers and great-grandfathers in the Civil War. Men from both sides were proud of their respective nations and the military service of their ancestors and ready to follow in their footsteps. The fortunes of war had placed them on unforgettable Bataan—symbolic to the Japanese as their hardest fought conquest in Southeast Asia, and to Americans as the most devastating defeat in their history—followed by the most brutal treatment imaginable to its men who became prisoners.

Map 1: The Philippines

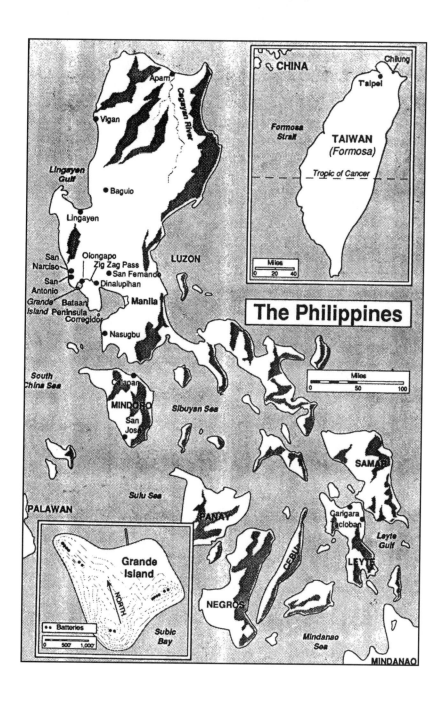

Chapter 1
NOTES

(1) *New York Times*, 10 April 1942, p. 1.
(2) *New York Times*, 10 April 1942, p. 1;
Whitman, John W., *Bataan: Our Last Ditch, the Bataan Campaign*, p. 605.
(3) *New York Times*, 10 April 1942, p. 1.
(4) *New York Times*, 10 April 1942, p. 4.
(5) *New York Times*, 28 January 1944, p. 1.
(6) *New York Times*, 28 January 1944, p. 1;
Falk, Stanley L., *Bataan: The March of Death*;
Knox, Donald, *Death March: The Survivors of Bataan*;
Villarin, Mariano, *We Remember Bataan and Corregidor*;
Whitman, *Our Last Ditch*, p. 605.
(7) *New York Times*, 29 January 1944, p. 1.
(8) *The Wainwright Papers*;
Headquarters Bataan Force G-2 Report #13, 6:00 P.M. 28 Dec. 1941.
(9) Headquarters Bataan Force Special G-3 Report #4, 11:00 A.M. 29 Dec. 1941.
(10) Morton, Louis, *The Fall of the Philippines*, p. 262.
(11) Romulo, Carlos P., *My Brother Americans*, p. 7.

THE JAPANESE 39th INFANTRY ARRIVES ON LUZON

It is not to be implied that all Japanese soldiers were as revengeful and full of venom as those pictured in Chapter 1. The Japanese conquerors of Bataan had been fighting a battle that was supposed to have been over in 50 days, but had dragged on for four months. They were in a foul mood, tired and disease-ridden. They showed little mercy for an enemy who had embarrassed them and whom they could not overcome until heavily reinforced. In contrast, ZigZag Pass was the first battle of the Pacific War for the 39th Infantry. None of its men were ever accused of atrocities or bullying of American soldiers or Filipino civilians. Their appearance in battle was late in the war when the Japanese soldier had a healthy respect for the Americans that was not evident early in the war.

The 39th Infantry, the enemy troops holding ZigZag Pass, was one of 15 Japanese regiments organized during the decade following Japan's humiliation by the European powers at the conclusion in 1895 of the Sino-Japanese War. Although this was to be its first and only battle of World War II, the regiment had trained in Manchuria since 1940 for this first test of its combat readiness. Its men had a venerable and storied tradition to uphold. Few Imperial Japanese Army regiments could boast of a more glorious history or were better trained.

In a ceremony replete with pomp and tradition, the 39th Infantry had been born 24 March 1898. At the Imperial Court in Tokyo, the Emperor Mutsuhito, with an appropriate inspirational message, presented an Imperial Standard to the Minister of War, who entrusted it to the regimental flag bearer, a second lieutenant. The bearer immediately entrained for 10th Division Headquarters in Osaka. Two days later, one of the division's two brigade commanders presented the standard to Colonel Naofumi Oka, the 39th Infantry's first leader. The brigade commander read the emperor's message to the entire regiment drawn up in the form of a horseshoe on the Jonan Parade Ground in Himeji. Then, Colonel Oka mounted his horse, and with saber drawn and trumpets sounding, led his regiment in a review to honor the regimental standard.[1]

Granting a standard as a symbol of Imperial authority dated back to the early 13th century. The practice was revived when the Emperor Mutsuhito ushered in the Meiji era in 1868. The Standard presented to Japanese regiments stood for a different set of values than the regimental flags used in armies of other countries. In Japan, the standard was regarded as an icon and served as an inspiration to the troops; in other armies, the regimental flag merely designated the unit.[2]

The Imperial Standard or battle flag, as it could also be called, symbolized the Samurai Spirit and the Bushido creed so essential to the success of the Japanese Army. The standard presented to Colonel Oka was to play an unusual and significant role in the history of the 39th Infantry.

During the Russo-Japanese War of 1904-05, as part of the 4th Army, the 10th Division with its 39th Infantry participated in the drive northward against Mukden from July 1904 to March 1905. The regimental commander, Colonel Norio Yasumura, was shot and killed instantly in a dawn attack in October 1904 against a key terrain feature. Five successive flag bearers, all company grade officers, and all killed or wounded, led the regiment and pressed the attack home. The blood of two of the bearers stained the flag. Throughout the next 40 years until the Army was disbanded in 1945, the 39th Infantry proudly carried the only battle flag in the Japanese Army known as the "blood-stained standard."[3]

The 10th Division received orders in June 1940 to move to Manchuria. As the 39th was preparing for the move from its home in Himeji, the regimental commander asked the flag bearer, 2nd Lieutenant Shigeya Wada, to repair the colors. A bullet in the Russo-Japanese War had weakened the flag's staff and portions of the flag were coming apart. Wada was unable to obtain permission from Tokyo, as was the custom, to make the repairs. With the help of the regimental blacksmith shop, he repaired the staff and sewed the tattered flag together himself.[4]

Indoctrination was a valuable part of the training in the Imperial Japanese Army. The regimental commander, Colonel Takeshi Sakai, supervised this phase of the training himself. He addressed the new recruits in "a loud but dignified voice," extolling the sanctity of the regimental colors, which had been "dyed by their ancestors' blood." The colonel made it clear that each soldier could do no less than fight as bravely as his forefathers against Russia and that he must be ready to lay down his life for his Emperor.[5]

The 10th Tetsu (Iron) Division conducted all of its training during the next four years in the harsh climate and rough, sparsely vegetated terrain of northern Manchuria. On 26 July 1944, the division received orders to entrain at its camp at Chiamussu, Manchuria, and then ship south. Everyone knew its final destination could only be the tropics. According to the 39th Infantry history, "the division had been training for armored warfare as part of larger units, and its degree of training was considered to be exceptionally high. However, it had not trained for the type of operations required for island defense in the south, particularly for coastal defensive fortifications."[6]

Colonel Sanenobu Nagayoshi, Commander 39th Infantry, IJA

The 39th Infantry's commander at this point in its history, Sanenobu Nagayoshi, was born 21 June 1894 in Kagoshima, Kyushu. He was the fifth son of a large family. In 1916, he was graduated from the Army Academy as a 2nd Lieutenant of Infantry and was immediately assigned to the 58th Regiment at Kurume in northwestern Kyushu. Promoted to major in 1934, he held his first important position, Chief of the Administrative Staff (Adjutant) 16th Division in Kyoto. From 1938 to 1940, he led a battalion in the fighting in China where he was awarded the Imperial Order of the Golden Kite 4th Class, the Imperial Order of the Rising Sun Small Cordon, and probably more important, ¥4000 in gold. In 1940, he was promoted to Lieutenant Colonel and in 1942 was Military Advisor to a provincial government in Manchuria. From there, he moved to the 39th Infantry at Chiamussu.[7]

Forming with a convoy, the regiment started south on 16 August. The American submarine *Ronquil* on its first patrol, under command of Henry S. Monroe, was lurking off northern Kyushu. Monroe shadowed the convoy and compelled it to take refuge for one night in Kagoshima harbor, Nagayoshi's hometown, at the southern end of Kyushu. Resuming the voyage, the convoy moved stealthily southward until 23 August when it was within sight of the scenic deep-water port of Chilung (or Keelung or Kiirun) at the northeastern tip of Formosa.

At 0400 hours in a misty rain, the *Ronquil* took aim at the 7,000-ton *Edogawa-maru*. This lead ship carried Colonel Nagayoshi, Headquarters, Company 39th Infantry, the 2nd and 3rd Battalions, the 37-mm Anti-tank

Company, the Communications Company and the Operations Company. By alert, evasive maneuvers, the ship's captain saved his valuable cargo by dodging the first torpedo, which missed by only six feet. The torpedo plowed into the starboard side of the 4,646-ton *Yoshida-maru #3*. Down it went with a loss of life of 166 men, mostly in the 1st Battalion. At 0700 hours the next day, *Ronquil* seriously damaged the 5,569-ton *Fukurei-maru*, which beached itself on Formosa's northern coast. Nagayoshi's ship reached port unscathed.[8]

The 10th Division started immediately to dig defenses on Formosa in expectation of an American invasion. The invasion came not from the sea, but from the sky. On 12 October, Admiral William F. Halsey's 3rd Fleet unleashed a powerful attack on Formosa to destroy installations and neutralize Japanese air power prior to the invasion of Leyte on 20 October. Task Force 38, supported by 109 B-29s of the XX Bomber Command based in China, pulverized Formosa in one of the most devastating raids of the Pacific War. In the three-day battle, American airmen destroyed more than 500 enemy planes, sank some two-score freighters and small craft, damaged many others and wreaked enormous destruction on ammunition dumps, hangars, barracks, shops and industrial plants. The 39th Infantry suffered no casualties in manning its anti-aircraft defenses during the raid nor did it inflict harm on the enemy.[9]

On 13 October, while the air raid was in progress, the Chief of Staff of the 10th Division, Colonel Sakae Tsuchiya, and Major Takenori Kashiwagi, the 39th Infantry's executive officer, were visiting the Navy 2nd Air Fleet Headquarters at Okayama, Japan. The naval officers gave a toast to the Imperial Japanese Navy for winning the great naval battle at Taiwan.[10]

The Japanese navy had reported sinking eleven enemy carriers, two battleships, three cruisers, and a light cruiser or destroyer and damaging eight carriers, two battleships, four cruisers, and fourteen unidentified ships. Major Kashiwagi reported these fictitious American losses upon his return, much to the joy of the men of the 39th Infantry, who felt that Japan was winning the war.[11]

In reality, the only damage the Japanese had inflicted on the huge American Task Force was to hit two cruisers with torpedoes. Both were towed back to Ulithi Atoll and repaired. The Americans lost 76 planes in the three-day raid.[12]

&* &* &*

At midnight on 6 November, lights still burned brightly in 10th Division headquarters. Messengers rushed orders to each of the division's scattered units. The 10th Division was moving to the Philippines! There could really be only one answer to the question "where?" Leyte was under siege by four American divisions. Reinforcements were badly needed, but first they had to run the American gantlet of submarines and planes patrolling the western shores of Luzon and Leyte.

"Hurry up and wait" was also an axiom in the Imperial Japanese Army. Shipping was at a premium. Even when shipping was available, it was touch-and-go whether ships would reach their destination. A month would elapse before the 39th Infantry would sail.

On 5 December, the regiment (minus the 1st Battalion) loaded into two transports at Takao (Gaoxiong)—the 10,000-ton *Arimasan-maru* with a speed of 20 knots and a former Japanese luxury liner, the 8,000-ton *Oryoku-maru*. The 39th was familiar with the *Arimasan-maru*, which had sailed in the convoy from Moji to Kiirun and had been damaged by the American submarine *Ronquil*. Tamotsu Nagai, Communications Sergeant of a machine gun company and editor of the company's reminiscences, remembered the now-repaired hole in its bow through which he had once looked inside.[13] The ill-fated *Oryoku-maru* was destined to be the "hell-ship" for 1,600 Allied and American prisoners of war crammed into three holds. American planes sank the ship on 15 December 1944 at the naval station at Subic Bay.

Soldiers with their weapons, equipment and bundles of personal belongings crowded the decks. Each machine gun squad prepared for anti-aircraft fire. A crewman reassured the nervous soldiers of the 39th, "The *Arimasan-maru* is a lucky ship! Torpedoes won't touch her." At 1500, the transport glided slowly out of the harbor and formed up with the convoy.[14]

Anti-submarine aircraft and two destroyers were to accompany the transports, but the aircraft never appeared. A soldier, in the regimental headquarters company, T. Takai, reminisced about the trip after the war. He reported that American planes or submarines would suddenly attack night or day and attempt to sink the convoy. Everyone aboard felt the convoy would probably be sunk. Crews held frequent shipwreck drills.

After the ships were well to sea from Takao, a near miss from a torpedo rocked the *Arimasan-maru* aft. Assuming the ship had been hit, Colonel Nagayoshi's first thought was to save the regiment's colors. He stripped the colors from the flagpole and bound the flag securely around his waist. If the ship sank, he was prepared to go down with the "blood-stained" flag.[15]

Unseasonable winds and choppy seas met the convoy in the Bashi Channel between Taiwan and Luzon. Packed into poorly ventilated holds, the infantrymen fell by the score to seasickness. By careful surveillance, constant zigzagging and maintaining a course close to islands, both transports miraculously reached Manila safely on 10 December.[16]

✸   ✸   ✸

Upon landing in Manila, Lieutenant General Yasuyuki Okamoto, commander of the 10th Division, and his Chief of Staff, Colonel Sakae Tsuchiya, were waiting at the pier. They escorted the 39th Infantry commander and his Executive Officer, Major Takenori Kashiwagi, to the 14th Area Army Headquarters, commanded by General Tomoyuki Yamashita, recently ordered to the Philippines to retrieve Japan's sagging fortunes.

As one of four lieutenant generals[17] leading the initial Japanese onslaught in 1941-42, Yamashita's 25th Army of three divisions had thrust like lightning down the Malay Peninsula in a campaign the British thought impossible. Given 100 days, Yamashita's skill, imagination, determination and decisiveness enabled his troops to conclude the campaign in 70 days, despite being outnumbered two to one. But in the Philippines, neither the 59-year-old "Tiger of Malaya," nor anyone else, could slow the United States advance for long in 1945.[18]

General Yamashita named Colonel Nagayoshi the commanding officer of the new "Nagayoshi Detachment." The core of the approximately 3,500-man detachment would be the 2nd and 3rd Battalions of the 39th Infantry, supplemented by the 6th Battery 10th Field Artillery Regiment, the 2nd Company 10th Engineer Regiment, an infantry battalion from the 23rd Division and a mobile gun platoon (the latter two units were later detached and reassigned).[19]

Staff officers from the 14th Area Army had dusted off an old plan to land a force on the northwest coast of Leyte at Carigara and attack the American forces now pressing hard against the nearly-spent Japanese 1st Division. Yamashita would have preferred to keep all his troops on Luzon, but he had little choice because of IGH's decision to fight the decisive battle of the Philippines on Leyte. Both he and his chief of Staff, Lieutenant General Akira Muto, felt the operation would fail, but decided to make this one last effort. According to Muto, Yamashita, "sacrificing himself to the will of Imperial General Headquarters," finally gave in. The landing would take place just after midnight 16 December.[20]

The 14th Area Army Headquarters conducted three map maneuvers and liaison conferences with the detachment staff and the Navy. General Yamashita and General Muto explained the urgency and importance of the mission to the officers at dinner the evening of 13 December preparatory to embarkation the next day.[21]

General Muto bluntly summarized the situation. "The Nagayoshi Detachment's attack is the key to success or failure in the battle for Leyte Island. If it goes well, more units will be sent; if not, this unit will be the last. I wish you success."[22]

General Yamashita provided a bottle of beer for each officer. Toasts were exchanged for success in battle and for the safety of the soldiers' lives. The officers pledged to accomplish the mission, but none doubted that the landing and attack would be suicidal. Few expected to return alive. Because the Americans completely dominated the air and seas, General Yamashita feared the detachment would not even reach Leyte. His exhortation to the officers to do their duty was, in reality, his condolences and apology for having to follow orders and send them to their deaths.[23]

However, the American invasion of Mindoro interrupted Yamashita's plans. Colonel Nagayoshi's old nemesis from the 39th's days on Formosa, Admiral Halsey, was determined to prevent Japanese planes based on Luzon from attacking the convoy carrying troops for the 15 December invasion. Halsey and his new Task Force 38 commander, Vice Admiral John S. McCain, put into effect an innovation that had been contemplated, but not tried because of a lack of planes. This was the "Big Blue Blanket" (B. B. B.), an umbrella of fighter-bombers maintained round-the-clock over Luzon's airfields, so that no enemy aircraft could take off. Those that tried would be destroyed in the air.[24]

McCain had greatly increased his striking power by doubling the effectiveness of his big carriers. He had modified his fighters so that each could now carry 2,000 pounds of bombs and fly a bombing mission unescorted.[25]

The "B. B. B." was a complete success. During the three days from 14 to 16 December, no Luzon-based aircraft attacked the Mindoro-bound convoy; those Japanese planes that did get through came from the Visayan fields. Task Force 38 flew 1,671 sorties of the fighter-bombers, which destroyed 270 Japanese planes, 208 of which were on the ground.[26]

The Japanese had monitored the American convoy since its departure from Leyte on 12 December. Because of its southern route through the Mindanao and Sulu Seas, they thought its destination might be Negros or Panay Islands. The 14th Army Area Headquarters alerted all air and ground units on these islands to prepare to resist a landing. The Army finally determined on the afternoon of 14 December that the convoy was headed for Mindoro. Fearing that the next American landing might come on Luzon's west coast or southwest of Manila, Yamashita issued orders that evening canceling the Nagayoshi Detachment's Leyte mission. He assigned the detachment to Major General Takashi Kobayashi's Manila Defense Force and ordered the detachment's immediate deployment to the Bataan Peninsula. The detachment was to travel the next day by land and water to repel any enemy landings on Bataan. Nagayoshi was authorized to assume command of Manila Defense Force elements already stationed on Bataan.[27]

It was just as well that the detachment's move to Leyte was canceled. The three-day umbrella over Luzon had other effects besides destroying Japanese planes. Early on the morning of 14 December, McCain's fighters sank three or four freighters and one or two LSVs (the Japanese LST) in Manila Bay. These were some of the craft that were to have borne the Nagayoshi Detachment to Leyte.[28]

With little time to develop a plan for the defense of Bataan, Nagayoshi faced the same problem—but with far fewer troops—that the Americans had faced in 1942: how to defend this rugged, mountainous, jungled peninsula—with no escape hatch—without control of the seas or air. Despite American intelligence estimates of 13,000 enemy soldiers in Bataan and Zambales Provinces,[29] there were actually only 4,000 troops defending this area—the Nagayoshi Detachment, the garrison troops already stationed at Olongapo, Bagac and Mariveles and the air personnel at San Marcelino.

The peninsula measures 30 miles north to south from ZigZag Pass to Mariveles and 20 miles at its greatest width from Moron to Orani. A gravel road (1942-1945) from Pilar on the east coast to Bagac on the west bisects the peninsula. The northern half is dominated by 4,222-foot Mount Natib and the southern by even higher 4,700-foot Mount Bataan. A hard surface north-south road on the east coast connected Dinalupihan and Mariveles. The less-defined road on the west coast north from Mariveles reached only as far as Moron.

Nagayoshi's mission had been clearly stated in 14th Area Army's new orders to the Manila Defense Force (Operational Policy Outline for Luzon dated 20 December 1944). The order directed in part: "4. Garrison forces in the Bataan area (Nagayoshi Detachment) will occupy established positions and endeavor to repel any enemy landing attempt in this area. If a landing is made, it will hinder an advance from the beachhead and endeavor to consume enemy strength."[30]

Therefore, expecting the main American landing to be at Subic Bay and its port of Olongapo, Colonel Nagayoshi chose elevated, mountainous, densely overgrown ZigZag Pass as the best ground for accomplishing his dual mission of repelling a landing and making the enemy pay for any advance from the beachhead. Through Zigzag Pass ran the only road between Olongapo and Dinalupihan and thence north to Clark Field or south to Manila. By fortifying ZigZag Pass, Nagayoshi felt he could interfere with a landing in Subic Bay and slow down any American attempt to reach the Central Plain of Luzon.

The detachment commander, therefore, decided to place more than half his troops in the northern sector of the peninsula to defend ZigZag Pass. Fearing American landings on the west coast of Bataan similar to those of the Japanese in 1942, he assigned about one-third of his force to central Bataan. He felt that well fortified Corregidor would discourage any initial American landing in southern Bataan; hence he stationed the fewest troops at Mariveles.[31]

The 3rd Battalion 39th Infantry would be the main force in the north, the 2nd Battalion in the center and the forces already in Mariveles would form the core of the defenses in the south. The main force embarked from Manila for Limay, across the bay on Bataan's east coast, the night of 15 December. Some of the boats had mechanical trouble and the lead boat became lost. Daylight found the boats still on the water, which attracted three American twin-fuselage P-38s. The planes, each equipped with a 20-mm cannon and four 50-caliber machine guns, hit three of the boats, killing 8 and wounding 14 in the Regimental Gun Company and 9th Company and destroying a 75-mm gun. The 5th and 7th Company men jumped into the bay and suffered no casualties. The remainder of the detachment did not depart Manila by land until the morning of 16 December because of mechanical difficulties with its trucks.[32]

To reinforce the troops he had brought to Bataan, Nagayoshi found a motley—but what proved to be a reasonably effective—assortment of units already on the peninsula. There were provisional company-size garrisons and naval personnel at each of the two main ports, Olongapo and Mariveles, and an independent infantry company from the 105th Division at Bagac. A sizeable contingent of air personnel operated the San Marcelino Airfield. An unknown number of Formosan laborers were available to help construct defenses.[33]

❖   ❖   ❖

Colonel Nagayoshi thought he had not a moment to lose. A rumor had spread that an American invasion in his sector would come Christmas

Day. Accordingly, he started Major Hironori Ogawa's 3rd Battalion (9th, 10th and 11th Companies) with heavy weapons toward ZigZag Pass with instructions to dig preliminary positions. From his temporary headquarters in Orion, Nagayoshi gave Major Ogawa his mission: march through Dinalupihan, establish a defensive position near Olongapo and stop the enemy landing expected at Subic Bay.[34]

Major Hironori Ogawa, Commander 3rd Battalion 39th Infantry

The 3rd Battalion left Limay after sunset 16 December and started its march to Balanga, the capital of Bataan Province. After provisioning themselves and the horses at Balanga, 1st Lieutenant Iwao Sakura, commander of the garrison infantry company at Olongapo, guided Ogawa's men, using the same trucks that had transported the 2nd Battalion and the artillery and engineers to Bataan. Traveling by night, the trucks bearing the 3rd Battalion shuttled their way without lights at only 10-15 mph.[35]

Ogawa and his key leaders reached the Olongapo area on 18 December ahead of their troops. About three miles northeast of the town they found a ridgeline in ZigZag Pass that afforded excellent defensive positions. Their objective was to prepare fortifications in depth designed to stop at least one enemy division. They complained of the difficulty (as the Americans were to discover later) in establishing positions for units and preparing attack and firing plans in dense jungle without adequate maps.[36]

By 22 December, they had prepared rough sketches of the terrain, assigned areas for the units and begun to place their men in their firing positions. Nagayoshi spent three hectic days gathering his forces, particularly the naval garrison in Olongapo commanded by Lieutenant (jg) Chusaku Ito, and urging his troops to dig in as best they could. The emergency battle preparations were complete by the evening of 24 December, but the tension-filled Christmas Day passed with no sign of the enemy.[37]

Colonel Nagayoshi expanded this area for his permanent defense of ZigZag Pass to about 4,000 yards in length along Philippines National Route 7. With the Santa Rita (Takamine) River as a rough midway point, the Japanese constructed their defenses on ridge lines perpendicular to the road at the eastern and western ends of this area. The eastern defenses came to be known by the Japanese as the East Pass, and the western defenses as the West Pass.[38]

The 50-year-old detachment commander initially established his main headquarters in Dinalupihan so as to maintain better communications with the Kembu Group occupying Clark Field and his detachment forces in central and southern Bataan. However, the Filipino guerrillas of Lieutenant Colonel Gyles Merrill, commander of all guerrilla forces in Zambales and Bataan provinces, constantly harassed the headquarters. Using 1,440-foot dome-shaped Mount Malasimbo northwest of Dinalupihan as observation post and site for mortars, the guerrillas made life miserable in Dinalupihan. Leaving most of the 5th Company to guard Dinalupihan, Nagayoshi moved into his new headquarters 23 January. In tribute to the guerrillas, the Japanese called Mount Malasimbo "guerri-yama."[39]

The new headquarters was dug into the side of Mount Kongo several hundred yards north of his battle command post in the East Pass. Nagayoshi designated Major Ogawa's line in the West Pass his main defenses (the American term was Main Line of Resistance (MLR)).[40]

On 23 January, Nagayoshi hastily formed a provisional infantry battalion (to be described later) composed of the airmen from San Marcelino. He placed this battalion under command of Major Takao Nakayama, who had been attached to the 39th Infantry when it left Manila for the Bataan Peninsula. The Nakayama Battalion prepared its defensive positions on a lower range of hills east of the East Pass with the primary mission of repelling any enemy advance from Dinalupihan.[41]

Nagayoshi assigned two 105-mm artillery pieces of the 6th Battery 10th Field Artillery Regiment to Major Ogawa. He also gave Ogawa Lieutenant Sakura's provisional infantry company and the naval personnel already encamped in Olongapo. These additions increased the number of troops defending ZigZag Pass, including headquarters personnel and the Nakayama Battalion, to slightly more than 2,000. Colonel Nagayoshi designated these forces the North Garrison Unit.[42]

On 28 December, the Nagayoshi Detachment came under command of the 2nd Tank Division. The Chief of Staff of the division visited Detachment Headquarters and brought with him a platoon of either two or three tanks. After forming the Nakayama Battalion, Nagayoshi allotted the platoon of tanks to Major Nakayama. The latter's positions east of the East Pass were located in better tank country—more open and less mountainous—than the terrain between the East and West Passes.[43]

In compliance with his orders to repel an American landing, Major Ogawa established an outpost at a "U" turn on Highway 7 a mile west of Olongapo. On 2 January 1945, riding his horse "Harukawa" (spring river), Ogawa personally led the Water's Edge Position Guard Troop (as this first outpost was named) through Olongapo to its assigned area. The force consisted of two 37-mm anti-tank guns and crews, a heavy machine gun squad and an infantry rifle squad. From a peninsula jutting into Subic Bay at the "U" turn, his men could fire on the landing, which was expected at Olongapo. The defenders could also ambush the Americans if they advanced from the west on Highway 7.[44] (See inset Map #4, p. 90.)

Highway 7 (view from Mount Koko)

Ogawa ordered 1st Lieutenant Iwao Sakura, commander of the 6th Company 2nd Provisional Battalion, to form a second outpost along Highway 7 about a mile west of the main line. The 14th Area Army had formed the 2nd Provisional Battalion of six companies in Manila in October 1944 from Japanese civilians and fully recovered wounded soldiers. The Sakura Company of about 150 men had come to Olongapo in November. Under its energetic and resourceful commander, the company had patrolled vigorously for more than a month out of Olongapo, scouting and raiding Filipino guerrillas.[45]

Colonel Nagayoshi distributed his remaining forces less liberally in central and southern Bataan. The Central Garrison Unit headquartered at

Bagac was composed of Major Shozo Yamamoto's 2nd Battalion, which was hardly more than the 6th Company. Nagayoshi had retained two-thirds of the 5th Company in ZigZag Pass as Detachment Headquarters Guard, and the 7th Company was assigned to guard the east coast road at Orion under command of the South Garrison Unit. Nagayoshi reinforced the 2nd Battalion with two extra 37-mm anti-tank guns, acquired on 14 December from the Manila Armory, and stationed the other two 105-mm howitzers of the 6th Battery 10th Field Artillery Regiment at Mariveles.[46]

☙ ☙ ☙

Disorganization, bordering on panic, seized the Japanese on Luzon in late December 1944 as they frantically prepared for the American invasion they expected at Lingayen Gulf. One of the 14th Area Army's main objectives was to prevent the capture of Clark Field. The Japanese had to guard against an American overland advance from Lingayen or the Bataan Peninsula or capture of the strategic airbase by airborne assault.[47]

The 14th Area Army had originally given the 2nd Tank Division the mission of thwarting such an attempt on Clark Field. When the Nagayoshi Detachment was detached from the Manila Defense Force in late December and placed under command of the 2nd Tank Division, the 14th Area Army considered sending Nagayoshi to Angeles to augment the defenses of Clark Field. By this time, however, the Nagayoshi Detachment was digging in on Bataan and could give only indirect support to Clark Field by impeding an American advance from Subic Bay to the Central Plain and then north to the airbase. Nagayoshi was never able to establish personal contact with Lieutenant General Yoshiharu Iwanaka, commander of the 2nd Tank Division, not even by radio.

Communications did not improve when 14th Area Army Headquarters reorganized the Kembu Group defending Clark Field and the mountains to the west on 11 January and assigned the Nagayoshi Detachment to its commander, Lieutenant General Rikichi Tsukada. Tsukada had his hands full with his new responsibilities, but he must have been pleased to have a force, however small, to protect his southern flank. He and Nagayoshi never established radio contact, much less meet. Nagayoshi did make contact once by sending a single officer courier to Kembu Group Headquarters.[48]

A curious 14th Area Army directive dated 28 January reveals how totally the Japanese high command was out of touch with reality: "An element of the Nagayoshi Detachment, at present stationed in Bataan Peninsula, will remain there to secure the neck of Bataan Peninsula while the main force of the unit will move to Angeles to attack enemy."[49]

Sending any element of the Nagayoshi Detachment to Angeles at that time was unthinkable. The move would have disrupted Nagayoshi's principal mission of garrisoning and defending the Bataan Peninsula and would most surely have been detected and thrown into disorder by American aircraft ranging daily over Bataan. The 14th Area Army apparently had no advance warning, nor did it suspect that a landing the next day by the American XI Corps would keep Nagayoshi fully occupied.

Map 2: Bataan Peninsula 1945

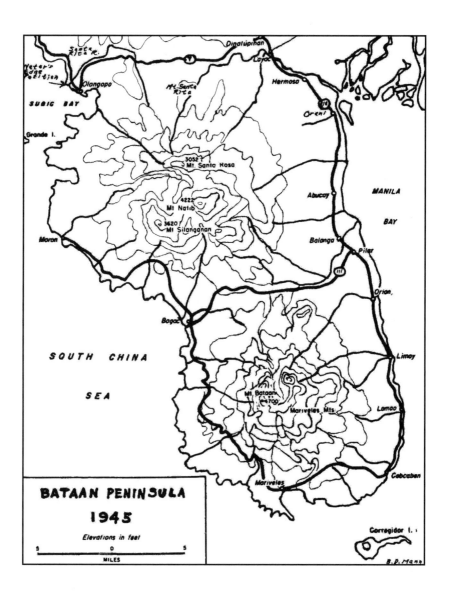

SUBIC BAY

SOUTH CHINA

SEA

MANILA

BAY

BATAAN PENINSULA
1945

Elevations in feet

5   0   5

MILES

B. P. Mann

Chapter 2
NOTES

(1) *History of the 39th Infantry Regiment*, edited and published by the 39th Infantry Association p. 20-23.

(2) *Ibid.*, p. 820-821.

(3) *Ibid.*, p. 820-823.

(4) *Ibid.*, p. 824.

(5) Hasukazu, Yokoyama, machine gunner 39th Infantry, Monograph *Memories of Chiamussu*, p. 1.

(6) *39th Infantry History*, p. 592.

(7) Mrs. Takako Nagayoshi, letter to the author, 29 June 1987.

(8) *39th Infantry History*, p. 592-594;
Alden, John D., *U.S. Submarine Attacks During World War II*, p. 126-127.

(9) Morison, Samuel Eliot, *History of United States Naval Operations in World War II*, Vol. XII: *Leyte*, p. 94-95;
39th Infantry History, p. 594-596.

(10) *39th Infantry History*, p. 596.

(11) Morison, *Leyte,* p. 108-109;
39th Infantry History, p. 594-596.

(12) Morison, *Leyte,* p. 106.

(13) *39th Infantry History*, p. 605-608;
Nagai, Tamotsu, Monograph *Memories of Takao*, p. 4.

(14) *Ibid.*, p. 5.

(15) *39th Infantry History*, p. 605-608.

(16) *Ibid.,* p. 605.

(17) The others: Masaharu Homma, 14th Army, Philippines; Shojiro Iida, 15th Army, Thailand-Burma; Hitoshi Imamura, 16th Army, Borneo-Sumatra-Java.

(18) Falk, Stanley F., *Seventy Days to Singapore*, p. 271, p. 276-278.

(19) *39th Infantry History*, p. 608.

(20) Falk, *Decision at Leyte*, p. 304.

(21) *39th Infantry History*, p. 608-610.

(22) *Ibid.*

(23) *Ibid.*

(24) Morison, *Leyte*, p. 55-57.

(25) *Ibid.,* p. 53.

(26) *Ibid.,* p. 57.

(27) *Reports of General MacArthur, Japanese Operations in the Southwest Pacific Area*, Vol. II-Part II, p. 443; *39th Infantry History*, p. 611-614.

(28) Morison, *Leyte,* p. 57.

(29) *Eighth Army G-2 Estimate of Enemy Troops on Bataan*

15 January 1945

Capones Islands	30	Hermosa	70
San Antonio	300	Orani	250
San Marcelino	1,200	Limay	800
Castillejos-Subic	2,000	Cabacben to Mariveles	5,000
Grande Island (naval)	1,000	Unlocated Garrison	
Olongapo	500	Troops	1,250
Dinalupihan	600	**TOTAL**	**13,000**

(30) *Reports of General MacArthur*, p. 454-455.

(31) *Disposition Japanese Troops for Defense of Bataan*

North Garrison Unit (ZigZag Pass)	2111	54%
Central Garrison Unit (Bagac)	1124	29%
South Garrison Unit (Mariveles)	658	17%
TOTAL	3893	100%

(32) *39th Infantry History*, p. 614-15.

(33) 15th Independent Air Unit; 38th Air Training Unit; 103rd Air Training Unit; BATAAN [Nagayoshi] Detachment Order 29 January 1945; *39th Infantry History*, p. 612-614.

(34) *Ibid.,* p. 616-617.

(35) *Ibid.,* p. 616. *How the Kato Company Fought: The Record of the 3rd Machine Gun Company, 39th Infantry Regiment*, Tamotsu Nagai, Editor, 1990, p. 157.

(36) Ogawa, Major Hironori, *Record of the 3rd Battalion, 39th Infantry Regiment in the "Big Asia War,"* p. 10-11.

(37) *Ibid.,* p. 13, 15-16; *39th Infantry History*, p. 622-623.

(38) Ogawa, p. 10; Smith, Robert Ross, *Triumph in the Philippines*, p. 315.

(39) DeJesus, Ramon V., *Zambales*, p. 56; *39th Infantry History*, p. 621; Interview with Tamotsu Nagai, 19 October 1992; *The Sho Army Operations, Part 2: The Decisive Battle for Luzon. Senshi Sosho Operations*, Vol. 60, p. 262.

(40) Ogawa, p. 10.

(41) Nagata, Yuchiro, letter to author, 24 June 1992;
39th Infantry History, p. 621.

(42) Ogawa, p. 15.

(43) *39th Infantry History*, p. 620.

(44) *Ibid.,* p. 620;
Ogawa, p. 12;
Kato Company History, p. 164.

(45) *39th Infantry History*, p. 633;
Sho Operations, p. 262.

(46) *39th Infantry History*, p. 616, p. 628-629.

(47) 14th Area Army Operations Order #15 January 1945, Monograph #7, p. 43;
Reports of General MacArthur, The Campaigns of MacArthur in the Pacific, Reprint 1994, Vol. I, 14th Area Army Plan for Defense of Luzon, 19 December 1944, Plate #76, p. 265.

(48) *39th Infantry History,* p. 602;
Statements of Japanese Officials on World War II, Statement of NAGAYOSHI, Sanenobu, 25 October 1948, General Headquarters Far East Command, p. 625.

(49) 14th Area Army Monograph

3

XI CORPS

Soon after the successful landing at Leyte on 20 October 1944, MacArthur's Headquarters Southwest Pacific Area (GHQSWPA) started planning for the invasion of Luzon. The planning took the form of a series of "Mike" operations. Mike-One was to be the main Sixth Army landing at Lingayen Gulf. Plans for several other landings were prepared, if needed, to augment the main landing. The location of these subsequent landings would depend on the enemy's dispositions and his reactions to the main landing.

Operation Mike-Two called for a landing at Dingalan Bay on the east coast of Luzon to protect the Sixth Army's left flank. In Mike-Three, the landing was to be at Vigan on the northwest coast 100 miles north of Lingayen Gulf. Mike-Four called for a landing at Nasugbu Bay or Balayan Bay on the Southwest Coast. These first four operations were planned through staff studies in October and November. Mike-Six (Batangas and Tayabas Bays farther south and east along the southern coast of Luzon) and Mike-Seven (southern Zambales coast) were not planned until January 1945. There was no Mike-Five.[1]

GHQSWPA assigned to the Eighth Army, commanded by Lieutenant General Robert L. Eichelberger, the responsibility for staging a subsidiary landing on Luzon following the main landing. The Eighth Army was to use the only combat troops under its command at that time (November 1944) to accomplish this mission: the 32nd Infantry Division, veterans of Buna, and the independent 112th Regimental Combat Team. XI Corps, Eighth Army's only corps headquarters, would direct the amphibious operation. The troops ultimately would pass to Sixth Army control.[2]

After a 20-day delay because of rain and unexpected strong Japanese resistance on Leyte, MacArthur put Operation Mike-One into effect. On 9 January 1945, the Sixth Army, under command of Lieutenant General Walter Krueger, invaded Luzon, landing at Lingayen Gulf on the west central coast. In essence, General Krueger repeated the earlier Japanese tactics employed by Homma's 14th Army in December 1941. The Sixth Army attacked southward with two Corps abreast, XIV Corps composed of the 40th and 37th Divisions on the right and I Corps composed of the

6th and 43rd Divisions on the left. By the last week in January, XIV Corps was poised for the critical phase of the campaign—the capture of Manila.[3]

As events unfolded after the main landing at Lingayen Gulf (Mike-One), Mike-Two became unnecessary because the Japanese removed their troops from Dingalan Bay for more effective use in northern Luzon. Mike-Three (Vigan) was scaled back to a division operation and then abandoned because Filipino guerrillas had secured this area. Mike-Four, re-designated Mike-Six, and Mike-Seven were still very much alive.[4]

After the initial Lingayen landing and first movements inland had proved successful, MacArthur, recently appointed to five star rank, called his principal commanders to a conference 12 January aboard cruiser *Boise*. Present were Vice Admiral Thomas C. Kinkaid, commander Seventh Fleet, Vice Admiral Theodore S. Wilkinson, commander VII Amphibious Fleet and the Army field commander, General Krueger. There the four planned a three-pronged assault on Manila.[5]

XIV Corps, to be reinforced by the 32nd Infantry and 1st Cavalry Divisions on 27 January, would spearhead the drive toward Manila from the north. The 40th Division on the Corps's right flank would overcome any Japanese resistance found at Clark Field and in the Zambales Mountains to the west.[6]

I Corps would cover XIV Corps's left flank and contain the Japanese forces in northern Luzon. General Krueger had reason to believe that the 2nd Tank Division and the 10th Division (minus the 39th Infantry), concentrated in the Munoz-San Jose area, posed an offensive threat.[7]

XI Corps would carry out the Mike-Seven operation. Staged by Eighth Army, the corps would land on 29 January on the southern Zambales coast of Luzon, hook in toward Manila from the west and open up Manila Bay by securing the Bataan Peninsula and the islands guarding the entrance to the Bay.

The GHQSWPA staff study for Operation "Mike-Seven," called "Zambales" by many of the participating units, had not been made until 14 January, two days after MacArthur's decision to invade southwestern Luzon. XI Corps's 32nd Division and 112th RCT had been assigned to the Sixth Army and were replaced by the 38th Division and the 34th Regimental Combat Team (RCT). Krueger, senior to Eichelberger, apparently wanted the veteran 32nd for his own operations.[8]

On 15 January, to cover all bases, MacArthur ordered General Eichelberger to execute Mike-Four, re-designated Mike-Six. Major General Joseph M. Swing's 11th Airborne Division under Eichelberger would land on 31 January at Nasugbu, 40 miles from the outskirts of

Manila. MacArthur and Krueger felt that this pincer from the southwest might ease XIV Corps's drive into Manila from the north.[9]

Mike-Three (the landing at Vigan) had been high in MacArthur's plans until it was learned after the Lingayen landing that Filipino guerrillas controlled Vigan. However, the 38th Division had been planning for this operation since Christmas Day when Eighth Army Headquarters called the division G-2, G-3 and G-4 together to start the planning. This operation called for the 38th Division, reinforced, to land at Vigan on the northwest coast of Luzon as protection for Sixth Army's left flank. This was to be a division operation not under any corps. The 38th Division staff worked on these plans until 19 January when XI Corps informed the staff that Mike-Three had been cancelled and ordered that planning start for the Mike-Seven operation.[10]

Major General Charles A. Willoughby, MacArthur's G-2 Chief of Intelligence, had another reason for landing XI Corps on the west coast of Luzon. He was afraid the enemy might slip into Bataan, as the Americans had done in late December 1941, and establish a strong defense in Bataan's rugged terrain. A XI Corps landing on the Zambales coast of Luzon and a subsequent rapid movement eastward to Subic Bay and thence to Dinalupihan would block any Japanese attempt to enter Bataan. Actually, the Japanese had no intention of following the American 1941-42 strategy, preferring instead to prepare their defenses in depth in the inhospitable mountains surrounding the central Luzon plain.[11]

On 17 January, MacArthur sent a radio message to General Krueger urging him to move rapidly southward because of "strategic considerations" and seize the Clark Field area. MacArthur noted that the known enemy dispositions would enable I Corps to contain the enemy on his left, while Krueger could move rapidly with his right [XIV Corps]. "If heavy resistance is encountered in the Clark Field-Bamban area, it will be completely dislocated by the execution of the Mike-Seven operation," MacArthur said.[12]

In summary then, as initially planned, there seemed to be three reasons for XI Corps to carry out Mike-Seven: first, to secure a supply base at Subic Bay to help relieve the burden of Sixth Army's ever increasing, lengthy supply line from Lingayen Gulf; second, to establish a blocking position at Dinalupihan to prevent the Japanese from moving into the Bataan Peninsula for a last ditch stand; and finally, to assist Sixth Army's drive south to Manila by helping to overcome resistance in the Clark Field area, if the Japanese proved to be more stubborn than expected.

XI Corps was one of five Army corps in three United States Armies in the Pacific.[13] Its history dated back to the Civil War. Under command of Major General Oliver O. Howard, the corps fought at Chancellorsville, where it received Stonewall Jackson's flank attack; at Gettysburg, where, on the first day, it was also roughly handled; and at Chattanooga where it redeemed itself. Disbanded at the end of the Civil War, the corps was reactivated 15 June 1942 at Chicago under Major General Lloyd R. Fredendall.

Major General Charles Philip Hall assumed command 20 October 1942 and commanded the corps for the remainder of the war. Corps headquarters moved to Finschhaven, New Guinea, in April 1944. As part of the Sixth Army, XI Corps conducted the Aitape campaign July-August 1944 and the Morotai campaign 15 September-5 October 1944. The corps moved to Leyte on 9 November and came under Eighth Army control.[14]

Major General Charles P. Hall, Commander XI Corps

General Hall, Class of 1911 USMA, was a 58-year-old Mississippian at the apex of a distinguished military career. His service in World War I added luster to a reputation already gained as a serious, thorough, hard-working infantryman in the Western United States and as mathematics instructor at West Point. Rising to the temporary rank of Lieutenant Colonel as Adjutant of the 3rd Brigade 2nd Division during World War I, he received the Distinguished Service Cross for extraordinary heroism at Vierzy, France, two Silver Stars, the French Croix de Guerre and the Purple Heart.

Between the wars, Hall completed the usual schools to which promising officers are assigned. He instructed tactics at the Infantry School at Fort Benning, Georgia, and even served for a time as Executive Officer to the Head of the School, future General of the Army George C. Marshall. He served his tour of duty in the Philippines with the 23rd Infantry at Baguio in 1931-33.[15]

In the Pacific, General Hall was already known as a resourceful, tough, hard-nosed, uncompromising commander. He was adept at taking complete charge of an operation and seeing it through to a successful conclusion with little supervision from above. At Aitape, New Guinea, he had interposed his corps between Sixth Army's main landing at Hollandia and the Japanese 18th Army advancing westward from Wewak. Maneuvering superbly an independent RCT and six regiments from four different divisions, Hall's XI Corps virtually annihilated the 18th Army in confused jungle fighting. At Morotai, he had commanded the 31st Division and the 126th RCT of the 32nd Division, the same size infantry force he would send ashore on Luzon.[16]

XI Corps's primary strength for the campaign on Luzon was the National Guard 38th Infantry Division, commanded by Major General Henry L. C. Jones. Two of its infantry regiments, the 151st and 152nd, were from Indiana and one, the 149th, from Kentucky. The "CY" in its shield-shaped division patch stood for a cyclone that descended on the division while it was encamped at Camp Shelby, Mississippi, during World War I. Arriving in France in October 1918, the division saw no action, but provided replacements for combat units.[17]

Its regiments were among the oldest in the nation. The 149th Infantry traced its history back to the 2nd Kentucky Regiment under Lieutenant Colonel Daniel Boone. The 2nd Kentucky fought at New Orleans in 1815 as part of General Andrew Jackson's hastily formed army. In the Mexican War, the 2nd fought under General Zachary Taylor at Buena Vista as well as with General Winfield Scott in the Vera Cruz-Mexico City Campaign.

Joining the Union side during the Civil War, the regiment ended the war with General Sherman's Army after serving in Virginia, Kentucky and Tennessee. The 149th was activated for the Spanish-American War and the Mexican border disturbance in 1916, but saw no combat. It was activated again in 1917 and assigned to the 38th Division at Camp Shelby.

Designated originally in 1810 as the 1st and 2nd Indiana Regiments, the 151st from northern Indiana and 152nd from southern Indiana had similar histories. Both fought with General William Henry Harrison at the Battle of Tippecanoe before Indiana became a state. Both served in Mexico in 1846-47 and as militia during the Civil War. Both were activated, but remained in the States during the Spanish-American War. As part of the 38th Division in World War I, they arrived in France too late to see action.[18]

When war threatened in 1940, the 38th was inducted into Federal Service in January 1941 and assigned again to Camp Shelby. Following additional training at Camps Carrabelle, Florida, for amphibious training, and Livingston, Louisiana, the division embarked for overseas duty on 30 December 1943.[19]

After landing in Hawaii in January 1944, the 38th engaged in all the training available for a division tabbed for southwest Pacific duty. The division manned the perimeter defenses of Oahu for six months. During this time, all personnel received training at a Jungle Training Center and took part in basic and advanced amphibious warfare exercises. Officers and NCOs attended Transport Quartermaster Schools where they learned combat loading of assault ships. In July, the division sailed to Oro Bay, New Guinea, where Australians trained selected personnel in long range patrolling.[20]

During the division's move to Leyte in November 1944, the 3rd Battalion 149th suffered casualties from enemy bombers. The regiment sent its 1st Battalion into action at Buri Airstrip on 7 December to help repel a Japanese paratroop assault. Later in the month, the division operated as a screening force behind more experienced assault troops against Japanese trapped in the Ormoc corridor.[21]

General Hall's other fighting component of XI Corps was a "mini-division," the 34th Regimental Combat Team (RCT). Organized like a division, but one-third its size, a regimental combat team had its own supporting artillery, tanks, engineers, et cetera. It could go into battle as an independent unit, as part of a corps or attached to a division. The 34th RCT consisted of the 34th Infantry Regiment, the 63rd Field Artillery Battalion, Company C 3rd Engineer Battalion, Company C 24th Medical

Battalion, 1st Platoon 603rd Tank Company, 24th Cavalry Reconnaissance Troop, the 383rd Quartermaster Truck Company and a detachment of the 592nd JASCO.[22]

Colonel William W. Jenna commanded the 34th Infantry and would also command the 34th RCT for the Mike-Seven operation. A native of New Hampshire, he moved to Leominster, Massachusetts, at an early age and was the first man from that district ever to be appointed to West Point. After graduation in the accelerated class of August 1917, he shipped to England for assignment. Instead of going to France as might be expected, 2nd Lieutenant Jenna was assigned as Assistant Military Attaché at the American Embassy in Greece for three years. In Athens, he became close friends with the young King Alexander and his wife and lived in a society few Americans would ever experience.

Between the wars, Jenna attended the requisite Army schools to prepare him for high command and from 1936 to 1940 served as Professor of French at West Point. When the Japanese struck at Pearl Harbor, he was on the staff of the Army commander, Lieutenant General Walter C. Short. He was soon promoted to full colonel and assigned to command the 34th, which he trained in Australia. After leading the 34th at Hollandia and Biak Island, he was hospitalized during much of the Leyte Campaign. He returned to the 34th in December 1944 near the end of operations on Leyte. The casual observer would never suspect that this debonair, slight-of-stature, sophisticated officer would win the Silver Star three times as an infantry combat leader.[23]

The 34h Infantry had been organized on 15 July 1916 at El Paso, Texas, as a unit in the Regular Army. The regiment fought as part of the 7th Division in Lorraine during World War I and was cited by the French Government with the Battle Honors of Lorraine. Between the wars, the 34th was equipped and organized as the first motorized infantry regiment in the Army. Scheduled to reinforce the Philippines in 1941, the 34th, ironically, was to have left the United States on 7 December.[24]

Arriving at Oahu on 21 December 1941, the 34th was immediately engaged in setting up the island defenses. On 12 June 1943, the regiment supplanted the 298th Infantry Regiment as a member of the 24th Infantry Division.

As part of the 24th Division,[25] the 34th trained in Australia and participated in special amphibious exercises on Goodenough Island off the northern coast of eastern New Guinea. Following a baptism of fire in the 24th Division's landing at Hollandia in April 1944, the 34th participated with the 41st Division in the cave fighting on Biak Island in June. As one of the regiments in the initial assault on Leyte 20 October 1944, it held that part of the 24th Division beach upon which General MacArthur made his triumphant return. Seventy-five straight days of grueling combat on Leyte followed.[26]

Chapter 3

NOTES

(1) Smith, Robert R., *Triumph in the Philippines*, p. 19n.

(2) *Ibid.*, p. 29.

(3) *Ibid.*, p. 211.

(4) *Ibid.*, p. 101-102, p. 310.

(5) Morison, Samuel E., *History of United States Naval Operations in World War II,* Vol. XIII: *The Liberation of the Philippines*, p. 184.

(6) *Ibid.*, p. 185;
Smith, *Triumph in the Philippines*, p. 187, p. 193.

(7) *Ibid.*, p. 187-190.

(8) GHQSWPA Staff Study, Operation Mike-Seven, 14 January 1945, p. 1.

(9) Morison, *The Liberation of the Philippines*, p. 189.

(10) Walters, Captain Edward E., *The Operations of the 38th Infantry Division in the Landing at San Antonio-San Narciso Area and the Advance to Dinalupihan,* Advanced Infantry Officers Course, 1949-1950, p. 8.

(11) Smith, *Triumph in the Philippines,* p. 311.

(12) Sixth United States Army: Report of the Luzon Campaign, 9 January-30 June 1945 in Four Volumes, Vol. I, p. 112-113.

(13) The other corps: I, X, XIV, XXIV. Armies: Sixth, Eighth, Tenth.

(14) XI Corps Historical Report Luzon Campaign, 4 April 1946, p. 5.

(15) West Point Assembly, 1953.

(16) 112th Cavalry RCT; 124th Regiment 31st Division; 126th, 127th, 128th-32nd Division; 163rd-41st Division; 169th-43rd Division; Smith, *Approach to the Philippines.*

(17) Fischer, Colonel Robert T., *An Abbreviated History of the 38th Infantry Division at the 50th Anniversary Activation in WWII*, 21-22 June 1991, p. 6.

(18) Regimental histories and biographies of World War II leaders of 38th Division units. 38th Division files National Records Center, College Park, Maryland.

(19) Fischer, *Abbreviated History of the 38th Infantry Division*, p. 8.

(20) Schoonover, Major James F., *The Operations of the 3rd Battalion 152nd Infantry in Zig Zag Pass, Luzon, 29 Jan.-14 Feb. 1945,* Advanced Infantry Officers Course, 1947-1948, p. 3.

(21) *Ibid.,* p. 3;
Regimental histories/biographies.

(22) Field Order #1 Hq RCT-34, 1200 20 January 1945;
34th Infantry After Action Report, Southern Zambales Operation,
p. 1.

(23) West Point Assembly, June 1975.

(24) Morton, Louis, *The Fall of the Philippines,* p. 35;
Taro Leaf, (24th Infantry Division Association Newsletter), Vol.
51, Issue #1, February 1997, p. 58.

(25) The 24th Infantry Division had been formed 1 October 1941 at
Schofield Barracks on the island of Oahu from elements of the
"square" four-regiment Hawaiian Division. Reflecting this early
history, the division's identifying patch is the "Taro Leaf" of a
plant used by native Hawaiians to make poi—a basic food in
their diet. The original infantry units of the 24th were the 19th,
21st, and 299th regiments. Later, the 299th, a Hawaiian National
Guard regiment, was replaced by the 298th, and on 12 June 1943,
the 298th was replaced by the 34th. By September 1943 the division had completed a move to Camp Caves near Rockhampton on
the East Coast of Australia for further training. One of the early
arrivals in the Pacific, the 24th had been bloodied at the start of
the war, losing three killed and eight wounded at Pearl Harbor.
The final training at Goodenough Island off the northern coast of
Papua, New Guinea, prepared the division for amphibious action.
In that role, the 24th spearheaded the landings at Hollandia and
Leyte, 6th Army's largest amphibious operations prior to
Lingayen Gulf. Casualties on Leyte were 2,342; next to the 7th
Division, the highest of any of the nine American divisions that
fought on that island until it was declared secure 8 May 1945.

(26) *Taro Leaf,* Vol. 51, Issue #1, February 1997, p. 58. (Text from
pamphlet *Brief History of the 24th Infantry Division*), 20 pages,
1954.

XI CORPS DEPARTS LEYTE FOR LUZON

On 24 January 1945, the 34th Infantry received replacements of 43 officers and 796 enlisted men who had arrived in the Philippines a week earlier. After five weeks aboard the USS *General R. L. Howze* (AP-134), they had been happy to set their well-polished boots on firm ground. They were part of the ship's human cargo of 3,145—227 officers and 2,918 male enlisted men. Among the officers were 21 nurses and 60 W.A.C.s. With little to do aboard the general transport, many EM competed to see whose shoes could sparkle brightest in the hot tropical sun.[1]

The 34th Infantry sorely needed the replacements despite their youth and limited amount of training. The regiment had reported on 11 January an average strength in its nine rifle companies of between two and three officers per company and 101 enlisted men.[2] The full TO&E (Table of Organization and Equipment) complement for a rifle company was six officers and 187 enlisted men. The additions brought the regiment to nearly full strength—3,001 against a Table of Organization strength of 3,068.[3]

The 38th Division received one officer and 315 enlisted replacements to bring its strength to 13,689 officers and men. This figure was still 348 men shy of its authorized Table of Organization strength of 14,037.[4] The untried division had spent a month preparing for one operation; now it was being called on to switch gears in one week for a landing in a very different type of area.

On Christmas Day 1944, Eighth Army Headquarters sent for the 38th Division G-2 (Intelligence), G-3 (Plans and Operations) and G-4 (Supply) officers to receive instructions for planning the Mike-Three operation at Vigan. It was to be a division operation not under any corps. The division worked on the Mike-Three plans until 19 January 1945 when the bombshell struck. XI Corps issued Field Order #3 informing the 38th Division of its embarkation one week later 26 January for San Antonio on the west coast of Luzon to engage in the Mike-Seven operation.[5]

The Navy and the 38th Division showed great flexibility and adaptiveness in discarding plans for the Vigan landing and devising new plans for their part in the Sixth Army operation to capture Manila. Confusion and chaos reigned as the 38th Division staff strove to cope with the entirely new operation. The 32nd and 1st Cavalry Divisions, loading on the same beaches for their voyage to Lingayen Gulf to reinforce the Sixth Army, further complicated matters. Since the 38th Division was far advanced in its planning for Mike-Three (Vigan), XI Corps wisely permitted the division to prepare its own loading plans for Mike-Seven. XI Corps assumed responsibility for loading the 34th RCT.[6]

Confusion increased as the deadline approached. Quartermaster did not deliver supplies according to schedule. Landing Ships, Tank, (LSTs) were beached and ready to load, but the loading of vehicles was held up because bulk cargo had not arrived on the beach for loading. In one instance, gasoline drums had to be transferred from one LST to make room for 500 tons of ammunition.[7]

Boxes of ammunition and supplies were stacked on the beaches at Tacloban as far as the eye could see. As an example of the chaos in this area, five truckloads of ammunition were directed to Dulag, the 38th Division's rear echelon 20 miles from the beach, only to be re-directed back to Tacloban for loading.

In the confusion, some units were not loaded intact on the same ship. In one instance, the personnel and equipment of one hospital were scattered among seven vessels. The personnel of the 3rd Field Hospital boarded too early, leaving no one ashore to load their cargo.[8]

Because the 38th Division's area of operations at Vigan in the Mike-Three operation was relatively small, motor transportation from D-day to D-plus-ten had not been a major concern. The division had planned to take a limited number of vehicles initially and depend on re-supply convoys on D-plus-five and D-plus-ten to complete its requirements. In Mike-Seven, these D-plus-five and D-plus-ten ships were not allotted for the operation. As a result the 38th Division never had enough vehicles for the demands of the extensive area it was to cover in Mike-Seven.

The division met the deadline of 26 January, but had to leave many needed items of supply and equipment among the approximately 2,000 tons of cargo left on the beach. A "considerable" number of personnel also remained on Leyte. These personnel and equipment caught up with the division in later convoys, but there was never enough shipping to supply the Mike-Seven Operation properly.[9] Sufficient shipping had not been allocated. When loading was completed on 25 January, 190 vehicles and their trailers remained on the beach, causing further serious shortages of transportation on Luzon.[10]

On 24 January, the 34th Infantry was already aboard ship in Tacloban Harbor preparing to embark on the Zambales operation. Both officer and enlisted replacements were deposited on the beach for a wait of several hours for lighterage to take them to the waiting APAs and AKAs anchored about a mile off shore. It was an overcast day, but without the usual Leyte rain that had slowed the Americans since November.

That night, the replacements joined their new companies in the holds below decks. One of the first orders to the replacements was to "get rid of that gas mask!" Following instructions of the Army authorities in San Francisco, each replacement had been issued a gas mask that he had carried with great care across the Pacific. The veterans looked on this excess baggage with disdain, but the gas mask did serve one useful purpose. Squad leaders instructed their men to cut off two of the rubber links of the hose of the mask. These links fitted snugly around each man's dog tags and kept them from clinking and giving away the infantryman's position when close to the enemy.

New officers were assigned directly to their companies and would lead their platoons in the amphibious assault. The enlisted replacements were considered too inexperienced to join the first waves in the landing. Having not even test fired their newly issued rifles, they would join their companies later during a lull in the battle.

The sudden influx of new second lieutenants in the 34th must have deflated more than one veteran platoon sergeant. These sergeants had led their platoons through thick and thin for months; now they had to hand over their platoons to young, "120-day wonders."

Verdun C. Myers, platoon sergeant 3rd Platoon G Company, was typical. Myers was part Indian, a tough Oklahoman, apparently in his late twenties, a veteran of all the regiment's training days and campaigns since Pearl Harbor. He was the epitome of what a platoon sergeant should be—brave, resourceful, caring and a natural leader. Myers had led his platoon through the fighting on Leyte and during the garrison preparations for the Zambales operation. He found it a bitter pill to swallow to relinquish his command to an untried youngster.

Many of the new second lieutenants groped for their first words to the soldiers entrusted to their care. Most would have hoped to handle the situation like Delmont E. MacAnallen of Akron, Ohio, of the OCS Class #363 from which most of the new 2nd Lieutenants had graduated. Assigned a platoon in F Company, the former Tech Sergeant's prudent remarks as relayed 40 years later by two veterans of the company, were approximately this: "Men, you have shown that you know what you are doing and don't need advice from a newcomer. Just continue to operate as you normally do, and I will help when needed."

There was the usual "scuttle-butt" aboard ship: "The 34th's mission is to join in the drive on Manila. It will move across the top of Bataan and attack Manila from the west." "The veteran 34th was selected for this operation to help the green 38th Division when it bogs down the first time it faces the enemy." "The 'old man' [Colonel Jenna] is depressed because he hasn't made brigadier general while some of his contemporaries have already reached one or two star rank." They were just that—rumors.

The next day, all hands practiced the preparations for the landing. The most precarious part of this operation, as far as the infantry was concerned, was climbing down the cargo net to the waiting LCVPs (Landing Craft, Vehicles and Personnel) bobbing up and down alongside the ship. Officers cautioned their men to unfasten the chinstraps of their steel helmets. In case a man fell into the Gulf, the steel helmet and helmet liner would come off and not drag his head under. Each man was further cautioned not to look up while climbing up or down as the steel helmet might slide off his helmet liner and plummet into the water. Inevitably, one man looked up and lost his steel helmet.

The navy coxswains of the LCVPs were the chief beneficiaries of these practices. The coxswains circled their boats several times, never making the dash inland, but practicing getting into position for that final maneuver. Following two such exercises the afternoon of 25 January, the convoy weighed anchor and departed for Luzon early the next morning.

An Oregonian, Rear Admiral Arthur D. Struble, Annapolis Class of 1915, commanded the convoy, designated Task Force 78.3. He had earned his laurels as Chief of Staff to Vice Admiral Alan R. Kirk, commander of naval operations for "Overlord," the Normandy invasion. Despite his short Pacific tenure, Struble had already commanded two amphibious operations: first, the task groups to occupy islands at the entrance to Leyte Gulf on 19 October 1944 prior to the main assault on Leyte; and second, the landings on Mindoro in December. He was later to command the amphibious landings at Inchon and Wonsan in Korea. To say the least, XI Corps was in capable hands on the high seas.[11]

GHQSWPA (MacArthur's Headquarters) had left no stone unturned to insure the success of this operation. XI Corps consisted of the 38th Division, the 34th RCT, corps troops including additional artillery, anti-aircraft artillery, engineers, quartermaster, ordnance, medical units and 5,500 airfield construction personnel, a total of 38,808 men plus 17,850 deadweight tons of equipment. All were loaded into two transport divisions and several Liberty ships with the usual complement of beaching craft. Army planes from Leyte furnished air cover. Surface cover came from light cruiser *Denver* and two destroyers under Rear Admiral Ralph S. Riggs. A screen of 14 destroyers and destroyer escorts and 11 big and 19 small minesweepers, plus an APD (Fast Destroyer Transport) debarking an underwater demolition team, completed Task Force 78.3.[12]

Even though American air power on Mindoro would discourage Japanese air attacks on the convoy and the landing area, Task Force 78.3 carried the same anti-aircraft artillery (AAA) units that had been designated for Mike-Three. This was considerable firepower (one 90-mm gun battalion and two 40-mm automatic weapons battalions) because the Japanese could have readily bombed the Mike-Three landing area at Vigan from Formosa. The AAA automatic weapons battalions were divided among the LSTs so that a platoon consisting of four 40-mm guns and four multiple machine gun mounts was assigned to each LST. Batteries of 90-mm guns were loaded on ships that would be unloaded on the flanks of the beach area with the third assault wave.[13]

The route of the convoy followed the much-traveled path from Leyte used by the Navy for the invasions and subsequent re-supply at Mindoro and Lingayen Gulf. South from Tacloban the fleet rounded the southern tip of Leyte and proceeded through Surigao Strait southwest into the Mindanao Sea. From there the ships sailed west into the Sulu Sea and then north through Mindoro Strait along the west coasts of Mindoro and Luzon to the landing site. It would take Task Force 78.3 approximately 60 hours to traverse the 800-mile route at an average speed of 13.3 miles per hour. It was easy to forget the war as the armada proceeded through the tropical islands in near perfect, usually sunny weather, with not even a squall to mar the tranquility.

✦　✦　✦

The site selected for the XI Corps landing is the only suitable beach on the west coast of Luzon south of Lingayen Gulf. The dominant feature of Luzon west of the Central Plains region is the rugged Zambales Mountains chain, which stretches from the Bolinao Peninsula at the Gulf to the tip of the Bataan Peninsula. Rough spurs of the range reach to the seashore along much of the coastline. All-weather Highway Number 7 snakes down the west coast from Lingayen through these foothills. When it reaches the only significant plains area in this part of Luzon, the road turns east through the town of San Antonio. The coast of this plains area is a six-mile stretch of beach that the planners named "San Antonio" for the largest town in the area.

From San Antonio, located two miles from the beach, Highway 7 runs five miles to San Marcelino with its airfield two miles northeast of town. The road travels another five miles from San Marcelino southeast to Castillejos where the Cabulisan Spur of the Zambales range creates a minor barrier. After reaching Subic Town at the top of Subic Bay five miles farther, Highway 7 twists south six road miles, hugging the coast, to the port of Olongapo and the Subic Bay naval base. From there the highway winds 14 miles east through the forbidding, mountainous jungle (in 1945) of ZigZag Pass to Dinalupihan. This is the only road connecting Subic Bay and Manila. Highway 7 is the natural route for any large-scale land movement of troops between the two areas.[14]

Highway 7 (view from Mount Koko)

GHQSWPA had assigned XI Corps three missions. First, it was to seize and occupy the six-mile wide beachhead at San Antonio by amphibious assault. It would then capture the San Marcelino airfield six miles from the coast and establish an airfield for the purpose of projecting American air power farther over Luzon and the South China Sea than was possible from the bases at Lingayen and Mindoro. Second, it was to secure Subic Bay and the port of Olongapo and establish an alternate Sixth Army supply base (eventually to be expanded into the major United States Naval Base in the Far East, which continued in operation until October 1992). Securing Subic Bay involved the capture of Fort Wint on Grande Island. Third, it was to drive rapidly through ZigZag Pass across the base of the Bataan Peninsula and seize and occupy the general line Dinalupihan-Hermosa to prevent any substantial Japanese withdrawal into the peninsula from the Central Plains. Speed was essential in securing Dinalupihan to shut off the Central Plains.[15]

XI Corps's plans for the landing assigned the 38th Division the northern area of the beach at San Narciso and the 34th RCT, the southern part at San Antonio. H-Hour was to be 0830 hours on "B-day" 29 January 1945 preceded by an hour's naval bombardment.

The 149th Infantry would move rapidly inland and secure the first major objective—San Marcelino Airfield. The 34th RCT would seize San Antonio and then advance along Highway 7 through the towns of San Marcelino, Castillejos and Subic to the second major objective—Olongapo.

The 152nd Infantry would follow the 34th and mop up any bypassed pockets of resistance, while the 151st would consolidate the beach area and guard the flanks at the beach.

The 38th Division would pass through the 34th at Olongapo and continue the attack eastward to Dinalupihan to accomplish the Corps's third major objective. Initial enemy resistance beyond the beach was expected in the pass through the hills south of Castillejos or along the coastal road between Subic and Olongapo. G-2 Eighth Army, however, in its After Action Report, believed the enemy capable of a "sustained defense to hold open the route [Highway 7] from Bataan peninsula to the central Luzon plain."[16]

General Hall's plans were based on assumptions he had made from the latest and most reliable intelligence reports. Although Eighth Army estimated approximately 13,000 Japanese to be in Zambales and Bataan Provinces, it reported that no identification had been made of a major combat unit in the area. Instead, Army intelligence emphasized that Subic Bay was a major debarkation point for troops destined for Central Luzon. Only anti-aircraft emplacements were mentioned as fortifications sighted.[17]

General Hall concluded that the entire Japanese strength on Bataan consisted of garrison and service troops and transients who would not present a cohesive force and who could not offer substantial resistance. Despite Eighth Army's belief that the enemy was capable of a sustained defense of the road (ZigZag Pass) between Subic Bay and Dinalupihan, Hall obviously thought the pass would be lightly defended. His subsequent actions would indicate that he expected to be through the pass and in Dinalupihan by 5 February.[18]

Aerial photographs might have helped solve the mystery of, "Where are the Japs and where will they make their stand?" Reports are conflicting regarding aerial photographs. Eighth Army stated in its AAR that 33,000 prints of 125,000 scale photomaps were distributed to the task force. If so, the maps did not cover the area where maps were most needed: ZigZag Pass. The commander of the 38th Division Headquarters Company reported that no aerial photographs of the ZigZag Pass area were available at the start of the operation.[19]

Another factor undoubtedly affected General Hall's thinking and may have shaped the nature of his offensive to accomplish the corps' missions. He had previously visited Olongapo and had prepared plans for its defense.

In 1932, Hall (then a major) had been assigned the problem of devising a defense of the Subic Bay area. He apparently thought the Japanese would follow the present American strategy of landing on the west coast of Luzon and moving overland to Subic Bay. Writing in 1949, Hall commented, "As a problem, the defense of the area was simple. It would require (other than Naval action) only beach watchers, possible delaying action from the San Antonio area, and a final defense along the hills and low pass two or three miles north of Subic [Town]. When we landed [in 1945], I expected the Nips to defend just north of Subic on a natural defensive position. Why the Nips defended ZigZag Pass so stubbornly when we were able to go down either side of Bataan will always be a mystery to me."[20]

From this statement, it appears that General Hall expected the Japanese to make their main effort at Castillejos Pass. In the initial planning stages of the operation, he apparently dismissed ZigZag Pass as a serious danger point. Instead of impressing him with the strong defense a determined enemy could establish in the rugged terrain of the ZigZag, the visit to Subic Bay in 1932 had the opposite effect. Hall seemed to belittle the defensive possibilities of the jungled hills of ZigZag Pass and to discount major opposition there.

☞   ☞   ☞

As the American convoy entered the waters off Luzon under a full moon on 28 January, the night before the scheduled assault, Colonel Jenna broadcast this message to all his troops over the ships' loudspeakers:

"The 34th CT has a most important mission. The Commanding General [General Hall] of this task force has placed his entire faith in this regiment of veterans, which proved its worth at Hollandia, Biak and Leyte. We will not let him down. Hit hard and destroy the Japs. Drive fast and go through to our objective. May God's blessing be on us and may His strength and courage carry us to a quick and complete victory."[21]

The 34th was used to hitting hard and driving fast, but Colonel Jenna could not conceive of the defensive stronghold Colonel Nagayoshi's men had built in Zambales's wild terrain.

There was a most serious poker game in progress that night among officers of the 2nd Battalion 34th Infantry aboard the USS *Saratoga APA 204*. The intent players seemed oblivious to everything except the money and the cards, an obvious ploy to get their minds off the morrow. Lieutenant Bishop, 1st Platoon Leader in G Company, was typical. His piercing, beady eyes missed nothing. Only God could have seen his cards as he slowly spread them close to his chest for a peek after each deal. Hardly noticing the shadowy forms moving about in the mammoth hold, other men cleaned their weapons, prayed, read their Bibles or in their own way prepared for whatever the morning would bring.

The Japanese soldiers in ZigZag Pass were also contemplating the approaching battle. Three lieutenants and two sergeants of the 9th Company and the 3rd Battalion communications sergeant were sitting in a bunker talking with the company commander. The conversation took an uncharacteristic twist. One of the lieutenants, a man who had fought in China and had formerly taught bayonet practice to recruits, was apparently shuddering from fright. The company commander turned on him. "What has happened to your bravery? You are now different from the rest of us." And then sarcastically, "You are trembling with eagerness to fight, aren't you?"[22] In a short time, XI Corps would wonder why anyone would question the willingness to fight of any of the defenders of ZigZag Pass.

Map 3: Southern Zambales–Northern Bataan Provinces

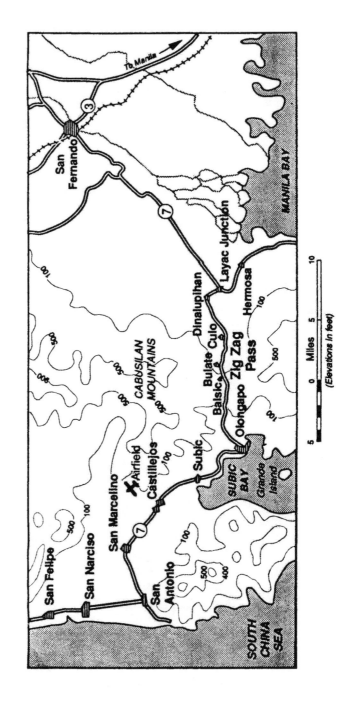

Chapter 4

NOTES

(1) After Action Report (AAR) of the Commanding General Eighth Army on the Nasugbu and Bataan Operations Mike-Six and Mike-Seven. Property of the Office of the Chief of Military History, p. 91;
War Diary—USS *General R. L. Howze* (AP-134), 15 December 1944 (Friday).

(2) Headquarters 34th Infantry, S-3 Report, 13 January 1945.

(3) Greenfield, Kent Robert, Palmer, Robert R., and Wiley, Bell I., *United States Army in World War II, The Army Ground Forces, The Organization of Ground Combat Troops*, p. 274.

(4) Walters, Captain Edward E., *The Operations of the 38th Infantry Division in the Landing at San Antonio-San Narciso Area and the Advance to Dinalupihan*, p. 10;
Greenfield et al, *The Organization of Ground Combat Troops*, p. 274;
Eighth Army AAR, p. 91.

(5) 38th Infantry Division Historical After Action Report, M-7 Operation, p. 11;
XI Corps Historical After Action Report, Luzon Campaign, M-7 Operation, p. 2.

(6) Eighth Army AAR, p. 124;
38th Division AAR, p. 12.

(7) Eighth Army AAR, p. 106.

(8) Eighth Army AAR, p. 122-124.

(9) 38th Division AAR, p. 11;
Walters, *The Operations of the 38th Infantry Division*, p. 9;
Eighth Army AAR, p. 111.

(10) Eighth Army AAR, p. 106.

(11) Morison, Samuel Eliot, *History of United States Naval Operations in World War II*, Vol. XII: *Leyte*, p. 119n.

(12) Smith, Robert Ross, *Triumph in the Philippines*, p. 312;
Eighth Army AAR, p. 124;
Morison, Vol. XIII: *Liberation of the Philippines*, p. 187-188.

(13) Eighth Army AAR, p. 98.

(14) Smith, *Triumph in the Philippines*, p. 310.

(15) General Headquarters Southwest Pacific Area, Staff Study
     Operation Mike-Seven, 14 January 1945, p.3.
(16) Eighth Army AAR, p. 94;
     38th Division AAR, 8, p. 15;
     XI Corps AAR, p. 4.
(17) Headquarters Eighth Army, G-2 Estimate of the Enemy Situation,
     15 January 1945;
     Headquarters 38th Division, G-2 Estimate of the Enemy Situation
     Mike Seven Operation, 16 January 1945, p. 1-3.
(18) Smith, *Triumph in the Philippines*, p. 314.
(19) Eighth Army AAR, p. 95;
     Walters, *The Operations of the 38th Infantry Division*, p. 9.
(20) Walker, Major Stephen M., *The Operations of Company A, 151st
     Infantry in the Attack Through ZigZag Pass 8-11 February 1945*,
     Advanced Infantry Officers Course, 1949-50, p. 6.
(21) Message—34th Infantry Journal Entry #37, 1700-28 January
     1945.
(22) *How the Kato Company Fought: The Record of the 3rd Machine
     Company 39th Infantry Regiment*, Nagai, Tamotsu, Editor, 1990,
     p. 224.

"ONLY CASUALTY FROM AN ILL-TEMPERED CARABAO"

(29 January)

Incessant blaring on the ships' intercom systems awakened the assault troops at 0330 on B-day 29 January. The Navy did not serve the traditional steak breakfast reserved for marines. The staple breakfast of bacon and eggs at 0400 was more than adequate. At 0500, the heavily laden riflemen formed on deck to board the unsteady LCVPs waiting below.

Each man carried at least 50 pounds of weapons and gear. His pack, with poncho strapped on, contained his personal belongings, a change of underwear, a change of socks and mess kit. To his cartridge belt were fastened canteen, first aid packet, entrenching tool and bayonet.

His most prized possession was his .30 caliber, 9 1/2 pound, gas-operated, semi-automatic, M-1 Garand rifle. Lieutenant General George S. Patton, Jr., called this masterpiece "the greatest battle implement ever devised." With eight-round clips, the average soldier could fire about 20 aimed shots a minute. The Garand gave the GI a decided advantage over the Japanese, who were still firing a bolt action, five-clip rifle of World War I vintage.[1]

Each American carried 12 clips of ammunition in pockets on his cartridge belt. He often carried 12 more clips in two bandoliers criss-crossing his shoulders. Many men strapped a fragmentation grenade to the front of each shoulder. The steel helmet completed the battle gear.[2]

One man in each squad carried a .30 caliber BAR (Browning Automatic Rifle), a cross between a rifle and a machine gun. Little changed since World War I, the gas-operated BAR with bipod and magazine weighed 19.4 pounds. Most soldiers used the BAR like a rifle, firing 300 to 350 rounds per minute even on slow automatic fire. This fire could be stepped up to 500 to 600 shots per minute on fast automatic. The BAR man normally carried 12 20-round magazines in a special cartridge belt with six pouches for two magazines each. He used the bipod when possible to increase his accuracy, but many times shot from the hip. Despite its intricate mechanism, the BAR was a potent weapon, particularly popular in close jungle fighting.[3]

Only the clanking, screeching sound of the davits, cranking to lower the boats into a calm sea, marred the dark early morning stillness. By 0630, the veterans had scrambled down the cargo-net ladders. Hitting the slippery deck of an LCVP rising on each wave crest, then falling in the trough, was difficult for the average soldier in the calmest of seas. The LCVPs began circling, preparatory to the dash inland. Only the air cover, the vigilant P-38s and P-47s from Leyte, provided realism to a major assault on Japanese-held territory without a deafening bombardment.

Admiral Struble had planned an hour's bombardment of the beaches starting at 0730. At first light, he had ordered destroyers *Isherwood* and *Young* to close the beaches and report their findings. His precautions paid off. Commander D. G. Dockum of *Young* reported that many Filipinos were in boats or on the beach. Guerrilla 1st Lieutenant Aureliano F. Tadena of the Philippine Resistance Army boarded *Young* and was whisked away to Admiral Struble's flagship, *Mount McKinley*. Tadena reported that American and Philippine flags were flying and that the nearest enemy was in Olongapo.[4]

Colonel Jenna had decided to land two battalions abreast and keep one battalion in reserve. The boats carrying the assault elements of the 34th formed without incident, the 1st Battalion on the left and the 2nd on the right. With spray flying, the LCVPs raced inland. When the boat ramps dropped in the sand at the scheduled time of 0830, instead of Japanese machine guns, Filipinos lined the beach and waved the troops in.

At the water's edge, nothing could be seen; the beach slope was too sharp. Once beyond the beach, the eye could catch a panorama of once cultivated fields, sunken roads and eroded gullies during this, the dry season. Dry streambeds wrinkled the landscape. Frequent palm groves, clumps of trees and undergrowth stretched in the distance to the Zambales Mountains along the horizon. The Japanese had learned that naval gunfire turned beach defenses into a shambles. Official Japanese doctrine at this stage of the war called for giving up the beaches and fighting in the hills.

The Filipino guerrillas under command of Lieutenant Colonel Gyles Merrill, formerly of the Philippine Scouts of the U.S. 26th Cavalry, had done their job. Soon after the landings at Lingayen Gulf on 9 January,

Merrill, commander of all guerrilla forces in Zambales and Bataan Provinces, had ordered Captain Ramon Magsaysay, a future president of the Philippines, to capture and occupy that part of western Zambales from San Felipe to Olongapo. In the area of the scheduled San Antonio landings, guerrillas had captured San Marcelino Airfield three days before the landing, overrun a "powerful" Japanese radio station at San Miguel and cleared the beach areas of Japanese from San Felipe to San Antonio.[5]

As early as 0100, Filipinos had been watching what Crispina Agaton described as "a sea full of fireflies"[6] as the American ships reached the landing site. By dawn, Filipinos had claimed the beaches. In the 34th RCT sector, 2nd Battalion 34th milled about the beach for more than an hour, waiting for all elements of the 34th to land and organize. The men joked and fraternized with their hosts. One agile Filipino shinnied up a tree and picked coconuts for G Company. "An old man danced a jig and waved an American flag."[7]

The 34th RCT's first day's mission was to push rapidly eastward and secure the pass between Castillejos and Subic 12 miles away. The Japanese might move into prepared positions there after hearing of the American landing. Even a Japanese platoon might slow the advance for a few hours.

General MacArthur would brook no delay. In his pleas to the Joint Chiefs of Staff in 1944 to liberate Luzon, MacArthur had boasted that his forces would be in Manila two weeks after the initial landing at Lingayen Gulf. In twenty days, leading elements of Sixth Army's XIV Corps had advanced only as far as San Fernando, still 30 miles from Manila.

MacArthur was not happy with Sixth Army's progress; therefore, its commander, General Krueger, was not happy. XI Corps was to come under Sixth Army control as soon as the beach area was secured and Corps headquarters could be established on land. MacArthur's and Krueger's demand for speed would breathe heavily down the chain of command onto General Hall. Their urging and Hall's natural competitive spirit and aggressiveness would make "speed" the XI Corps watchword.

The 2nd Battalion 34th was the initial spearhead of the corps's advance. The fully motorized 24th Division Reconnaissance Troop commanded by 1st Lieutenant Richard V. Collopy of Chillicothe, Ohio, would take over the point as soon as his Troop could unload, assemble and start moving. The 1st Battalion 34th was to consolidate the beachhead; the 3rd, which landed after the 1st and 2nd, was to load on trucks and leapfrog the 2nd Battalion.

At 0950, the 2nd Battalion moved out for San Antonio along a hard dry streambed. In San Antonio, the battalion stepped onto Provincial Highway 7, an all-weather road with a firm bed and solid crown. In towns and on the approaches to towns the road had been macadamized. Because the guerrillas had reported no Japanese along the highway or in the pass between Castillejos and Subic, the Americans dispensed with flank guards and moved fast. "Every crossroads was lined with Filipinos with flowers in their hands."[8] Collopy's Reconnaissance Troop passed 2nd Battalion at 1115 and pushed on to Subic Bay before dark without enemy contact.

By the end of the first day, 2nd Battalion 34th had hiked 12 miles along Highway 7 through San Antonio, San Marcelino and Castillejos to a bivouac in the wooded hills between Castillejos and Subic Town. The 3rd Battalion followed by foot and truck and encamped south of 2nd Battalion about 3,000 yards south of Castillejos. The 1st Battalion, moving entirely by truck, shuttled just beyond Castillejos to a point behind the 2nd Battalion.[9]

The new replacements, some of whom had joined their companies, soon learned the veterans' routine for digging in while it was still daylight. Each company dug its own perimeter of foxholes, three men to a hole. One dug with an entrenching tool, one stood guard and the third cut brush with a machete. The latter cleared a good field of fire so the enemy could not sneak too close after dark. During the night, one man stood guard for two hours on a rotating shift while the other two slept. The company commander located his command post near the center of the perimeter. Each platoon leader dug in behind his platoon. The Japanese were so adept at infiltrating that there was general agreement to shoot anyone moving about after dark.

The ingenuity and adaptiveness of the American GI were amazing. He would readily dig a rough foxhole night after night and move on the next day. But let him stay one extra day in the same place and he immediately created a home by fastening two ponchos together and stretching them over a cross pole above the foxhole. He would carve shelves around the edges for various personal items and pieces of equipment. He would constantly improve the hole's comfort by meticulously adjusting the two ponchos just right to shield against sun or rain. He would build the ring of dirt around the hole ever higher to give more protection from bullets and shell fragments.

✵   ✵   ✵

The 38th Division accomplished its first-day missions with dispatch. Regular Army Major General Henry L. C. Jones, the division commander, elected to land his 151st, 149th and 152nd regiments abreast from north to south. Because of the narrowness of the beach, battalions landed in column. There was no opposition except the cheering Filipinos. They crowded the beaches and hindered the landing until they were organized into work gangs in the afternoon to help unload the ships. A soldier in F Company 151st Infantry was the only casualty of the day. He "was gored by one of the notoriously ill-tempered Filipino carabao" and evacuated to the LST hospital ship.[10]

Filipinos help unload ships 1st day, 29 January 1945

General Jones was born in Nebraska, but moved to Nevada in his early years. He was graduated in 1906 at age 19 from the University of Nevada with a degree in engineering. A year younger than General Hall, he had acquired all the experience necessary to qualify as a division commander. Entering the Army in 1911, he served his Philippine tour of duty in 1914-17. After transferring to the field artillery, he served as an instructor at Fort Sill, Oklahoma, during World War I. Between the wars he attended the requisite Army schools and was an honor graduate at the Command and General Staff College.

In July 1941, Jones was made brigadier general and named commander of the 1st Division Artillery. He became commander of the 38th in April 1942 and the following month attained the rank of major general. As the 38th Division prepared to engage in its first combat, General Jones had supervised and been responsible for its training for nearly three years.[11]

By 1600, the 38th Division's 149th Infantry had secured the day's principal objective, the San Marcelino airfield. Filipinos assisted the GIs by carrying packs and equipment. Colonel Paddock, the 151st Infantry commander, placed his 1st Battalion on the extreme left for left flank protection of the beachhead. To protect the right flank, he moved his 3rd Battalion across the entire beachhead with little interruption to traffic.[12]

The 152nd Infantry's mission was to follow the 34th

Major General Henry L. C. Jones,
Commander 38th Infantry Division

RCT and mop up any resistance bypassed by the 34th. Colonel Stillwell, commander of the 152nd, finding no resistance, sent his 3rd Battalion, commanded by Major Harry Mangold, to San Marcelino. The 3rd Battalion was to provide additional protection for the airfield. Mangold formed his battalion in perimeter northwest of the airfield during the afternoon. By nightfall, the battalion's motor vehicles had been unloaded and brought into the perimeter.[13]

The 152nd Infantry would be the guinea pig. By its assignment and position in the B-day plans, the regiment would be the first to face the enemy in ZigZag Pass.

🌑   🌑   🌑

At the beach, the operation was not moving as smoothly. Units and supplies had not always been loaded at Leyte in reverse order. This meant delays in unloading and in forming units in their proper marching order, a nuisance for an unopposed landing, but deadly serious if the enemy had defended the beach.

Reefs cannot always be seen in aerial photographs. The LSTs encountered reefs in their assigned landing areas and lost time looking for suitable beaches. Not until 1430 was an adequate beach found. In some cases, supporting troops on these LSTs unloaded miles from their objective areas.

Bulldozer operators were responsible for pushing sufficient sand against the LSTs' lowered ramp to provide a firm path for vehicles to clear the LSTs. If the drivers were lax or inept, trucks stalled in the water and deep sand. At times, unloading personnel did not use wire mats properly to keep trucks from sinking. Using 20-20 hindsight, Eighth Army recommended that a loading officer be assigned to each ship in the future to avoid these pitfalls.[14]

Serious problems developed because of careless handling of supplies. The ships carried 30 days of all four classes of supplies—Class I Food, Class II Clothing, Class III Petroleum Products, Class IV General—plus five units of fire for combat troops and three units of fire for service troops. All the supplies were unloaded immediately on the initial beaches at San Antonio and San Narciso. Within two days, the supplies had to be displaced 22 miles forward to Olongapo. This meant double handling of every pound of supplies. As a result, because of the great tonnages involved, the long turnaround time and limited truck transportation, more than 1,000 tons of supplies remained in the initial beach dumps two weeks after the landing.[15]

With careful planning, immediate supply requirements would have been unloaded the first day on the landing beaches and the remainder retained on the ships as a floating reserve. After two days, the ships could have moved directly to Subic Bay and the supplies unloaded when needed. Since XI Corps had scheduled the landing on Grande Island and occupation of Subic Bay for 30 January, it is difficult to understand why all the supplies were unloaded on the landing beaches on 29 January.

An important bright spot was the handling of ammunition. The 186-man 636th Ordnance Ammunition Company had landed by 1100, ready to receive, segregate and stack ammunition in the beach dumps as soon as unloading started. Filipino civilians lightened many a tired soldier's load by joining the American labor details.[16]

In retrospect, it is easy to criticize slip-ups in the Mike-Seven Operation and to wonder why certain actions were taken and decisions made that today seem odd and illogical. We must consider the enormous pressure under which all hands were operating. Schedules for landing operations were tight. Mike-Seven and Mike-Six landings were two days apart. Both were loaded at the same time. Mike-Three had to be changed to Mike-Seven in a week's time. Two reinforcing divisions for Mike-One were loaded during this same period. Those personnel responsible for loading the ships—Army and Navy quartermaster units, beach masters,

Eighth Army and XI Corps staff planners—accomplished this immense task in the last two weeks of January in one small area—Tacloban Harbor, Leyte.[17]

The wonder is that the operations went as smoothly as they did and that there were no major, damaging snafus. Personnel involved were strained to the utmost to coordinate loading operations. Despite the anxiety and pressure, in their After Action Reports, these same personnel were hard on themselves and sometimes on others as they strove to improve their performance and not repeat the same mistakes.

🌶   🌶   🌶

During the daylight hours of 28 January, Lieutenant Abe, commander of the Water's Edge Position Guard Troop at Kalaklan Point, observed American destroyers scouting the channel in Subic Bay on both sides of Grande Island. He reported that at dusk he saw about 40 ships moving north beyond Subic Bay.

On 29 January, Lieutenant Abe radioed Major Ogawa, commander of the 3rd Battalion 39th Infantry in ZigZag Pass that the enemy had landed on the west coast of Luzon about 20 miles from Subic Bay. Ogawa assembled his officers that evening in his well dug-in headquarters bunker atop the highest point in his defenses, offered a victory toast and swore to destroy the enemy.[18]

Chapter 5
NOTES

(1) Bruce, Robert, *The U.S. M1 Garand Rifle*, p. 18, p. 21.
(2) O'Donnell, Michael J. and Sylvia, Stephen W., *Uniforms, Weapons and Equipment of the World War II GI*, p. 92, p. 156.
(3) *Ibid.*, p. 94, p. 141.
(4) Morison, Samuel Eliot, *History of United States Naval Operations in World War II*, Vol. XIII: *Liberation of the Philippines*, p. 187-188.
(5) DeJesus, Ramon V., *Zambales*, p. 56, p. 58.
(6) Letter to author from daughter, Alpha Canonizado, 6 September 1995.
(7) Smith, Pvt. Arthur D., K Company, *34th Infantry Monograph,* p. 1.
(8) *Ibid.*, p. 2.
(9) 34th Infantry Journal, p. 2.
(10) 151st Infantry After Action Report (AAR), p. 2; 38th Division AAR, p. 15.
(11) 38th Division Officer Biographies. National Records Center, College Park, MD.
(12) 38th Division AAR, p. 15; 151st Infantry AAR, p. 1-2.
(13) Schoonover, Major James F., *The Operations of the 3rd Battalion 152nd Infantry in Zig Zag Pass, Luzon, 29 Jan.-14 Feb. 1945*, Advanced Infantry Officers Course, 1947-1948, p. 6.
(14) *Report of the Commanding General Eighth Army on the Nasugbu and Bataan Operations, Mike Six and Mike Seven*, p. 77, p. 99.
(15) *Ibid.*, p. 105, 107.
(16) *Ibid.*, p. 116.
(17) *Ibid.*, p. 106.
(18) Ogawa, Major Hironori, *Record of the 3rd Battalion, 39th Infantry Regiment in the "Big Asia War,"* p. 18.

FIGHT AT THE WATER'S EDGE POSITION

(30 January)

When General Hall stepped ashore at 0800 on 30 January, XI Corps passed from Eighth Army to Sixth Army control. Hall's objective for the day was to capture Olongapo so that XI Corps could be supplied by sea, and the ever-lengthening overland supply route from San Antonio abandoned. His plan called for the 34th RCT to follow Highway 7 and secure Olongapo and for the 2nd Battalion 151st Infantry to seize Grande Island, the "Corregidor" of Subic Bay.[1]

Subic Bay was the focal point of operation Mike-Seven. With its protective Grande Island near the entrance, the bay had always been significant in both Spanish and American plans for defending the Philippines. The Spanish first entered Subic Bay (called *Subig* by the natives, a spelling that persisted into the 20th century) in 1572. Although impressed with the bay's deep water, sheltered anchorages and strategic location, the Spanish established their main naval base and shipyard at Cavite on Manila Bay's southern shore. But Cavite, with its shallow water and unhealthy living conditions, rampant with malaria and other diseases, finally convinced the Spanish in 1868 to look for another base.

In 1885, the Spanish began construction of a naval base at Subic Bay. Filipino laborers, under Spanish direction, worked off their heavy tax burden by constructing a foundry and other shops for ship repair and by enclosing these structures with a wall on the landside for defense. Spanish plans called for shore batteries to be installed at the entrance to the bay and on Grande Island to complete the fortifications.[2]

When the United States declared war on Spain 25 April 1898, the Spanish Admiral Montojo took his fleet to Subic Bay, but found the defenses not as strong as he had anticipated. He returned to Manila Bay and his fate is too well known to be recounted here.

In the first decade of the 20th century, the Subic Bay Naval Station served as a training ground for U.S. Marines. Hikes were usually five days long, the Marines cutting their way through dense undergrowth, wading streams and swamps, crossing mountains. Admiral C. J. Train, commander of the Asiatic Fleet, called Subic Bay the most valuable school any Marine ever had. He especially praised "their practice marches . . . into a most wild and difficult country, their building of bridges and practice of everything that is a soldier's duty in the field."[3]

During the war scare with Japan in 1907, President Theodore Roosevelt quietly began to build up both the Army and Navy defenses of Subic Bay. Major General Leonard Wood, commander of the Philippine Division in Manila, considered the naval base at Olongapo indefensible from the landside. He thought it would require a defensive line of about 35 miles of permanent fortifications manned by 80,000 men, and if no permanent works were built, by 125,000 men. General Wood envisaged defenses necessary to hold "all this difficult country" three times as extensive as those manned by the Russians at Port Arthur in 1904-05. Congressional appropriations for a major naval base in the Philippines lagged behind, and in 1908 Roosevelt started pushing for funding for a major base at Pearl Harbor.[4]

Despite cutbacks in appropriations for the Subic Bay Naval Base in the 1930s, Olongapo thrived, and by the beginning of World War II, boasted a population of 15,000. Until 1932, Olongapo could be reached from Manila only by sea. By a coincidence already mentioned, General Hall made the trip by automobile at the beginning of construction of the road from Dinalupihan to Olongapo. "I finally made it over the pass to the Naval Base at Olongapo, but it took a lot of help from Filipinos and twelve hours to do it," he wrote in 1949.[5]

Lying directly athwart the shipping lanes from the South China Sea through the bay to Olongapo, Grande Island, with its Fort Wint, had been a key point in America's pre-war defensive scheme for the Philippines. Although its huge naval guns had been spiked when the Americans withdrew in 1942, the island could be a formidable obstacle if still in possession of the Japanese.

☞ ☞ ☞

Colonel Jenna picked the 3rd Battalion to lead the advance this day since that battalion was closest to the objective, Olongapo. The battalion commander, Lieutenant Colonel Edward M. Postlethwait from Kansas City, Missouri, Class of 1937 West Point, loved the Army and had entered West Point as a private from the 14th Home Cavalry. His battalion, with A Company attached, was to earn undying fame and a Presidential

Citation for its role as the amphibious landing force in the seizure of Corregidor.[6]

The 3rd Battalion 34th moved out at 0810 and entered Subic Town 45 minutes later with no sign of the Japanese. Then, the 24th Recon Troop took the lead again with 3rd Battalion in trucks close behind and 1st Battalion about a mile back. 2nd Battalion remained at its bivouac in the Castillejos-Subic Pass in regimental reserve.[7]

Highway 7, running south from Subic Town, hugged the coast under the precipitous, jungle-covered cliffs of a long ridge called Kalaklan on American maps and Mount Todai (lighthouse) by the Japanese. About a mile west of Olongapo, the road bent sharply left 180 degrees in a hairpin turn, ran 200 yards north, then made a 90 degree turn right. Olongapo lay southeast across a narrow bridge spanning the Kalaklan River. A spit of rocky ridge with a lighthouse at the end projected about 300 yards seaward from the base of the "U" of the hairpin turn. The lighthouse at the tip of the peninsula was known as Kalaklan Point.

Major Ogawa had selected this location primarily to help repel the expected American landing near Olongapo. He had entrusted the defense of this area to 2nd Lieutenant Hiroshi Abe, a platoon leader in the anti-tank company of the 3rd Battalion 39th Infantry. Abe's principal armament consisted of two 37-mm anti-tank guns with 600 rounds of ammunition. Located on the eastern side of the projecting spit of rocky

Lighthouse in 1993; view from road at "hairpin" turn

ridge, the anti-tank guns were sited to fire into the bay against the American landing force.

In addition to himself and his own platoon of 30 men, Abe was reinforced by the eight-man .30 caliber heavy machine gun squad of Sergeant Tadashi Ogaki from the battalion's machine gun company, a seven-man infantry squad with a light machine gun from the 10th Company, three men from the Olongapo naval garrison specially trained in explosives to blow the bridge, and engineer Sergeant Isoo Miyake. Abe's troops, numbering 50, had constructed an elaborate system of interconnecting pillboxes, caves and trenches, with the aid of Sergeant Miyake's drilling and blasting, and had stocked them with abundant food and ammunition.[8]

Lieutenant Abe had organized his "Water's Edge Position" into three mutually supporting components to protect the anti-tank guns and to delay the Americans. The strongest component was a pillbox located on the peninsula. Here Abe entrenched Sergeant Ogaki's heavy machine gun to sweep both sections of the road forming the hairpin turn and also to fire on the bridge. Another pillbox position was dug into the bank above the road at the 90-degree turn onto the bridge. The 10th Company squad's .25 caliber light machine gun in this pillbox protected the bridge and covered both the 200 yards of road from the "U" turn to the bridge and the anti-tank gun positions. The remainder of the squad occupied a cemetery above the road at the hairpin turn where it could cover the position on the lighthouse spit of land as well as the road by which the Americans would approach.[9]

Lieutenant Abe dug in the anti-tank guns in pillboxes on the eastern side of the peninsula in back of the beach against an almost perpendicular bank of earth. Sited to fire toward Olongapo harbor, they were of no use against an attack along Highway 7 to their rear. The explosive specialists from Lieutenant (jg) Chusaku Ito's Olongapo Naval Garrison were to halt the Americans by demolishing the bridge. Lieutenant Abe also had Sergeant Miyake set explosive charges to blow a hole in the road about midway between the "U" turn and the bridge to create an anti-tank ditch.[10]

A culvert under the road near the bridge would serve, if needed, as an egress in defilade for the troops on the peninsula to cross the road by squeezing through the culvert, climbing the 15-foot high bank to the cemetery, and escaping to the relative safety of Mount Todai. Characteristic of all Japanese defenses, an extensive trench system connected major points, enabling the defenders to move from one position to another unobserved. G-2 XI Corps reported that an experienced observer, who had been on Saipan, stated that the defenses at the lighthouse position were the most extensive he had seen.[11]

About 1 1/2 miles north of Kalaklan Point, the 24th Reconnaissance Company received artillery fire without damage or casualties. The artillery fire was later determined to be friendly. Apparently, the 63rd Field Artillery Battalion, which had unlimbered at Subic at the top of the bay, was trying to lay down fire in front of the leading elements. There was no artillery observer forward, and the reconnaissance unit was moving faster than expected.

Company I, leading the 3rd Battalion 34th, was in rear of the reconnaissance troop. 1st Lieutenant Paul J. Cain of Urbana, IL, I Company's commander, immediately had his company dismount from the trucks and move by foot. Not knowing the source of the artillery fire and not wishing to bypass any Japanese, Cain sent the 3rd Platoon, commanded by 2nd Lieutenant John W. McFayden from Milwaukee, WI, and Platoon Sergeant Personeni up the ridge to cover his left flank.[12]

Watching from their secluded positions, the well dug-in Japanese engaged the 24th Reconnaissance Troop about noon as it tried to make the "U" turn. Lieutenant Collopy's men immediately returned fire with .30 and .50 caliber machine guns and 37-mm anti-tank guns mounted on jeeps. But routing the enemy from his well-prepared positions was a job for the rifle companies. Lieutenant Cain sent 2nd Lieutenant Lewis Richtiger's 1st Platoon up the bank to take and occupy the cemetery and 2nd Lieutenant Kenneth E. Yeomans's 2nd Platoon forward to knock out the heavy machine gun pillbox position on the peninsula. This was a job well suited for the daredevil Yeomans of Somerville, MA, who was later killed on Mindanao.[13]

A sergeant in Richtiger's platoon in the cemetery produced "probably the longest expert rifle shot fired up to that time by the 34th in combat." He spied a Japanese soldier apparently trying to blow the bridge. Calmly, at a range of 300-350 yards, he zeroed in and found his mark. Another Japanese tried; he got him also. A total of three Japanese tried in vain to blow the bridge.[14]

Not sure of the enemy strength, Lieutenant Cain called for more firepower. Colonel Postlethwait dispatched the RCT's heavy armament, the 1st Platoon 603rd Tank Company and the 34th regiment's Cannon Company, which were forward with the 3rd Battalion. Most cannon companies in the Pacific were armed with the 105-mm gun mounted on an M-3 Sherman tank chassis. Cannon Company 34th, however, had two platoons of two vehicles each equipped with 75-mm guns called SPMs (Self-Propelled Mounts) and one platoon with the standard 105-mm mount. One of the platoons of 75-mm SPMs was in the vanguard this day.[15]

In a drizzling rain, Yeomans, supported by the SPMs, attacked the machine gun on the peninsula with two squads and sent Sergeant John Mitchell's third squad down the road toward the bridge. Cannon Company's lead 75-mm SPM tore into Sergeant Ogaki's machine gun on the peninsula. Three men were killed: Atsumi Hirai was shot in the head, Toshimichi Yamauchi received a shell fragment in the stomach, and Shinichiro Otani died from a shell fragment in the neck.[16]

During the firefight, scout James L. Adams of one of Yeomans's squads was wounded in the hip while crossing an exposed area. Sergeant Roger Guilliam of Defiance, OH, and company aid man, Pfc. Victor Hinze of Racine, WI, dashed across the exposed area amid a hail of machine gun and rifle fire. After administering aid in the prone position, Guilliam and Hinze attempted to drag Adams to safety. The fire was so intense they were pinned down for 30 minutes until friendly fire enabled litter bearers to rescue Adams.[17]

The Japanese machine gun dug into the bank caused even more trouble. Squad Leader Mitchell, Pfc. William E. Rose and Pvt. William F. Allen all fell mortally wounded. In barely six months after graduation from high school the previous June, Allen had received basic training, been shipped overseas, and been killed his first day in combat.[18]

At about this time, Sergeant Miyake blew the hole in the road 100 yards beyond the hairpin turn. According to Cain, the "demolition did not do a very good job." The lead SPM could not advance, but could still fire at anything that moved.

The tank trap did not hold up the column long. Men of C Company 3rd Engineer Battalion brought steel mats, usually used to keep vehicles from bogging down on sandy beaches, and covered the anti-tank ditch. The survivors of Abe's outpost, after returning to the main lines, told a sad story. They reported in amazement that the Americans unloaded steel plates full of many small holes, assembled the plates into a bridge, and even "tanks started forward on the steel plates as if nothing had happened."[19]

The action was over by 1600. Cain assigned McFayden's 3rd Platoon the task of clearing the peninsula of Japanese. The reconnaissance company, the tanks and Cannon Company rolled into Olongapo, followed by K and L Companies. I Company had shed the first American blood of the campaign, losing three men killed and one wounded. An artillery forward observer and a man from Cannon Company were also wounded. The Americans estimated they killed 14 Japanese.[20]

The 105-mm howitzers of the 63rd Field Artillery Battalion shifted their fire to Olongapo to complete its devastation. The retreating enemy had already started burning what he could not remove. From Cain's position at the hairpin turn, Olongapo "looked like it was pretty much all on fire." But some of the warehouses in the former American naval base that were only partially destroyed were repaired and later used for the XI Corps ordnance shops.[21]

Lieutenant Abe's superiors had expected too much of him. With only 50 men, he was no match for an infantry company, much less the infantry battalion behind. Following orders to emplace his 37-mm AT guns to fire on ships in Olongapo harbor, his heaviest armament was useless against an attack from the rear. His machine guns were quickly put out of action once the SPMs' 75-mm guns came into play. Apparently with no electrical detonators, his men could not conceal themselves to blow the bridge at a distance. But Abe's determined resistance had kept the Americans away from the main positions in ZigZag Pass for at least another day.[22]

After 3rd Battalion (less I Company) moved into Olongapo, 1st Battalion passed through and fanned out north and east of the captured port. Company I dug in for the night around the hairpin turn. Movement could be heard along the beaches of the peninsula, but the men on guard could not tell whether the enemy was withdrawing or reinforcing his positions.

Olongapo burning after artillery bombardment, 30 January

Under a now moonlit sky, the Japanese survivors waded along the west side of the peninsula or escaped through the trench system to the culvert and reached the cliffs above the cemetery. Anti-tank gunner Heiichi Nakamura saw the man in front of him shot by an I Company rifleman. Nakamura managed to worm his way through the culvert and climb Mount Todai to safety.[23]

Anti-tank gunner Heiichi Nakamura in 1992 observing
culvert through which he crawled to safety after skirmish
at Water's Edge Position, 30 January 1945

Sergeant Ogaki and three of his men carried a fourth, Pfc. Toyoji Narukawa, who had been wounded by a cannon shot in the right thigh. While the group was struggling up Mount Todai, Narukawa whispered, "I cannot go farther; if I did, I would be a burden to you." Left alone, he committed suicide with a grenade. The four survivors of the Ogaki squad, carrying their machine gun salvaged from the fight, made their way back to ZigZag Pass the next day.[24]

Abe was one of those who escaped. He reported to 2nd Lieutenant Kitano of the Sakura Company, whom Major Ogawa sent to learn the details of the battle, that the enemy he faced was about 1,000 strong with eight to ten tanks. He thought he had been attacked by a battalion and had caused approximately 100 casualties. He had destroyed some enemy automatic weapons, but admitted the loss of one of his anti-tank guns.

According to American reports, he had lost through destruction or abandonment both machine guns, both anti-tank guns, four pillboxes filled with explosives and many caves containing ammunition and food in abundance.[25]

The 34th's enlisted replacements had not landed with the leading waves, but had assisted in unloading supplies at the beach. Some of these men were still trying to catch up with their units. Twenty assigned to A Company reached Olongapo late in the afternoon over the bridge, still smoldering after its attempted destruction. They found a town marked with fires and dark smoke. Scattered shots from the retreating enemy still posed a danger. Filipinos hugged the Americans and tearfully thanked them for coming. The GIs responded with cigarettes. According to Private William J. McKenna of Albany, CA, "It is 1900 and still we haven't found A Company. We decide to spend at least another night on our own. We move into one of the empty houses in the town."[26]

While 1st and 3rd Battalions 34th were liberating huge chunks of important territory, 2nd Battalion experienced a slow and frustrating day. The battalion could not move from its bivouac of the night before until the 152nd Infantry relieved at 1225. By that time, the 24th Reconnaissance Troop had made first contact with the enemy. Not knowing the extent of the resistance in Olongapo, Colonel Jenna ordered the 2nd Battalion to be trucked forward either to help 3rd Battalion or to be available for pursuit. Major Snavely, the 2nd Battalion commander, did not receive the radio message to entruck, because in that hilly country, radio contact was not reliable. This was the first instance of a problem that was to plague all units from time to time throughout the campaign.

Snavely ordered his battalion to move by foot as soon as the first elements of the 152nd arrived. The men were soon strung out along both sides of Highway 7 with movement slow and jerky because of the action at Kalaklan Point. At about 1700, the battalion stopped to dig in at a small valley that opened from the bay halfway between Subic Town and Olongapo. Even though the Japanese were miles away, 2nd Battalion dug foxholes in respect for the unpredictable enemy.[27]

General Hall had to be pleased with the first two days of the operation. More than 35,000 troops had landed, and the supplies for the combat forces had been unloaded. His corps had advanced 25 miles to Olongapo and beyond, opening port facilities for supply by sea. His forward

Olongapo Cemetery in 1993; first enemy contact 30 January

elements on the plain north of Olongapo had not drawn fire from the main body of the enemy he now suspected was in ZigZag Pass.

2nd Battalion 151st had secured Fort Wint on Grande Island by 1130 without opposition. Army planes and warships of Task Force 78.3 had given the island a good pasting on 29 January and early on 30 January. Minesweepers had found only one mine that was of 1941-42 vintage. The battalion recaptured seven early century American coast defense guns and a "considerable quantity" of artillery ammunition in good condition. None of it, however, could be utilized in the Mike-Seven operation.[28]

Major Ogawa had originally sent Lieutenant Ito's naval contingent to occupy Grande Island. On 20 January, when American planes started bombing the island every day, he recalled Ito's men. Thereafter, he sent only a small force at night to alert Lieutenant Abe if American ships started moving up the bay.[29]

Two bomb disposal squads were immediately put to work disarming unexploded bombs at the Olongapo Naval Base and on Grande Island. Most were American high explosive parachute bombs in which the fuse had failed to arm. The parachute had compressed the bomb fins, thereby preventing the rotation of the arming vane.[30]

Having finished his initial tasks easily, Hall felt confident he could comply rapidly with the crucial order he had received earlier in the day. This was an advance copy of Field Order #46 from General Krueger at Sixth Army Headquarters outlining the actions each of his three corps would take to achieve the common mission: the liberation of Manila.

The recapture of Manila had been MacArthur's goal ever since that now distant day in March 1942 when he had left Corregidor by PT boat bound for Australia. Planning and fighting the long campaigns through New Guinea, Biak, Morotai and Leyte and the fighting with Washington to invade the Philippines had all been directed toward this moment. MacArthur had hoped to be in Manila for his 65th birthday 26 January, but it was not to be.

Sixth Army's Field Order #46 called for preparations that would lead to an all-out assault on Manila. The spearhead would be a XIV Corps two-pronged drive by the 37th Division on the right and the 1st Cavalry Division on the left. The 1st Cavalry, reinforced by the 44th Tank Battalion, was to organize a fully motorized force. This so-called "flying column" would be composed of three serials, two of which would include a cavalry squadron (similar to a battalion of infantry), a medium tank company, a 105-mm howitzer battery and other supporting elements. The other serial would be a reinforced reconnaissance unit. Brigadier General William C. Chase, commander of the 1st Cavalry Brigade, would command the "column" slated to move on 1 February.[31]

According to Field Order #46, General Hall's XI Corps was to "advance vigorously eastward, establish and maintain contact with XIV Corps along the line Hermosa-Dinalupihan." I Corps was to block the southward advance of enemy troops from the Cagayan Valley and continue to attack to the east and southeast on 1 February, capture San Jose and secure a line that would include Cabanatuan, 55 miles from the outskirts of Manila.[32]

General Hall's plan to implement his part of Field Order #46 called for the 38th Division to pass through the 34th RCT on 31 January at the junction of a trail and Highway 7 approximately 3,000 yards northeast of the 34th's leading element, A Company. At the trail junction, the 152nd Infantry would continue the attack eastward along Highway 7 to Dinalupihan. The 149th Infantry would turn left at the trail junction and follow the trail about one mile north to the barrio of Santa Rita. From there, the 149th would take a little used Negrito[33] trail and make a wide sweep north and east to reach Dinalupihan rapidly and hook up with XIV Corps. The XI Corps order directed the "advance [of the 149th and

152nd] to be so conducted that the two columns, moving along separate axes, could be mutually supporting."[34]

General Hall expected to finish his work in northern Bataan by 5 February (see page 47). He had already radioed General Krueger that he would "do [my] utmost to attain speed in reaching Dinalupihan and blocking roads in that area."[35]

Lieutenant Colonel Gyles Merrill, who commanded Philippine guerrilla forces in Zambales and Bataan Provinces, had joined General Hall at XI Corps Headquarters. He warned that 2,000 to 5,000 Japanese troops armed with machine guns, mortars, anti-tank guns, tanks and artillery, dug in or in pillboxes, were guarding ZigZag Pass blocking the way to Dinalupihan. Many were believed to be naval personnel evacuated from their base at Olongapo.

General Hall and his G-2, Colonel John W. Patton, seem to have taken this estimate with a grain of salt. It did not agree with the estimate they had formed on Leyte—that ZigZag Pass would be lightly held.

Besides, there were conflicting intelligence reports. Merrill also said that the general movement of the Japanese on Bataan was northeast, suggesting a withdrawal. A guerrilla officer reported that many of the enemy in ZigZag Pass did not have guns, were malaria ridden, and were without medicine. Analysis of documents taken from enemy dead at Olongapo indicated the presence of only air training units, naval units and freight depot personnel. No sign of combat troops. There were even wild guerrilla reports of 1,000 Formosans armed with bamboo spears and mounted Japanese cavalry patrolling the numerous trails leading from Highway 7.

No wonder G-2 took most reports with a grain of salt! The enemy force in ZigZag Pass did not seem very imposing, certainly not one that could hold up a United States Army Corps for long. The 152nd Infantry was to march into the pass against a force estimated since the landing to number as few as 900 and as many as 5,000. The only agreement among the reports (except for Merrill's) was that the Japanese troops were of low-caliber, ill equipped, and non-combat.[36]

Chapter 6
NOTES

(1) Headquarters XI Corps, Field Order #3, 19 January 1945.

(2) Anderson, Lieutenant Commander Gerald R., *Subic Bay From Magellan to Mt. Pinatubo*, p. 2-9.

(3) *Ibid.*, p. 32.

(4) Morton, Louis, *Military and Naval Preparations for the Defense of the Philippines During the War Scare of 1907*, p. 95-104.

(5) Walker, Stephen M., *The Operations of Company A, 151st Infantry in the Attack Through ZigZag Pass 8-11 February 1945*, p. 6.

(6) West Point Assembly, September 1986, p. 169.

(7) 34th Infantry After Action Report, p. 19.

(8) *How the Kato Company Fought: The Record of the 3rd Machine Gun Company 39th Infantry Regiment*, p. 33, p. 164; Ogawa, Major Hironori, *Record of the 3rd Battalion, 39th Infantry Regiment in the "Big Asia War,"* p. 18.

(9) Kato Company History, p. 34 (map).

(10) *Ibid.*, p. 167.

(11) Nakamura, Heiichi, interview, 19 October 1992; XI Corps G-2 Report #3, 31 January 1945, p. 1.

(12) Letter from Cain to author, 22 August 1994.

(13) *Ibid.*, 22 August 1994.

(14) Letter from Major General Chester A. Dahlen (ret) to author, 2 August 1986.

(15) 34th Infantry AAR, p. 22-23.

(16) Kato Company History, p. 164.

(17) Summary of official commendation of Sergeant Guilliam and Pfc. Hinze.

(18) Telephone interview with Cain, 27 April 1998.

(19) Kato Company History, p. 167.

(20) Casualties 34th RCT listed by company, name and date. Zambales Operation, The National Archives.

(21) Letter from Cain to author, 22 August 1994; Historical Report of XI Corps Ordnance Activities During the M-7 Operation, 14 January-30 June 1945, p. 14.

(22) Nagai, Tamotsu, interview by author, 13 May 1991.

(23) Nakamura interview, 19 October 1992.

(24) Kato Company History, p. 164.

(25) Ogawa, *Record of the 3rd Battalion*, p. 19;
XI Corps reported two machine guns and two 37-mm AT guns
captured at Kalaklan Point. One of the 37-mm guns with
ammunition was prepared for demolition. G-2 XI Corps Report
#4, 1800-1 February 1945;
34th Infantry AAR, p. 37, also reports two machine guns
captured. Surviving Japanese contend that Sergeant Ogaki
returned to the West Pass with his heavy machine gun.

(26) McKenna, Pvt. William J., A Company 34th Infantry diary.

(27) 34th Infantry AAR, p. 24-25.

(28) Report of the Commanding General Eighth Army on the Nasugbu
and Bataan Operations (After Action Report), p. 107.

(29) Ogawa, *Record of the 3rd Battalion*, p. 17.

(30) Eighth Army AAR, p. 118.

(31) *Ibid.*, p. 215.

(32) Field Order #46, 2300-30 January 1945, Sixth United States
Army Report of the Luzon Campaign, 9 January-30 June 1945,
Vol. I of four volumes, p. 148.

(33) Pygmy hill people of Luzon.

(34) Smith, *Triumph in the Philippines*, p. 314;
Message, XI Corps to 38th Division 2020.

(35) Radio, Hall to Krueger, 1100-30 January 1945.

(36) XI Corps G-2 Reports #1, #2, & #3; 29 January, 30 January and
31 January 1945, respectively.

PART II
The Japanese Dominate the Battlefield

MAJOR OGAWA'S DOMAIN

With the 152nd Infantry poised to move through the 34th and attack into ZigZag Pass, the Japanese dispositions in the pass must be considered. Because 14th Area Army had provided only an essentially useless 1:500,000-scale map of the area, Major Ogawa's troops had made their own small-scale maps. Most of the soldiers came from Himeji and Hyogo Prefecture in southwest Honshu. Therefore, the officers named the key defensive terrain features after well-known places at home or used the Japanese word to describe a certain feature. Since the Americans also lacked small-scale maps and never got around to naming the key features, we will use the Japanese designations in describing the battlefield.

Major Ogawa's 3rd Battalion 39th Infantry was as different as night and day from the hastily organized, rear area troops XI Corps expected were defending the pass. Colonel Nagayoshi felt that the 39th's training as part of a division and army in the cold plains and mountains of northeastern Manchuria would handicap the regiment in the narrow confines of a tropical island. In jungled mountains, it would be difficult to mount an attack of any size, and large-scale maneuver was out of the question. But battle in ZigZag Pass would prove that the ardor, elan and defensive skills of Colonel Nagayoshi's men compensated for any offensive liabilities. Although they knew reinforcement was impossible, morale was exceedingly high. They were sick of training! They were confident of their ability and eager to tangle with the Americans.

The 3rd Battalion was reinforced with regimental heavy weapons, with artillery and tanks—albeit only two pieces of each—and the provisional Nakayama Battalion of airmen turned infantrymen in its rear. In its six weeks in the pass, Ogawa's battalion had dug in expertly on ground that was as suited for defense as any that could be devised for a theoretical problem at the Military Academy in Tokyo. Morale was high. Although malaria and typhoid fever had caused at least three deaths and had affected several men, all the sick had returned to their stations for the impending battle.[1]

Major Hironori Ogawa was graduated from the Military Academy in August 1937 after an 11-year army career as an enlisted man. After fighting in China and serving a tour as a regimental aide-de-camp, he became commander of the 3rd Battalion 39th Infantry in December 1943 and was promoted to major 1 December 1944. He had been cited by his superiors for the excellent defenses his battalion had dug north of Chiamussu, Manchuria, in the numbing cold of January 1944.[2]

💣 💣 💣

Ogawa chose for his Main Line of Resistance (MLR) the West Pass where three ridgelines met at a point on Highway 7 as the road formed a "2" on the American maps. (See Map #4, p. 90.) A long twin-topped, southeast slanting ridge south of the road formed the southern anchor of the position. The northern end of this ridge abutted the road at the upper part of the "2." The ground west of this ridge receded rapidly so that the ridge, when observed from the "horseshoe" (another prominent configuration of Highway 7 on American maps), looked like a steep, solid wall. Ogawa named this ridge Mount Ege after an ancient battlefield in Japan. He assigned the battalion's 9th Company, commanded by 1st Lieutenant Yoshio Shinfune, to control this area.

North of the road at about the same point where Ege joined the highway, two ridges, one slanting from the northwest, the other from the northeast, converged to make this area a veritable hell to break through. The western oval-shaped ridge, named Mount Hissho (must win; certain victory), inclined gradually northwest, then rose steeply into a menacing 2,000-yard long east-west ridge 600 yards north of and roughly parallel to Highway 7.

This prominent massif, with its dark cliffs, towered over the battlefield. Mount Koko, as the prominence was named, gave the Japanese a bird's-eye view of the lengthy American approach march from Olongapo along Highway 7 as well as all of their own defensive positions. Koko was certainly Major Ogawa's "most trusted subordinate" as this eagle's nest was so aptly named. Ogawa established his forward battalion headquarters atop Mount Koko and turned over its defense to his 11th Company under 1st Lieutenant Ukichi Ogata.

1st Lieutenant Ukichi Ogata, Commander 11th Company 39th Infantry

Mount Koko from Highway 7

The third of the three ridges converging at the "2" was actually triple-domed. The dome near the road, with high ground extending east one-third the distance to the next turn of Highway 7, was called Mount Minami (south). To the northeast at about 600 yards, the ground rose considerably higher to two relatively sharp peaks. The northern peak was named Mount Kita (north) and the southern, at a distance of about 150 yards, was named Mount Kasuga for a popular mountain in Nara Prefecture.

Besides being heavily fortified, Kita/Kasuga was a good observation post, a perfect mask for heavy weapons located in its rear, and a protected area for troops to form for a counterattack. 1st Lieutenant Masanobu Miyazaki's 10th Company dug the emplacements for the eventual defense of this vital northeastward slanting ridgeline with its 300-yard base paralleling the road. Because this triple-domed ridge would not come under attack until Koko and Hissho had fallen, the 10th Company constituted Major Ogawa's initial reserve.[3]

The organization of a Japanese infantry company was similar to that of the Americans. Although smaller, it packed considerable firepower. A company contained three platoons of four squads each. Three of the squads were rifle squads, each augmented by a Nambu .25 caliber light machine gun. The fourth squad contained three 50-mm grenade launchers, called "knee mortars" by the Americans. The launcher consisted of a mortar tube mounted on a stubby, curved base plate. This versatile, light (10.25 pound) weapon could fire the standard hand grenade, which could be adapted for firing from the launcher, or hurl its own 1.75 pound shell up to 700 yards. Because it was fired by a trigger arrangement (and not by gravity action as with American mortars), it could be aimed by one man at a very low angle above the horizontal at pillboxes or other close stationary targets. The eight-second-delay fuse on the grenade and a time-delay device on the shell enabled the launcher to fire through the jungle canopy without fear of premature explosion. Thus, each Japanese company mustered nine light machine guns and, in effect, nine light mortars. Ogawa estimated his three considerably under-strength rifle companies averaged 97 men each.[4]

In comparison, an American rifle company's heavier weapons were concentrated in a weapons platoon containing two air-cooled light .30 caliber machine guns and three light (60-mm) mortars. But each American company could also bank on the brutal firepower of a Browning Automatic Rifle in each of its nine rifle squads.[5]

On paper, the individual Japanese rifleman was at a serious disad-vantage compared with his American counterpart. His rifle was the Arisaka .25 caliber Meiji 38, substantially the same weapon his grandfa-ther had used in the Russo-Japanese War. Basically, the Meiji 38, using a five-round clip, was a copy of the German bolt action Mauser of 1898. Despite being saddled with a weapon definitely inferior in firepower and rapidity of fire compared to the Garand, the Japanese soldier's morale and offensive spirit never wavered.[6]

✒   ✒   ✒

Ogawa had constructed a second line to fall back on when the first inevitably fell to the preponderance of American manpower and matériel. This line, running north-south across Highway 7 about 900 yards east of the first, was also anchored by strong hill positions. North of the road, Mount Shinshu (Land of the Gods) was studded with pillboxes and spider holes connected by tunnels to entrance caves in the rear off Highway 7.

South of the road was forbidding Mount Fumetsu (indestructibility), actually two hills, with the higher to the south or the left front of the Japanese, giving added protection against an American flank attack from the south. Both Shinshu and Fumetsu crowded the road, thus forming another narrow, dreaded defile like the one between Ege and Minami.

View of Highway 7 from Mount Ege

Ogawa designated Fumetsu the "last-ditch" rallying point after all other positions had fallen.[7]

The slope of the land further toughened the almost impregnable Japanese positions. Highway 7 climbs noticeably and steadily through the horseshoe in its approach to the narrow pass between Ege and Minami on the MLR. From there, the road declines gently downhill 900 yards to the similar narrow pass between Fumetsu and Shinshu. Then the road plunges suddenly and steeply through a hairpin turn to the Santa Rita River down terrain that descends sharply to the east from the Fumetsu and Shinshu positions. The Americans would be constantly ascending and looking up to reach the high ground as they approached the MLR through the horseshoe. When they eventually reached the second line, it would avail little to outflank and attack these positions from the rear because of the near vertical approach to Fumetsu and Shinshu from the river valley.

✦　✦　✦

Ogawa's men worked feverishly and unceasingly to dig in and fortify this near perfect defensive terrain the Gods of War had granted them. Working night and day, the 3rd Battalion used all the expertise and cunning gained in fortifying previous positions against expected invasions by the Russians in Manchuria and the Americans on Formosa. The work went on 24 hours a day. Just a bag of "ship biscuits" for meals, bemoaned Tamotsu Nagai, the articulate Communications Sergeant of the 3rd Battalion Machine Gun Company. It was "very hard, disturbing work."[8]

Wherever possible, the men dug positions on the reverse slope of knolls so as to fire on the enemy after he had passed the position. They tunneled into the hillsides to obtain maximum protection against artillery fire. Japanese soldiers were adept at cutting lanes for firing machine guns through jungle growth and covering their tracks so it was almost impossible to see the cuts. They covered individual holes with dirt and logs and connected the positions with camouflaged trenches. To confuse the Americans and disperse their superior firepower, Ogawa ordered many false positions constructed, some even near the real positions.

Probably the most important facility as far as the individual Japanese soldier was concerned was the shelter cave for each unit. This large room was more strongly built than other positions and served as a haven in a storm of artillery fire. A squad of men, or more in an emergency, could find shelter during unusually heavy bombardments.

The 2nd Company 10th Engineer Regiment set demolition charges in the road approaching the West Pass. The Americans found some of these mines imbedded in the "horseshoe" section of Highway 7 installed in an ingenious manner. They were buried in the road with a long fuse attached. The fuse was carried under the surface to the roadside through a pipe to a well-concealed foxhole. A camouflaged soldier with a pull ring attached to the fuse detonated the charge at the appropriate time. Other brave individuals would emerge from well-camouflaged holes by the side of the road to make suicidal attacks on tanks by placing demolition charges on the treads.[9]

The fortifications in ZigZag Pass were so extensive and formidable that the Americans assumed the enemy had constructed the works during most of the three years of Japanese occupation. Major Ogawa emphatically states in his memoirs that his troops constructed all the works after the landing 16 December 1944 using only materials readily available, i.e., trees and earth. They adroitly concealed the dirt accumulated from the diggings. Aided by the natural camouflage of rapid jungle growth, the positions were almost impossible to detect from the air and difficult at best at ground level.[10]

There are references in 38th Division records to "concrete" pillboxes and barbed wire defenses. The survivors contend that they brought no cement or barbed wire with them and did not construct any defenses of this type. The concrete pillboxes reported may have been left over from the American defenses of 1941-42.[11]

♦ ♦ ♦

Major Ogawa located his precious few heavy weapons with great care to complement his 27 each light machine guns and grenade launchers (see Map #5, p. 91). He placed his duo of 105-mm howitzers under 2nd Lieutenant Shigeo Otani about 200 yards west of the "hairpin" at the northern end of Mount Shinshu. The guns could be moved out of their caves to cover much of the battlefield either by direct fire on the area between Mount Shinshu and Mount Minami or, directed by an observer on Mount Koko, by indirect fire on the areas west of Mount Minami along Highway 7.

Ogawa situated his next heaviest armament, two 90-mm mortars, under Master Sergeant Masatoshi Fujimoto of the Regimental Gun Company, back of the Kita/Kasuga twin peak. Fujimoto directed the fire of the mortars from Mount Koko and could cover Highway 7 from the West Pass almost back to Olongapo.[12]

The means of acquiring the mortars is somewhat of a mystery. The 39th Regiment's history says they were "received" with 430 shells on 12 January and test fired on 14 January. Survivors of the battle allege that the mortars came by the still operating original supply route by sea. Supplies and food from Manila were ferried across Manila Bay to Orani and then transported by trucks, when available, or by oxcart. Test firing could not be done in the hills and jungle because ranges could not be measured accurately. Instead, the mortars were emplaced on Mount Todai and fired across the mud flats of Olongapo. Soldiers chained the distance to the center of impact to obtain exact measurements.[13]

There is strong evidence that the Japanese used 120-mm mortars extensively during the battle (see Chapter 17, pages 233-234), but neither Ogawa nor the 39th Infantry nor Kato Company histories mention them.

The battalion commander kept the gun of Squad Leader Sergeant Okuda of 1st Lieutenant Katsutaro Yuasa's two 75-mm regimental guns with him atop Mount Koko. He would use this gun to provide plunging fire into the area of the "2" where he expected the battle to be decided. He located the other 75 slightly north of his 105s to augment the howitzers. He sited his two 70-mm battalion guns under 2nd Lieutenant Yoneji Yanase south of the road between Ege and Fumetsu to fire directly into the West Pass at the top of the "2." Ogawa's dispersion of his guns guarded against total loss from artillery concentrations, but precluded massing his own fires.[14]

The 37-mm Anti-tank Company, commanded by Captain Masaaki Ichinose, dug its positions on a knoll adjacent to Highway 7 at the northern end of Mount Ege. This area, which was the key point in Major Ogawa's primary defensive line, was called the Jukaki-dai (heavy firearms knoll). Three heavy machine guns added their firepower. The soil was so hard in this area that the Operations Company (similar to Service Company in American regiments) was called in to help dig the positions.[15]

Ogawa had already lost two of his 37-mm anti-tank guns at the Water's Edge Position, leaving him with only two 37s to deal with American armor in the pass. Captain Ichinose straddled Highway 7 at the "2" with the two remaining guns. The one south of the road was sited to fire at the enemy emerging from the "2." The northern gun could fire on the rear of tanks as they started down the road toward the hairpin or against American infantry in the defile west of Mount Ege.[16]

Positioning the heavy machine guns of 1st Lieutenant Kiyotaka Kato was the most critical element of the defense. The men of the heavier weapons could hold out indefinitely in their caves during bombardments, as could the infantry. In the final analysis, only the American infantry with their grenades, flamethrowers and close-in firepower could ultimately overcome the strong Japanese emplacements. The most effective weapon against infantry was the heavy machine gun, hence the impor-

Cave used by Lieutenants Kiyotaka Kato and Masanao Kobayashi on northern end of Mount Ege (later renamed for Captain Ichinose)

tance of locating these weapons where they could cause maximum damage.

The Japanese heavy machine gun was the Type 92 7.7-mm (.30 caliber) air-cooled "woodpecker," well known in the Pacific because of its slow, 450-rpm rate of fire and unmistakable, distinctive sound. Its fins for cooling and two pistol grips were also distinctive features. Type 92 meant that production started in 1932. The gun itself and the tripod broke down into two 60-pound backbreaking loads. Ammunition was fed by 30-round metal strips also called bullet boards, a design deficiency from conception that was never corrected. This was a serious matter when compared to the American Browning .30 caliber water-cooled heavy machine gun with its 250-round belt feed and 600-rpm rate of fire.[17]

Major Ogawa and Lieutenant Kato, commander of the Battalion Heavy Machine Gun Company, placed the company's 12 guns with care among the rifle companies. Three of the four guns of 2nd Lieutenant Takashi Koyama's 1st Platoon joined the 11th Company to defend vital Mount Koko. The guns of Sergeant Shiro Takamura and Sergeant Koji Morimoto were sited along the ridge to deliver plunging fire onto Highway 7 at the "2" or defend against attacks up the sides of Mount Koko. Sergeant Toshio Takenaka's gun was sited to fire to the west. With a maximum range of 4,500 yards, the rounds would carry almost to Olongapo. The fourth squad of Sergeant Tadashi Ogaki (down to four men after its return from the Water's Edge Position) set up at the Jukaki-dai at the northern extremity of Mount Ege.

2nd Lieutenant Masanao Kobayashi's 2nd Platoon of four squads defended the remaining portion of the initial MLR. Sergeant Haruo Morinaka's gun at the southern end of Mount Ege would discourage attempts to outflank Ege or itself fire into the saddle between the two domes of Ege. The squads of Sergeant Tadao Ueno and Sergeant Misao Kanazawa dug their guns in at the crucial northern end of Mount Ege (the Jukaki-dai) near Highway 7 with Kanazawa's gun being nearest the highway. Sergeant Yoshitada Yamauchi's squad, situated north of the road at the inner curve of the "2," would be the first to fire on the Americans as they emerged from the horseshoe.

Sergeant Takamura's squad of the 1st Platoon atop Mount Koko had the additional, important duty to halt the Americans as they attempted to cross the Hissho ridgeline to outflank Sergeant Yamauchi. Warrant Officer Kazuichi Ishihara's 3rd Platoon was assigned the initially less critical areas on the Shinshu-Fumetsu line. Sergeant Kyujiro Iga and Sergeant Kuniharu Hijikata dug their squad positions north of the road on Shinshu; Sergeant Masao Togo and Sergeant Motohiro Onishi prepared their positions on Fumetsu south of the road. Sergeant Iga had another significant role to play and initially dug in behind Mount Kita. Sergeant Togo had the additional responsibility of protecting the battalion 70-mm guns located between Fumetsu and Ege.[18]

These heavy machine gun squads were by no means immobile. They were not confined to one fixed bunker position. The squads moved their guns into other prepared positions as the battle developed.

At the 75-mm gun position at Mount Shinshu, the Japanese built a huge "U" shaped cave, which was large enough to house a company of soldiers. This cave had three entrances, two in the rear facing the valley of the Santa Rita River, the other entrance on top. Each entrance was covered with logs and dirt. There were other caves nearby for ammunition, food, a kitchen, even one with well water, all designed to serve the troops for a long battle.[19]

The Americans were to find every prominent hill and knoll honeycombed with a labyrinth of foxholes linked by tunnels or trenches to the gun positions. Each foxhole was five to six feet deep covered with logs and earth, leaving an opening to the front and one to the rear. Each foxhole was connected to the next by a shallow communications trench. The sites were so well camouflaged by rich foliage that many were unrecognizable until an American soldier was about to step on them.

The only means of silencing the fire of each foxhole or emplacement was a direct hit by artillery or mortars or an attack by individual riflemen. In abundance were spider-holes, command post caves and caves containing food, ammunition and supplies. Each hilltop was a fortress, which had to be reduced in turn. A maze of trees, underbrush, vines and bamboo thickets effectively concealed all these installations.

The weakness of the Japanese position was its lack of width, which was inevitable with the limited number of troops available to Major Ogawa. To the north of Mount Koko was a plateau whose northern slope was a steep cliff varying from 40 to 100 feet in height that formed the south bank of the Santa Rita River. Unfortunately, Major Ogawa did not have enough troops to occupy this forbidding area and force the Americans to scale the cliffs or extend their lines farther north. On the Japanese left, the situation was similar. Ogawa could not extend his lines beyond Mount Ege, much less occupy the highest point on the battlefield farther south—Mount Kosaku (maneuver; scheme)—or Familiar Peak as it appeared on American maps.

Ogawa probably realized that his flanks were vulnerable, but in the final analysis, protection of his flanks was the least of the Japanese commander's worries. His mission was to prevent the use of Highway 7

View from Mount Koko: Mount Ege in foreground, Mount Santa Rita
at left, Mount Kosaku (Familiar Peak) at right in distance

by the enemy. Each of his fortified knolls and ridges was a fortress designed to accomplish this end. Every American flanking attack turned into a frontal assault because of the 360-degree defense employed on each hill.[20]

The state of Japanese supplies in the pass is a moot point. Ammunition and food were never abundant according to surviving evidence; yet the Americans found ample supplies abandoned when they overran positions. The supply line established on 16 December by boat from Manila to Orani was apparently still in operation the last days of January. Mortars, ammunition, food and other supplies were landed at Orani and then transported to the West Pass by whatever means available—carabao and oxcart as a last resort. If lack of ammunition and food was a problem, the fault must have been in distribution once the battle started and not from the total amount available.

We must also consider the overall problem of supply and distribution for 14th Area Army in December and January. With 262,000 troops scattered in three groups on Luzon and with supplies probably never equal to that of the Americans, supplying the Nagayoshi Detachment was a low priority. Besides, daylight movement was always subject to the careful scrutiny of the United States Army Air Corps, and Filipino guerrillas made movement at night hazardous.[21]

Map 4: Area of Operation of the North Garrison Unit

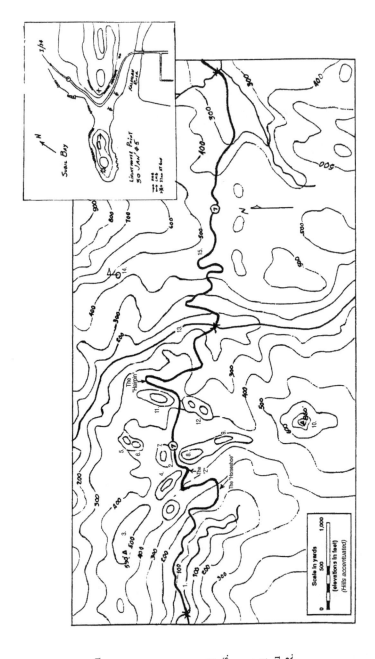

Key Terrain Features

1. Kalaklan R.
2. West Pass
3. Mt. Koko
4. Mt. Hissho
5. Mt. Kita
6. Mt. Kasuga
7. Mt. Minami
8. Ichinose Hts.
9. Mt. Ege
10. Mt. Kosaku
11. Mt. Shinshu
12. Mt. Fumetsu
13. Santa Rita R. (Takamine)
14. Mt. Kongo
15. East Pass

Map 5: Location of Japanese Weapons

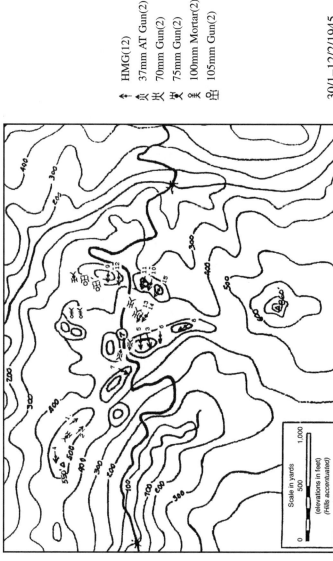

Scale in yards

0   500   1,000

(elevations in feet)
(Hills accentuated)

	HMG(12)
←	37mm AT Gun(2)
	70mm Gun(2)
	75mm Gun(2)
	100mm Mortar(2)
	105mm Gun(2)

30/1–12/2/1945

Heavy Machine
Guns

1. Takamura
2. Morimoto
3. Ohgaki
4. Takenaka
5. Ueno
6. Kanazawa
7. Yamauchi
8. Morinaka
9. Iga
10. Togo
11. Ohnishi
12. Hijikata
13. Masuda
14. Nishioka
15. Kubota

Chapter 7
NOTES

(1) *How the Kato Company Fought: The Record of the 3rd Machine Gun Company 39th Infantry Regiment*, Tamotsu Nagai, Editor, 1990, p. 33.

(2) Ogawa, Major Hironori, *Record of the 3rd Battalion, 39th Infantry Regiment in the "Big Asia War,"* p. 54.

(3) *Ibid.*, p. 10 (map).

(4) *Ibid.*, p. 15;
History of the 39th Infantry Regiment, edited and published by the 39th Infantry Association, Appendix #14;
Handbook on Japanese Military Forces, War Department Technical Manual TM-E 30-480, 1 October 1944, p. 28;
Barker, A. J., *Japanese Army Handbook 1939-1945*, p. 49-55.

(5) TO&E No. 7-17, War Department, 26 February 1944.

(6) Barker, *Japanese Army Handbook 1939-1945*, p. 31.

(7) Ogawa, *Record of the 3rd Battalion*, p. 10 (map), p. 42;
Kato Company History, p. 199.

(8) Kato Company History, p. 160.

(9) *39th Infantry History*, p. 624-25;
34th Infantry AAR, p. 66-67.

(10) Ogawa, *Record of the 3rd Battalion*, p. 11.

(11) The references to concrete and barbed wire are typical of the overestimation by the Americans of Japanese resources in the pass. Other examples are references to: (a) Pre-registration of heavy weapons. There was virtually zero pre-registration because of limited supplies of ammunition. (b) 47-mm anti-tank guns. The Japanese had no 47-mm AT guns in the pass. (c) Heavy weapons. Estimates of heavy weapons by the Americans (at least one battalion of artillery) were much greater than the ten Ogawa noted on his map of the battlefield: two each of 105-mm howitzers, 75-mm guns, 70-mm guns, 37-mm anti-tank guns, and 90-mm mortars. There were perhaps six 120-mm mortars under control of Nagayoshi Detachment Headquarters. Neither Ogawa nor the survivors of the Kato Company mention these mortars in their writings about the battle.

(12) Ogawa, *Record of the 3rd Battalion*, p. 10 (map).

(13) *39th Infantry History,* p. 620;
      Tamotsu Nagai, letter to author, 29 September 1998.
(14) Ogawa, *Record of the 3rd Battalion*, p. 10 (map).
(15) Kato Company History, p. 186.
(16) Ogawa, *Record of the 3rd Battalion*, p. 10 (map).
(17) Barker, *Japanese Army Handbook 1939-1945*, p. 47;
      Hogg, Ian V., *The Encyclopedia of Infantry Weapons in World War II,* p. 79.
(18) Kato Company History, p. 31-47.
(19) *39th Infantry History,* p. 625.
(20) 38th Division Historical Report M-7 Operation, 19 January 1945 to 30 June 1945 (AAR), p. 17-18.
(21) Tamotsu Nagai, letter to author, 29 September 1998;
      Smith, Robert Ross, *Triumph in the Philippines*, p. 95.

8

THE 152nd INFANTRY ATTACKS

(31 January)

Lieutenant Colonel Charles E. Oglesby, commanding the 1st Battalion 34th Infantry, was eager to resume the pursuit and re-establish contact with the enemy. Nicknamed "egg-head" because he kept his head practically shaved, Oglesby was West Point Class of 1940. Like Postlethwait of the 3rd Battalion, he was from Missouri and also like him had served in the U.S. Cavalry before entering West Point. Never luke-warm, Oglesby could be expected to approach any task "with deep conviction, thoroughness, and self-denying discipline."[1]

Colonel Oglesby's mission for the day was to secure the trail junction on Highway 7 where General Hall planned to pass the 38th Division through the 34th RCT. Oglesby assigned this mission to Company A, his lead company, commanded by 1st Lieutenant Gilbert Heaberlin of Longview, TX.

During the night, the company had guarded a bridge on Highway 7 crossing the Kalaklan River about 2,500 yards north of the Olongapo dock. Preservation of this bridge was critical to maintaining rapid pursuit. The Japanese had already burned two other bridges north of Olongapo. The pursuit had been slowed while succeeding columns forded the river beside one bridge and circumvented the other by using a railroad bed.

Company A had easily repulsed about ten Japanese who had tried to burn their bridge around midnight. Colonel Oglesby planned an early breakfast at 0445 for A Company and to have Heaberlin on his way at daybreak. For some unexplained reason, the company not only did not eat at 0445, but received no breakfast at all before resuming the march at 0745.[2]

Beyond A Company's position, Highway 7 was flanked on the left by the Kalaklan River and on the right by a narrow gauge railroad which ran from Olongapo to a point about 400 yards beyond the trail junction (the railroad was later torn up and the ties used as ammunition dunnage and to corduroy roads to bypass destroyed bridges).[3]

Rising abruptly from the Kalaklan Valley floor were two hills to the right on the other side of the railroad. The hills afforded good observation of a considerable length of Highway 7. Major Ogawa had placed the Sakura Company (see page 24) in the vicinity of these two hills to man the Outpost Line of Resistance. Lieutenant Sakura possessed only two machine guns as armament heavier than the rifle. He had fortified the two hills, particularly the saddle between the hills, and had also dug defensive positions north of the road.[4]

Fully aware of the danger posed by these two hills, Lieutenant Heaberlin assigned one platoon as right flank security with orders to seize the first hill. He sent a second platoon forward as advance guard astride the highway while the rest of the company followed a short distance behind.

The advance guard was the first to make contact. At 0815, several well-concealed defenders of the Sakura Company threw grenades and fired from tall grass along the railroad bed, wounding the platoon leader, 1st Lieutenant Lawrence S. Weiss, slightly and hitting the lead scout, Ben L. Guzman, twice in one leg and once in the shoulder. Still full of fight, Guzman crawled as close as possible to the enemy, then rose to his feet and leveled a salvo at a sniper. The Japanese swept the road with machine gun fire. Without regard for their own safety, Scouts Robert Howe and Harold Rock from another squad and Weiss's runner, Jack Laird, crawled across the road and reached Guzman, who was sinking fast from loss of blood. They succeeded in dragging him back across the road, still under sporadic machine gun fire, where the company medic administered first aid.[5]

Heaberlin quieted the Japanese position with 60-mm mortar fire, but decided to bypass it. He recalled the platoon from the first hill, which the platoon leader reported was laced with unoccupied prepared defensive positions. The company then forded the river and proceeded by another trail unopposed to its objective. Inexplicably, two empty machine gun emplacements Heaberlin noticed to the left of the trail were unmanned.

At 1115, after placing his company in position to secure the trail junction, Heaberlin led one platoon back southwest along Highway 7 to flush out the opposition he had bypassed. He had moved cautiously 900 yards when Sakura's men, firing after the platoon had passed their position, pinned the platoon down. Disengaging without further casualties, Heaberlin led the platoon back to the trail junction. He reported that the hostile force consisted of two or three machine guns and a mortar (not reported by Japanese sources) located in the saddle between the two hills.[6]

Shortly after 1400, the 20 replacements for A Company completed their two-day chase and reached the road junction. The group looked starry-eyed at the sweaty, dirty men who were now their brothers-in-arms. A bewhiskered, grim, shirtless man whom everyone seemed to know and respect, Lieutenant Heaberlin, called the replacements to gather round him. He described the trouble the company had run into that morning and told of the two men who had been hit. Heaberlein's radioman laughingly displayed his canteen with water leaking from a bullet hole.[7]

Like a hovering "big brother," Captain James B. Ransohoff of the XI Corps G-3 section, flying an L-4 artillery spotter plane out of San Marcelino airfield, had witnessed the day's early action. He had reported the initial halt of A Company 34th when it received its first fire and later when Lieutenant Heaberlin had taken one platoon back along Highway 7 after securing the trail junction. Through Ransohoff's extension of his vision, General Hall missed very little of what was happening at the front.[8]

The 152nd and 149th regiments, which had encamped along Highway 7 back of the 34th, spent the better part of the day approaching ZigZag Pass. As soon as General Jones received the news that the trail junction was secure, he ordered the 152nd forward. Diligently trying to follow the orders for speed, Colonel Stillwell attempted to maintain the fast pace of the last two days. He marched his 152nd regiment in the order of 1st, 3rd and 2nd battalions with all its vehicles along the soon well-worn Highway 7. Colonel Skelton's 149th Infantry close behind added to the logjam.

In the meantime, Colonel Oglesby had brought up B Company to relieve the hungry men of "A". He committed B Company against Lieutenant Sakura's positions, but without success. At 1500, Lieutenant Colonel Delbert D. Cornwell's 1st Battalion 152nd Infantry arrived at the trail junction. After a briefing by Oglesby, Cornwell prepared to continue the advance eastward on Highway 7.[9]

This activity at the trail junction and the two-regiment procession of the 149th and 152nd winding out of Olongapo did not go unnoticed by the Japanese on Mount Koko. Suddenly, mortar and artillery fire started falling on B Company 34th and the 1st Battalion 152nd. Major Ogawa caused great confusion among the tightly packed vehicles and men by unleashing long-range machine gun and mortar fire. Lieutenant Sakura's men in the saddle and on the high ground south of the road added their firepower. Miraculously, there was only one casualty, a man in the 3rd Battalion 149th Infantry wounded.[10]

Colonel Cornwell reported machine gun fire coming from the large hill mass (Mount Koko) to his left front. Cornwell sent two patrols up the hill to try to find the source of the machine gun fire.

Colonel Stillwell ordered up his 3rd Battalion, commanded by Major Harold B. Mangold, to support Cornwell at the trail junction. He directed Mangold to leave the road and move north to envelop the right flank of enemy positions on Mount Koko holding up the 1st Battalion.

Mangold led with L Company and advanced up a draw toward the top of the mountain. As the lead scouts neared heavy jungle, they drew fire from Lieutenant Ogata's men near the top. The L Company commander brought his machine guns forward to combat this new enemy opposition, but Mangold told him to hold up because the 1st Battalion was patrolling in the area. L Company dispatched a patrol to locate the source of the firing. The patrol leader returned empty handed in about two hours. He reported undergrowth so thick that he had covered less than 400 yards.[11]

Colonel Stillwell was upset that the Japanese strongpoint to the right of the road (Lieutenant Sakura's position) was still active. He said he could wait no longer for B Company 34th to knock out the resistance and would take care of it himself. Although artillery was not yet available, he ordered his 2nd Battalion, commanded by Lieutenant Colonel Charles H. Rice, to do the job, utilizing 60-mm and 81-mm mortars for support. Following the route of A Company 34th's flank platoon in the morning, F Company 152nd dug in for the night atop the first hill after being pinned down by rifle and machine gun fire. The company suffered the regiment's first battle casualty—the death of Staff Sergeant Hieden.[12]

1st Battalion 152nd moved gingerly along Highway 7 into the pass unaffected by the firing in its rear. Colonel Cornwell led with B Company commanded by 1st Lieutenant William P. Todd of Laurens, SC. Todd deployed Lieutenant McCann's 1st Platoon to the right of the road and the 2nd Platoon under Tech Sergeant George H. Franklin of Clarksville, IN, to the left. Since the 2nd Platoon had no officer, Lieutenant Todd doubled as its platoon leader. Led by two scouts of the lead squad in each platoon, XI Corps began its first attack in ZigZag Pass.[13]

The scouts carried a .45 caliber sub-machine gun, either the Thompson or its gradual replacement during the war, the lighter and less expensive "grease gun." The Thompson weighed ten pounds without its 30-round magazine and boasted a rate of fire of 700 to 800 rounds per minute. The "grease gun" fired its 30-round magazine at a rate of 350 to 450 rounds per minute. With magazine, oiler and sling, the "grease gun" weighed 8.9 pounds. Although .45-caliber ammunition was heavy, scouts loved both weapons for their short, quick bursts that were deadly in jungle fighting.[14]

Because of rough terrain, the 1st Platoon soon lagged behind. Todd pulled the 2nd Platoon onto the highway into the lead and increased the pace. A Japanese soldier appeared round a bend in the road and then disappeared so suddenly that no shots were fired.

The platoon had slowed down, and Todd and Franklin found themselves 40 yards in front serving as lead scouts. Taking refuge behind a huge boulder as they approached a curve, they could see an open field, unmistakably cleared for a field of fire. Fortunately for Todd and Franklin, an artillery observation plane was scouting the Japanese positions. When Franklin started to move, the pilot cut his motor and shouted, "No, no, no!" The message was clear—STOP—the enemy was in front; it was time for the battalion to dig in.[15]

Major Ogawa had planned an elaborate reception for the Americans during their first night in the pass. He had organized a group of chosen and specially trained men led by 2nd Lieutenant Shozo Nakano of the 9th Company for the "Kirikomi-tai" (night attack). The raiding force was composed of a squad each from the three rifle companies, each squad with its own light machine gun and each squad reinforced by one heavy machine gun and light mortar.

The Nakano force's mission was to penetrate to the rear areas and create general havoc: shoot up tents, ammunition and supply dumps; disable tanks, vehicles and artillery pieces with "Molotov cocktails" and mines. Major Ogawa had placed routine harassing mortar and artillery fire on the enemy units that could be pinpointed before dark. After assembling at sunset and receiving encouragement and a glass of sake from the Emperor provided by Ogawa, Nakano's men melted into the jungle gloom.[16]

The organization of the raiders is a good example of the Japanese practice of splitting up and detaching units in preparing for special missions. The Japanese also applied this principle to battalions, regiments and divisions. They split and detached units at will, ignoring the cohesion that is lost and the confusion that results when men are fighting in unfamiliar circumstances under unknown or little known commanders.

Organizing a mission of this type, an American commander would have designated a rifle platoon as the basic unit and reinforced the platoon with specially trained men and armament depending on the mission.

Pfc. Halbert Smith of C Company 152nd remembered: "That night being our first in the pass, we dug in about six inches. When the first rounds started falling, you could hear mess kits, shovels—everybody using anything to dig in deeper!"[17]

Machine gun ammo carrier Pfc. Melvin McCathern of D Company was odd man and dug in by himself. To stay awake, he pulled the pin on a hand grenade surmising that the thought of a grenade burst would keep him awake. He dozed off, awaking just in time after his relaxed hand released pressure on the handle and actuated the grenade. He threw it out of the foxhole and no one was hurt.[18]

1st Battalion 152nd headquarters had dug in for the night in the vicinity of a sawmill slightly east of the Highway 7 bridge over the Kalaklan River (only a narrow stream at this point near its source). B Company under Lieutenant Todd had advanced several hundred yards farther until darkness had forced them to dig in. Todd brought forward the 3rd Platoon of 1st Lieutenant O. B. White of Belton, TX, which became the regiment's point along the highway.

At about 2030, a BAR man in the 3rd Platoon started to fire on a group of Japanese advancing down the road. His weapon misfired, but the noise of the jammed action sent the enemy scurrying down the hillside. Sergeant Ray Cotner's lead squad threw grenades down the bank with unknown results.

This commotion, of course, caused consternation in the rear. At Colonel Stillwell's order, Company M started firing 81-mm mortars. They plummeted rounds 300 yards *behind* the lead positions. This was a dangerous practice because the gunners had no way of knowing the exact location of the lead units. Stillwell even came forward by jeep to investigate the action, another dangerous practice on a night when the enemy was infiltrating.[19]

Mortar and artillery fire from both sides continued throughout the night while Lieutenant Nakano's men worked farther toward the rear. Company C's perimeter was adjacent to a thick stand of bamboo. The company's automatic fire spraying the bamboo caused a weird cacophony that added to the confusion. One of the Japanese riflemen shot and killed the Executive Officer of the 2nd Battalion 152nd, Major Shirley N. Duer, about midnight. Captain John Byus, the F Company commander, replaced him. Next morning the 152nd Infantry counted casualties of three KIA, five WIA and one MIA from the night's encounter.[20]

♦ ♦ ♦

During the harassing long range Japanese mortar and machine gun fire earlier in the afternoon, the 2nd and 3rd Battalions 149th Infantry turned left at the trail junction and advanced one mile to Santa Rita with no further opposition. The regiment had moved up 12 miles entirely by foot during the day. This march was child's play compared to the eastward trek it was to start the next day.[21]

From his observation post atop Mount Iwa (big boulder), a ridge extending west of Mount Koko, Master Sergeant Sueo Tanaka reported the 149th's left turn immediately. Major Ogawa could do nothing to impede this wide flanking move. There were not enough troops to man his thin main line adequately much less oppose every diversionary effort. Ogawa was probably relieved that this American column did not join in the assault on his main line.[22]

$$ \bullet \quad \bullet \quad \bullet $$

While 1st Battalion 34th and the 149th and 152nd Regiments had borne the brunt of the third day's work, the other units had moved and accomplished their missions according to plan. The 151st Infantry was securing the beachhead and the long supply line with aggressive patrolling.

For the second day in a row 2nd Battalion 34th had an easy time. At 0930, after a leisurely hot breakfast, the battalion marched from its previous night's bivouac on Highway 7 to Olongapo. Its mission for the day was to secure Olongapo and its environs. Company E guarded a position at the northern end of the slough that formed the harbor; Company F and the battalion anti-tank platoon defended the beach. Company G, with one platoon of H Company heavy machine guns attached, occupied the former Japanese "water's edge position," the scene of the campaign's initial skirmish, Kalaklan River Bridge, the lighthouse point, and the cemetery north of the point.[23]

Lieutenant Mann's 3rd Platoon, supported by one of the machine guns, dug in across the base of the narrow peninsula leading to the lighthouse. Captain Rucker G. Innes, the G Company commander, told Lieutenant Mann that his platoon, if attacked from the landside, could make a "little Bataan" of the peninsula (the captain never explained whether he was serious or pulling the lieutenant's leg!).

That night G Company received two attacks. The first came about 2030 on the Kalaklan River Bridge by two Japanese in a boat. One, a corporal, was killed by the 1st Platoon defending the bridge, but the second got away. The second attack came from rats that the unobliging enemy had not driven from the cemetery. Disturbed by the Americans digging in, the rodents had fought for the foxholes, drawing several shots,

Kalaklan River Bridge, Highway 7; Mount Koko in the distance

Lighthouse point

but had not lost a single rat. They had brushed faces with two or three men and stolen food from another. The attack had occurred in 2nd Platoon territory, and the sergeant, Thomas Martin, a swarthy Hawaiian, regaled the whole company in his broken English at daybreak with tales of the night's "battle" with the rats.

3rd Battalion 34th had scoured the area east and south of Olongapo, but had found no opposition. Company L sent a patrol by boat as far south as Cubi Point. To date all the action had occurred in Zambales Province. By reaching Cubi Point, L Company was definitely south of the boundary between Zambales and Bataan Provinces. Thus the 34th Infantry, as the regiment's After Action Report proudly proclaimed, was the "first among victorious American troops to return to the hallowed peninsula of Bataan."[24]

Chapter 8
NOTES

(1) Grube, Captain Harry T., S-1 & Asst. S-3 34th Infantry, interview describing 24th Division campaigns transcribed by World War II Publications, Inc., Indianapolis;
West Point Assembly, Obituary, September 1985.

(2) 34th Infantry After Action Report, p. 28.

(3) *Ibid.,* p. 31.

(4) *Ibid.,* p. 32;
Ogawa, Major Hironori, *Record of the 3rd Battalion, 39th Infantry Regiment in the "Big Asia War,"* p. 15.

(5) 34th Infantry AAR, p. 32-33;
Pfc. Guzman was awarded the Silver Star Medal for this action;
Summary of official commendations for Pfcs Howe and Rock, and T/5 Laird.

(6) 34th Infantry AAR, p. 32-33.

(7) McKenna, Pvt. William J., Company A 34th Infantry, diary, p. 4.

(8) Ransohoff, Captain J. B., memo to Colonel Charles S. Monteith, Jr., XI Corps G-3, 31 January 1945.

(9) Journal, 2nd Battalion 149th Infantry, 1635;
Journal, 152nd Infantry, 1500;
34th Infantry AAR, p. 34.

(10) Ogawa, *Record of the 3rd Battalion,* p. 20;
Morrissey, Captain George E., Surgeon 1st Bn 34th Infantry, diary p. 30;
Journal, 3rd Battalion 149th Infantry, 2015.

(11) Schoonover, Major James F., *The Operations of the 3rd Battalion 152nd Infantry in Zig Zag Pass, Luzon, 29 Jan.-14 Feb. 1945,* Advanced Infantry Officers Course, 1947-1948, p. 8.

(12) 34th Infantry AAR, p. 34;
Journal, 152nd Infantry, 1450.

(13) Franklin, T/Sgt. George H., Company B 152nd Infantry, letter to author, 6 August 1991;
Journal, 152nd Infantry, 1532;
Journal, 1st Battalion 152nd Infantry, 1350.

(14) O'Donnell, Michael J. and Sylvia, Stephen W., *Uniforms, Weapons and Equipment of the World War II GI,* p. 149.

(15) Franklin letter, 6 August 1991.

(16) Ogawa, *Record of the 3rd Battalion*, p. 19;
History of the 39th Infantry Regiment, edited and published by
the 39th Infantry Association, p. 633.

(17) Smith, Pfc. Halbert, Company C 152nd Infantry, interview by
author, 27 July 1991.

(18) McCathern, Pfc. Melvin, Company D 152nd Infantry, interview
by author, 27 July 1991.

(19) Cotner, Sergeant Ray, Company B 152nd Infantry, interview by
author, 27 July 1991;
Franklin letter, 6 August 1991.

(20) Smith interview, 27 July 1991;
Journal, 152nd Infantry, 2400.

(21) Journal, 2nd Battalion 149th Infantry, 1830.

(22) Nagai, Sergeant Tamotsu, Communications Sergeant, Machine
Gun Company 3rd Battalion 39th Infantry, interview, 14 May
1991.

(23) 34th Infantry AAR, p. 34.

(24) *Ibid.,* p. 44.

"THAT NIGHT WAS ONE OF TERROR"

(1 FEBRUARY)

The first of February promised to be a big day for XI Corps. With two regiments poised to strike eastward, General Hall expected to accomplish the third of his four objectives (to seal off Bataan Peninsula) in short order. The right prong of his attack, the 152nd Infantry, was already in ZigZag Pass astride Highway 7; his left, the 149th, had assembled well north of the Japanese right flank and was ready to move cross-country to Dinalupihan.

Forty-seven-year-old Colonel Winfred G. Skelton commanded the 149th Infantry. With more than 25 years Army experience since graduation from West Point in 1919, Colonel Skelton was the senior regimental commander in the 38th Division. A native of Fairfield, IL, he had come to the Pacific in November 1943 as commander of the 111th Infantry, an old Philadelphia regiment created by Benjamin Franklin. When the 111th was placed in reserve in Hawaii, Skelton, seeking combat, had transferred to the 149th in July 1944.[1]

His command this day would be his 2nd and 3rd battalions (the 1st was in division reserve), Company C 113th Medical Battalion, and a platoon of Company A 113th Engineers. Only essential items of equipment were to be carried. Packing everything on their backs, including a complete portable surgical hospital, Colonel Skelton's men moved out early on the morning of 1 February. Filipino guerrillas and Negritos, the pygmy hill people of Luzon, were on hand to guide the regiment to Dinalupihan.[2]

With the 149th on its way, we return to the 152nd commanded by Colonel Robert L. Stillwell. Born in Princeton, IN, in October 1894, he had matured in Evansville and had graduated from Indiana University. After Army service as a sergeant major in the Mexican disturbance in 1916 and as a 2nd Lieutenant in World War I, he began a lifelong career in the Indiana National Guard. Organizing Company A 152nd Infantry in

Evansville, he literally grew up with the regiment. He advanced through all the ranks to become its colonel in 1940. He knew his men well; he had recruited and trained them. In a word, Colonel Stillwell was the 152nd.

Stillwell had selected three very able men to lead his battalions. The 1st: Lieutenant Colonel Delbert D. Cornwell, an accountant from Indianapolis, formerly regimental S-3; the 2nd: Lieutenant Colonel Charles H. Rice, an executive in a machine company in Warsaw, IN; and the 3rd: Major Harold B. Mangold, an executive with Servel, Inc., in Evansville.[3]

Colonel Stillwell's first objective, and perhaps his most important one, was to learn the nature of the Japanese defenses in the pass and locate the enemy strong points. After conferring with Colonel Jenna, who was forward with the 1st Battalion 34th, Colonel Stillwell put his plan for the day in motion at 0830. General Hall—already becoming impatient with the slow progress—considered this time "unpardonably late."[4]

Stillwell's plan called for Colonel Cornwell's 1st Battalion in the lead to continue the advance along Highway 7. Colonel Rice's 2nd Battalion, after spending the night dug in facing the Sakura Company, was to reduce this strongpoint and then attack eastward south of the road. The 1st Battalion 149th would follow 2nd Battalion 152nd on a wider front to clean out any remaining pockets of enemy resistance. Major Mangold's 3rd Battalion was to attempt again to outflank the Japanese entrenchments on Mount Koko by a wide envelopment to the left of the road.[5]

We can dispense with the 3rd Battalion first since it met no opposition. The battalion, nevertheless, spent a strenuous day hacking and chopping to cut a path through thick bamboo. At 1800, the battalion started digging in for the night about 300 yards north of the road with not much to show for its day's work.[6]

Colonel Cornwell's 1st Battalion advanced cautiously into the jungled, mountainous area of sharp ridges and steep ravines that was ZigZag Pass. Immense tangled growth threatened to engulf the narrow, hard-surfaced but long-neglected Highway 7. While more rugged terrain than ZigZag Pass was to be found on Luzon, few pieces of ground combined to the same degree both roughness and dense jungle. Route 7 contorted crazily through the pass, following a treacherous path of least resistance. The jungle flora was so thick that one could step five yards off the highway and not be able to see the road. It was easy to imagine a son of Nippon behind every tree and around every bend in the road. One could search far and wide and not find a more sinister spot for an infantry battle.[7]

With A Company in the lead, the 1st Battalion had moved only a short distance when at 0845 two "woodpeckers" on the left (probably those of Sergeants Yamauchi and Takamura) pinned down the lead platoon. A sniper killed the lieutenant platoon leader when he stood up and attempted to get his platoon moving. With his men unnerved by this sudden turn of events and hugging the earth, the company commander, Captain Ralph Pharr, called forward the platoon of two tanks attached to the battalion. The M-4 Shermans soon silenced the machine gunners.

Moving approximately 1,000 yards along the road, 1st Battalion hit stiff resistance. Warrant Officer Hitoshi Takao's platoon of the Shinfune 9th Company had moved from Mount Ege and was contesting every foot of the way. Calling for 150 hand grenades, Cornwell soon had his men involved in a vicious firefight at close range with a practically unseen foe.[8]

An hour later, Cornwell ordered his forward elements to pull back so that the artillery could shell the unyielding enemy positions. An artillery observation plane directed fire, hovering over the battlefield so low that Communications Sergeant Tamotsu Nagai of the Kato HMG Company felt that "it almost touched the trees in the jungle." Impressed with the abundant matériel of the Americans, Nagai thought, "How can they keep shooting like this without ever stopping?"[9]

1st Battalion resumed the attack, but the artillery had done little good. The Japanese were still firmly entrenched and the 1st Battalion attacks stalled for the rest of the afternoon.

In the meantime, 2nd Battalion 152nd had also had a trying time. Continuing its attack against Lieutenant Sakura's stubborn defenders, Colonel Rice sent E and F Companies into thick growth on the steep hill across the road from B Company 34th's position at the trail junction. At about this time, a cub plane, circling overhead, saw figures moving along the top of the hill. Taking the figures for the enemy, the pilot informed the 152nd headquarters.

Recognizing the figures as Americans, men of B Company and 1st Battalion 34th Headquarters Company watched in horror as the 152nd's own mortars pounded the figures severely, killing a half dozen men and wounding more. 2nd Battalion 152nd reported at 0945 that some of its personnel had been injured by friendly mortar fire, a gross understatement of the actual facts. When Sakura's position was finally overrun, Colonel Rice estimated the size of the defending force to be approximately 80-100, judging from the bedrolls and other supplies captured.[10]

Early in the day, General Hall sensed that the advance of the 152nd was not going well. He wrote to General Krueger later, "I personally visited the Division Commander on the morning of 1 February and insisted that he advance more rapidly. I pointed out to him very carefully the necessity for a rapid advance.

"I suggested to him [General Jones] that if he had any person in whom he had no confidence, he should promptly and cold-bloodedly get rid of him immediately . . . On the afternoon of 1 February, I called him up again and told him that the advance looked very slow to me in view of the few casualties and the lack of known opposition . . . I again urged him to make sure that his advance was pressed and that he get the lead out of the pants of his people."[11]

The officers and men of the 152nd, after suffering casualties of 14 KIA, 43 WIA and 1 MIA, were beginning to fathom the defenses in ZigZag Pass. They knew the enemy was strong in the area of the horseshoe that was easily identified on their maps. They felt he was in force on the long ridge to their left. From where else could he observe and bring down such devastating mortar and artillery fire? They sensed they had reached the main Japanese positions, and it was time to pound these positions with all the artillery at hand before advancing farther.[12]

In this wild region, the 152nd Infantry had difficulty orienting itself. Bad radio communications (already experienced by 2nd Battalion 34th Headquarters) led to misunderstandings. Part of the difficulty arose from using a map with co-ordinates completely different from the standard 1:50,000 maps used by other units. *Familiar Peak* was the name of the map used by the 152nd for this area of the ZigZag whereas other units used a map entitled *Subic*. Maps issued to the 149th and the 152nd used a letter/number co-ordinate system that had to be converted to the all-numbers coordinate system on the maps issued to Corps, Division, and the 34th Infantry. Confusion was the natural result.

These errors were compounded when unit locations were reported to Division and Corps Headquarters. Colonel Charles S. Monteith, Jr., XI Corps G-3, on his overlay to accompany his daily report of 1 February at 1800 hours, located leading elements of 1st Battalion 152nd 500 yards east of the horseshoe. A more careful analysis after the war placed the 1st Battalion 200 yards west of the horseshoe after its bitter all-afternoon fight. Company A had reached the southeast corner of the horseshoe, but was forced back by a wall of Japanese fire. 2nd and 3rd Battalions were behind the 1st Battalion.[13]

Aerial photographs may have helped, but none were available for ZigZag Pass until after the 38th Division had been fighting for four days. Even then, it was extremely difficult to identify Japanese positions concealed by the dense undergrowth. Since Eighth Army's planning time for the Zambales Operation was limited, only six photographic missions were flown, producing 33,000 scale 1:25,000 maps. These covered the landing area and the initial areas of the move inland. It is unfortunate that no one in Eighth or Sixth Armies had the foresight to photograph the most likely area of resistance—ZigZag Pass.[14]

As American pressure mounted on the afternoon of 1 February, Major Ogawa, unwilling to be bullied, planned another night action. The core of his attacking force, called a combat patrol by Ogawa, was two squads of 2nd Lieutenant Momoyo Jyohoji's 1st Platoon of the 11th Company. The Iga Squad of the Kato HMG Company reinforced them. Artillery and mortars, of course, would lend support by firing at known targets. Using Mount Koko as both an observation post and staging area, Jyohoji's men picked their route and targets during the daylight hours and then debouched down the hillside toward Highway 7 as darkness settled. At the same time, Warrant Officer Hitoshi Takao of the 9th Company led a raiding party from Mount Ege. Both forces had the mission of creating havoc and destroying vehicles and heavy weapons.[15]

Major Ogawa was making the Americans jittery. At 1730, an airborne artillery observer spotted what he estimated to be a battalion of Japanese in the vicinity of the hairpin "moving west along Highway 7." This force was expanded to "1,000 Japs" by the 152nd Infantry and so reported by Division G-2. This completely erroneous report impelled Colonel Stillwell to move Mangold's 3rd Battalion back to its perimeter of the previous night to cover the north side of the highway.[16]

Darkness did not end the day of frustration for the men of the 1st Battalion 152nd. At 1930, Japanese gunners concentrated their fire on the headquarters perimeter and motor pool, and Lieutenant Jyohoji's troops started infiltrating between the perimeters of the rifle companies. At about 2000, Japanese mortars and artillery opened up on the 3rd Battalion with unusual accuracy, probably because the battalion was occupying the same foxholes of the previous night.[17]

Company M's 81-mm mortars and heavy machine guns discouraged any serious attacks by Jyohoji's men, but their fire helped the Japanese locate the 3rd Battalion positions in the darkness. Casualties during the night included the commanding officer of K Company, Captain Thomas Yasm; his executive officer, 1st Lieutenant Vincent Kimberlin; the battalion S-3, 1st Lieutenant James Cunningham; and the heavy weapons company commander, Captain James Vest.[18]

Company L Machine Gun Sergeant Don Kreis of Milford, IN, remembered that battalion headquarters (where his gun was located) dug in deeper and with more care compared with 31 January. Rumor had it that the estimated battalion of Japanese reported by the artillery observer would counterattack that night. Hearing noises outside their perimeter, everyone thought the enemy was attacking in force. Kreis's machine gun was at the outer edge of the perimeter and firing toward the enemy's expected best line of approach. According to Kreis, "The fire was so intense from our battalion that the whole sky turned pink."[19]

The writers of the 39th Infantry history also remembered: "Enemy flares showed the ghastly scene of destruction caused by incessant mortar and artillery fire." Major Ogawa summed up the situation accurately: "The confusion in the valley was far beyond description." From his crow's nest on Mount Koko, Ogawa always referred to the enemy as being in the valley.[20]

The 38th Division G-2 reported at 2130 that "Japs [were] working around 152nd, doubtful how long communications will stay in." Lieutenant Jyohoji performed his mission well. At 2245, both the 138th and 163rd F.A. Battalions were forced to stop firing because of enemy infiltration into their positions. The Japanese continued to pour mortar and artillery fire most of the night on the 152nd Infantry strung out along Highway 7 west of the horseshoe.[21]

The shelling that accompanied the Japanese attack on the 152nd also reached B Company 34th, still manning the roadblock at the trail junction. "That night was one of terror as the Japs repeatedly dropped mortar shells on our position while a few of them attempted to penetrate our perimeter," Pfc. Douglas W. Thornton, Jr., of Atlanta, GA, recalled.

Several foxholes to Thornton's left, an enemy soldier jumped in with its two GI occupants. One of them, a replacement, panicked and jumped into an adjacent hole. On guard was Guiseppe Ciancarlo, a former Italian soldier who was drafted while visiting relatives in the U.S.A. and trapped here by the war in Europe. Ciancarlo greeted this unfortunate replacement with a chop to his face with a machete! Ciancarlo quickly realized that his victim was a GI and stopped before killing him.[22]

This poor fellow staggered by Thornton's hole the next morning on his way to the hospital with a slash to the bone from his ear to his chin. Captain Morrissey, 1st Battalion surgeon, called the machete cuts on his face and arms the worst he had ever seen. The barrage killed one man and wounded six in B Company, including a sergeant and another of the new replacements.[23]

Sergeant Iga's heavy machine gun squad of Jyohoji's patrol stayed behind the American lines for two days, harassing several rear area units and even firing into the lights of Olongapo. The lone Japanese casualty was a rifleman shot by his own men on the return to Mount Koko.[24]

How had the 149th Infantry fared during the day? Colonel Skelton's objective was a point on the trail directly north of Bulate, a barrio on Highway 7 about four miles east of the horseshoe. This was a rather ambitious undertaking for a one day march over an unknown trail through wild, mountainous terrain. At 1300, the colonel reported his co-ordinates to General Jones that placed the 149th at a point 1,200 yards north of Highway 7 and two miles east of the horseshoe. Everything was going well, but then a chain of events started that would make a grown man cry.[25]

General Hall had directed that the 149th and 152nd stay within supporting distance of each other, an order General Jones considered incongruent with the corps commander's obsession with speed. Nevertheless, in conformity with his orders, Jones had instructed the 149th to "patrol to Highway 7 gaining contact with 152nd, if practicable."[26] Now with the 152nd bogged down at the horseshoe, Jones felt the 149th was extending itself too far east for mutual support. He ordered Colonel Skelton to halt about 2,500 yards west of the day's objective. Well before dark, Skelton reported he was digging in with his leading

The "horseshoe" on Highway 7 from Mount Koko

elements 750 yards north of Highway 7 opposite barrio Balsic, a mile west of Bulate.[27]

General Jones doubted this report, believing that Skelton was well north of his reported location. The 38th Division Artillery had been firing close to the trail the 149th was supposed to be marching, and there had been no protest from Colonel Skelton. He said that he could hear the fire, but it was not close. Jones also based his conclusion on a report of a 38th Division liaison plane, which placed the 149th almost three miles northwest of the regiment's reported location.[28]

General Hall, who happened to be at the 38th Division CP in Olongapo when Skelton radioed, also doubted the report. An XI Corps artillery plane had placed the regiment 1 1/3 miles northwest of Skelton's claim. General Jones naturally believed his observer's report, while General Hall was just as adamant that the XI Corps report was correct. And, of course, Colonel Skelton still insisted he was right. He had considered the guides unreliable and had sent them back. Jones told Hall that he would verify the 149th's position before taking further action and did so by dispatching a second plane.

Analysis in a more peaceful time several years later proved that nobody was right. The trail XI Corps thought paralleled Highway 7 did not exist, but instead swung off to the northeast two miles east of the Santa Rita River. Part of the area in question was unmapped and appeared as white blotches on maps the pilots used; they could only guess at the location of the 149th. In reality, Skelton was two miles due north of the point he had reported reaching.[29]

When General Jones's second artillery observer reported the 149th 4,000 yards north of the proper trail, Jones radioed Colonel Skelton at 2100 to return to Santa Rita and start over. But poor communications again reared its ugly head; Skelton never received the message. In summary, when General Jones bedded down the night of 1 February, he was completely out of touch with one of his lead regiments (the 149th), and there were doubts how long communications would stay in with the other (the 152nd).[30]

General Hall played down the opposition in his nightly radio report to General Krueger: "Forward elements bivouacking 11,000 yards east Olongapo on trail. Conducted mopping up operations northwest of Olongapo." Why he used the direction "northwest" (repeated in the message) is not known. All of the day's action was northeast of Olongapo.[31]

The message reflects the totally different perspective of command headquarters and the men in the front lines. To General Hall and his staff, the attack was a two-pronged affair with two regiments driving eastward to reach Dinalupihan. The left regiment, the 149th, was now 11,000 yards northeast of Olongapo, unopposed and in the lead; the regiment on the right, the 152nd, was mopping up the opposition in the rear. To the men of the 152nd and later the 34th, the fight in the pass was the main issue, a life or death struggle; the flank march of the 149th seemed mythical to them, a little known corollary to the main effort.

Back in the rear areas, the 34th Infantry had no taxing assignments during the day. Company B rechecked the area where the Japanese had initially delayed the advance on 31 January, but 2nd Battalion 152nd had done its work well. Company I 151st Infantry relieved G Company 34th at about 1600 at Kalaklan Point and bridge, and "G" moved several hundred yards east to a slight rise overlooking Olongapo. The only significant activity of the 3rd Battalion was K Company's unopposed patrol 2,000 yards east on Telegraph Trail.[32]

Colonel Jenna informed all his units that surrender leaflets would be dropped the next day 2 February. One side was printed in Japanese. On the other side in large bold letters under the caption SURRENDER was printed:

"Attention American soldiers. This leaflet guarantees humane treatment to any Japanese desiring to surrender. Take him immediately to your nearest COMMISSIONED OFFICER. By order C. G. U.S. Forces."

This was routine; no one really expected the enemy to surrender.

This leaflet was just one of ten different types used in the campaign. The Psychological Warfare Branch of G-2 Eighth Army supplied one officer and one non-commissioned officer to supervise the dissemination of 175,000 surrender leaflets during the operation. The branch supplied special artillery shells for wide dispersion. From D-Day to D-Day-plus-three, planes dropped 783,000 leaflets from San Antonio to Olongapo directing the activities of Filipino civilians.[33]

Japanese shelling extended even to the 2nd Battalion 34th's encampment in Olongapo. At dusk in the G Company area and at E Company nearby, several stray artillery shells sent the men scurrying for cover. No one was hurt, but it was a reminder in the rear areas that the war was very close.

Chapter 9
NOTES

(1) West Point Assembly, Skelton obituary, September 1983, p. 133.
(2) 38th Division Historical Report M-7 Operation, 19 January 1945 to 30 June 1945 (AAR), p. 16.
(3) Regimental histories and biographies of World War II leaders of 38th Division units, 38th Division files, National Records Center, Suitland, Maryland.
(4) 152nd Infantry Journal.
(5) Memorandum, Hall to Jones, 4 February 1945.
(6) Schoonover, Major James F., *The Operations of the 3rd Battalion 152nd Infantry in Zig Zag Pass, Luzon, 29 Jan.-14 Feb. 1945*, Advanced Infantry Officers Course, 1947-1948, p. 8-9.
(7) Smith, Robert Ross, *Triumph in the Philippines,* p. 315.
(8) 1st Battalion 152nd Infantry journal;
Ogawa, Major Hironori, *Record of the 3rd Battalion, 39th Infantry Regiment in the "Big Asia War,"* p. 22.
(9) *How the Kato Company Fought: The Record of the 3rd Machine Gun Company 39th Infantry Regiment*, Tamotsu Nagai, Editor, 1990, p. 214.
(10) Morrissey, Captain George E., Surgeon, 1st Bn 34th Infantry diary p. 30;
152nd Infantry journal;
Jones comments, 20 December 1956, p. 3.
(11) Letter, Hall to Krueger, 3 February 1945.
(12) 152nd Infantry Journal.
(13) XI Corps G-3 Periodic Report #4, 1800-01 February 1945;
Smith, *Triumph in the Philippines*, p. 318.
(14) Report of the Commanding General Eighth Army on the Nasugbu and Bataan Operations (AAR), p. 95;
Walters, Captain Edward E., *The Operations of the 38th Infantry Division in the Landing at San Antonio-San Narciso Area and the Advance to Dinalupihan,* p. 33.
(15) Ogawa, *Record of the 3rd Battalion*, p. 21-22;
Kato Company History, p. 177-178.
(16) XI Corps G-2 Report #4, 1800-01 February 1945;

Entry #5, 38th Division G-2 Journal, 1855-01 February 1945;
Schoonover, *The Operations of the 3rd Battalion 152nd Infantry,*
p. 9.

(17) 1st Battalion 152nd Infantry journal;
152nd Infantry journal.

(18) Schoonover, *The Operations of the 3rd Battalion 152nd Infantry,*
p. 9.

(19) Kreis, Sergeant Don, Company L 152nd Infantry, letter to author,
4 February 1988.

(20) *History of the 39th Infantry Regiment,* edited and published by
the 39th Infantry Association, p. 634;
Ogawa, *Record of the 3rd Battalion,* p. 22.

(21) 38th Division G-2 message to XI Corps G-2, 2030-01 February
1945.

(22) Thornton, Pfc. Douglas W., Jr., Asst. Squad Leader B Company
34th Infantry, letter to author, 30 October 1989.

(23) *Ibid.;*
Morrissey diary p. 30.

(24) Iga, Sergeant Kyujiro, Squad Leader 3rd Platoon Heavy Machine
Gun Company 3rd Battalion 39th Infantry, interview, 14 May
1991.

(25) 38th Division G-3 Periodic Report #40, 1800-01 February 1945.

(26) 2nd Battalion 149th Infantry journal entry 1830-31 January 1945.

(27) Smith, *Triumph in the Philippines*, p. 325-326.

(28) Jones comments, 20 December 1956, p. 1-2.

(29) Smith, *Triumph in the Philippines*, p. 326.

(30) *Ibid.*

(31) Priority G-3 radio message to CG Sixth Army signed Hall, 1800.

(32) 34th Infantry AAR, p. 43.

(33) Eighth Army AAR, p. 96.

THE 152nd INFANTRY REPULSED

(2 FEBRUARY)

Colonel Stillwell had placed his Command Post (CP) with his 2nd Battalion for the night. At dawn 2 February, he was anxiously waiting at the 152nd aid station as the casualties started coming down the road from the pass. It had been impossible to move the wounded during the night. To a compassionate man like Colonel Stillwell, the agony and suffering that men he had trained so diligently had endured all night was almost more than he could bear. The night's casualties included two company commanders and, added to the 5 KIA and 17 WIA during the day of 1 February, raised the total to 14 KIA, 43 WIA and 1 MIA in the past 24 hours. Most of the casualties were in the hard-hit 1st Battalion. Colonel Cornwell was to have a difficult time getting his battalion ready for another go at the Japanese on 2 February.[1]

Some of the mortar shells that fell during the night in the 1st Battalion Headquarters Company perimeter were of 81-mm size (the Japanese had no 81-mm mortars in ZigZag Pass) and had hit the trees and their roots on the west side. Lieutenant Brown of D Company visited M Company, located farther back on the road, and found that their 81-mm mortars "had fired during the night at a range that would put them [the shells] in our area."[2]

General Jones felt isolated as he groped for a way to force the pass with the only troops under his command: the still relatively green 152nd Infantry and the division reserve, the 1st Battalion 149th. "Even though all the enemy was in the pass, the best I could get for the attack was a regiment and a battalion," Jones lamented.[3] The flanking movement of the 149th was essentially a Corps conceived and directed operation. For some reason that is not clear, General Hall was using both the 151st and 34th regiments to guard and patrol the rear areas.

The 2nd Battalion 151st under Lieutenant Colonel L. Robert Mottern, which had taken Grande Island, was encamped near the 38th Division CP.

Although old at 50 for a battalion commander, Mottern was full of fight and begged General Jones to let him get into the fray. Jones called General Hall and told him he could put the 2nd/151st to good use. General Hall became incensed and shouted over the phone that he (Jones) already had more troops than he needed to break through the pass and not to ask for reinforcements.[4]

XI Corps staff concocted a novel plan for the 152nd to execute this morning, which fortunately was never attempted. The regiment would form a moving "V" with the open end facing east on Highway 7. The 3rd Battalion would move on the left or north side of the road, 2nd Battalion on the right or south side, with the 1st Battalion marching behind on the highway. According to Colonel Monteith, XI Corps G-3, "Wings of 'V' will sweep slopes of hills forcing enemy defenders into vortex where 1st Battalion will be in position to destroy them."[5]

Such a maneuver might have worked on open ground against a lightly held position, but the scheme was entirely impractical for ZigZag Pass. In the tangled undergrowth and on steep slopes, men could move off the trails or the highway only with great difficulty and exertion. Besides, as the regiment advanced around the horseshoe, it would be vulnerable to flanking fire from the entrenched Japanese. Unplanned events that morning postponed an attack of any sort until afternoon.

✦ ✦ ✦

After a brief stopover at the 152nd Infantry regimental CP, General Jones arrived soon after daybreak at the CP of the 3rd Battalion 152nd. The battalion was scheduled to pass through the 1st Battalion and advance on the north side of the road. Major Mangold's men were slow in starting. They had been severely harassed by the infiltrating Japanese during the night, they had been under heavy mortar fire, and they were just getting out their dead. One company commander had been killed. They were grumbling that their breakfast had not arrived.

Jones discovered that the infiltrators were reported to have seized the section of Highway 7 between the 1st and 3rd Battalions. Major Mangold had sent a platoon forward to check this report. General Jones caught up with the platoon, which had encountered a small force, apparently a Japanese rifle squad with its light machine gun. At the general's order and under his watchful eye, the platoon drove the Japanese away. Jones went back to start the 3rd Battalion—still with no breakfast. This was no job for a major general, and Jones made a mental note that "all this supervision should have been done by the regimental commander."[6]

Captain Ransohoff was airborne early to observe the day's activities. At 0850, he reported the 149th Infantry on a trail about 3,000 yards north and 2,000 yards east of the horseshoe. The men were sitting by their foxholes and had not started. He reported at 0930 that leading elements of the 152nd were at the northwest corner of the horseshoe, but not advancing. Although there was no evidence of the enemy, division artillery was blasting the road east of the horseshoe.[7]

Returning to the Division CP, General Jones found the corps commander waiting for him. It was by now mid-morning and General Hall had heard no reports of advance at the front. His purpose in visiting the Division CP was obvious: to emphasize to General Jones again his utter dissatisfaction with the progress made to date. General Jones said he was also dissatisfied and that he would return to the 152nd Infantry CP and get the regiment moving.

Obviously having lost confidence in the 38th Division commander, General Hall proceeded immediately to the 152nd CP himself ahead of General Jones. He talked frankly with Colonel Stillwell and his staff and with Brigadier General Roy W. Easley, the Assistant Division Commander for Infantry, whom Jones had dispatched forward to get the day's action started. In essence, Hall repeated his familiar refrain: "GET GOING!"[8]

Hall then visited the Battalion CPs, all of which were on the road. He found that the 1st Battalion commander had no idea where the enemy was and that he had only one patrol out. He received no satisfactory reply when he asked the 3rd Battalion commander why he was so late moving to the attack. "There appeared to be a general lack of appreciation on the part of most officers of the fact that this is not a maneuver but war," Hall emphasized later in a memorandum to Jones.[9]

General Hall also noted he heard no gunfire and that no resistance had been encountered since soon after daybreak. Colonel Stillwell assembled the battalion commanders in the 152nd CP, and Hall reiterated in no uncertain terms his demand for speed. After leaving the CP at 1220, he concluded that the explanations he had heard "were not in line with what he would expect from an outfit willing to fight."

Infuriated and frustrated by the lethargy of the 152nd, General Hall returned to the 38th Division CP and ripped into General Jones: "The exhibition of your Division is in my mind the worst I have ever seen."[10]

With due respect for General Hall's position and wide experience, this would seem an unfair indictment of an entire division. After the war, General Jones even denied that Hall had made the accusation. Of the 38th's three regiments, only the 1st Battalion 149th had seen previous action (that for less than a week on Leyte). The remainder of the 149th and the entire 151st had yet to face the enemy, and this was only the 152nd's third day.

Part of the problem was General Hall's apparent misunderstanding of the strength of the Japanese defenses at the horseshoe. There had been little opposition in reaching the pass, indicating to him that the enemy now opposing the 152nd formed at most an outpost line of resistance. If this were true, the main line was probably several hundred yards or perhaps a mile east. He believed that the 152nd had found "nothing that an outfit ready to go forward could not overcome quickly." Colonel Stillwell and General Jones, on the other hand, sensed correctly that the 152nd had reached the Main Line of Resistance.[11]

Disregarding the possibility that the opposition was greater than anticipated, General Hall seemed to have reached the eleventh hour with General Jones. He resolved that unless General Jones could show him the next morning that he had taken drastic action to assure future aggressiveness of his division, he would relieve him of command. In Hall's mind, it was evident that if the extraneous facts were removed—three days with practically no advance and extremely small casualties—the relief was entirely warranted.[12]

Artillery had been used sparingly as the 152nd felt its way into the pass. Only 1,200 rounds were fired prior to 2 February and these were mainly to harass the enemy or were fired on random targets. Only 174 rounds preceded the attack on 1 February and none on 2 February. Although General Jones stepped up the artillery fire during the attack later in the day, he felt the position could not be taken without pulling back, registering the artillery fire, and then pounding the fortifications thoroughly with the four light (105-mm) and two medium (155-mm) battalions available.

As Jones analyzed the problem: "The trouble was not how to attack the position, but how to attack the position in accordance with the corps commander's desire for speed, speed and more speed. I knew he would not permit me to take time for artillery adjustment or any type of coordinated attack. He was already reprimanding me for moving too slowly and threatening to relieve me from command."[13]

It would have been hard to convince Communications Sergeant Tamotsu Nagai of the Kato HMG Company that the Americans were not using enough artillery. Returning in the afternoon to Mount Ege from Mount Koko, he was appalled at the devastation caused by the American artillery during the day. "The area used to be covered with thick trees. What happened?" he asked Nagaharu Kobayashi, a heavy machine gunner of the Morinaka Squad in the 9th Company's area on Mount Ege. The gunner replied, "The company commander told us to shoot when the enemy in front of us seemed to be close. I had no sooner pulled the trigger than we received a heavy bombardment. We did not see the enemy; I was really surprised to be told to fire."

Nagai was surprised, too. Japanese tactics called for machine gunners not to reveal their positions by haphazard firing, but to fire only when the enemy came into their sights and then as quickly and unexpectedly as possible. Helping to clean up and re-camouflage the position, Nagai grumbled to himself about the impropriety of the 9th Company commander's order.[14]

Lt. Colonel Jesse E. McIntosh, Commander 152nd Infantry

General Jones was as displeased as General Hall with the 152nd Infantry's performance. On his own initiative—but certainly with the corps commander's admonition of the previous morning ringing in his ears—Jones relieved Colonel Stillwell of his command. In his place, he named the 152nd's executive officer, Lieutenant Colonel Jesse E. McIntosh of Tipton, IN, as the new regimental commander.[15]

Both his superiors and men in the ranks considered Colonel Stillwell to be an adequate regimental commander and a good administrator who was intensely interested in his men. In the heat of battle, however, he apparently could not stomach seeing good men die nor did he execute sound judgment. There were disturbing reports, which naturally led to many rumors, that men of the 152nd were firing on each other. Two instances implicated Colonel Stillwell as mistakenly ordering mortar fire to be placed on his own troops. Unimposing and mild-tempered, Stillwell did not look the part nor did he play the role of a combat regimental commander.

After General Hall left the 38th Division CP in early afternoon, his dominating thought was how to break the stalemate at the horseshoe. He had expected to reach Dinalupihan by 5 February after eliminating the weak, hastily gathered rear echelon troops he believed were standing in his way. Now he was uncertain and confused by the innovative tactics and tenacious defense of the enemy.

Radio Operator Jim Frederick of Greensboro, NC, returning from a swim in the bay, was surprised when a general in a jeep pulled up beside him as he walked along a road in Olongapo. "What company is this; where is your company commander?" the general asked. Jim answered smartly, "E Company 34th Infantry, sir; I will find Captain Pullen for you."[16]

Pullen directed General Hall to the 34th Command Post. There an action plan unfolded that General Hall hoped would solve his problem. Dissatisfied with the progress of the 152nd Infantry during the first three days of battle, General Hall would replace it with the veteran 34th and place the 34th directly under XI Corps control.

But the 34th Infantry was not the same battle-hardened regiment that General Hall knew had spearheaded the 24th Division's slashing attack across the northern part of Leyte. The 34th's aggressiveness and daring had doomed Japanese plans to win a decisive victory in their first battle in the Philippines. Gone was the incomparable regimental commander who had led this drive, Aubrey S. Newman, wounded severely in the stomach when the regiment was nearing its principal objective, Carigara.

An even greater loss were the 184 men killed and 564 wounded (many never to return to the regiment), a total of 748, 78 percent of whom were in the rifle companies.[17] Most of these had trained in Australia and received the special amphibious and jungle training on Goodenough Island. They had lived together, trained together and fought together. In place of these veterans were 839 replacements, most fresh from basic training, with no experience with each other or in unit training together, and only one week's acquaintance with the men of the 34th prior to combat.

After the long harangue in the morning, the 2 February attack finally got underway at 1255 with no preliminary artillery preparation. Colonel McIntosh's plan of attack called for the 3rd Battalion to pass through the 1st Battalion and continue the advance along the north side of Highway 7. The 2nd Battalion would attack eastward on the south side of the road, and the 1st Battalion would follow Mangold's 3rd Battalion.

At the turn into the horseshoe, Mangold sent his leading Company L to clear the enemy from Mount Hissho. Using flamethrowers against scattered resistance, the company had difficulty orienting itself as it advanced through the jungle maze 300 yards north of the open end of the horseshoe.

Learning that the 1st Battalion was beginning to place heavy mortar concentrations on Mount Koko, Mangold ordered L Company to return to the road.[18]

Even with the aid of tanks, the 3rd Battalion could make little headway against the well-designed Japanese defenses. In late afternoon under General Jones's observation, Company K attacked up a steep slope to reduce a bunker covered by strong interlocking machine gun fire. Major Mangold brought up two tanks, which moved a short distance along the road in front of the position. The tanks did not go far. According to Jones, "about ten machine guns opened up on them." Supporting infantrymen creeping along the road beside the tanks did not give adequate protection. When the lead tank passed a small clearing, a daredevil Japanese soldier rushed out of the jungle with a pole charge to disable the tank. He was cut down by small-arms fire just before he reached the tank. General Jones concluded that, "obviously tanks could not be used [in ZigZag Pass] except to assist in reconnaissance."[19]

By this statement, Jones showed a lack of imagination and a narrow mentality reminiscent of World War I. There are many instances of tanks being used effectively in Pacific jungle fighting, and they would be used effectively later in ZigZag Pass. Besides their destructive power, tanks always give a psychological uplift to the attackers and have a demoralizing effect on the defenders.

An example of a method which might have helped K Company in the situation described above was used on Mindanao. When tanks and infantry advanced along a jungle road, the tank would first fire its 75-mm gun down each side of the road. Then supporting infantrymen would move approximately 50 yards along the road, dispatching any Japanese stunned by the blast who had been waiting in their foxholes to throw an explosive charge at the tank. The tank would then move forward and stop abreast of the leading infantrymen, and the process would be repeated. The tankers would not move without infantry protection on each side.

During this action, the 3rd Battalion found a Japanese sketch map, which was promptly forwarded to Division G-2. The sketch, which had been classified by the Japanese as "most secret," was translated, and on 7 February, distributed in the form of an overlay for the American maps. The overlay showed the main enemy defenses in the pass from Mount Koko to the Santa Rita River. Subsequent actions confirmed the accuracy of the map.[20]

Colonel Rice's 2nd Battalion moved forward aggressively south of the road because of the southeastward slant of the Japanese lines, until opposed by the Yamada Platoon of the 10th Company. Major Ogawa had ordered Lieutenant Miyazaki, commander of his reserve, to reinforce Mount Ege to repel any threat against the southern portion of his line. Since the 2nd Battalion was far in advance of the 3rd, Colonel McIntosh pulled the 2nd Battalion back to the highway at the end of the day.[21]

The 1st Battalion initially followed the 3rd Battalion. Shortly after noon, D Company's Sergeant Jean Ancelet of Indianapolis noticed an antenna protruding from the jungle of trees on the ridge to the left of the road. It appeared that the Japanese were using a radio to direct their mortar and artillery batteries, which had periodically and accurately shelled the 1st Battalion.

Lieutenant White of B Company led his platoon on a patrol to destroy this suspected Japanese observation post. At an open space where bamboo had been cut to provide a field of fire, the patrol found itself in a fire and hand grenade fight with Sergeant Takenaka's heavy machine gun crew and some of Lieutenant Ogata's 11th Company men. The 1st Battalion 152nd journal reported "2 Japs killed and 1 probable." The men killed must have been Sergeant Takenaka himself and Pfc. Juichi Kamiyama, whom Lieutenant Kato reported as being killed by grenades on Mount Koko on this day.[22]

The only American casualty was Lieutenant White, who was shot in the shoulder. Sergeant Cotner helped him down the hillside to the road before the lieutenant collapsed. Several B Company men gathered around White, attracting the attention of Japanese mortar observers on Mount Koko. Luckily, the mortar barrage that automatically followed wounded only one man. Although the patrol did not find the antenna, and thus did not accomplish its mission, it had started a series of advances on this ridge that would be the key to the reduction of ZigZag Pass.[23]

At dusk, 2nd and 3rd Battalions started digging in along the western leg of the horseshoe and back along Highway 7. The 1st Battalion occupied its bivouac of the previous night at the sawmill. Casualties for the day were 5 KIA, 26 WIA and 1 MIA.[24]

General Jones, because of either erroneous reports or confusion by units in identifying their locations on the maps, grasped an entirely different picture of the day's fighting. He thought the 2nd and 3rd Battalions 152nd were digging in east of the horseshoe and that the 1st Battalion was well into the horseshoe. The 38th Division staff was clearly befuddled. The G-2 report at the end of the day stated that the Japanese had reinforced their positions early in the evening of 1-2 February with an estimated 700-1,000 men. In spite of their stubborn resistance, the report continued, they [the Japanese] were driven back approximately 1,800 yards during the day![25]

Actually, the 152nd's attack on 2 February had accomplished very little except for the routine patrol action by the 1st Battalion that eventually led to the capture of Mount Koko.

When General Jones returned to his CP at nightfall on 2 February, he found that General Hall had taken over and "was bringing in the 34th RCT to pass through the 152nd Infantry and open the pass. The Division G-3 was at that time down at the Corps CP getting the orders."[26]

Japanese morale reached its zenith after the repulse of the 152nd on both 1 and 2 February. Not only had the staunch defenders stopped the infantry, but also the American tanks had not proved to be as fearsome as they seemed. As we shall see, the tanks would be used to greater advantage as the battle progressed, but never as effectively as expected or desired.

Although there had been no preliminary artillery fire for the 152nd's attack on 2 February, nearly 2,500 rounds were fired during the day, principally at Mount Koko and Mount Ege. However, Lieutenant Ogata's 11th Company had suffered few casualties from the shelling. Major Ogawa had nothing but praise for the Ogata Company for driving the enemy back.

During the night, at Captain Ichinose's suggestion, Ogawa moved a 37-mm gun squad, which had no gun, to reinforce 1st Lieutenant Kyokai Sunami's platoon of the 9th Company dug-in near the road at the northern end of Mount Ege. This was the area where Ogawa and Ichinose believed the battle would be won or lost.[27]

The 149th's flanking move to Dinalupihan continued to go haywire. At about 2100 on 1 February, General Jones had radioed Colonel Skelton to return to Santa Rita and start over. Skelton never received the message.

On 2 February, with his column still halted and awaiting new orders in the same place Captain Ransohoff had observed from the air earlier that day, Skelton had frantically attempted to raise General Jones by radio three times. Only the third message got through. He wanted to inform Jones that his guerrillas said he need only follow the trail he was on to come out on Highway 7 near Dinalupihan.

Believing the 149th Infantry was already returning to Santa Rita, Jones had seen no need to reply to Skelton's first two requests for new orders. After the third request, Jones replied at 1145, "Return at once. Can use you to better advantage here."[28] It is not known for sure what General Jones meant by this message, but it can be interpreted as a desire to use the 149th to help break the impasse at the horseshoe.

Colonel Skelton spent the remainder of the day marching his troops back to their starting point at Santa Rita. Dog tired and fuming at anyone who would listen, he reached the 38th Division CP at 1930. There he found orders for him from XI Corps to start at 0700 the next morning to try again to reach Dinalupihan. General Hall had lifted the restriction that the 149th keep within supporting distance of the 152nd on Highway 7. Now Skelton could move as he wished and as fast as his men could traverse the rugged slopes.[29]

The movements of the 149th Infantry were to have an important bearing on General Jones's career. General Hall gave him a written reprimand, a severe indictment to be found in a career officer's file. The charges were that (1) the 149th took the wrong trail (which by later analysis was found not to exist) and (2) Jones ordered the regiment to return to Santa Rita by its original route instead of having it march due south cross-country until it found the proper trail. One is inclined to accept Jones's reflections on the second charge: "I will admit that I never even considered that solution. In that rough, mountainous jungle with deep-cut canyons, I thought that it would be much easier and faster to come back by trail and then go east on the proper trail."[30]

The second day of February had been a good one for the 34th Infantry. The only casualty was Pfc. Hershel O. Ryan of the 3rd Battalion Headquarters Company, wounded by mortar fire. Every man knew the morrow would be different. All units had been notified at 1530 that the 34th would be moving into the pass the next day. "I am putting my faith in Colonel Jenna and the 34th RCT tomorrow," General Hall radioed General Krueger as he retired for the night.[31]

Chapter 10
NOTES

(1) 152nd Infantry journal;
     XI Corps G-3 message to 38th Division G-3, 1126-2 February 1945.
(2) 1st Battalion 152nd Infantry journal, 0845.
(3) Jones comments, 20 December 1956, p. 11.
(4) *Ibid.*
(5) Telephone Monteith (XI Corps G-3) to Kirby (38th Division G-3), 1045.
(6) Jones comments, p. 4.
(7) XI Corps G-3 (Air Reconnaissance Report of Captain Ransohoff)
(8) Letter, Hall to Krueger, 3 February 1945.
(9) Memorandum, Hall to Jones, 4 February 1945.
(10) *Ibid.*
     Letter, Hall to Krueger, 3 February 1945.
(11) Letter, Hall to Krueger, 3 February 1945;
     Smith, Robert Ross, *Triumph in the Philippines*, p. 320.
(12) Letter, Hall to Krueger, 3 February 1945.
(13) Jones comments, p. 5.
(14) *How the Kato Company Fought: The Record of the 3rd Machine Gun Company 39th Infantry Regiment*, Tamotsu Nagai, Editor, 1990, p. 215.
(15) Smith, *Triumph in the Philippines*, p. 319.
(16) Frederick, Pfc. James, Company E 34th Infantry, letter to author, 5 February 1988.
(17) Roster of Killed and Wounded—Leyte, 34th Infantry files, National Records Center.
(18) Schoonover, Major James F., *The Operations of the 3rd Battalion 152nd Infantry in Zig Zag Pass, Luzon, 29 Jan.-14 Feb. 1945*, Advanced Infantry Officers Course, 1947-1948, p. 10.
(19) Jones comments, p. 4.
(20) Schoonover, *The Operations of the 3rd Battalion 152nd Infantry*, p. 10.
(21) Ogawa, Major Hironori, *Record of the 3rd Battalion, 39th Infantry Regiment in the "Big Asia War,"* p. 24;

Smith, *Triumph in the Philippines*, p. 318.

(22) Ancelet, Sergeant Jean, Company D 152nd Infantry, interview by author, 27 July 1991.

(23) Cotner, Sergeant Ray, Company B, interview, 27 July 1991.

(24) 152nd Infantry journal.

(25) Smith, *Triumph in the Philippines*, p. 319;
38th Division G-2 Report #5, 1800-2 February 1945.

(26) Jones comments, p. 4.

(27) Ogawa, *Record of the 3rd Battalion*, p. 24-25.

(28) 38th Division G-3 journal entry #31, radio, Jones to Skelton 1145;
Smith, *Triumph in the Philippines*, p. 326.

(29) Message No. 1, CG XI Corps to CG 38th Division, 2100-2 February 1945.

(30) Jones comments, p. 3.

(31) Letter, Hall to Krueger dated 3 February 1945, an "amplification of the radio I forwarded you tonight 2200." Letter obviously sent 2 February 1945.

THE 34th INFANTRY ATTACKS

(3 FEBRUARY)

It was nearly midnight on 2 February before Colonel Jenna returned to the regimental CP from XI Corps Headquarters with his orders for 3 February. By 0230, he had formulated his own plans and passed on verbally to the battalion commanders his orders to comply with the Corps directive: "34th CT . . . under Corps control, will pass through leading elements 38th Infantry Division in their present positions and attack vigorously direction DINALUPIHAN."[1] Reinforced by the attached 603rd Tank Company and a detachment from Company B 27th Engineer Battalion, and guided by 12 guerrillas from Corps Headquarters, the 34th would try to smash through the Japanese obstructing Highway 7. The 149th Infantry would depart Santa Rita and try to reach Dinalupihan via a different trail. This time, Colonel Skelton would have his full regiment (the 1st Battalion 149th had been released from division reserve). Corps specifically ordered "the 149th to advance rapidly and not—repeat not— slow its advance to conform to the advance of the 34th Infantry if that regiment should be slowed down." The 1st and 2nd Battalions 152nd Infantry would patrol north and south of Highway 7 respectively behind the 34th.[2]

Colonel Jenna designated his 1st Battalion to lead the attack since Oglesby's men were closest to the pass and had already explored much of the ground leading to the entrance. 2nd and 3rd Battalions would follow in that order in fifty 2.5-ton trucks of the 383rd Quartermaster Truck Company.[3]

At 0700 sharp, a grim 2nd Battalion climbed aboard the "6x6s" in the middle of Olongapo and began the gradual ascent to the battleground. The trucks would return to pick up the 3rd Battalion. After traversing a wide plain, gently sloping upward, the trucks passed through rougher ground with increasing jungle vegetation. Suddenly, huge trees rose from both sides of the road, blocking the sunlight and casting an instant gloom.

It was like entering a tunnel, of course not totally dark, but in sharp contrast to the brilliant sunshine on the plain.

Many of the replacements had not joined their companies until the 34th reached Olongapo. Sergeant Donald M. Bayles of Southold, NY, a squad leader in C Company, said he hardly had time to learn the names of the new men in his squad before heading up to ZigZag Pass.[4]

The 152nd Infantry was still occupying its positions of the previous night when the 34th arrived to relieve them. 3rd Battalion 152nd's leading elements were camped along the western leg of the horseshoe. The remainder of the battalion, the 2nd Battalion, and the 1st were strung out along the road all the way back to the sawmill. As the 34th caravan wound into the pass, elements of six battalions of infantry at various times were moving forward or backward along a 3,000 to 4,000 yard stretch of road.

The company commanders of the 152nd had found it so difficult to orient themselves on their maps that no one could locate the enemy positions with certainty. Therefore, Colonel Jenna decided to use his 1st Battalion to probe the enemy's defenses and get a feel for the situation before committing his other two battalions.[5] Accompanied by General Jones, Colonel Oglesby gained what information he could from Major Mangold, the 3rd Battalion 152nd commander. At 0930, 1st Battalion 34th moved out with two companies abreast, A Company on the right side of the road, C Company on the left, with B Company in reserve.[6]

Movement had barely started when the road curved to the right to start that 850-yard loop known as the horseshoe—"that great loop . . . embroidered with many little loops." Somebody in the 34th later counted 11 little loops. Each changed the direction of the highway ever so slightly, but enough to mask the road beyond. Having passed one turn, the lead scout could see only to the next turn.

To add to the misery of the troops traversing the horseshoe, the ridge to the left of the road within the "U" branched out into five noses, like five fingers, at its southern end. Each finger had been excavated for the roadbed. Thus at five points on the loop, nearly perpendicular banks of earth jutted upward from the left side of the road.

To the right of the road, the ground fell away into deep gullies between each of the five fingers until a point about three-fourths the way round the loop. Here the steep ridge of the northern end of Mount Ege rose to the right of the road, forming a defile off the right side of the road for much of the eastern leg of the horseshoe. At its open end to the north, the horseshoe measured about 200 yards across a sharp, steeply rising ridge. The western leg measured 250 yards north to south; the southern leg 275 yards west to east; and the eastern leg 325 yards south to north.

The broadest point in the center measured 300 yards. The road climbed appreciably throughout the length of the horseshoe.

Each lead company dispatched flanking patrols to its side of the road, as vegetation and terrain would permit. Within 45 minutes, one of C Company's patrols was atop the ridge inside the horseshoe, which gave good observation of the terrain lying south of the road and immediately east of the loop. The two lead companies, Headquarters Company and D Company had proceeded along two legs of the horseshoe.[7]

About one-third the way along the eastern leg, A Company was stopped by a tank trap—a huge tree felled to block the road with a mined area in the road on both sides of the tree. Five volunteers from the three Japanese heavy machine gun squads on Mount Ege were hidden in holes beside the road, each with an explosive meant to destroy a tank. These soldiers were the "kamikaze" of the Japanese infantry. Single men were expected to volunteer before married men because it was suicidal to attack a tank surrounded by infantry.

A Company beat off the attackers using rifle fire and grenades. Three of the five attackers were killed. The premature explosion of his own bomb blew up one of the Japanese, Toshio Nakase of the Ueno Squad. Toshiyoki Yoshida and Genichi Hirotani of the Kanazawa Squad "attacked the tanks and met heroic deaths." In describing this attack, the Kato HMG Company history reveals the disgust with the American tactics: "Walking soldiers precede the tanks. They start shooting at anything that seems suspicious. We cannot get close to them [the tanks]."[8]

Oglesby called for the engineers to remove the obstructions so that his unharmed tanks could move forward. At about 1000, he radioed his reserve, B Company, still at the northwest corner of the horseshoe, to move overland across the ridge eastward and close the open end of the loop.[9]

Commanded by 1st Lieutenant Thomas C. Rhem of Memphis, TN, B Company started moving up a trail off the highway. Skirmishers of Lieutenant Ogata's 11th Company, who had moved down the ridge to previously prepared positions, barred the way. Their well placed shots caused several casualties, among them Lieutenant Rhem with a painful wound in the hip. Although barely able to walk, Rhem refused evacuation. He was to lead two more attacks before he left the line at 1830 on orders from the battalion commander.[10]

Farther back along the trail that ran through a compact stand of bamboo, Assistant Squad Leader Thornton of the 1st Platoon "was terrified to hear a rifle shot immediately behind [him]." He quickly turned around and was shocked to see a sergeant grimacing with pain from a shot in the foot. It was never known whether this self-inflicted wound was intentional, but the sergeant never returned to the company.[11]

The move by B Company brought stern retaliation from the Japanese. At about 1100, artillery, mortar, machine gun and rifle fire rained down on the company and the remainder of the battalion from positions north and east of the open end of the horseshoe. Sergeant Bayles of C Company looked up and saw a mortar shell tumbling end-over-end and coming right down on him. He dove into a depression in the ground about two seconds before it exploded, showering him with dirt, but causing no damage.[12]

The 152nd Infantry was still retiring after its relief by the 34th. With two regiments of infantry strung out along the road in the valley below him, Major Ogawa considered this an appropriate time to rake the entire road. Master Sergeant Fujimoto at Ogawa's headquarters on Mount Koko laid down immediate, accurate fire from his two 90-mm mortars located behind Mount Kita and also directed fire for Lieutenant Otani's two 105-mm howitzers at Mount Shinshu. The barrage caused casualties in both regiments, but the results were spotty.

The leading elements of E Company at the head of 2nd Battalion 34th were just turning into the horseshoe followed in order by F, G, Hq, and Headquarters Companies. 2nd Battalion suffered no casualties, but the barrage damaged several Headquarters Company and H Company vehicles.[13]

3rd Battalion 34th was not so lucky. Lieutenant Paul Cain, commanding I Company, later reported, "Suddenly and without warning we were in the midst of an artillery barrage. When the smoke had settled, we had one man killed, five wounded and two men shell-shocked." Among the casualties were two sergeants, a corporal and three replacements, one of whom was the man killed.[14]

Cain not only had the Japanese barrage to contend with, but also the withdrawing 152nd Infantry. Jammed within a space of less than 1,000 yards along the highway was the 3rd Battalion 152nd moving back to the sawmill area and the 3rd Battalion 34th advancing toward the horseshoe. Little wonder that Ogawa gave this area special attention. The narrow road became so congested and dangerous that Colonel McIntosh finally ordered the 3rd Battalion 152nd to halt in place and return to the sawmill the next day.[15]

Captain Donald B. Cameron of Cleveland, OH, the 2nd Battalion 34th surgeon, attributed the lack of casualties in the 2nd Battalion to Japanese accuracy. "They were obviously zeroed in to cover the road. When the barrage started, our men leaped into the ditches by the side of the road and were unharmed. The Jap rounds beat into the road and tore up several vehicles."[16]

Old timers immediately noticed one aspect of this barrage that boded evil. These artillerists and mortar men were a cut above the average Japanese gunner. Correct guessing gained through long experience enabled the Japanese observers and gunners to lay their first rounds directly on target without bracketing fire. They could "fire for effect" with their first rounds. American reports attribute their accuracy to pre-registration, but we know now that ammunition was too precious to waste before the battle. An artillery observation plane finally spotted these audacious gunners and silenced them with counter-battery fire.[17]

It was evident that these Japanese were not the transients and rear echelon troops that General Hall and the XI Corps staff had believed were defending ZigZag Pass. They were as skilled and tenacious as any the 34th Infantry had encountered. It is significant that on 3 February the Corps G-2, Colonel John W. Patton, identified the veteran 39th Infantry definitely as the force barring the way in the pass. Corps finally admitted that the Americans were facing Japanese combat troops—something the 152nd Infantry had strongly suspected since 31 January.[18]

● ● ●

From the fire he had received, Colonel Oglesby sensed there was a pocket of Japanese dug-in just south of Highway 7 at the northern end of the long north-south ridge (Mount Ege). This high ground near the road completely dominated the ground east of the horseshoe. Oglesby was correct in his assumption. The Japanese had concentrated a mass of fire-power in this area called the *Jukaki-dai,* the Heavy Fire Arms Position or the Heavy Weapons Plateau. Here was a 37-mm anti-tank gun protected by the Ueno and Kanazawa HMG Squads and several riflemen. They were in a commanding position to resist infantry advancing along the road or attempting to attack the northern end of Mount Ege from the west. It would be senseless for the 1st Battalion to turn the corner out of the horseshoe before investigating this suspected pocket of resistance.[19]

Oglesby ordered C Company to leave the road where the battalion had stopped, move northeast and investigate. 1st Lieutenant Oakley W. Storey, the company commander, elected to take a more southern approach to seize higher ground and then attack the suspected pocket from the south. The company made contact about 1140 with some of Lieutenant Shinfune's 9th Company men and engaged in a sharp firefight without being able to advance appreciably.

As the enemy dispositions became clearer, Oglesby realized that a solid wall of strong defenses on dominating terrain blocked B Company north of Highway 7 and C Company south of the highway. To relieve the pressure, he ordered Lieutenant Heaberlin to take A Company on a wide flanking movement to the southeast and hit the southern flank of the enemy halting C Company. Company A left the road and moved as rapidly as the dense foliage would permit.

But the jungle was to frustrate Oglesby's battalion as it had Stillwell's regiment. Trying to maneuver south, east, and then north, Heaberlin worked through the woods and ridges by compass, laying wire to insure his communications with Battalion Headquarters. Once off the road, there were no recognizable terrain features; orientation of map to ground was entirely by estimate and difficult at best. Apparently, Familiar Peak to the south could not be seen because of tall trees. Heaberlin, believing his company to be moving east parallel to Highway 7, was actually moving more nearly south toward the peak.

At about 1300, new sources of rifle and machine gun fire on Mount Ege made their presence known. C Company pulled back to allow artillery fire to blanket the area. The concentrations had little effect. When the men of C Company tried to move back to the area they had vacated, heavy mortar and machine gun fire greeted them.

First Scout Edd M. Gonzales of New Mexico did what every good scout was supposed to do. With no regard for his own safety, he advanced alone against an enemy pillbox firing his submachine gun until he was hit in the arm. His brave act forced the Japanese to disclose several positions, which were marked for future destruction.[20]

Lieutenant Storey attempted to knock out these strong points with his own 60-mm mortars and D Company's 81s, but to no avail. When he committed his reserve platoon round the south flank, it was stopped by a counterattack by the Yamada Platoon of the 10th Company. Pfc. Bernard Schneller of Carlton, OR, the C Company aid man, distinguished himself in the firefight that followed. Ignoring the fight, he moved up and down the firing line giving aid wherever needed and assisting in the evacuation of casualties of almost one-third of the platoon. Calling for covering artillery fire, C Company withdrew 250 yards and dug in for the night.[21]

Ogawa commended Lieutenant Shinfune and his 9th Company, which, despite many casualties, had repelled every enemy advance. Platoon Commander 1st Lieutenant Kyokai Sunami had especially distinguished himself. Manning a light machine gun on the front line, he had stopped C Company until late in the afternoon, but had finally died a brave death from a bullet to his chin.[22]

During the artillery fire near dusk covering C Company's withdrawal, the best reporter on the Japanese side of the battle was wounded. Sergeant

Company C 34th Infantry attacks along Highway 7, 3 February 1945
Courtesy of Charles W. Card, Houston, TX

Tamotsu Nagai of the Kato HMG Company was sitting in an "octopus trap," a Japanese foxhole that enabled a soldier to sit with relative security during bombardments and then stand and look out for the enemy during lulls in the firing. Nagai had taken off his bayonet and hung it on the dirt wall to the right of his head, loosened the chin strap of his helmet, and bent his body to the left, closing his ears with his index fingers against the incessant din of artillery fire.

Suddenly he saw a "bright red color" and felt a strong impact as if held tightly and struck on the head with a big log. He felt he was falling into a dark, void space as if he were descending in an elevator. He remembered seeing these things happening to him as if all the frames of a high-speed movie projector were shown in a second. When he regained consciousness, he felt dizzy. When he touched his face with his right hand, it was slimy with blood from his temple. Surprisingly, he felt no pain. He stopped the bleeding by pressing his carotid artery with his left hand and applying an emergency triangular bandage with his right.

Sensing that the emergency treatment was not enough, Nagai decided to go to the 9th Company Headquarters' cave for better treatment. As the firing subsided, he crawled out of the octopus trap and started for the cave about 20 meters (65 feet) to his left front. Still feeling dizzy, he could only

Sergeant Tamotsu Nagai,
Communications Sergeant 3rd
Battalion 39th Infantry, 1944

crawl. Intending to go left, he went to the right. American artillery resumed. Nagai lay flat on the ground and felt the shock waves from the rounds moving over him. The earth shuddered and dirt covered him. He needed to get back to the octopus trap, but he couldn't remember which way to go. It was getting dark. Each time the artillery fired, Nagai felt it was all over for him. "Time passed so slowly."

At last, gaining courage to continue his search, he finally found Lieutenant Shinfune's cave. Somebody asked, "Who's there?" Nagai couldn't remember the password. However, he knew by the voice that it was Sergeant Kunio Ogura, with whom he had been a recruit. "I am Nagai of the Kato Troop. I got it in the head."

Ogura led him into the cave, but the occupants would not treat his wound. They said they were not adequately equipped to handle casualties from other companies; there weren't enough medical supplies to go around. They permitted Nagai to stay overnight, but he could get no treatment for his wound.

Nagai remembered Company Commander Shinfune sitting by candlelight tearing up documents. Comparing the present battle with a crucial one in Japanese history, Shinfune philosophized, "This is the great war of the Minato-gawa. It's going to be death in an honorable defeat. Right? Let's all die together."[23]

Nagai groaned all night from the pain caused by vibrations from American artillery fire and even from other soldiers in the cave walking round him. The blanket at the cave entrance swayed with each explosion. Feeling lucky to be alive, he was glad to leave this oppressive atmosphere the next day.[24]

Sergeant Nagai in 1991

We return to B Company 34th waiting off the road near the northwest corner of the horseshoe. With no further opposition, the company moved forward after the late morning's artillery barrage, meeting little resistance initially, but becoming engaged in a heavy firefight at 1600 with the Japanese riflemen supporting the Yamauchi machine gun position. In the rear of the company, Assistant Squad Leader Thornton and a rifleman were scouting a certain area looking for the enemy. With Thornton in the lead, they crawled cautiously from their position on the trail, fully expecting to come face-to-face with a Japanese lurking in the tall grass. Rifle shots from the rear quickly ended their patrol. Turning around, Thornton saw his companion, a Hispanic, contorting his face in agony and pointing to one of his knees. Four or five inches of flesh had been blasted away, exposing the bone. The damage had been done by one of the recent replacements. He had panicked and thoughtlessly fired at the grass waving in the wind.[25]

In February, when darkness comes early, it was standard practice to start digging in by 1630. Both B and C Companies, however, pushed their attacks beyond 1700 before pulling back to the first good defensive terrain. B Company returned to the edge of the road near the northwest corner of the horseshoe.[26]

Although the Japanese had thwarted Oglesby at every turn, the 1st Battalion 34th's attack was of deep concern to Major Ogawa. He had rushed to Mount Ege at the first sign of a possible American penetration. He was dismayed by the totally different appearance of the northern slope of Ege near the road that had been devastated by American artillery fire.

Trees were down everywhere; it was impossible to use the transportation trench to supply the front line machine gun positions from the rear. The log and dirt roof over the Kanazawa Squad's machine gun had been destroyed. A squad of riflemen protecting the Ueno heavy machine gun near the road had been wiped out.

During the night, Lieutenant Kato tried to close the gap left by the destroyed rifle squad with a work squad brought up from the rear. The ground was so hard the replacement squad could dig in only knee deep.

After A Company 34th's wide swing to his left, it was obvious to Ogawa that he might annihilate this group of Americans separated from the main force. The Sakura Company had withdrawn in good order from its outpost line the night of 31 January, and after returning to Mount Fumetsu, had rested 1-2 February. Ogawa ordered Lieutenant Sakura to send one squad to reinforce the hard-pressed men of the 9th Company at the northern end of Mount Ege. With the remainder of his company, he was to attack at dusk the Americans isolated between the horseshoe and Mount Kosaku (Familiar Peak).[27]

At about 1630, Lieutenant Heaberlin picked a knoll for A Company to dig in for the night. He sent a seven-man patrol commanded by Squad Leader Sergeant Garrett, "a short, blond guy from Georgia," toward the firing he had heard in the afternoon to see if any Japanese were in his area. The patrol set off down the slope and into the jungle. After wandering for 15 minutes, Garrett realized he was lost.[28]

As darkness approached, an enemy patrol opened fire. Garrett's men hit the ground, but did not return fire. After about 20 minutes, Garrett tossed a couple of phosphorus grenades in the hope that A Company would see the smoke and reveal its position. After the smoke rose through the jungle growth, a pre-arranged burst from a Tommy gun disclosed A Company's direction. Moving as fast as the undergrowth would permit, the patrol breathlessly charged up the knoll to the perimeter—scared and tired—but safe.

By this time, A Company had started digging its perimeter for the night. Lieutenant Sakura's attack came so suddenly that two men on outpost never made it back to the perimeter. One of Sakura's machine guns opened up right in front of replacement Bill McKenna's foxhole. "My hole was only about three inches deep, and I literally crawled inside my helmet," McKenna remembered. The machine gun fire skipped across the perimeter, bullets kicking up dirt in McKenna's face and knocking the sight off his rifle.

The firing stopped, and a Japanese voice shouting and yelling in a frenzy harangued the Americans unintelligibly. Then there was another moment of silence. With an eerie, chilling, blood-curdling chorus of "Banzai," the attack erupted about ten yards to McKenna's left on a gentler slope. A machine gun and BAR positioned there cut the Japanese down as they came screaming up the slope. The Japanese withdrew, giving McKenna and his foxhole buddy, Tony Ratto, time to dig deeper and wider.[29]

With A Company pinned down, close-in artillery fire, dependent solely on instant communications with the supporting battery, was the only way to repulse such an attack. Corporal Leonard N. Grannon of Washington, IN, was the radio operator with the forward observer from the 63rd F.A. Battalion assigned to A Company on its flanking march. Corporal Grannon's radio failed to work when the attack started. Undaunted, he exposed himself, with total disregard for his own safety, above ground in the midst of the prone infantrymen to repair his radio.

His bravery and coolness under fire saved the day. Artillery shells were soon winging in and, in blunting the attacks, saved many lives and possibly saved A Company from total destruction.[30]

But the Japanese were not through after one charge. A single voice screamed, like a cheerleader exhorting the crowd. Company A fixed bayonets and pulled grenades from their pack straps. Lieutenant Sakura's men attacked again, yelling even louder. With visibility only five yards, McKenna and Ratto sprayed the area in front with their M-1s, firing several clips each into the near darkness. The noise was terrific—the gunfire, the Japanese screaming as they charged up the knoll—but again, they were beaten back.

When it became completely dark, the Japanese mounted a third charge, but with less enthusiasm and less force, and A Company's perimeter quickly silenced the Japanese rifles. At about 2000 hours, American artillery started pouring in shells in earnest all around the perimeter. Some rounds exploded close enough to shower half-spent steel on the foxholes. The Americans kept up sporadic firing all night at any suspicious sound in the jungle.

Despite appalling casualties, including the death of its leader, the Sakura Company had surrounded and neutralized A Company. A/34th was reasonably safe with an artillery observer who consistently brought in rounds only 25 yards outside the perimeter, but the company was effectively removed as a factor in 1st Battalion's attack.[31]

◆　　◆　　◆

What had the 34th accomplished during the day? 1st Battalion had pushed around the horseshoe, eliminating a tank trap in the process, and was staying for the night. The front line (if one were to be drawn) was about 400 yards long. It would run northwest to southeast from B Company's perimeter near the northwest corner of the horseshoe across Highway 7, bisecting the eastern leg of the horseshoe, to C Company's perimeter 200 yards south of the "2" and 250 yards west of the Ege ridge. Isolated A Company was dug-in about halfway between the horseshoe and Mount Kosaku.

These gains had not come lightly. Casualty records compiled after the battle show for 3 February B Company with 6 KIA and 6 WIA, C Company with 5 KIA and 16 WIA, and A Company with 2 KIA and 4 WIA during its 3 days of isolation. Among C Company's wounded were two of the replacement officers. The casualties, as usual, came in bunches late in the afternoon in an unseasonable, heavy rain for the battalion surgeon, Captain George E. Morrissey of Davenport, IA. Colonel Oglesby praised Morrissey for his calm efficiency and indifference to enemy fire, which inspired his own men as well as the wounded, who knew he would assure proper treatment and rapid evacuation.[32]

One thing was certain. One battalion of the 34th could not get the job done where three battalions of the 152nd had failed. Neither of the other two battalions of the 34th had been called on. After reaching the turn into the horseshoe, 2nd Battalion 34th remained in place and dug in for the night along the road. 3rd Battalion dug in farther back.

Colonel Jenna had considered alternatives for reinforcing the 1st Battalion attack early in the afternoon when Oglesby was slowed down by the defenses at Mount Ege and Mount Hissho. He wanted to send the 2nd Battalion on a wide flanking movement south of the Japanese defenses. He abandoned the idea because the guerrillas did not know of a suitable trail. He learned that Intelligence estimates (which would prove to be incorrect) of Japanese strength south of the road would necessitate what he considered an extreme movement south to effect an encirclement.[33]

The 152nd Infantry patrolled vigorously during the day. The regiment used the sawmill near Highway 7 where the road crossed the Kalaklan River near its source as a staging area and jump-off point for patrols and attacks. Colonel Cornwell's 1st Battalion continued its special interest in the high, steep ridge on its left whose dark cliffs at the top seemed to frown and glower at every movement in the valley below.

One 1st Battalion patrol met opposition from three bunkers, reported as concrete protected by barbed wire, on the western portion of this ridgeline. The battalion marked the bunkers for destruction the next day. Another patrol reported finding in a ravine near the horseshoe 104 enemy dead (not reported in Japanese records). If true, these Japanese must have been killed by artillery fire on previous days and hidden. The 152nd patrols lost two KIA and six WIA on 3 February.[34]

Thus, a day General Hall had expected to be the turning point in the campaign merely added to his frustrations. The 34th Infantry had been stopped cold, but was deeply imbedded in the horseshoe. At least the 149th Infantry, that General Hall had expected to be in Dinalupihan on this date, was now on the right trail and making satisfactory progress.

Soon after 1st Battalion 34th launched its attack, Hall received this message from Commanding General XIV Corps:

"Friendly troops will be in Dinalupihan-Hermosa area on arrival (ahead of) Eleventh Corps—Signed, Griswold"[35]

Lieutenant General Oscar W. Griswold, graduate of the Class of 1910, had been one year ahead of Hall at West Point. Those who knew

General Griswold say he intended no malice; his message merely stated a fact. But perhaps he was also good-naturedly needling a good friend. Any response that General Hall made to Griswold's message was not recorded.

Colonel Monteith, XI Corps G-3, confirmed this news the next day in a handwritten message to his counterpart at 38th Division Headquarters:

"One platoon 40th Recon Troop reached Dinalupihan without enemy contact, proceeds to Hermosa today. Company G 185th Infantry scheduled to arrive Dinalupihan 031900. Elements 1st Cav entered Grace Park, Manila 031835."[36]

The full import of the last sentence of this message was not realized at the time. In a matter of days, the commander of those 1st Cavalry Division elements was to become well known to the 38th Division.

Although the infantry of the 38th was barely involved with the enemy during the day, General Hall's poor opinion of the division continued to fester. His conviction that General Jones was not the man he wanted to command the troops in ZigZag Pass seemed to harden even further. He had already revealed his feelings with severe criticism of the 38th Division and 152nd Infantry in his letter to General Krueger written 2 February but dated 3 February, mentioned in Chapter 9.

General Krueger radioed his terse reply to this letter at 0737-4 February:

RE YOUR LETTER 3 FEBRUARY. STRATEGICAL CONSIDERATIONS DICTATE THAT YOUR CORPS MUST ADVANCE RAPIDLY AND VIGOROUSLY TO EFFECT ABLE [A] JUNCTION WITH FOURTEENTH CORPS AND CARRY OUT YOUR ASSIGNED MISSIONS PROMPTLY. TAKE WHATEVER ACTION IS NECESSARY TO ACCOMPLISH THIS END. ADVISE ACTION TAKEN.

Sgd KRUEGER[37]

Chapter 11

NOTES

(1) CG XI Corps to CG 38th Infantry Division, Message #1, 2100-2 February 1945.

(2) *Ibid.*;
CG XI Corps to CG 38th Infantry Division, Message #2, 2100-2 February 1945.

(3) *Ibid.* (Messages #1&2)

(4) Bayles, letter to author, 28 October 1988.

(5) 34th Infantry AAR, p. 53.

(6) *Ibid.,* p. 56.

(7) *Ibid.,* p. 57.

(8) *How the Kato Company Fought: The Record of the 3rd Machine Gun Company 39th Infantry Regiment*, Tamotsu Nagai, Editor, 1990 p. 39, p. 187, p. 218.

(9) 34th Infantry AAR, p. 58.

(10) 34th Infantry files, National Records Center.

(11) Thornton, Pfc. Douglas W., Jr., letter to author, 30 October 1989.

(12) 34th Infantry AAR, p. 58;
Bayles letter.

(13) Yoshikawa, Takehiko translator and Mann, B. David, editor, *The Untold Story Behind the Battle of Bataan in 1945*, Appendix #15;
34th Infantry journal;
34th Infantry AAR, p. 59.

(14) Special report in 34th Infantry S-3 journal;
Casualties Zambales Operation, National Archives, Washington, D.C.

(15) Walters, Captain Edward E., *The Operations of the 38th Infantry Division in the Landing at San Antonio-San Narciso Area and the Advance to Dinalupihan*, p. 21;
Schoonover, Major James F., *The Operations of the 3rd Battalion 152nd Infantry in Zig Zag Pass, Luzon, 29 Jan.-14 Feb. 1945*, Advanced Infantry Officers Course, 1947-1948, p. 11.

(16) Cameron interview by author, 1 October 1988.

(17) Nagai, Tamotsu, Communications Sergeant, Machine Gun Company 3rd Battalion 39th Infantry, interview, 14 May 1991; 34th Infantry journal.

(18) Enclosure #1 to XI Corps Periodic G-2 Report #6, 3 February 1945.

(19) Ogawa, Major Hironori, *Record of the 3rd Battalion, 39th Infantry Regiment in the "Big Asia War,"* p. 26; Kato Company History, p. 186.

(20) 34th Infantry AAR, p. 59-63; Summary of official commendation of Pfc. Gonzales.

(21) 34th Infantry AAR, p. 62; Ogawa, *Record of the 3rd Battalion*, p. 27; Summary of official commendation of Pfc. Schneller.

(22) Ogawa, *Record of the 3rd Battalion*, p. 26.

(23) Kato Company History, p. 215-216; The War of the Minato-gawa refers to the crucial battle fought near the river by that name near Kobe by more than 100,000 Samurai warriors in January 1336 between forces from Kyushu and Kyoto for control of central Honshu. The Minato-gawa symbolized for Shinfune the annihilation of his company he expected during the following days.

(24) Kato Company History, p. 215-217. Narration by Tamotsu Nagai.

(25) 34th Infantry AAR, p. 62; Thornton letter to author, 30 October 1989.

(26) 34th Infantry AAR, p. 63.

(27) Ogawa, *Record of the 3rd Battalion*, p. 26-27; Kato Company History, p. 39.

(28) McKenna, Pvt. William J., A Company 34th Infantry diary, p. 4.

(29) *Ibid.,* p. 5-7.

(30) Corporal Grannon was awarded a Silver Star Medal for this action.

(31) McKenna diary, p. 5-7.

(32) 34th Infantry AAR, 63; Casualties Zambales Operation, National Archives, Washington, D.C.; Morrissey, Captain George E., Surgeon, 1st Battalion 34th Infantry diary, p. 30; Summary of official commendation of Captain Morrissey by Colonel Oglesby.

(33) 34th Infantry AAR, p. 64-66.

(34) 152nd Infantry journal;
      Message G-3 38th Division, journal entry #65, 1845-03 February
      1945;
      38th Division G-2 Report #6, 03 February 1945.
(35) Message CG XIV Corps to CG XI Corps, 0955-03 February
      1945, journal entry #29.
(36) Message XI Corps G-3 to G-3 38th Division, (handwritten, no
      time given) 04 February 1945, journal entry #28.
(37) CG Sixth Army to CG XI Corps, 0737-04 February 1945.

JAPANESE CANNONADE
(4 FEBRUARY)

Through the probing attacks of his 1st Battalion on 3 February, Colonel Jenna had gained a better picture of the Japanese defenses. He knew that the enemy held strong positions that blocked the road east of the horseshoe. He knew that mortars and artillery were emplaced several hundred yards to his left front that could deposit accurate fire on most of the regiment at a moment's notice.

Artillery forward observers (for reasons not clear) regarded a high prominence approximately 2,000 yards east of the horseshoe as the key to the Japanese defenses. On 2 February, the Japanese had pushed the 3rd Battalion 152nd off the high ridge on the left side of the road north of the horseshoe. This significant action did not seem to enter into Colonel Jenna's thinking. His thoughts were of the high ground east of the Santa Rita River.

At 2130 on 3 February, he issued orders to his battalion commanders outlining an ambitious plan that, if successful, would break the logjam in ZigZag Pass. The regiment would attack eastward, 1st Battalion on the right, south of the road, 2nd Battalion on the left, north of the road, Highway 7 inclusive to 2nd Battalion, with 3rd Battalion initially following 2nd.

The attack would occur in phases. 1st Battalion, after B Company's relief by 2nd Battalion, would secure the twin-topped ridge (Mount Ege) that had eluded C Company the day before. 2nd Battalion's mission was to seize the high ground (Mount Shinshu), 1,000 yards east almost to the hairpin loop, believed to be the general location of the mortars and artillery that had bombarded the regiment on 3 February. Line of departure for 2nd Battalion would be the ridge (Mount Hissho) in front of B Company.

3rd Battalion would then move through 2nd and secure a crossing of the Santa Rita River 700 yards beyond 2nd Battalion's objective. The 3rd would then ascend and capture the high ridge (the East Pass) east of the river, which appeared from maps and aerial photographs to command all the ground east and west. The key to the 3rd Battalion's attack was the 2nd Battalion's objective, the ridgeline overlooking the valley of the Santa Rita River. Guns for direct fire and observers for artillery on this ridge could bring down a devastating fire to cover 3rd Battalion's advance down to the river and up to its final objective.[1]

Major Ogawa had correctly judged American intentions. As a result of the incursions of B and C Companies 34th and the 152nd probes on 3 February, he had reinforced Mount Koko and Mount Hissho with a squad from the Nakamura Engineer Platoon and another squad from the rear. He had reinforced the northern end of Mount Ege (the Jukaki-dai) with three squads. These were a squad each from the Sakura Company and the Ichinose AT Company, in addition to the work squad from the Operations Company Lieutenant Kato had placed there.

The soil was so hard at the Jukaki-dai position that the reinforcements could dig only 50 centimeters (20 inches) deep before daybreak. The Ogaki Squad of the Kato HMG Company, having returned from the Water's Edge Position, was also defending this area. Ogawa assigned responsibility for this most critical part of his line—the defile at the top of the "2"—to his senior company commander, Captain Masaaki Ichinose of the Regiment's 37-mm Anti-tank Company.[2]

After an all-night artillery and mortar duel between the combatants, 2nd Battalion ate a hurried breakfast of ten-in-one rations (these rations came in a large cardboard box containing cans and boxes of food that

would feed ten men for one day). Major Harry L. Snavely of Lancaster, PA, commanded the 2nd Battalion. A graduate of Lehigh University, Snavely had transferred to the 24th Division from the 503rd Parachute Infantry. He fitted comfortably into his new position. His nickname, "Snapper," was a natural for the radio code name for the battalion.

Snavely had been named 2nd Battalion Commander in early January when the prior commander, Lieutenant Colonel James F. Pearsall, Jr., Class of 1937 West Point, had gone stateside on leave. In preparing for the attack, Snavely

Major Harry L. Snavely, Commander
2nd Battalion 34th Infantry

moved his battalion several hundred yards along the road to relieve B Company and then reconnoitered the ridge in front of B Company as far forward as he dared. Next, he sent patrols to check out the road into the horseshoe and the high ground inside the horseshoe.

When the patrols reported no contact along the first leg of the horseshoe, Snavely obtained permission to alter the plan for the 2nd Battalion. Instead of attacking eastward cross-country from the horseshoe, he would take the more rapid course of moving along the road. If stopped on the road, he would attempt flanking movements to his left to envelop the enemy positions. He may have been swayed to follow the highway because of B Company's bad experience in leaving the road the previous day.[3]

1st and 2nd Battalions began their attacks shortly after 1000. Snavely and Colonel Oglesby, the 1st Battalion commander, coordinated a preparatory artillery barrage that was four times heavier than any fired in preparation for an attack to date. Major Ogawa admitted that this barrage caused much damage to the 9th Company defending Mount Ege. Both Oglesby and Snavely would call for artillery fire when needed as their attacks developed.

Oglesby started his attack with B Company on the right and C on the left, with the objective being the twin-nosed Ege ridge whose summit was about 300 yards east of the eastern leg of the horseshoe. Company A could not help. Lieutenant Heaberlin reported by radio after his sleepless night that he was surrounded and unable to fight his way out. Sakura's men had found and cut his wire communications with Battalion.[4]

Artillery had saved A Company. The artillery observer laid in his fire all night by radio as close as 25 yards from the perimeter without once dropping a round inside. Company A men were in general agreement that they would have been severely mauled or wiped out without the artillery fire. The company counted 35 dead Japanese around its perimeter, but many more had apparently been removed by their comrades.[5]

Captain Ransohoff flew over at the start of the 1st and 2nd Battalions' attacks. He observed a few men making short rushes across the open ground in the vicinity (02.8-96.7). He reported artillery falling about 200 yards in advance of these troops. From the co-ordinates, this was C Company. Extremely heavy artillery or mortar fire was falling on a hill at (03.0-96.8). By the co-ordinates, 38th Division artillery was pounding the 1st Battalion's objective.[6]

At about 1045, Captain "Tuffy" Pullen's E Company, leading 2nd Battalion, advanced cautiously along the road out of the horseshoe and turned right into the "2." The Japanese on the 1st Battalion's objective controlled the top of the "2" as the road turned into a relatively straight 900-yard stretch. Therefore, another purpose of the 1st Battalion's attack was to divert the enemy's attention while E Company slipped around the top of the "2."

Ogawa had been careful to site all positions to be mutually supporting. Company E had been protected from observation and fire on its left by a high bank, but as the road rounded the top of the "2," the bank gave way to a gently rising slope. As the leading 2nd Platoon of Sergeant James H. Bibby of Verona, NJ, made this turn, the First Scout, Pfc. Harry W. Potter of Tyronza, AR, spotted an enemy pillbox and warned the platoon to halt. Immediate heavy fire from Sergeant Yoshitada Yamauchi's machine gun at the top of the slope followed. Pfc. Potter fired back, hitting one enemy soldier, and continued firing until his grease gun jammed. The Japanese began laying in intermittent mortar fire that was to plague E as well as B and C Companies for the rest of the day.[7]

Captain Pullen, Bibby, and Pullen's radio operator, Jim Frederick, were with the lead scouts and came under the enemy fire. "Captain Pullen never lost his cool. He just stood out in the road sucking a cigarette with all hell breaking loose around him," Bibby remembered.[8]

Sergeant Bibby urged Pullen, with Pfc. Potter's guidance, to lay 81-mm mortar fire on the machine gun. Frederick had just gotten through to H Company when a Japanese rifleman knocked out the communications, the bullet piercing both the radio and Frederick's left shoulder. Bibby called a medic, T/5 Karl E. Nyren, who bandaged the wound and gave Frederick a shot of morphine so that he could work his way back down the road to an ambulance. Frederick was closely followed by Nyren, who minutes later was shot in the arm about one inch away from the spot where he had also been hit on Leyte.[9]

Pullen sent a platoon up the bank with orders to assault the machine gun pillbox position or button it up so it could be attacked from the road. This platoon no sooner reached the top of the bank than it was pinned down by a machine gun from the left rear. This was the gun of Sergeant Shiro Takamura, which had been purposely sited on Mount Koko to stop the Americans as they crossed over the ridge of Mount Hissho.

Riflemen from Lieutenant Shinfune's 9th Company in a gully in rear of E Company peppered the road with well-aimed shots that gave the rest of the battalion second thoughts about leaving the horseshoe and coming to the aid of E Company. Replacement 2nd Lieutenant Charles J. "Robbie" Robinson of Pennsylvania sent a squad into the gully to root out Shinfune's men, but the latter were well covered by a light machine gun positioned on the northern slope of Mount Ege.

Concentrating on the machine gun to his left front, Captain Pullen called for 81-mm mortar fire from both D and H Companies. The forward artillery observer with E Company started to bracket the enemy position with 105-mm rounds. The high bank on E Company's left afforded good protection from the Japanese machine guns, but made it hazardous to fire artillery. One low tree burst would splatter the company with shell fragments, while high shots would land harmlessly beyond the enemy.[10]

Lieutenant Colonel Chester A. Dahlen (pronounced DAYlen), the Regiment's Executive Officer, had come forward to investigate the slow progress. A 1933 graduate of West Point from Minnesota, Dahlen had commanded the 3rd Battalion 21st Infantry during the Hollandia campaign. As regimental exec on Leyte, he had assumed command of the 34th when Colonel Newman was wounded. Equally at home as a staff officer or unit commander, Dahlen had shown a master's hand in preparing the orders for the Zambales Operation.

Dahlen was on the side of the road in close proximity to Major Snavely and his artillery forward observer, who were having trouble adjusting the close-in artillery fire. An incoming round, adjusted to be close, was a tree burst above the three. Of the 25-30 soldiers (including two colonels from Corps) in a 25-yard radius, Dahlen was the only one hit. A shell fragment caught him in the right buttocks. "It really blew a hole; you could drop a grapefruit in it," Dahlen recalled.

While waiting for the medics, Dahlen learned the trouble. The Division Artillery was in low angle fire configuration including the 34th's own supporting 63rd F.A. Battalion. That accounted for the tree burst. Dahlen ordered the Forward Observer to get the 63rd in high angle fire, which the 63rd had used in all the 34th's previous fighting. The medics evacuated Dahlen after he told Major Snavely to report to Colonel Jenna what had happened and the orders he (Dahlen) had given to the 63rd F.A. Battalion.[11]

Sergeant Hanford Rants of Downey, CA, 2nd Battalion Wire Chief, and Pfc. T. R. Grissom were with Dahlen laying wire as they advanced. They were sickened by the smell of powder and burning flesh from the wound in the colonel's rump. Grissom poured sulfa into the wound. Rants was thinking, "Had that large shell fragment been one foot my way, it would have gone into the middle of my back and ended it all for me."

As soon as the American artillery stopped firing, the Japanese infantry were back at work. They shot the two medics evacuating Colonel Dahlen. During the melee, they cut the telephone lines to the rear. Sergeant Rants and one of the wiremen, Pfc. John Six, started back to search for the break and splice it. A lone enemy rifleman, with what sounded to Rants like a U.S. M-1 rifle, covered a curve in the road about ten yards long. Rants and Six ran the gantlet through a hail of bullets, found the break and spliced it. They raced back and again successfully dodged the three or four shots the rifleman could squeeze off as they passed through that ten-yard no-man's land.

But in their haste and fear, they did not check the line before returning and were shocked to find there was still another break in the line. They had counted eight shots fired at them in the first trip, so they knew what to expect as they got ready to repeat their run. Miraculously, they made it through both ways again and successfully spliced the line, counting eleven shots in the second round trip. Perhaps in an understatement, Rants recalled, "The fear felt at a time like this is almost paralyzing."[12]

Despite a renewed hammering by artillery and 81-mm mortars, the Japanese returned a rapid fire when E Company tried again to round the "2" after noon. Sixth Army had made 1:25,000 aerial photographic maps of ZigZag Pass available for the first time on 3 February. Major Snavely discovered a trail on one of the maps that seemed to lead into the enemy positions from the north. He ordered F Company to leave the road at the lower curve of the "2" and follow this trail. But the wily Japanese were not to be flanked so easily; they soon drove Fox Company back to the road with heavy rifle and machine gun fire from the rear of the slope.[13]

Company E was stalemated and remained stationary until mid-afternoon. During the lull, Lieutenant Robinson received the surprise of his life. As he jumped back after peering round a bend and drawing fire, a Red Cross worker handed him a cup of coffee. This was Weldon B. Hester, who was accepted like a brother by the 34th.[14]

On the other side of the road, B and C Companies advanced almost to their objective without meeting resistance. The thick undergrowth and trees made it difficult to determine the location of friendly troops. At about 1250, the scouts of B Company glimpsed troops moving to their front on slightly rising ground. Scattered shots were fired from both sides. Colonel Oglesby, believing the troops to be C Company, called to them not to fire, that his party was friendly. He had no sooner spoken than a grenade exploded near him. His eye was torn, the side of his face was badly lacerated, and one arm and his chest were pierced in many places.

No one could say with certainty who actually threw the grenade. The few witnesses, however, felt they had definitely met an enemy patrol. If it had been an American grenade, exploding as close as this one had, it would have blown the colonel's head off.[15]

Upon receiving news of this mishap, Colonel Jenna ordered Major Carl O. "Speedy" Mann (no relation to the author), executive officer of the 3rd Battalion, to assume command of the 1st Battalion. B and C Companies did not wait for Major Mann to arrive, but continued to advance. B Company reached the saddle between the two domes of Mount Ege, and C Company approached the northern end of Mount Ege.[16]

1st Lieutenant Masanobu Miyazaki, Commander 10th Company 39th Infantry

Company E 34th's push around the "2" into the heart of Major Ogawa's defenses and B Company's occupation of the Mount Ege saddle compelled the battalion commander to use his reserves. Most of the 10th Company of Lieutenant Miyazaki, led by Miyazaki himself and reinforced by the Morimoto heavy machine gun squad and a squad of engineers, rushed to the threatened points. Their firepower stopped C and E Companies but did not drive them back.

Warrant Officer Taro Yamada, who had led the counterattack against C Company 34th the previous day, was killed during Miyazaki's counterattack. Ogawa praised Yamada and Master Sergeant Sadao Nakano, who also died in the counterattack. Both men used their swords bravely until cut down by C Company's bullets.[17]

After F Company's short flanking maneuver had failed, Major Snavely decided to expand the flanking idea. From the northeast corner of the horseshoe, he would lead F and G Companies west, then north, and attempt to pick up the same trail he had observed on the aerial photograph. The two companies would then take the Japanese positions holding up E Company from the rear. If opportune, he would bypass those positions and drive on to the battalion's objective. At about 1300, the 2nd Battalion (minus E Company) left the road with F Company again leading.

With B and C Companies now occupying ground that might dominate the Japanese positions holding up E Company, Captain Pullen tried once more to break the stalemate. At about 1430, he sent one platoon up over the bank to work its way round the open slope, while a reinforced rifle platoon from C Company advanced from the south toward the road. This movement brought instant shellfire from the Japanese that killed four and wounded three men of Easy Company's rear elements resting in the ditch along Highway 7.

Sergeants Ueno and Kanazawa were not to be caught napping. Their heavy machine guns effectively pinned down the platoon from C Company advancing from the south. The platoon leader asked the leader of the mortar squad attached, Sergeant Joseph P. O'Malley of Newark, NJ, to lay 60-mm fire on the closest machine gun. Placing his mortar in the only defilade he could find, a shallow shell hole, O'Malley initially silenced the machine gun. Learning that all the men in the light machine gun squad attached to the platoon were casualties, O'Malley turned over his mortar squad to his second in command. Lieutenant Storey ordered the platoon to withdraw. O'Malley covered the platoon's pullback with accurate fire from the machine gun, with which he had only a slight working knowledge.

Major Mann arrived soon afterward. Upon investigating the situation, Mann recommended using heavier armament.[18]

It was evident from the fierce enemy resistance that the Japanese had strengthened their front line. General Hall blamed the 152nd Infantry. He cited the regiment's lack of aggressiveness that had allowed the enemy to bring up reinforcements that had caused additional casualties and time lost.[19]

Interlocking bands of machine gun fire from the Yamauchi, Ueno and Kanazawa Squads blocked every approach. Japanese riflemen, still well concealed despite being pounded by artillery, protected the machine guns. A renewed American heavy mortar and artillery barrage might overcome this opposition, but much time would be lost in extricating E Company, which was quite close to the Japanese positions. It would also be risky to adjust the artillery and mortar fire with F and G Companies only in sporadic contact by radio, moving along the hillside of Mount Koko. Instead, Major Mann called for flamethrowers and three tanks, which were parked in the 3rd Battalion area.

By 1515, Mann, Pullen and the tank commander had planned their assault. While the tanks concentrated on the right side of the road against the northern end of Mount Ege, Pullen's E Company would try once again, this time with flamethrowers, to overpower the troublesome Yamauchi heavy machine gun on the left at the top of the "2." Only two tanks could get into firing position. Supported by a squad of E Company riflemen, the first tank rounded the top of the "2." The tanker attempted to close down the Japanese machine guns to his right with his own machine gun fire and relieve the pressure on C and E Companies.

Unable to silence these machine guns with .30 caliber fire, the tanker swung his turret with its 75-mm gun. Directed by lead scout Harry Potter, the same who had first spotted the Yamauchi Squad, the tank obliterated Sergeant Kanazawa's heavy machine gun with one shot. The shot instantly killed Sergeant Kanazawa and three of his men clustered around the gun. A shell fragment in the right side of his chest wounded a fifth victim of the shot, squad member Chikara Goto. He recovered at the Kato Company command cave, only to be killed in March by Filipino guerrillas.[20]

The shot brought return fire from Captain Ichinose's 37-mm anti-tank gun north of the road, which answered the tank round for round. The two were masked; neither could hit the other. The anti-tank gun's shots smacked hard into C Company now near the northern end of Mount Ege. Heavy Japanese mortars and artillery joined in, finding their marks many times in C Company. The company commander, Lieutenant Storey, was hit, but refused evacuation until wounded again the next day.

It was no better in B Company in Ege's saddle where the Nipponese constantly raked the company's recently won positions with machine gun fire. At about 1630, Master Sergeant Kanechika's 75-mm gun, sited to fire on the "2" from atop Mount Koko, forced the tanks to withdraw. Stripped of their support, B and C Companies dug in for the night on the nearest defensive ground.[21]

This action south of Highway 7 finally gave Captain Pullen the chance to overcome the pesky Yamauchi heavy machine gun north of the road that had pinned down E Company all afternoon. Led by men wielding flamethrowers, E Company's riflemen annihilated the nine-man Yamauchi squad. After their work was done, Captain Pullen pulled his men back for the night behind a sheltering bank along the road.

Corporal Matsuo Masuda, soon to be a heavy machine gun squad leader himself, and Sergeant Major Sawada from a cave back of Mount Ege had observed E Company's assault on Yamauchi. Masuda and Sawada first noticed that Yamauchi's gun had stopped firing. They knew that was strange because they both knew Squad Leader Yamauchi well. He was not a man who would stop firing while the enemy was still in his sights. After the battle the two crept forward to within shouting distance of the gun position. "Yamauchi, are you all right?" Sawada approached, calling him. There was no answer.

Upon reaching the position, they found a ghastly scene. Yamauchi with a bullet to his head had fallen face down in the firing trench holding a pistol in his right hand. His Assistant Squad Leader, Chicao Nanba, a shell fragment in his belly, was slumped over the gun barrel still gripping the trigger. Superior Private Tetsuji Matsumoto with a bullet in his head was in the act of feeding a 30-round bullet board into the gun.

The other six squad members had been overcome by the flamethrowers. Konishi, Honma and Setogawa had died from explosions induced by the flames. Yamada, Saeki and Kuko, who had put blankets over their heads against smoke from the flamethrowers, had died from asphyxiation in the back of the gun crew's cave. Masuda and Sawada immediately realized what had happened. All the infantry support for the machine gun position had been killed, leaving the Yamauchi Squad at the mercy of the flamethrowers.[22]

The men of F and G Companies 34th warily picked their way single file along a twisting jungle trail up the ridge towering over them. After winding approximately 700-800 yards, F Company encountered an enemy outpost at 1535, which withdrew from F Company's fire. At 1600, the scouts of F Company were within 50 feet of the top when a crisp fusillade broke out from the crest of the ridge. With no place to lay down a base of fire to cover an advance, Captain Tassin, the F Company commander, sent his 2nd Platoon 100 yards to the northwest to outflank this resistance.

Again, within only a few feet of the top, a murderous enemy fire broke loose. While the 2nd Platoon of F Company bore the brunt of this fire from the Ogata 11th Company, the remainder of F Company and all of G sat and waited, not knowing what was happening at the head of the column. It was too late in the day to think of attacking or flanking this newly found enemy line. Snavely ordered the companies to move rearward to the first defensible ground and dig in for the night.[23]

The open space selected was not covered with foliage, as were the areas adjacent to the road. F Company started to dig near the top of a knoll with G Company joining one of its flanks and starting to extend down the hillside. Suddenly, at about 1730, the earth shuddered as a torrent of shells fell savagely on the open, exposed companies. The barrage first engulfed F Company at the upper end of the open space and then sped down the hillside to G Company. There was no warning, no bracketing fire, just ear shattering explosions and buzzing shell fragments, made even more deadly by treetop detonations. The immediate guess was 90-mm mortars, but this was immaterial as men hugged the earth and hoped no fragments would find them.

Sergeant Major Masatoshi Fujimoto, directing fire from his observation post on Mount Koko, could not miss this target. The first shells from his mortars, located behind Mount Kita, found their mark; there was no need to adjust fire. Many shells exploded in the trees, spreading their zinging fragments over a wide area. Faint cries of "medic, medic" could be heard among pauses in the ear-splitting roar of incoming rounds.[24]

Every round seemed to do damage. Single shells left gaping holes in squads huddled together with no cover. Men who lay prone or sought cover behind trees were hit, and men remaining upright were spared. With no immediate counter battery fire forthcoming, withdrawal off the ridge was the only recourse. Panic was never a factor, just a quiet resignation to evacuate the dead and wounded and pull out. The aid men of the regiment spent a very full night caring for the 50-plus casualties estimated that evening.

The mortar attack was violent, but mercifully short. Company G's casualties were one killed and 24 wounded, about evenly divided among the four platoons. When a final count was made in F Company, 11 had been killed and 52 wounded. Many slightly wounded could be added to this total of 88 casualties in the two companies who were evacuated to hospitals. Snavely ordered a withdrawal, as the battalion was in no shape to receive an attack should the Japanese so choose.[25]

Captain D. Bertram "Doc" Cameron, Surgeon 2nd Battalion 34th Infantry

Then came the arduous, heart- and back-breaking labor of carrying the dead and wounded back down the trail. The available litters were soon used up. Many soldiers improvised litters from ponchos and bamboo poles from the thick stands of bamboo in the area. Many able-bodied men served as litter bearers, returning to the scene of the disaster two and three times bearing litters. The lightly wounded assisted the more seriously injured, the walking wounded. Captain Cameron and his medical team at the Battalion aid station did yeoman's work far into the night.[26]

Several mortar rounds fell on E Company along the road in the vicinity of the "2" at about the same time as the barrage on F and G Companies. The resulting four killed and two wounded in Easy worsened the evacuation problem. Among those killed by the first rounds were the weapons platoon leader, the platoon sergeant and the platoon guide. With shells still exploding, Staff Sergeant Erie Erickson of Blairstown, NJ, took charge of the platoon and ran to the aid of the wounded and dying. He organized the men into litter teams to evacuate the casualties and then moved the platoon to a new position ready to repulse a counterattack.[27]

The same barrage also caused five casualties in a section of two H Company machine guns attached to and dug-in with E Company. The section leader, Tech Sergeant Edward J. Benik of Maquah, WI, immediately organized his men into carrying parties to remove the wounded with ponchos and rifles being used for litters. Mortar rounds continued to fall and Japanese snipers continually made any movement hazardous.[28]

Medical personnel at all levels worked ceaselessly, selflessly, gallantly to succor the never-ending stream of casualties. Chest and fracture cases swamped the 18th PSH (Portable Surgical Hospital), located in the dry rice paddies north of Olongapo. The 18th was soon sending its overflow to the 1st PSH and the 36th Evacuation Hospital in the city. Lieutenant Silber of the 2nd Platoon G Company, who survived, had been hit in the chest by a mortar shell fragment. "You could literally see his heart beating in his chest cavity, and he was alive!" a regimental staff officer commented.[29]

Collecting company personnel, usually used to transport casualties from the battalion and regimental aid stations to the rear, served as litter bearers forward of the aid stations. Six ambulances plied the road all night between the horseshoe and the two PSHs. Personnel Carriers, 2 1/2 ton trucks, anything that could move, transported the wounded to the clearing stations and hospitals in the rear. Litters, blankets, plasma and bandages moved in a steady stream toward the front.[30]

Service Company driver Lorne L. Curtis of Eldred, PA, was delivering rations to the 2nd Battalion from supply dumps in the rear. As he proceeded along Highway 7, Japanese artillery and mortar fire forced him to de-truck and seek cover in the ditch beside the road. Upon arrival at 2nd Battalion headquarters, Curtis's truck was the first available as the F and G Company casualties started coming in. Quickly unloading his rations, Pfc. Curtis started loading casualties. But a call from E Company sent Curtis farther up the road through continuous artillery fire to load 4 litter cases and 12 walking wounded. Thus, beginning his trip with rations, Curtis returned to the regimental area with an entirely different cargo.[31]

Despite being wounded, Captain Innes, the G Company commander, and all surviving officers of F and G Companies and H Company attached remained in the area until the last casualty was evacuated. F Company Sergeant Jere A. Kuehn of Parkdale, AR, and Pfcs. Mariano R. Chavez of Los Lunas, NM, and John P. Lynch of Clarksburg, WV, gunner and ammunition bearer from H Company, distinguished themselves. Kuehn remained at the site to bandage, administer sulpha drugs and evacuate the wounded. Chavez and Lynch administered first aid and helped carry the wounded back to the road. They immediately turned around and returned to the barrage area to carry more wounded and abandoned equipment down the trail.[32]

Innes's successor, company exec Lieutenant Calhoun, ordered one officer to assemble a small covering force of ten men, form a hasty defensive line, and be prepared to resist any counterattack the enemy might launch. Many wondered why the Japanese did not counterattack or impede the withdrawal with another barrage. But the hard-pressed enemy, preferring to conserve ammunition, allowed the 2nd Battalion to remove its dead and wounded with no further interference.

F and G Companies were back on the road before dark. The dead were neatly stretched out by the side of the road in the dim light, each body hastily covered by a poncho with only the combat boots protruding. One of the G Company men, who had been through Leyte, wrote to his wife that the war was getting worse, that ZigZag was the worst he had seen.[33]

Japanese mortars and artillery fired intermittently all night, the shells rumbling in the ravines south of Highway 7. The best refuge for 2nd Battalion was to bed down in the ditch beside the road against the steep banks and hope none of the shells landed in the road. One can only imagine the thoughts of the men huddled in ZigZag Pass that night with shells sometimes crashing a mere 50 feet away. What was happening? How would they ever get at the Japanese? When and how would it all end?

Colonel Jenna's plans for breaking Japanese resistance in the pass had ended in disaster. As night fell, the 1st Battalion was pinned to its foxholes southeast of the horseshoe, 2nd Battalion was strung out along Highway 7 from the vicinity of the "2" around the horseshoe, and 3rd Battalion was even farther removed to the west, having never been committed during the day.[34]

The 1st Battalion 152nd Infantry patrols of 3 February had found enough enemy positions on Mount Koko to warrant a full-scale attack on 4 February. The steep ridge of Mount Koko on the left of the advancing troops was designated Hills 301 and 401 from west to east on the 152nd's maps. Colonel McIntosh, the 152nd commander, joined the 1st Battalion Headquarters to prod the attack.

At 1035, A and B Companies left the sawmill and started climbing an old logging trail. Company A reached Hill 301 at 1150 against no opposition, but B Company, taking over the lead, found that the approaches to Hill 401 were a different matter. This was the highest prominence of the Mount Koko ridge, well covered by Lieutenant Ogata's 11th Company and the Takenaka HMG Squad. Communications Sergeant Katsumi Fujiwara commanded the squad after Takenaka's death on 2 February.

Finding stiff resistance from Fujiwara's rapid fire, the 1st Battalion companies returned to their previous night's perimeters near the sawmill. Company B, in the forefront of the action, suffered 12 of the 15 casualties (all wounded) in the conflict.[35]

At the end of the day, General Hall, sensing the need for a unified command at the front, detached the 34th Infantry from XI Corps control and attached it to the 38th Division. General Jones reasoned differently: "The order placing me in command [of the 34th] came in by telephone about 10:00 P.M. February 4 . . ." Jones wrote later. "When the G-3 read the order to me, my remark was that I was being placed back in command so that the Corps in some way could push the blame on me for the failure of the 34th Infantry. I believe without question that was the real reason for the order."[36]

General Hall also asked Jones for his plan to break through ZigZag Pass. The central feature of General Jones's one-page plan was to reduce the enemy centers of resistance methodically as opposed to the frontal assault. He admitted his method was comparatively slow, but felt it was the only one that offered any promise of success. All operations would be of battalion strength. The terrain and enemy dispositions would govern each battalion operation. The plan would be changed to some other method if it did not work. Jones wanted to feel free to stop and rest the units (if necessary, all of them) when they became exhausted.

Initially, because of the strength and aggressiveness of the enemy, a battalion would be assigned the mission of capturing a definite terrain feature and holding until ordered to move. The centers of resistance at some distance from the road would be given priority. It was from those that the enemy came down to the road and caused so much trouble. Once these centers were captured, it would be easier for the Americans to gain control of the road by coming down from the high ground.

Jones admitted he could not present a complete overall plan. He offered his plans for the next day: the 1st Battalion 152nd Infantry would attack the strongly fortified center of resistance it now faced, Hill 401 (Mount Koko); the 2nd Battalion 152nd Infantry would comb an area south of the road and locate any center of resistance in that area; the two lead battalions of the 34th RCT would be assigned areas to capture close to the road on their immediate fronts. The exact areas would be determined later, when the information the two battalions possessed about the terrain and the enemy points of resistance became known.[37]

There is no record of General Hall's reaction to this plan. Only time would tell if General Jones was on target to break the stalemate at the horseshoe.

⚫　⚫　⚫

The day had not gone well for the Japanese, particularly for the Kato HMG Company. Fifteen machine gunners had been killed. E Company 34th's flamethrowers and riflemen had obliterated the entire nine-man Yamauchi Squad; four in the Kanazawa Squad had been felled by one tank round. Pfc. Shigeru Mori of the Ueno Squad had died from artillery fire. Pfc. Seiichi Kamo of the Takamura Squad on Mount Koko had been shot in the head by a B Company 152nd rifleman.[38]

American artillery must have seemed incessant to the Japanese. The preparatory bombardment preceding the 34th and 152nd attacks had been five times as great as on any previous day. The total of 2,700 rounds for the day was the heaviest yet. Sometime during the day, a shell fragment

found and killed Captain Ichinose while he was trying to fill the gap in the line caused by the annihilation of the Yamauchi HMG Squad. Ichinose's bravery and leadership were legendary in the 39th Infantry. Ogawa named the Jukaki-dai, now a battered hump abutting Highway 7, the ICHINOSE-DAI (Ichinose Heights) in honor of this loyal and resourceful commander. Warrant Officer Shigeru Uwane took command of the remaining troops defending this essential position.[39]

Major Ogawa had successfully repulsed all attempts by the 34th to force its way through the pass. Managing his interior lines adroitly, he had met each thrust resolutely and had demor-

Captain Masaaki Ichinose, Commander 37-mm Anti-tank Company 39th Infantry

alized and frustrated the Americans with the uncanny accuracy of his mortar and artillery fire.

But how long could he move squads and platoons to repel the relentless attacks of companies and battalions backed by overwhelming artillery? How long could he afford to lose brave leaders like Ichinose, Yamada, Sadao Nakano, Kanazawa and Yamauchi and his meager supply of veteran soldiers? These problems must have weighed heavily on Ogawa and especially on the men in the trenches as they prepared to resist the next day's assault, and the one the following day, and the one after that.

Chapter 12

NOTES

(1) 34th Infantry AAR, 68-72. This plan is not found in XI Corps or 34th Infantry journals, but described in detail in the 34th Infantry AAR. It is not known whether this was the actual plan or the conjecture of the writer of the AAR.

(2) Ogawa, Major Hironori, *Record of the 3rd Battalion, 39th Infantry Regiment in the "Big Asia War,"* p. 27;
How the Kato Company Fought: The Record of the 3rd Machine Gun Company 39th Infantry Regiment, Tamotsu Nagai, Editor, 1990, p. 39.

(3) 34th Infantry AAR, p. 72-73.

(4) *Ibid.,* 73-74;
Ogawa, *Record of the 3rd Battalion,* p. 27.

(5) McKenna, Pvt. William J., A Company 34th Infantry diary, p. 7; 34th Infantry journal.

(6) Ransohoff, Captain James B., XI Corps G-3 report, 1015-04 February 1945.

(7) 34th Infantry AAR, p. 74-75;
Recommendation of Bronze Star Medal for Pfc. Potter for this action and subsequent actions.

(8) Bibby, Sergeant James H., E Company 34th Infantry, letter to author, 31 December 1988.

(9) Frederick, Pfc. James, E Company 34th Infantry, letter to author, 5 February 1988.

(10) 34th Infantry AAR, p. 75-76.

(11) Dahlen, Lt. Colonel Chester A., Exec. Off. 34th Infantry, letter to author, 6 October 1986.

(12) Rants, Sergeant Hanford, Hq. Co. 2nd Battalion 34th Infantry, reminiscences written several years after the war.

(13) 34th Infantry AAR, p. 78;
Schoonover, Major James F., *The Operations of the 3rd Battalion 152nd Infantry in Zig Zag Pass, Luzon, 29 Jan.-14 Feb. 1945,* Advanced Infantry Officers Course, 1947-1948, p. 8.

(14) Weldon B. Hester from South Dakota, the American Red Cross Field Director for the 34th Infantry, operated under U.S. Army

Regulations. His duties, like those of other Field Directors, consisted of furnishing comforts to the soldiers; establishing refreshment stations and places of rest and recreation; transmitting correspondence, literature and gifts to servicemen and women; and collecting and exchanging information concerning wounded or prisoners of war.

Hester's primary visible benefit to the infantry was a "movable feast"—the Red Cross Center. Heading a contingent of ten men, Hester had hit the beach at San Antonio 29 January in the fourth wave (H-hour plus nine minutes), hand-carrying onto the beach enough supplies to set up a hot coffee service. A nearby stream furnished fresh water. Within an hour he was serving coffee to the 3rd Engineers of the 34th RCT. Later he made his way to the front lines when the 34th was committed to the battle.

Hester had provided like service for even the minor landing of the 34th at San Isidro Bay on the northwestern coast of Leyte in December 1944. He would serve 100 gallons of coffee the first day on Corregidor to the 3rd Battalion 34th. The Red Cross utilized limited service personnel and was never a burden in combat. On the contrary, its services were welcomed and encouraged by the regimental and battalion commanders.

(15) 34th Infantry AAR, p. 79-80.

(16) Called "Speedy" by Lt. Colonel Leslie L. Wheeler, CO of the 34th in the latter stages of the Mindanao campaign and in occupied Japan. Wheeler was 24th Division G-2 at the time of the Battle of ZigZag Pass;
34th Infantry AAR, p. 80.

(17) Ogawa, *Record of the 3rd Battalion*, p. 28.

(18) 34th Infantry AAR, p. 78-79, p. 83;
2nd Battalion 34th Infantry AAR, period 6 January-24 February 1945;
Recommendation of Bronze Star Medal for Sergeant O'Malley for this action.

(19) Memorandum, Hall to Jones, 4 February 1945.

(20) 34th Infantry AAR, p. 83;
Kato Company History, p. 189;
34th Infantry Journal.

(21) 34th Infantry AAR, p. 83-84.

(22) Kato Company History, p. 39, p. 184-185.

(23) 34th Infantry AAR, p. 84-85.

(24) Nagai, Tamotsu, Communications Sergeant Machine Gun Company 3rd Battalion 39th Infantry, interview, 14 May 1991;

(25) 34th Infantry, Zambales Operation, Casualties by Company and Date;
34th Infantry AAR.

(26) 2nd Battalion 34th Infantry AAR, period 6 January-24 February 1945.

(27) *Ibid.*;
Recommendation of Bronze Star Medal for Sergeant Erickson.

(28) Recommendation of Bronze Star Medal for Sergeant Benik.

(29) Grube, Captain Harry T., S-1 and Asst. S-3 34th Infantry, transcription by World War II Publications, Inc., Indianapolis, IN, of interview describing 24th Division campaigns, p. 122.

(30) 2nd Battalion 34th Infantry journal.

(31) Recommendation of Bronze Star Medal for Pfc. Curtis.

(32) 2nd Battalion 34th Infantry AAR;
Summary of official commendations of Sergeant Kuehn and Pfcs Chavez and Lynch.

(33) Letter read later in rest camp by author in capacity as censor.

(34) 34th Infantry journal.

(35) 1st Battalion 152nd Infantry journal.

(36) Message G-3 XI Corps to CG 38th Division, 2050-4 February 1945;
Jones comments, 20 December 1956, p. 6.

(37) Plan included with 38th Division journal National Records Center.

(38) Kato Company History, p. 39-41.

(39) 38th Division Artillery Unit History, M-7 Operation Luzon, 16 January-30 June 1945, Annex #3 (Summarized in Appendix C);
Ogawa, *Record of the 3rd Battalion*, p. 27;
History of the 39th Infantry Regiment, edited and published by the 39th Infantry Association, p. 640.

THE 34th INFANTRY RETIRES

(5 FEBRUARY)

General Jones lost no time in framing a detailed plan for 5 February. At 2300 on 4 February, he issued Field Order #11 orally to Colonel Jenna of the 34th and Lieutenant Colonel McIntosh of the 152nd. Written confirmation followed at 1330 the next day. The 34th Infantry was to "attack without delay, capture enemy fortified area" about 1,000 yards northeast of the horseshoe that had been 2nd Battalion's objective the previous day. The 34th also was to "hold present positions astride Highway 7 and south thereof."

1st Battalion 152nd was to attack and capture the position called Hill 401 (Mount Koko) that had defied the battalion on 4 February. 2nd Battalion 152nd would attack toward Familiar Peak and relieve the pressure on A Company 34th. The 3rd Battalion 152nd, in division reserve, would remain in its present location on Highway 7 west of the horseshoe and support one of the other battalions, if needed.

In Paragraph #3 of the order, General Jones placed a restriction on the 38th Division Artillery that was to cause much confusion and grief later: "Div Arty will keep all fire east of SANTA RITA River except missions called for by the regiments. Such missions will be examined carefully to see that other troops are not endangered. East of SANTA RITA River all known enemy works will be destroyed using precision fire when necessary. Massed fires of short duration will be placed on areas east of SANTA RITA River which may be occupied by the enemy."[1]

The word "east," appearing three times in the paragraph, is confusing. It would seem that the 38th Division staff member who prepared the order meant to say "west" either the second or third time he used the word "east."

Taking the order verbatim, an artillery forward observer with the leading infantry platoons in constant radio or wire contact with his battalion's guns could not fire until his request had gone through Division

Artillery and been approved. By that time, the enemy would have inflicted further damage on the lead troops or moved out of range of observation.

Colonel Jenna did not like General Jones's order and argued against its adoption. He particularly did not like the mixture of regiments on both sides of the road and especially splitting the 152nd Infantry on each side of the 34th. He preferred using Highway 7 as a clear line of demarcation, with the 34th assuming responsibility for objectives south of the road and the 152nd north of the road. This shift of battalions and getting into new positions would probably consume half the day. General Jones, ever mindful of General Hall's emphasis on speed, rejected Jenna's suggestion.[2]

In compliance with Field Order #11, Colonel Jenna ordered his 1st and 2nd Battalions to remain in place, but to patrol vigorously to maintain contact with the enemy. He ordered the 3rd Battalion to make an extensive reconnaissance preparatory to attacking and capturing the position 1,000 yards northeast of the horseshoe (Mount Shinshu). At about 0800, elements of five battalions started on missions to maintain pressure on the Japanese.[3]

But as the day unfolded, it was the Japanese, not the Americans, who maintained pressure and continued to dominate the battlefield. As a portent of what was to come, the aggressive enemy began with a destructive early morning mortar barrage. The target this time was H Company 2nd Battalion. Violating a basic infantry tenet—leaders must not congregate while under enemy observation—the company commander, 1st Lieutenant Haskel P. Miller, Supply Sergeant Leo P. Heck of Cedar Rapids, IA, and section leader Sergeant Lew Downey of Muskegon, MI, were sitting by the side of the road discussing equipment shortages. Suddenly mortar rounds fell in their midst, severely wounding Lieutenant Miller and wounding Sergeant Heck in his upper left arm and in both legs. Both Downey and Heck, the latter ignoring his own wounds, administered first aid to the company commander and stayed with him until he was evacuated to the rear.

Pfc. James W. McFee of Parkersburg, WV, started giving first aid and helping to evacuate another of the H Company wounded. He then remembered that his jeep and trailer load of 81-mm ammunition was in the center of the shelling. He ran through the barrage, turned his jeep around with great difficulty and sped away.[4]

Company B 34th patrolled to the east, and a combined E and F patrol under the F Company commander covered an area north and northwest of the 2nd Battalion 34th's position. Discovering little information, these patrols returned before mid-morning when the artillery preparation for the 1st Battalion 152nd attack was to begin.[5]

When the preparatory firing started, the Japanese, not to be outdone, returned with counter battery fire, and the cannonade gradually spread over the entire front. Again the enemy singled out the 34th for another general raking. By 1030, B and C Companies were receiving heavy mortar fire. Casualties of 1 KIA and 10 WIA were soon reported, even though the companies were well dug-in.

But it was the 2nd Battalion 34th, still licking its wounds from the murderous mortar barrage of the night before, that took the meanest blow of all. At 1130, four enemy high explosive rounds landed on the trunks of the trees over the foxholes of the 2nd Battalion command post. Sergeant Major, Operations Sergeant, staff officers, staff personnel, papers, maps and equipment flew to the four winds in the concussion.[6]

Wire Sergeant Rants remembered the scene. Tech Sergeant Arthur G. Blackburn (S-3 Operations) was left with no body below his waist and died quickly after some pitiful, appealing gestures. T/4 Melvin V. Ennes had one eye and half of his face blown away, but lived to tell the tale. One soldier was screaming from a face that had no lower jaw. The left wrist and hand of Staff Sergeant William G. Wilkinson lay several yards from its owner. 1st Lieutenant James E. Cain, an artillery observer, was blown in half. Sergeant Wilkinson and Pfc. Evon H. Gustafson, also killed by the salvo, were initially buried on the spot.[7]

Minutes before this barrage, Captain Austin, the 2nd Battalion Exec, had walked down the trail from the Battalion CP to the road. There he found a normal scene of medical jeeps, an artillery observation team, stacks of rations, and soldiers talking. Austin began a conversation with an artillery sergeant. Suddenly, he was seized with cramps in the pit of his stomach and had an uncontrollable urge to vacate that place. He raced to his foxhole, put on his helmet, and waited—but not for long. The concussion of three mortar shells, about half a second apart, swept over him in a roar of dirt and smoke and screaming metal.

After about 15 or 20 more rounds (not that close), the familiar cries of "medic" brought Austin back down the trail. On the way he passed Battalion Sergeant Major Raymond M. Heller's foxhole. He found Heller dead, blown out of the hole, his shirt blown off and his back blackened from the explosion. His record case and papers were scattered over the area.

Back on the road, Austin found chaos. He remembered ration boxes turned black by the shelling. The jeeps' windshields were blown out, and their tires were flat. Several of the men who had formed the peaceful scene a few moments before had been killed or wounded.[8]

T/5 Kenneth S. Seitner, Captain Cameron's "foxhole buddy," had had a premonition. After the bombardment of the regiment the morning of 3 February, when his unoccupied jeep had been destroyed, he told the 2nd Battalion surgeon that he did not expect to come out of ZigZag Pass alive. He repeated the premonition when the casualties from F and G Companies started coming in to the Battalion Aid Station the evening of 4 February. Seitner had been one of those waiting on the road and was killed instantly by the Japanese hail of steel.[9]

Major Snavely was sitting on the parapet at one end of the Battalion CP foxhole when the rounds hit. Snavely had been blown out of the hole with the Sergeant Major and the Operations Sergeant, but they had absorbed the force of the blast. Uninjured but shaken, Snavely called Regimental Headquarters and asked to displace his CP to a less exposed location. With the help of Captain Austin and Captain Cameron, Snavely moved 2nd Battalion Headquarters and the wounded to a deep ravine about 200 yards back along the road, "so rapidly that many weren't even bandaged."[10]

Captain Harry T. Grube, Regimental Adjutant, saw Snavely coming down the road with his headquarters company behind him. Grube remarked that Snavely was covered with blood and dirt, his hand was unsteady, but he was in complete command.[11]

A soldier was sitting on the ground shaking. He said to Doc Cameron, "What have you got for a man's nerves?" Doc said, "Well, I got aspirin." The soldier said, "Oh, no, I don't need aspirin. I already had aspirin."[12]

In the same barrage that decimated 2nd Battalion Headquarters, B and C Companies again came under heavy bombardment. 1st Lieutenant Thomas C. Rhem, B Company commander, was wounded and evacuated with difficulty. The 1st Sergeant of C Company, Edward Revock, was also wounded. More than 50 C Company men were suffering from psychoneurosis (shell shock) or wounds that required hospitalization. Company B, better protected by the terrain, suffered less on this day but on a par with C Company for its three days in the pass.[13]

When the Japanese barrage started, it was natural to reply with counter battery fire. But the unusual restrictions General Jones had placed on the artillery for supporting fires came into play. The 34th regimental journal (written at the end of the day) describes the frustration and veiled anger. "Between 0930 and 1100 elements of both 1st and 2nd Bn's [sic] came under extremely heavy Jap arty fire. Supporting arty counter battery fire was delayed until 1115 because it was necessary to obtain a release from Div arty. Because of the failure of Div arty to release its consent for supporting fires, the Bn's [sic] suffered heavy casualties. At 1130 Jap arty was still active and the 2nd Bn CP received a direct hit, resulting in an estimated four KIA and three WIA."[14]

The 2nd Battalion 34th was effectively removed from the battle. By striking at its headquarters, the Japanese in one blow had rendered the battalion "hors de combat" or at least incapable of further offensive action.

Colonel Jenna acted quickly after learning the condition of his lead battalions. He fired off the following message to General Jones:

I AM CONVINCED THAT THE ENTIRE JAP POSITION OPPOSING XI CORPS CANNOT BE CRACKED UNLESS THERE IS A WITHDRAWAL TO A POINT WHERE ENTIRE CORPS ARTY AND ALL AVAILABLE AIR WORKS IT OVER WITH EVERY POSSIBLE MEANS FOR AT LEAST 48 HOURS. MY 1ST AND 2ND BNS HAVE SUFFERED TERRIFIC CASUALTIES, AND IT IS BECOMING QUES-TIONABLE HOW LONG THEY CAN HOLD UNDER THIS POUNDING. REQUEST CORPS BE NOTIFIED OF CONTENTS OF THIS MESSAGE.[15]

General Jones was only too happy to pass this message on to "Corps." This is exactly what he had been preaching for days.

With American artillery again in full control, Colonel Jenna ordered the 2nd Battalion to withdraw to a position along the road about 400 yards west of the horseshoe. This movement, covered by E Company, was completed by 1300. At about 1500, Jenna ordered 3rd Battalion to occupy 2nd Battalion's previous positions and 1st Battalion to withdraw to a position about 1,000 yards west of 2nd Battalion.[16]

As 2nd Battalion was retiring along Highway 7, E Company's Sergeant Bibby spotted a swagger stick lying in the road. "I recognized it as the one Father Moran (the Catholic Chaplain) always carried. I felt sure he must have been hit, but a couple of days later I ran into him and was able to return the stick."[17]

General Jones summed up his disgust with Colonel Jenna and the 34th Infantry: "To be run out of position by mortar fire is unusual . . . I asked that the whole regiment be pulled out as incapable of further action."[18] He had rather go it alone with only his own division.

At 1735, Jenna visited the front for the second time during the day. He had received a message from the commanding general XI Corps that had to gladden the heart of every soldier in the 34th. General Hall had decided that the 34th Infantry had had enough; he would replace the 34th with the 151st Infantry starting on the morrow 6 February.[19]

Men of G Company hugging the bank on the inside of Highway 7 for the second consecutive night, with enemy shells thundering down the ravines across the road, had mixed emotions about the withdrawal. Little was known of the paralysis of command at Battalion Headquarters. Knowledge of the mauling B, C, E and F Companies had taken from mortar and artillery fire had not spread widely in G Company. On the one hand, all would be happy at leaving the hell that was ZigZag Pass. On the other hand, G Company had suffered relatively few casualties and some thought the retirement was premature. No one wants to retreat without putting up a good fight. But the 34th Infantry's work in ZigZag Pass was finished. Now the 38th Division alone would face the challenging task of rooting the Japanese from their heavily fortified hills and caves.

&* &* &*

The 1st Battalion 152nd Infantry's attack on 5 February, initially successful, did not go well either. The battalion had captured Hill 301 on 4 February and attacked toward Hill 401, but had returned to its perimeter at the sawmill for the night. Its mission on 5 February was to repeat its advance of the previous day, then attack east and capture Hill 401 (Mount Koko). The battalion would then sweep the ridge all the way to the horse-shoe.

1st Battalion moved out at 0930 in the order of C, B and A Companies behind an artillery and mortar barrage. Enemy mortar fire halted C Company at 1045 with a barrage that Pfc. Ray Mathena of the 3rd Platoon would never forget. Wounded along with a medic by the same shell, he pulled the shell fragments from his chest by himself.[20]

The company commander, 1st Lieutenant Louis Rathje, requested help from D Company's mortars. After D Company had quieted the Japanese, C Company moved forward slowly against several strongly built bunkers. Staff Sergeant Earl Dillon of the 3rd Platoon took a grenade blast at four or five feet that blew the stock off his rifle and bent the barrel. Shell fragments hit both legs, both arms, his chest and his stomach and went through his shoes into his feet. Hit at 1100, he was not carried off the hill until 1700. An ambulance took him to Olongapo more dead than alive. Medics at the 18th PSH set him aside with a group of dead bodies. One of the hospital staff soon realized the mistake and one of the surgeons stayed with Dillon almost constantly for four days until satisfied that he would recover.[21]

The Fujiwara Heavy Machine Gun Squad (formerly Takenaka) halted C Company again in early afternoon. The only surviving member of the squad to return to Japan, Toshio Ono, said the Americans attacked like owls. When Sergeant Fujiwara crawled out of the trench to snatch a carbine dropped by an American, another U.S. soldier, hiding in a tree, shot Fujiwara to death through the chest.

Ono guessed where the "owl soldier" was hiding by the sound of the shot and sprayed the tree with his machine gun. Ono was immediately shot in the right cheek and chin, but not seriously. Pfc. Masahiko Kurokawa took his place as gunner. After being treated for his wound, Ono made up reserve bullet boards. Suddenly, he was aware that the machine gun had stopped firing. Kurokawa had been shot dead through the chest.

Ono noticed an American BAR protruding from shade about 20 meters to his right. He thought this must have been the gun that killed Kurokawa, so he fired a full board of 30 rounds into the shady area. After he had changed bullet boards, a U.S. soldier emerged from the shade and started running. Ono fired a burst, and the soldier leaped in the air and fell dead. Ono continued to fire until the barrel became too hot to handle. After it had cooled, he lugged all 122 pounds of machine gun and tripod to his platoon leader's (2nd Lieutenant Koyama) cave.[22]

Colonel Cornwell came to the front to assess the strength of the enemy defenses. He committed B Company so that C could remove its casualties. Lieutenant Todd, B Company commander, was still smarting from his repulse of the previous day when his company was pinned down and unable to retaliate. This time he elected to attack through a stand of bamboo rather than risk a wide flanking maneuver that would consume time and might uncover new perils. But first brave men had to remove armed grenades the Japanese had strapped to the bamboo shoots.

After struggling through the bamboo against increasing enemy fire, the company was pinned down yards short of the hilltop crowned with the usual bunkers and trench system. Wielding a BAR, Lieutenant Todd, with Colonel Cornwell not far behind, got his men to their feet and led a wild charge to the top. Despite Lieutenant Todd's painful leg wound, B Company carried the position. For this heroic action, Lieutenant Todd received the Distinguished Service Cross, the only one awarded during the campaign.[23]

🔥 🔥 🔥

It was now 1600, and per Battalion order, B and C Companies and one platoon of A started digging in for the night atop Mount Koko. If the 1st Battalion men had realized the true value of their conquest, they would have known the enemy would not surrender without an all-out battle.

After the heavy American artillery fire and the attacks of two battalions against his 11th Company on 4 February, Lieutenant Ogata realized he would be overwhelmed the next day. Therefore, he changed his tactics for the fighting on 5 February. He instructed his men to resist sparingly, to permit the Americans to overrun the company's position, and then come out of their caves unexpectedly and drive the enemy back.

As Cornwell's weary men began digging, all hell broke loose. Out of the ground around them, out of spider-holes camouflaged near their half-dug foxholes—all over the ridge they had fought for—the Japanese emerged firing from their hiding places. The cunningly conceived trap nearly threw the 1st Battalion into complete rout.

Fortunately, the officers of the battalion had the qualities of leadership and the men were disciplined enough to survive the pummeling that followed. They couldn't see the enemy. If they fired their weapons, they might shoot their comrades. They couldn't assemble and group together to resist, for every movement drew deadly fire from the phantom enemy. Not dug-in, they could not bring down mortar or artillery fire on themselves. A squad leader in the 3rd Platoon of B Company thought his whole squad was lost and went berserk. He was eventually evacuated to a hospital where it finally took a straitjacket to calm him. Withdrawal was the only possible recourse.[24]

Cornwell's men moved rapidly down the slope and across the road into a draw west of 2nd Battalion 34th. The laborious work of a full day's battle had come to naught. By nightfall, 1st Battalion 152nd had returned to the same perimeter foxholes near the sawmill it had occupied for the last three nights.[25]

The battalion lost 9 KIA and 33 WIA for the day. The big loss was in company grade officers and key NCOs. All of Company B's officers were evacuated with wounds. Soon after, three platoon sergeants: Franklin, Chasteen, O'Bryan and 1st Sergeant Robert Maraman, all of B Company, received battlefield commissions. All officers in C Company but one were killed, as were three platoon sergeants. Captain Albert S. Thomas, Jr., Assistant Regimental S-3, and Captain Howard A. Smith, S-3 1st Battalion, were assigned respectively as COs of B and C Companies.[26]

General Jones thought that the enemy had redeployed and reinforced Mount Koko after the precipitate pull out of the 1st and 2nd Battalions 34th. No evidence to support this theory could be found. Major Ogawa had reinforced Mount Koko with two squads on the night of 3 February, but that was before the decision to withdraw the 34th had been made.

At 1735, 34th Infantry Headquarters learned of the 1st Battalion 152nd Infantry's hasty withdrawal off Mount Koko and movement farther back on Highway 7. This left the 2nd Battalion 34th's left flank completely unprotected. It was too late in the day for Major Snavely to make dispositions to cover this flank. Instead, Snavely called for close-in intermittent artillery fire to be placed at dark to within 100 yards of the 2nd Battalion Headquarters perimeter. Following orders received at 1500, Colonel Postlethwait moved his 3rd Battalion 34th into the positions north of the road vacated by 2nd Battalion. 3rd Battalion was now 150 yards beyond 2nd Battalion on Highway 7. Pvt. James C. Shields, Jr., of Lake City, FL, a replacement machine gunner, was killed, and eight were wounded from the friendly artillery fire called in to protect 2nd Battalion.[27]

During the last two days of bloody battle, Major Ogawa had baffled all attempts by three American battalions to break his Koko-Hissho-Ege main line. His infantry had driven 1st Battalion 152nd back to its starting place, and he had forced the 1st and 2nd Battalions of the 34th to retire, mainly with highly accurate mortar and artillery fire. But the continuing war of attrition, arduous fighting and high American casualties also spelled hard times for the Japanese. Besides losing the incomparable Captain Ichinose, Ogawa had seen five experienced and irreplaceable platoon leaders fall. One of these, brandishing his saber, was the courageous Lieutenant Jyohoji, who had led the successful infiltration of the American lines on 1 February. With no chance for reinforcement, sergeants from the ranks would have to serve as replacements for the officers.

The vicious combat on Mount Koko and at the top of the "2" had convinced Major Ogawa that he must make changes during the night to bolster his weakened lines. He decided to abandon Mount Koko and move Lieutenant Ogata's 11th Company, now reduced to 30 men, to Mount Shinshu to constitute the reserve. He removed his own headquarters to Mount Fumetsu.

Ogawa reassigned the three heavy machine gun squads originally emplaced on Koko under Lieutenant Koyama. He sent the Takamura Squad to defend Mount Minami, the next logical terrain feature north of the road to be attacked, and the Morimoto Squad, reinforced by a squad of engineers, south of the road to defend Mount Ege. These two squads contained seven men each. The leaderless four survivors of the Takenaka Squad helped replace the losses in Koyama's remaining squads. His four-man Ogaki Squad, reactivated after its return from the Water's Edge Position, would help the Ueno Squad defend the hard-hit Ichinose-dai.[28]

The move off Mount Koko was not made without mishap. Sergeant Okuda, Squad Leader of the 75-mm regimental gun on Koko, had been killed, as were all the squad's five horses. Two of his men were seriously wounded. The remaining cannoneers disassembled the 75-mm gun and hand carried it to Mount Shinshu to join the other 75 for fire in tandem.

As the Takamura HMG Squad moved off the mountain, Pfc. Motoyoshi Yamauchi carried a heavy load of explosives on his back. Moving through the jungle, the branch of a tree brushed across the explosives and armed a fuse. Realizing he could not shed his pack in time, he jumped into a depression and yelled to the others, "Get down!" He was killed in the explosion, but his brave and unselfish act saved several lives.[29]

Ogawa's front line north of Highway 7 now became the Kita-Kasuga-Minami ridge defended by Lieutenant Miyazaki's 10th Company. South of the road, the line would still run through the Ichinose-Ege ridge and be defended by the remainder of the 37-mm AT Company and Lieutenant Shinfune's 9th Company.

The 70-mm battalion guns were located between Mount Fumetsu and Ichinose Heights south of but near the road. Sited to fire into the West Pass, they would now play an important role in stopping future American attacks against Minami and Ichinose. The heavy machine gun squads of Sergeant Masao Togo and Sergeant Sanji Onishi would support them.

2nd Lieutenant Oda, commanding the Olongapo shipyard workers and Japanese engineers stationed in Olongapo, submitted a "blood-written petition" to become a suicide unit. Major Ogawa accepted the request with gratitude and placed Oda's men under Lieutenant Ogata. Ogawa assigned the 20 survivors of the Sakura Company under the one remaining officer, 1st Lieutenant Akashi, the task of guarding the north side of Fumetsu near the road.[30]

A sick bay had been hastily improvised in back of Mount Ege to take care of the increasing numbers of wounded. Engineer Superior Private Omae carried Sergeant Nagai to the cave. "Although my wound had been treated, it hurt so bad," Nagai wrote later. He couldn't wear a helmet because of the bloody triangular bandage on his head that smelled terrible. The more seriously wounded were evacuated at night to regimental headquarters at Mount Kongo.[31]

In a special order, Ogawa reminded his battered, but still determined troops that they had already inflicted more damage on the Americans than anticipated. He exhorted them to fight to the end, to dig deeper and constantly improve their positions, to work in pairs to avoid loneliness and to make maximum use of their extensive cave system to protect themselves during enemy bombardments.

He reviewed the American tank tactics, advising his men to cut down the three infantry soldiers on each side of the tank before trying to destroy the tank. He grudgingly commended the Americans for digging in close to the Japanese lines after an attack and fortifying their perimeters with heavy weapons. Lastly and ominously, he warned his men to conserve ammunition, particularly grenades.[32]

Good news came from the American right flank south of Highway 7. Colonel Rice's 2nd Battalion 152nd reached Λ Company 34th in early afternoon against no opposition. The company rejoined its battalion at 1740, thus ending a three-day saga that had given Colonel Jenna great concern.

Colonel Skelton could finally report success. After their bivouac the night before on the Filipino guerrilla stronghold, Mt. Malasimbo, the 3rd Battalion 149th Infantry had reached Dinalupihan at 1305. Still finding no opposition, men of the 2nd Battalion 149th had reached the Central Plains and relished their first view of Manila Bay.

Taking no chances for misunderstanding, General Jones dispatched Major Sitton of the 38th Division G-3 section in a cub plane to deliver his instructions to the 149th. He ordered the regiment to occupy the line Dinalupihan-Hermosa with one battalion to prevent enemy forces from entering Bataan and to be prepared, less that battalion, to move west via Highway 7 on division order.[33]

With the 34th Infantry's relief imminent, we can assess its role in the battle. What had the regiment accomplished during its three days in the pass? In terms of real estate acquired, the score was virtually zero. The 34th had moved at best only 200-300 yards forward of the point where it had relieved the 152nd. It had located, identified and destroyed certain enemy strong points that would have prevented further advance until reduced. Company A, by its incursion south and southeast, had provoked a strong enemy reaction that it had repulsed with few casualties.

In its hard fighting on 4 February, the bloodiest day for the Americans during the battle, the 34th had wrecked the heart of the Japanese Main Line of Resistance: the three heavy machine guns covering the top of the "2." Company E had killed all nine members of the Yamauchi Squad (six with flamethrowers) and had escorted tanks to a position where they had dealt savagely with the Kanazawa Squad. Starting the day with but six men, only two members of the squad remained alive at day's end. Only the Ueno Squad, still seven strong, and the four-man Ogaki Squad could offer machine gun support after 4 February at this most critical point of the Japanese line.

The greatest contribution made by the 34th was to convince General Hall and the XI Corps staff that the Japanese possessed a strongly held defensive position on formidable terrain. The 34th had been sufficiently bloodied to show that the enemy was not to be ejected from his stronghold except through massive firepower by artillery and from the air.

General Hall admitted to General Krueger, "I have been hard to convince, but now there is no doubt in my mind about being up against a well defended Jap position . . . The resistance has been extremely strong for the last two days. The enemy has obviously sited and registered his automatic weapons and artillery on every road bend and all commanding ground in this area . . . It is a tough nut to crack . . . It is the best fortified place I have ever seen."[34]

The 34th Infantry suffered enormous casualties during its short stay in ZigZag Pass compared with its other battles. A count made several days later, after the MIAs had been accounted for, showed that 61 men had been killed and 258 wounded to such an extent as to require hospitalization. To this total of 319 must be added at least 25 cases of severe psychoneurosis or shell shock.

The great majority of the casualties came on 3, 4 and 5 February and were almost half the regiment's 748 casualties in 77 days of fighting on Leyte. The 1st and 2nd Battalions suffered more than 80 percent of the regiment's casualties in ZigZag Pass, with the rifle companies, as usual, bearing the brunt. Both the 1st and 2nd Battalion aid stations received direct hits from enemy mortar or artillery fire, adding to the problem of evacuation and care of the wounded. Forty percent of the casualties were replacements—the same percentage of replacements to the total strength.[35]

"Doc" Cameron, 2nd Battalion surgeon, summed up the plight of these dazed, bewildered replacements, strangers to the veterans and to each other, suddenly thrust into a terrifying battle in a strange land. "The ZigZag was the only time I ever saw an American soldier break down emotionally. These wounded kids were coming in crying and when I asked them what unit they were from they said, 'I don't know—maybe ? Company.'"[36]

☛   ☛   ☛

Despite the setbacks of 5 February, General Hall was unusually optimistic in an evening letter to General Krueger. "The situation as of tonight looks much better to me. It has eased my mind as to what we are up against for one thing. The 34th RCT has done a good job since being here. I am taking it out of the line and substituting for it the 151st Infantry, the remaining regiment of the 38th Division not heretofore available to General Jones. The 151st is anxious to go, and I want to try it out."[37]

Another reason for General Hall's optimism was the readiness for operations of the San Marcelino airfield. The Japanese had used the airfield sparingly during their occupation, and there were numerous soft spots that needed repair. Like most Philippine airfields, it was dusty during the dry season and mucky during the rainy season. To solve this problem, the engineers reconstructing the field found pits immediately adjacent to the airdrome that produced a combined gravel and clay topping. This combination formed a firm surface and held down the dust. By 5 February, the engineers had completed one runway 6,000 feet long and 100 feet wide and two 100-foot by 800-foot strips for small planes. At 0900, on 6 February, 16 P-47s would start bombing the ZigZag with 500-pound bombs and napalm.[38]

Chapter 13

NOTES

(1) 38th Division Field Order #11, 1330-05 February 1945, Item 3c (confirming verbal orders issued previous night).

(2) Smith, Robert Ross, *Triumph in the Philippines*, p. 322.

(3) 34th Infantry AAR, p. 90;
34th Infantry journal Message #4, CO 34th RCT to CG 38th Div, 0855-5 February 1945.

(4) Summary of official commendation of Sergeant Heck and Pfc. McFee; Sergeant Downey was awarded a Bronze Oak-Leaf Cluster for this action.

(5) 34th Infantry journal;

(6) 2nd Battalion 34th Infantry AAR;
34th Infantry AAR, p. 93.

(7) Rants, Sergeant Hanford, Hq. Co. 2nd Battalion. 34th Infantry, reminiscences written several years after the war.

(8) Austin, Captain Paul, Exec Off 2nd Battalion 34th Infantry, monograph written c. 1960.

(9) Cameron, Captain Donald B., 2nd Battalion 34th Infantry surgeon, letter to author, 1 July 1987.

(10) 34th Infantry AAR, p. 93-94;
Morrissey, Captain George E., Surgeon, 1st Battalion 34th Infantry diary, p. 31.

(11) Grube, Captain Harry T., S-1 34th Infantry, transcription by World War II Publications, Inc., Indianapolis, IN, of interview describing 24th Division campaigns, p. 122.

(12) *Ibid.,* 122.

(13) 34th Infantry AAR, p. 92-93.

(14) 34th Infantry journal.

(15) Radio Jenna to Jones, 1136-05 February 1945, Entry #629, 34th RCT journal file;
Smith, *Triumph in the Philippines*, p. 323;
34th Infantry AAR, p. 99.

(16) 34th Infantry AAR, p. 95.

(17) Bibby, Sergeant James H., Co. E 34th Infantry, letter to author, 31 December 1988.

(18) Jones comments, 20 December 1956, p. 8.

(19) 34th Infantry AAR, p. 99-100.

(20) 1st Battalion 152nd Infantry journal, 04 and 05 February 1945;
Mathena, Pfc. Ray, C Company 152nd Infantry, interview, 27
July 1991.

(21) 1st Battalion 152nd Infantry journal;
Dillon, Staff Sergeant Earl, C Company 152nd Infantry, interview, 27 July 1991.

(22) *How the Kato Company Fought: The Record of the 3rd Machine
Gun Company 39th Infantry Regiment*, Tamotsu Nagai, Editor,
1990, p. 183.

(23) Colonel Cornwell was awarded the Silver Star for his command
of this action;
38th Infantry Division AAR, "Avengers of Bataan" Luzon
Campaign, p. 3.

(24) 1st Battalion 152nd Infantry journal;
History of the 39th Infantry Regiment, edited and published by
the 39th Infantry Association, p. 641;
Cotner, Sergeant Ray, Company B 152nd Infantry, interview by
author, 27 July 1991;
34th Infantry AAR, p. 97. This action is not mentioned in 152nd
Infantry or 38th Division reports.

(25) 34th Infantry AAR, p. 97. The hasty withdrawal is not mentioned
in 152nd Infantry or 38th Division report;
1st Battalion 152nd Infantry journal.

(26) Franklin, Tech Sergeant George H., Company B 152nd Infantry,
letter to author, 6 August 1991;
1st Battalion 152nd Infantry journal.

(27) 2nd Battalion 34th Infantry AAR covering period 6 January-24
February 1945.

(28) Kato Company History, p. 192, p. 195.

(29) *39th Infantry History,* p. 642;
Kato Company History, p. 192.

(30) *39th Infantry History,* p. 642;
Ogawa, Major Hironori, *Record of the 3rd Battalion, 39th Infantry
Regiment in the "Big Asia War,"* p. 31.

(31) Kato Company History, p. 218.

(32) Ogawa, *Record of the 3rd Battalion*, p. 32.

(33) 34th Infantry journal;
XI Corps G-3 memorandum for information, 1700-05 February
45;

XI Corps G-3 memorandum for file, 1400-05 February 1945.

(34) Letters, Hall to Krueger, 4 and 5 February 1945.

(35) Casualties Zambales Operation, National Archives, Washington, D.C.;
The William W. Jenna Papers, Archives, U.S. Army Military Institute, Carlisle Barracks, PA, Medical Service 34th RCT, p. 11.

(36) Cameron, letters to author, 30 July 87 and 17 June 1990.

(37) Letter, Hall to Krueger, 5 February 1945, National Archives, Washington, D.C.

(38) Sixth United States Army Report of the Luzon Campaign, Engineers Section, p. 98.

THE TURNING POINT
(6 FEBRUARY)

Nothing in the American records indicates a Japanese attack or infiltration the night of 5-6 February. Yet one hate-filled Japanese officer, vowing to avenge the death of his men, made a bold, stubborn sortie.

Since late afternoon 4 February, 2nd Lieutenant Masanao Kobayashi, leader of the 2nd Platoon of the Kato HMG Company, had been brooding over the annihilation of his Yamauchi Squad and the decimation of his Kanazawa Squad. Unwilling to permit their deaths to go unavenged, he revealed his rancor to Lieutenant Kato.

There was mutual respect between the two; the company commander had been his mentor since their days in Manchuria. Kato presented his sword to Kobayashi, telling him that if he must avenge the deaths, to think of the sword as Kato himself being with him. Kobayashi gathered up 15 grenades and boldly marched off Ichinose Heights toward the American lines around midnight—never to be heard from again.[1]

After the disappointing day of 5 February, General Jones found his resources even further depleted on the 6th. The 34th Infantry was moving out of the pass to make room for the 151st, only one of whose battalions would arrive this day. 1st Battalion 152nd, after its hard fight of the previous afternoon, was in no condition to continue the attack. Colonel Cornwell issued orders at 0900 that his "companies would rest today . . . troops to clean ordnance, clothes, bathe and rest."[2] The 149th Infantry was in Dinalupihan under XI Corps control. The division commander had only the 2nd and 3rd Battalions of the 152nd ready for action on the morning of 6 February.

Jones moved 3rd Battalion 152nd into the positions vacated by 2nd Battalion 34th and decided to move the battalion of the 151st Infantry, when it arrived, into the old positions of 1st Battalion 34th. Since 2nd Battalion 152nd was off to the south near Familiar Peak, this seemed to General Jones "a God-given opportunity to adjust the artillery—which we had needed so badly."[3]

The four light and two medium battalions in Division Artillery had been pounding suspected Japanese installations in the rear areas, but most of their fire along the MLR had been directed at targets of opportunity. To adjust the artillery properly, it was necessary to pull the troops back, "zero in" on known and suspected enemy guns, infantry positions and supply dumps, and then saturate these areas with metal before resuming the attack.

General Hall visited the front at mid-morning and became infuriated when he discovered that the infantry was not attacking. He immediately went to General Jones's CP and asked what he was doing. Jones said he was adjusting his artillery. When Hall asked on what he was registering his artillery and how long it would take—Jones said, "All day." Hall told him "to cut out such precise stuff, get his patrols out and find out what he wanted to shoot at."[4]

It felt more than merely "adjusting his artillery" to Sergeants Iga and Hijikata on Mount Shinshu. They described the shelling on this day as a "heavy bombardment" with the 105-mm positions nearby getting the worst of it.[5]

The roar of planes joined the crash of artillery. At 0900, 16 P-47s of the 309th Bombardment Wing, flying from San Marcelino, bombed and strafed suspected targets considerably beyond the frontline troops. The targets covered an area along Highway 7 starting 500 yards west of the Santa Rita River and extending 3,000 yards east.

In the first of three flights, each plane carried two 165-gallon wing tanks filled with napalm. In the second flight at 1000, each plane carried two 500-pound demolition bombs with instantaneous nose and tail fuses. The third flight at 1100 repeated the first flight's dose of napalm.[6]

Machine Gun Company commander Hiyotaka Kato watched as the Thunderbolts unleashed the first oblong missiles that tumbled end-over-end into the jungle and along the road. Balls of flame and billowing black clouds of smoke erupted when the napalm canisters exploded. Kato's first thought was that the Americans had no bombs and were dropping drums of gasoline. Painfully aware of the Nagayoshi Detachment's scarcity of ammunition, particularly for mortars and artillery, Kato assumed that the Americans were also running short of ammunition.[7]

Pilots participating in the air strike estimated that 60 percent of their bombs fell in the target area, but observed little ground activity. They silenced the only machine gun that fired on them. After each swoop made by the P-47s, Pfc. Thornton of B Company 34th recalled hearing in the distance a defiant rifle shot from a determined enemy soldier.

The Thunderbolts dropped four tons of bombs and 3960 gallons of napalm and fired 63,000 rounds of .50 caliber ammunition. These are not impressive totals compared with other World War II bombings, but air power, even hundreds of yards in advance of the front lines, must have seemed like manna from heaven to the GIs mired at the horseshoe.[8]

On the way back to his own headquarters around noon, General Hall reached the decision he had been considering since 2 February: he would relieve General Jones and replace him with Brigadier General Roy W. Easley, the 38th Division Assistant Commander. Soon after arrival at his CP, he had his Chief of Staff, Brigadier General John A. Elmore, direct General Jones to report to him. General Jones, fully aware of his tenuous relationship with General Hall, arrived promptly with his bedding roll and personal baggage on his jeep trailer. Hall told him he was "canned" and remarked later that Jones did not seem surprised.[9]

Although General Hall insisted after the war that he did not make up his mind to relieve General Jones until noon of the 6 February, the 38th Division staff was obviously aware that something was brewing. At 1640 on 5 February, the Chief of Staff of the 38th Division, Colonel Albert J. Hastings, informed the Division G-1 that Jones was about to be relieved. Late that night, the G-1 Section prepared orders for Easley's assumption of command. In interviews after the war, neither Hall nor Elmore could offer any explanation for this strange set of circumstances. In retrospect, it may have been that the 38th Division staff sensed the relief was coming and prepared itself accordingly, or that Jones, feeling his relief was imminent, alerted his chief of staff.[10]

His relief obviously rankled Jones for the remainder of his life. In January 1957, he wrote that when he was relieved, he objected so vehemently that XI Corps, to justify its actions, changed orders, twisted the facts and falsified documents. It "made every effort to discredit me," he stated.[11]

In his relief order, Hall blamed Jones for a "lack of aggressiveness on the part of his division, unsatisfactory tactical planning and execution, and inadequate reconnaissance measures. He failed to produce the results with his division, which might be reasonably expected." But Hall softened the blow. "Nothing in this letter [referring to his letter of 4 February to General Jones which was attached] is to be considered as reflecting in any way on General Jones's personal courage or his willingness to cooperate to the best of his ability nor on his loyalty to his division or higher headquarters."[12]

His military career shattered, General Jones reported immediately to Sixth Army Headquarters for reassignment to the United States. He will appear no more in this battle history. The Army had been his life, and he had advanced steadily to a position of great responsibility. Like General Hall, he was a man of strong convictions. Where had he gone wrong? He felt he had done well considering the corps commander's emphasis on speed. He could see no real mistake or blunder he had made except to order the 34th Infantry to attack on 5 February. "The order . . . was not good because I was asking the 34th Infantry to do something which they were not going to do."

Jones felt strongly that his action to adjust the artillery fire on 6 February, which precipitated his relief, was the proper action. He could think of no way he could have fought the battle differently, given the conditions imposed by General Hall. "My positive conclusion is that there was nothing that I could have done to keep my command."[13]

💣   💣   💣

The differences between General Hall and General Jones warrant further analysis. As a starting place, neither trusted the other. Hall did not think Jones competent to command a division and had no confidence in the 38th Division under his command. Jones was convinced Hall was out "to get him" and show up the 38th Division in the process.

When the 152nd Infantry was repulsed after three days in the pass, Hall felt that aggressive leadership was missing and replaced the 152nd on 3 February with the 34th under corps control. Jones considered the replacement as showing up himself, the 38th Division and the 152nd Regiment. "He [Hall] was absolutely certain that the 34th would brush aside any resistance and advance rapidly through the pass." When the 34th failed to produce, Jones interpreted Hall's attachment of the regiment to the 38th Division on the night of 4 February as a way to get himself (Hall) "off the hook" and blame Jones for the failure.[14]

It is not difficult to understand General Jones's mistrust of General Hall and the XI Corps. Instances have been cited showing that General Hall and the XI Corps staff underestimated the Japanese and were reluctant to admit that the corps faced a strong adversary. At times, the staff even seemed to take a cavalier and glib attitude toward the 38th Division. This attitude was never more evident than in its Advanced Copy of the After Action Report (AAR) on the ZigZag phase of the corps' campaign on Luzon. This AAR coverage of the events of 1-5 February is a good example.

After briefly describing the actions of 29-31 January, the AAR glosses over the 1-2 February fighting in one paragraph: "Slow progress was made by the 152nd Infantry operating against a stubborn enemy west of the ZIGZAG area along Highway 7 for the following two days." A long paragraph describes the entry of the 34th Infantry into the battle on 3 February with the first mention of the obstacles—terrain and strong enemy defenses—in the pass.

The AAR summary of the attacks of 4-5 February for brevity, over-simplification, ambiguity and inaccuracy is incredulous: "Meanwhile the 34th RCT had advanced east along the highway, to positions fifteen hundred yards north of FAMILIAR PEAK, where on 4 February, the leading battalion was almost completely surrounded by the enemy. These elements of the 34th RCT withdrew the following day to positions astride the highway sixteen hundred yards northwest of FAMILIAR PEAK, which had been gained by severe fighting against a tenacious enemy in well prepared positions." Even a trained observer would have difficulty deciphering the corps' description of the fighting on these two days.

After mentioning the relief of General Jones and a paragraph commending the supply and engineer personnel, the AAR covers the last eight days of the campaign in one sentence. "Vicious fighting continued in the vital ZIGZAG Pass area with the 149th Infantry [remember, the 149th was under corps control] attacking to the west and the remainder of the division advancing eastward."

Inaccurate to the end, the corps AAR closes the section on ZigZag Pass by stating that 4,000 enemy had been killed to open the highway. This figure is only slightly less than *twice* the entire number of Japanese troops actually in the pass.[15]

In short, the reader of the report cannot help but notice the emphasis on the 34th Infantry, the flank march of the 149th Infantry (which was strictly an XI Corps operation), and the air strikes. Only brief mention is made of the 151st and 152nd Regiments and no mention is made of the artillery (all under command of the 38th Division).

General Hall considered initial light casualty figures as proof that the 152nd was not aggressive. He contended that most of the 152nd's casualties had occurred at night and not during the actual fighting in the daylight hours. He said that, according to the medical officer of the 1st Portable Surgical Hospital, most of the gunshot wounds came from calibers larger than the Japanese .25 caliber.[16]

The unmistakable inference was that many of the 152nd Infantry's casualties resulted from their own panic and careless fire at each other and not from enemy action. Jones, of course, backed up his own troops. He wrote after the war that "the 152nd Infantry had done so much better than the 34th Infantry . . ."[17]

If casualties are considered as a criterion of satisfactory performance for the first six days of the battle, the statistics favor General Hall. In comparing the casualties of the lead regiment in the pass 31 January-5 February, the 152nd reported 98 battle casualties during its first three days in the pass, 31 January-2 February. The 34th reported 308, or more than three times that number during its three days, 3-5 February.[18]

This is not to disparage the 152nd. Through 6 February, that regiment reported 222 battle casualties, reflecting its hard fighting on 5 and 6 February. Its casualties for the entire battle totaled almost as many as the other three regiments combined (see Appendix B).

The rift between the two generals extended into tactics. Jones was critical of the need for taking Grande Island, which he called "another wild goose chase . . . Information was readily obtainable that there wasn't a Jap on the island."

Jones was also critical of sending the 149th Infantry to Dinalupihan. He contended that the tactical situation on the Central Plain of Luzon changed from the time the Zambales Operation was planned and the actual date of the landing. He felt that the rapid, practically unopposed march of the XIV Corps south from Lingayan Gulf proved the absence of Japanese troops in Central Luzon, thereby voiding the necessity of sealing off the Bataan Peninsula.[19]

General Jones's statements may be accurate, but his reasoning is illogical. Two vital missions of XI Corps as determined by GHQSWPA and Sixth Army were securing Subic Bay and sealing off Bataan Peninsula. Subic Bay could not be considered secure until Grande Island was occupied, regardless of intelligence reports. The flank march to Dinalupihan was a brilliant maneuver, not only sealing off the peninsula, but also enabling General Hall to effect the classic double envelopment. If General Jones was forthright in these criticisms of corps tactics and not just trying to find fault, he does not seem to have had a clear grasp of the corps' mission.

General Jones's chief criticism of General Hall was the latter's demand for speed with little thought given to artillery support, terrain or the nature of the enemy's defenses. Jones said, "The primary requirement of the corps' order was speed . . . He [Hall] told me in anger that we did not need artillery support and should not delay the attack [through the pass] to adjust the artillery."[20]

General Hall's insistence on speed originated with his two bosses, MacArthur and Krueger. It was strengthened by Hall's underestimate of the number and caliber of Japanese troops in ZigZag Pass and of the stout defenses they had constructed. Jones argued that Hall had a preconceived idea, implanted in his mind on Leyte, that ZigZag Pass would be lightly defended, and, therefore, could be taken in short order. (see Chapter 4, page 47.)[21]

If General Hall really thought speed was important, Jones reasoned the corps commander could have lifted the restriction placed on the 149th Infantry on 1 February to stay within supporting distance of the 152nd in the pass. "If he wanted the 149th to reach DINALUPIHAN in the minimum time, he could have told me to let them keep on going regardless of the trail they were on."[22]

In a final slap at the futility of speed, General Jones aptly summarized the campaign: "It actually took four regiments 15 days, hacking from all sides, to open the pass, and they had to kill 2,400 [Japs] to do it."[23] General Jones also overstated the number of troops he faced. The North Garrison Unit of the Nagayoshi Detachment was about 2,100 strong.

A second Jones criticism was Hall's reluctance to use artillery and save American lives. Supply problems emerged after the second day. The supplies that landed 29 January had to be moved overland to Olongapo to keep up with the front line troops. A shortage of trucks hampered this movement. It is reasonable to assume there may have been limited ammunition available the first two days of February, but nothing in the records indicates a dearth of artillery ammunition or any reason why more artillery rounds could not have been fired.

General Hall had at his disposal six howitzer battalions (four 105-mm and two 155-mm) in 38th Division Artillery plus 155-mm "Long Tom" rifles and 8" howitzers under Corps control. In the first eight days of the campaign (30 January-6 February), Division Artillery fired 15,770 rounds plus 63rd F.A. Battalion expenditures not included in the division records. This is not as much ammunition as was fired in one day later in the campaign. Why would Hall limit this power until incontrovertible evidence dictated a greater use of artillery? By his insistence on speed and using artillery sparingly, Hall may have prolonged the campaign by not permitting Jones to reconnoiter thoroughly, pre-register his artillery, and direct a "set-piece" battle.[24]

A third Jones criticism—not utilizing all the troops available—also appears to have merit. A more sound and prudent strategy would have been for the Americans to attack from the outset with two regiments abreast along Highway 7, with the road as the dividing line. The 34th Infantry did practically nothing 31 January-2 February during the 152nd's first three days in the pass. Encamped between Olongapo and the trail junction captured 31 January, the 34th was readily available to join the 152nd in the attacks of 1 and 2 February. But speed was the over-riding factor. It was quicker and seemed easier to attack along the road where troops could move rapidly and be supplied without difficulty. An attack on the flanks would have required cutting new paths of communication and result in slower movement.

In the final analysis of the rift between these two strong-willed and stubborn men, we can detect a gnawing antagonism beneath the surface, often called a clash of personalities. Others would term it a difference in style. It was probably inevitable that a break in their relationship would come sooner or later. When this happens, the one with higher rank prevails. Jones' two superiors held all the cards and played them. With their reputations and careers on the line, General Hall and General Krueger dismissed General Jones—the unpleasant task they felt was necessary to accomplish their mission.

💣   💣   💣

The remainder of the day's activities were anti-climatic after the bombshell of General Jones's relief had filtered down to the troops. As temporary commander of the division, General Easley's main concern was to get an attack started to relieve General Hall's obvious displeasure with inactivity. His only battalion ready to attack was Major Mangold's 3rd/152nd, which had completed its relief of 3/34th at 1020. At 1400, Mangold moved out along the road with tanks at the front and patrols to the side.[25]

Major Ogawa countered by moving two squads of the Sakai Platoon of Lieutenant Ogata's reserve to Ichinose Heights. Lieutenant Miyazaki called up the wounded men who could still fight from Mount Shinshu to help repel the American advance. The increased firepower of the rein-forcements plus the two 70-mm guns located between Ichinose and Fumetsu pinned down the leading Company L at the top of the "2."[26]

Major Mangold started a flanking maneuver to the left up toward the ridge from which 1st Battalion 152nd had been driven the day before. Company L found several bodies of 1st Battalion men left where they had fallen. The company suddenly received fire from all sides as it moved up to occupy a low ridge. Men began falling from machine gun and rifle fire. Major Mangold ordered K Company forward with stretchers to evacuate the wounded. There were so many casualties that K Company had to leave the dead and remove only the wounded.[27]

Mangold pulled back and formed his battalion in line of companies left to right, I, K and L, with the tanks moved off the road in support as far as the undergrowth and steep terrain would permit. The objective was the hill (Mount Hissho) directly north of the bottom of the "2." Fighting until 1830 when darkness had nearly set in, the battalion finally overcame the stubborn defenders: several infantrymen from the 10th Company including the LMG of Sergeant Nishimoto and a 37-mm anti-tank squad of Warrant Officer Shigeru Uwane.

3rd Battalion 152nd stayed in place and dug in for the night. The bloody fight had cost the battalion 10 KIA and 19 WIA. However, the Americans had pierced and occupied another section of the original Japanese MLR, and the way was now open to crack the Kita-Kasuga-Minami line.[28]

Major Ogawa was especially pleased with the work of Warrant Officer Uwane and LMG squad leader Sergeant Nishimoto, whose squad ended the day with only two survivors. Uwane and Nishimoto, who had been surrounded, made their way through the American lines around midnight to report. Ogawa praised them as heroes defending key positions. He asked them to defend to the last man, because retention of Ichinose Hts. was vital to the success of the entire operation.[29]

1st and 2nd Battalions 152nd were not engaged during the day. After its rough action the previous day, 1st Battalion rested before moving forward along the road behind 3rd Battalion to be available for immediate support. Colonel McIntosh returned 2nd Battalion to the highway from its advanced position near Familiar Peak and sent it to occupy Hill 301.

3rd Battalion 151st Infantry started arriving in the morning and occupied positions at the northwest corner of the horseshoe. General Jones had planned to move 3/151st into the old positions of 1st Battalion 34th. However, General Easley did not wish to expose 3/151st immediately to the wrath of the Japanese mortars.[30]

💣   💣   💣

News from the 149th Infantry was good. Colonel Skelton occupied Layac Junction and the line Dinalupihan-Hermosa with his 3rd Battalion. Upon division order, he started his 1st and 2nd Battalions westward along Highway 7 toward ZigZag Pass. By the end of the day, lead elements had reached Culo, more than one-third the distance, without opposition. A single C-47 cargo plane spent the day ferrying supplies to the 149th Infantry Headquarters at Dinalupihan.

All supplies for the 149th were delivered by air during the remainder of the campaign. C-47s from San Marcelino dropped the supplies and then returned for another load. Machine guns, mortars and other heavy items came in by parachute, but rations and ammunition arrived by free fall. This was a poor way to deliver supplies, but there was no airfield at Dinalupihan. Cartons of rations would break and scatter over the drop zone. The free drop was hard on mortar ammunition. The shock from hitting the ground caused many bent fins on the shells and numerous erratic rounds when fired.[31]

Dinalupihan was a crossroads town, a bottleneck, through which passed all civilian traffic (as it does today) between Bataan and the Central Plain of Luzon. The town was also a center for guerrilla activity. On the night of 6 February, the 149th's leading Company C was dug-in along Highway 7 in the vicinity of Culo. Several patrols of guerrillas were to pass through the company's perimeter that night, and Regiment had instructed C Company's men to be certain that it was the enemy—not the guerrillas—in their sights before they fired. After a number of Filipino patrols had passed through, relaxation and carelessness set in. Eight Japanese tagged along behind the last patrol and threw grenades at close range before the startled Americans recovered their composure. All eight were killed in the resulting melee, but two C Company men were also killed.[32]

For the 34th Infantry, the sixth of February was, like the third of February, a day of entrucking and moving—except in reverse. Desultory artillery fire crisscrossed the battlefield. While waiting for G Company to receive its marching orders, 1st Lieutenant Edward S. Symanski, the weapons platoon leader, was sitting with a comrade under the jungle canopy. After a tall tree burst, shell fragments could be heard tinkling down through the leaves. One sliver nicked Symanski in the leg between the end of his pants and the top of his socks. The "wound" drew blood, and Symanski gained the first of two Purple Hearts he would eventually take back to the States.

By late afternoon, the 34th had completed its move to the coast where it had landed 29 January. 1st Battalion encamped at San Felipe, slightly north of the 38th Division's landing site; 2nd Battalion crossed the Pamatuan River at San Antonio and bivouacked on the north slope of Mount Rongosto; and 3rd Battalion moved to old positions in Olongapo. Regimental Headquarters and Field Train and other elements of the combat team set up bivouacs between San Antonio and San Felipe. Anti-tank Company and the 24th Recon Troop moved to the foothills between Castillejos and Subic, where General Hall had expected the Japanese to make their stand. From there they could protect and, if needed, defend the San Marcelino airstrip. The 34th's supporting 63rd FA Battalion remained with the 38th Division Artillery.[33]

The 2nd Battalion was hot, tired, mad and bewildered by its rough reception in ZigZag Pass. Hardly anyone had seen a live Japanese. "Doc" Cameron made sure the battalion started its recuperation in style. Defying strict orders, he provided each man that night with the staple cocktail of the Pacific—grapefruit juice and 100 proof alcohol!

&* &* &*

When darkness arrived in ZigZag Pass 6 February, the forces on a front line which had not changed appreciably in five days were equal: one American battalion faced one Japanese battalion. Despite this bleak outlook for the GIs at the time, 6 February was the turning point of the battle. Three events this day finally started tilting the scales in favor of the Americans.

First, the air strike. Bombings would demoralize the enemy and destroy his supplies of food and ammunition. The fiery napalm would flow into his caves and trenches and burn away the undergrowth camouflaging his bunkers. Second, the approach of the 149th Infantry from the east. This pressure would soon squeeze the Japanese between all three regiments of the 38th Division. Third, the relief of General Jones.

Regardless of the causes or who was right, the differences between General Hall and General Jones had brought the operation to a virtual standstill. It was a cancer that would not go away. With the 34th Infantry now completely out of the picture, it was essential that General Hall have full confidence in the 38th Division commander, whoever he would be. The 38th Division had been assigned to General Hall as part of XI Corps for the Zambales Operation, and with the division came its commander, General Jones. Having dismissed General Jones, General Hall could now choose his own commander.

Map 6: Olongapo–Dinalupihan

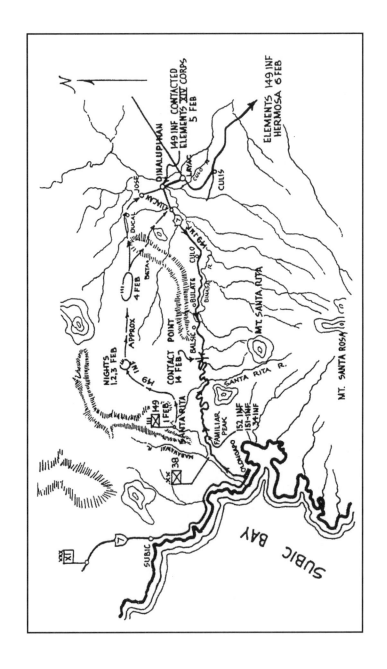

Chapter 14

NOTES

(1) *How the Kato Company Fought: The Record of the 3rd Machine Gun Company 39th Infantry Regiment*, Tamotsu Nagai, Editor, 1990, p. 190-191.

(2) 1st Battalion 152nd Infantry journal.

(3) Jones comments, 20 December 1956, p. 9.

(4) Hall comments, 15 March 1952.

(5) Kato Company History, p. 205, 209.

(6) 309th Bombardment Wing Field Order #1, 05 February 1945.

(7) Kato, Hiyotaka, letter to author, 18 March 1990.

(8) 309th Bomb Wing Final Mission Report, 1145-06 February 1945; Thornton, Pfc. Douglas W., Jr., Asst. Squad Leader B Company 34th Infantry, letter to author, 30 October 1989.

(9) Hall comments.

(10) Smith, Robert Ross, *Triumph in the Philippines*, n. 55, p. 329.

(11) Jones supplementary letter to comments, 26 January 1957, p. 2.

(12) XI Corps Memorandum to CG Sixth Army, 06 February 1945, Subject: Relief from command of Major General Henry L.C. Jones.

(13) Jones comments, p. 5; Jones supplementary letter, p. 2-3, p. 6-7.

(14) Jones comments, p. 6, 8.

(15) XI Corps Advanced Copy of Historical Report, Luzon Campaign, p. 8-12.

(16) Letter, Hall to Krueger, 3 February 1945.

(17) Jones comments, p. 9.

(18) Casualties reported in 34th Infantry and 152nd Infantry journals.

(19) Jones comments, p. 11.

(20) Jones supplementary letter, p. 4, 6.

(21) Jones comments, p. 5.

(22) *Ibid.,* p. 2.

(23) *Ibid.,* p. 11.

(24) 38th Division Artillery Report (Appendix C in this volume).

(25) 152nd Infantry journal.

(26) *History of the 39th Infantry Regiment,* edited and published by the 39th Infantry Association, p. 644.

(27) Kreis, Sergeant Don, Company L 152nd Infantry, letter to author, 4 February 1988;
152nd Infantry journal.

(28) *39th Infantry History,* p. 644;
152nd Infantry journal.

(29) Ogawa, Major Hironori, *Record of the 3rd Battalion, 39th Infantry Regiment in the "Big Asia War,"* p. 35;
39th Infantry History, p. 644.

(30) 152nd Infantry journal;
Avengers of Bataan: 38th Infantry Division Historical Report M-7 Operation (AAR), p. 21.

(31) XI Corps G-3 Periodic Report #9, 1800-06 February 1945;
Brinson, Captain Arthur, Cavalry, monograph: *The Battle of ZigZag Pass*, p. 8, delivered at the Armored School, Fort Knox, KY, 5 May 48. At the time of the battle Brinson was C Company 149th Infantry Exec.

(32) *Ibid.,* p. 6-7.

(33) 34th Infantry AAR, p. 109-110.

PART III
The Americans Prevail

BREAKOUT TO THE
SANTA RITA
(7 FEBRUARY)

Brigadier General Roy W. Easley, the new commander of the 38th Division, realized that he must take a radically opposite direction from the tactics used by his predecessor. He had the two regiments from Indiana on line who were familiar with each other and with whom he was familiar, an advantage not enjoyed by General Jones. Of one thing Easley was certain: he must use more imaginative tactics than General Jones had exhibited so far.

Despite fighting seven days in the pass, no one had a firm idea of the overall Japanese scheme of defense. The 38th Division staff suspected that the southern flank might be the Japanese Achilles heel. Major Ogawa's unsuccessful attempts to knock A Company 34th back from its isolated position near Familiar Peak and 2nd Battalion 152nd's unopposed march to the relief of this company suggested a weakness south of the road. Perhaps another wide flanking movement, this time to the south and east, would force the enemy to weaken his MLR to meet the threat of encirclement and reveal a seam in his defense that could be exploited.

When General Hall placed a call on 5 February for the 151st Infantry to relieve the 34th in the pass, the Hoosiers were scattered from Olongapo to the west coast of Luzon. The 2nd Battalion, under operational control of the 34th Infantry, was responsible for the security of Olongapo. The 3rd Battalion was patrolling the area from San Marcelino to Olongapo. Company A was responsible for the security of the San Marcelino airstrip. The remainder of the 1st Battalion was patrolling north of San Felipe.[1]

The 151st's commander was a 49-year-old Illinoisan, Colonel Ralf C. Paddock. After attending the University of Illinois for two years, Paddock enlisted in the Marine Corps in June 1917. Commissioned 2nd Lieutenant a year later, he served as an instructor at the Marine Corps Officers School at Quantico. At the end of World War I, he embarked on a career in the shoe business in Frankfort, IN, but could not get the military out of his system. In 1921, he joined the reorganized Indiana National Guard and steadily advanced to become regimental commander. Never forgetting that many men went overseas in 1917-18 without adequate training, Paddock resolved early in his military career that his men would learn to fight and survive.

Paddock's three battalion commanders had joined the Indiana National Guard in the 1920s. Commanding the 1st was 36-year-old Major Robert Stewart, born in Colorado Springs but later residing in Shelbyville, IN. He had risen steadily in rank since joining the Guard as a private.

Lieutenant Colonel L. Robert Mottern commanded the 2nd. The "old man" of the regiment, Mottern was even one year older than Colonel Paddock. A native Indianan, he was employed by Swift and Company in Indianapolis at the outbreak of the war. Aggressive and feisty, Mottern is the spokesman quoted in the 151st's After Action Report.

Lieutenant Colonel William L. Funkhouser of Indianapolis commanded the 3rd Battalion. At 34, he was among the youngest field grade officers in the division prior to combat promotions, having progressed from private to lieutenant colonel in 16 years.[2]

In late afternoon of 5 February, Lieutenant Colonel Norman L. Thompson, the 151st Infantry Executive Officer and former Assistant Adjutant General for the state of Indiana, and Captain Robert A. Stine, the regimental S-3, reported to XI Corps Headquarters. Their purpose was to

Colonel Ralf C. Paddock,
Commander 151st Infantry

Lt. Colonel Robert Mottern,
Commander 2nd Battalion
151st Infantry

coordinate the relief of the 34th Regiment by the 151st. Even though 2nd Battalion 151st was in Olongapo and the battalion nearest the pass, E Company was still enroute to the Philippines from Oro Bay, New Guinea. Therefore, Colonel Paddock designated his full strength 3rd Battalion as the first element of the regiment to move into the pass. The 3/151st departed San Marcelino airstrip by truck at 0800 on 6 February and arrived in the pass later that morning.

Thompson and Stine had also visited division headquarters and conferred with the commander of the departing 34th Infantry. Colonel Jenna warned them what to expect. "Their [Japanese] defensive setup is the most intricate maze of pillboxes and caves I have seen in the Southwest Pacific Area."[3]

By the end of the day 6 February, General Easley had crafted a new approach to attacking the defenses in ZigZag Pass. He resolved to outflank the Japanese by sending the 3rd Battalion 151st south to skirt round the enemy's left and strike for the Highway 7 bridge over the Santa Rita River 1,800 yards east of the horseshoe. At the same time, the 152nd Infantry would resume its frontal assault against the enemy's Main Line of Resistance.

The 3rd Battalion 151st's flanking movement was a preliminary move to link up with the 149th Infantry. Easley gave the battalion the mission of first securing Familiar Peak (Mount Kosaku), then patrolling to the river and following the patrol with two rifle companies. After reaching the river, Funkhouser's men were to secure the bridge, then move east south of the road and make contact with the Kentuckians. Even though the bridge was antiquated and of little value because it could not bear heavy traffic, the move might open up a new front to disconcert the enemy and speed the union with the 149th.[4]

After its relief by the 3rd Battalion 34th as security for Olongapo, 2nd/151st closed the sawmill area at 0920 on 7 February and was designated regimental reserve. Farthest from the action, the 1st Battalion entrucked before daybreak and reached Olongapo at 0700, closing the pass at 1015. However, Company A was particularly hard pressed to keep its appointment for the ensuing battle.

Reinforced with a platoon of heavy machine guns from D Company, A Company had provided security for San Marcelino Airstrip since 30 January. The company dug in about 400 yards east of the strip and then patrolled the area extensively from its perimeter. The engineers repairing the strip worked round the clock, utilizing searchlights at night.

At about 0200 on 6 February, two Japanese planes flew over the brightly lit strip and dropped about 25 anti-personnel bombs. Work was not interrupted as none of the bombs fell on the strip. Instead, nearly all fell in the totally dark A Company area 400 yards away. The action resulted in 11 hospital casualties in A Company plus 2 in a nearby AAA gun crew. The puzzle of how the Japanese pilots missed the airstrip and hit A Company in the dark was never solved.

After this brush with disaster, A Company received orders later in the day to entruck at 2000 hours and meet the 1st Battalion in Olongapo. The trucks failed to show at the appointed time. After a four-hour wait, the company commander, Captain Stephen M. Walker, a 1930 graduate of the Virginia Military Institute, motored by jeep to XI Corps Headquarters at San Antonio to investigate the cause for the delay. After three hours of negotiations, Walker finally located sufficient vehicles to move his company. Fortunate to breakfast with another company at the airstrip, Walker's men finally boarded trucks at 0630 7 February for Olongapo.[5]

General Easley wanted to exert maximum pressure against the enemy along the MLR. He ordered the 152nd Infantry, supported by tanks, to resume its attack eastward. Colonel McIntosh, CO of the 152nd, planned to attack north of the road with his 1st and 2nd Battalions and along Highway 7 with the 3rd Battalion. This meant that Major Mangold's 3rd Battalion, now dug in on Mount Hissho, would have to force the West Pass on the road between Ichinose Heights and Mount Minami at the top of the "2."[6]

The defenders in this area were 20 survivors and the 2 guns of the 37-mm Anti-tank Gun Company under Warrant Officer Shigeru Uwane, originally entrenched on either side of the road at the top of the "2." Sergeant Nishimoto's LMG squad and two squads of Lieutenant Ogata's 11th Company reserves under command of Warrant Officer Ichiro Sakai would provide rifle protection.[7]

2nd Battalion, already occupying Hill 301, would attack east and southeastward along the top of the ridge (Mount Koko). 1st Battalion would mop up behind the 2nd. Apparently, because Colonel Cornwell was familiar with the ridge following the 1st Battalion's attack over the same ground 5 February, McIntosh specified that Cornwell would command both battalions.[8]

Meanwhile, the 1st and 2nd Battalions of the 149th would draw the noose tighter round the Japanese by continuing their attack westward, with Bulate being the objective for the day. An artillery concentration and air strike between the east and west forces was to precede the 152nd's attack and pave the way for the 149th's advance. In a rare instance, the artillery, in positions in the rice paddies northeast of Olongapo, could support both the attacks of the 152nd eastward and the 149th toward the west.[9]

The 152nd's two-battalion attack was the most successful so far of the ten-day campaign. Artillery blasted the Kita-Kasuga-Minami-Ichinose ridgeline and the Japanese defenses at Shinshu, concentrating in that area again on Lieutenant Otani's 105-mm howitzers. Major Ogawa called the artillery fire and incendiary bombs (napalm) "really severe."

At Shinshu, Sergeant Hijikata reported, "The place for stocking food used by Battalion Headquarters was destroyed completely." Sergeant Iga said that his position at Shinshu, once covered by jungle, "had turned into a red-brown bare mountain." Heavy Mortar Platoon Leader Master Sergeant Masatoshi Fujimoto with Lieutenant Miyazaki at Mount Kita was appalled by the change in appearance of the mountain caused by the Americans' constant bombardment. "No words could describe it," he said. "It was just terrible."[10]

Early in the day, Sergeant Tadao Fujiwara's 70-mm gun with its 15-man crew became disabled, and at about 1330 a direct hit by an artillery shell destroyed the gun. This cut Lieutenant Yanase's battalion gun section in half. The mishap left only Corporal Uichi Mano's 70-mm gun, except for machine guns, on the south side of the road to combat the American tanks coming through the West Pass.[11]

Major Ogawa's withdrawal from Mount Koko the night of 5 February (not known by the Americans) assured a successful attack north of the road. Expecting another bitter fight for Hill 401 as he had experienced on 5 February, a surprised Colonel Cornwell with the leading 2nd Battalion, quickly overran this long ridge that was the key terrain feature on the battlefield. The Japanese had left booby-traps on their own as well as American dead, but nothing else to impede the 2nd Battalion's advance.[12]

After sending patrols to the north to guard his left flank, Colonel Cornwell led the 2nd Battalion down the eastern end of the ridge toward the western slope of Mount Kasuga until stopped by mortar fire and elements of Lieutenant Miyazaki's 10th Company.

Valiant fighting along the Kita/Kasuga/Minami line by the Shimuzu Platoon of the 10th Company, 20 soldiers of the 37-mm AT Gun Company under Warrant Officer Shigeru Uwane on Ichinose, the machine gunners of the Takamura Squad, who had moved from Mount Koko on 5 February, and the Nakamura Engineer Platoon finally brought the attack to a halt. Even though they were under close observation from artillery observation planes, the Japanese could not be displaced.

The 2nd Battalion dug in place and the trailing 1st Battalion dug company perimeters 300-500 yards west. Disregarding his own personal safety, Sergeant Ancelet of D Company roamed the 1st Battalion Headquarters and D Company perimeters and located and disarmed several booby traps.[13]

•   •   •

In the meantime, the 3rd Battalion had started the 152nd Infantry's attack on the right. Company I with the platoon of 1st Lieutenant A. R. Bell and two tanks in the lead advanced along the road into the "2." As the platoon and tanks rounded the last curve at the top of the "2" and approached the defile between Mount Minami and Mount Ege, a Japanese suicide unit ambushed the tanks from both sides of the road. They caused general mayhem by killing Lieutenant Bell and disabling both tanks.

Realizing the folly of continuing head-on assaults, Major Mangold moved I Company with M Company's heavy machine guns to a knoll north of the "2." He moved Companies K and L south of the "2" between the horseshoe and Mount Ege and emplaced his 81-mm mortars north of the highway in the upper curve of the "2." The mortars were so close that the gunners had to use maximum elevation to hit targets on Ichinose Heights.[14]

At 1500, following an air strike and heavy artillery and mortar preparatory fire, Companies K and L assaulted the northern tip of Mount Ege (Ichinose Heights). Sergeant Kreis of L Company remembered taking his light machine gun squad to the first platoon to give added fire-power. The platoon's lieutenant had been shot in the head and killed. Kreis's first gunner was killed as they crawled into position for firing. Before he could set up the gun, he received orders to help the third platoon. As he reached them, their lieutenant was shot in the right shoulder. Kreis's own lieutenant in charge of the fourth platoon (weapons platoon) was "shot in the leg, and the bullet came out his knee cap."

This furious resistance came from the platoon of 2nd Lieutenant Yoshimitsu Shimizu of the 10th Company, defending Mount Minami. Platoon Leader Shimizu was killed by the blast of a tank shell during this battle for Ichinose Heights.[15]

When the 3rd Battalion was closely pinned down by devastating mortar and machine gun fire, Major Mangold came to the front in the thick of the fighting. Moving from one company to another, he success-fully coordinated and led the hotly contested advance.[16]

By late afternoon, K and L Companies had overrun two strong Japanese positions, one each on Ichinose Heights and Mount Minami. Two pillboxes next to the road on the rear slope of Ichinose still held up the advance.

Major Mangold placed a five-minute 81-mm mortar concentration on the two pillboxes. The mortar barrage was of WP (white phosphorus), causing the Japanese holed up in the pillboxes and surrounding trenches to break and run across the road toward Mount Minami. Company M's machine guns cut down an estimated 20 of the enemy caught in the open.[17]

Major Ogawa singled out Lieutenant Shimizu for praise as well as Lieutenant Miyazaki's entire company for finally halting the attack. He was also lavish in praise of the Takamura and Ueno HMG Squads on Minami and Ichinose respectively, and Warrant Officer Shigeru Uwane's 37-mm Anti-tank Platoon on Ichinose.

The 3rd Battalion commander did not accept lightly this incursion by another 3rd Battalion into the most heavily fortified portion of his line. Near sundown, Japanese mortars and artillery gave a terrific pounding to the Americans trying to consolidate their newly won positions in the Ichinose-Minami area. They particularly concentrated along the curves of the "2."[18]

Captain Ransohoff from his observation plane reported, "This fire was the heaviest concentration I have observed the Japs use. I could see trucks burning, and it sounded and looked as if ammunition dumps were exploding." As usual, the Japanese spread this 30-minute barrage over the entire regiment. "There were many casualties, as yet not counted. Several vehicles destroyed. Several fires started in area," Colonel Wilson, the 38th Division G-2, telephoned to G-2 XI Corps late in the afternoon.[19]

Men of Sergeant Lester H. Keller's squad were removing their heavy machine guns from a D Company weapons carrier when the barrage struck. The first round hit 1st Lieutenant Sheridan R. Brown of Oregon, standing in the road. With both legs mangled, he scrambled under a burning ammunition truck. Oblivious to the danger and still under heavy fire, Sergeant Keller of Shoals, IN, dragged Lieutenant Brown from under the truck to the ditch by the side of the road—all in vain. Lieutenant Brown died later in the hospital.[20]

All of the members of one of M Company's mortar sections became casualties when a direct hit ignited mortar ammunition in one of the company's trailers. The 3rd Battalion aid station located at the bottom of the "2" came under heavy Japanese mortar fire. The battalion surgeon was killed and his assistant wounded. Nearly half of the aid station personnel were killed or wounded.[21]

Many wounded from both the 2nd and 3rd Battalions were strewn along the sides of the road where they had been carried on litters from the firefight on the ridge. A few soldiers in the aid station awaiting treatment were wounded a second time. Under the intense mortar fire, some men, taking cover as best they could, helped the walking wounded move stretcher cases off the road into sheltered places.

Major Kenneth W. Brewer of New Albany, IN, 3rd Battalion Exec, saw in a flash what had to be done to relieve the chaos. He ran down the road to the battalion CP near the aid station and commandeered two 6 x 6 kitchen trucks, with their drivers, parked along the road. He led them back up the road where he drafted several soldiers and the walking wounded to load the litter cases onto the trucks. Then he sent the trucks down the road to the regimental aid station about a mile west on Highway 7. Several trips were required to evacuate the approximately 60 WIAs caught in the open by the mortars.[22]

Major Kenneth W. Brewer, 3rd Battalion 152nd Infantry Executive Officer, lost 30 pounds during the two-week battle

The Japanese harassed the 152nd Infantry all night. They placed intermittent mortar fire on the 3rd Battalion, but concentrated their efforts on the 1st and 2nd Battalions threatening Mount Kasuga. Led personally by Lieutenant Miyazaki, the 10th Company counterattacked at dusk and forced the leading elements of 2/152nd to give up their advanced positions on the western slope of Mount Kasuga. Miyazaki continued the attack after dark, but his men could not penetrate the Americans' perimeters.[23]

"It was so dark you couldn't see your hand in front of your face," Pfc. Clyde S. Townsend of New Albany, IN, described the action on the D Company perimeter in an article that appeared in his hometown newspaper. "Japs were barking like dogs around the foxholes and making weird, frightening noises." Suddenly one came walking straight for Townsend's position firing a light machine gun from the hip. Townsend's foxhole mate moved out of the perimeter and cut down the intruder, but received a bullet wound. An enemy bullet also hit Townsend, but under fire he "crawled out of his foxhole and pulled his wounded buddy back to safety."[24]

Next morning, the 152nd Infantry counted 17 KIA, 110 WIA and 2 MIA lost on 7 February. The 129 total casualties were the most suffered by one regiment in one day during the ZigZag battle, except for the 178 of the 34th Infantry on 4 February. Little wonder that the 152nd called the Japanese MLR "Bloody Ridge."[25]

This attack by the 2nd and 3rd Battalions was perhaps more significant than the high command realized. It was the first time the GIs had forced their way into Major Ogawa's main line and slugged it out hand-to-hand with the foe. The 3rd Battalion finished the day's battle firmly ensconced between Minami and Ichinose, two of the most strongly held Japanese positions. The 2nd Battalion perimeter in front of Kasuga had set the stage for an XI Corps breakthrough of the vital Kita-Kasuga-Minami ridge.

The Americans had also accomplished another major objective by clearing the long ridge (Mount Koko) north of Highway 7. 2nd Battalion 152nd had made the final sweep on 7 February, but this vital terrain feature, that so effectively dominated the road approach to the Japanese Main Line of Resistance, had been 1st Battalion territory from the start.

It is not clear from the records who first realized the importance of this ridge, but the available evidence points to General Jones. It was he who first suggested following the ancient maxim of taking the high ground first. In his plan formulated on 4 February, Jones recommended that his men take the high ground from which "the enemy came down to the road" before trying to attack along the road (see pages 160-161). No real progress could be made until the enemy was cleared from his commanding perch on Mount Koko. Never again would the 38th Division be harassed from this eminence with well-observed artillery and mortar fire and well-conceived and executed night raids.

After the Japanese had evaluated the results of the day's action, Colonel Nagayoshi believed that the real objective of the American attack north of the road was his headquarters area at Mount Kongo (neither the existence of the headquarters nor its location was known by the Americans). Therefore, he moved his advance command post from the East Pass (the top of the ridge east of the Santa Rita River) to Mount Kongo. He assigned the 5th Company as security for the move and as Detachment Headquarters Guard to strengthen security at his headquarters. The Operations Company (similar to the Service Company in

American regiments) would man the Battle Command Post at the East Pass.[26]

🔥   🔥   🔥

3rd Battalion 151st began its flanking move to the south and east at 0925 after an artillery barrage and air strike. The battalion ducked under Japanese mortar fire as it emerged from the horseshoe and had one platoon atop Familiar Peak at 1330. Colonel Funkhouser dispatched a patrol toward the river and ordered I and L Companies to follow. With orders to capture the bridge but not to cross Highway 7, the lead elements reported reaching the bridge at 1630. The two companies dug in for the night along the river about 500 yards south of the bridge.[27]

Although the banks of the Santa Rita River are steep and the river unfordable at the bridge, infantry could ford the stream in many places. The only two casualties suffered by the battalion came from the mortar fire at the beginning of this daring venture that exposed the hollow shell of the enemy's defenses south of the pass.

The 149th Infantry had moved farther than expected by the end of the day—but against no opposition. Captain Ransohoff reported in late afternoon that the lead elements were in the vicinity of Balsic, 1,800 yards west of the day's objective, Bulate. They were moving along at a fairly good pace considering that the lead scouts had already entered the "ZigZag defile proper." The lead elements of the 1st Battalion dug in at Balsic for the night; 2nd Battalion halted 200 to 300 yards behind the rear of the 1st Battalion.[28]

Thirty-six-year-old Lieutenant Colonel Arthur C. Bonnycastle commanded the 1st Battalion. The Anchorage, KY, native had joined the National Guard in 1925 at age 17 and had been an industrial lubrication salesman for Standard Oil Company before the war. His battalion had already received its baptism of fire during the five-day battle for Buri Airstrip, Leyte, in December 1944.

Lieutenant Colonel Silas B. Dishman of Barboursville, KY, commanded the 2nd Battalion. According to 38th Division records, he joined the National Guard a month before his 15th birthday. He had been a civil engineer with the State Highway Department before the war.[29]

🔥   🔥   🔥

The day XI Corps finally started making a dent in the Japanese defenses was also a busy day for Brigadier General William C. Chase. Called by General MacArthur "an unsurpassed front-line fighter,"[30] he had led the "flying column" of the 1st Cavalry Division into Manila on 3 February and freed 3,700 internees at the University of Santo Tomas.

On 7 February, MacArthur "put his hands on my shoulders, congratulated me and said, 'Chase, well done! I have recommended you for promotion to Major General and have ordered you over to take command of the 38th Division, which is bogged down in ZigZag Pass east of Subic Bay.'"[31]

Chase escorted his chief to several locations in Manila, which had an emotional attachment for the former Marshal of the Philippines, and then to the front lines where the 1st Cavalry was fighting. He then bade adieu to his division commander, Major General Verne D. Mudge, and flew to Sixth Army Headquarters for a briefing by the Army's staff.

Major General William C. Chase, Commander 38th Infantry Division

"General Krueger fed us a fine big dinner and then told me very gruffly that he had had to relieve the commander of the 38th and that he wanted me to get them going—but fast!"[32] The new commander then flew to XI Corps Headquarters at San Marcelino where General Hall briefed him. Finally at 2100 hours 7 February, Chase arrived at 38th Division Headquarters with his aide, Captain Freidinger.

Before retiring for a few hours of rest, Chase approved General Easley's attack plans for 8 February and issued General Order #4 to the 38th Division: "The mission of this division is to recapture BATAAN and avenge the stigma of that 1942 defeat. I want all units to MOVE IN AND KILL JAPS. LET'S GO!"

With his closely clipped moustache, General Chase presented the same dapper, cocksure appearance as General Hall. Soon to be 50 in March, he was in the prime of a strictly military career. A New Englander by birth and ancestry, Chase was graduated from Brown University in 1916 with a Phi Beta Kappa key.

He had enlisted in Battery A, a horse-drawn artillery unit in the Rhode Island National Guard, in 1913. The afternoon of his graduation, he joined his battery, which had been mobilized for duty on the Mexican border. He saw no action, but the young sergeant passed the officers' examination while in El Paso and was commissioned a provisional 2nd Lieutenant of Cavalry in the regular army. During World War I, Chase commanded a company in the 11th Machine Gun Battalion of the 4th Division and fought in the second Battle of the Marne (Aisne-Marne offensive), the drive against the St. Mihiel salient, and the Meuse-Argonne campaign.

In the town of Sergy in late July 1918, Chase's brigade was attached to the 42nd "Rainbow" Division. Chase remembered in his autobiography that the fighting was bitter with heavy casualties. His company was not directly involved, but it was here that he first met Douglas MacArthur, Chief of Staff of the 42nd. "I remember going forward one night when our 4th Division relieved the 42nd and seeing MacArthur for the first time. He was unarmed, carried a riding crop and obviously had a magnetic effect on all with whom he came into contact."[33]

In World War II, General Chase became a marked man after he successfully led a reconnaissance in force and secured Los Negros Island in the Admiralties on 1 March 1944. This feat enabled MacArthur to complete the isolation of the large Japanese base at Rabaul with its thousands of combat-ready troops and in effect close out the Solomon Islands campaign. The Navy established a major United States base at Seeadler Harbor at this site to support further operations to the west in New Guinea and northwest in the Philippines.

The 1st Cavalry Division was an infantry division, but retained the World War I square division organization. Chase was commander of the 1st Cavalry Brigade of two regiments and led this brigade in the invasion of Leyte. For once, MacArthur disappointed him. "General MacArthur chose to make his historic 'I shall return' landing in the Philippines near Palo in the sector of the 24th Infantry Division. The fortunes of war . . . kept us out of the headlines at this most historic time," he lamented.[34]

Chase regained the limelight on 23 October, after Tacloban fell, and escorted MacArthur, Osmena (President of the Philippines), and numerous generals and admirals into the city in a hastily organized victory parade. MacArthur spoke to the assembled Filipinos and American officials from the steps of the capitol.[35] Commanding the "flying column" into Manila was merely the final icing on the cake; Chase richly deserved promotion to Major General and command of a division.

Chapter 15
NOTES

(1) 151st Infantry After Action Report (AAR), p. 3.

(2) Regimental histories and biographies of World War II leaders of 38th Division units, 38th Division files National Records Center, College Park, Maryland.

(3) 151st Infantry AAR, p. 4.

(4) *Ibid.*

(5) Walker, Major Stephen M., *The Operations of Company A 151st Infantry in the Attack Through ZigZag Pass*, Advanced Infantry Officers Course, Fort Benning, Georgia, 1949-1950, p. 10-12.

(6) 152nd Infantry journal;
1st Battalion 152nd Infantry journal.

(7) *History of the 39th Infantry Regiment,* edited and published by the 39th Infantry Association, p. 644.

(8) 1st Battalion 152nd Infantry journal, 0735.

(9) 38th Division G-3 message to XI Corps, 1935-07 February 1945.

(10) *How the Kato Company Fought: The Record of the 3rd Machine Gun Company 39th Infantry Regiment*, Tamotsu Nagai, Editor, 1990, p. 205;
39th Infantry History, p. 644.

(11) Ogawa, Major Hironori, *Record of the 3rd Battalion, 39th Infantry Regiment in the "Big Asia War,"* p. 37;
39th Infantry History, p. 644.

(12) 1st Battalion 152nd Infantry journal, 1110.

(13) XI Corps G-3 Memo, 1200-07 February 1945;
39th Infantry History, p. 644;
152nd Infantry journal;
Headquarters 38th Infantry Division General Order #6, 04 March 1945, Silver Star Medal Awards.

(14) Schoonover, Major James F., *The Operations of the 3rd Battalion 152nd Infantry in Zig Zag Pass, Luzon, 29 Jan.-14 Feb. 1945*, Advanced Infantry Officers Course, 1947-1948, p. 12.

(15) Kreis, Sergeant Don, Company L 152nd Infantry, letter to author, 4 February 1988;
Ogawa, *Record of the 3rd Battalion*, p. 38.

(16) Major Mangold was awarded the Silver Star for this action, Division General Order #6.

(17) Schoonover, *The Operations of the 3rd Battalion,* p. 12-13.

(18) *39th Infantry History,* p. 644;
Ogawa, *Record of the 3rd Battalion,* p. 38.

(19) Memo, Ransohoff to Monteith, G-3 XI Corps, 1800-07 February 1945;
Telephone message, 38th Division G-2 to Major Weaver G-2, section XI Corps.

(20) Sergeant Keller was awarded the Silver Star for this action.

(21) Schoonover, *The Operations of the 3rd Battalion,* p. 12.

(22) As related by Brewer in letter dated 7 March 1980 to Colonel Robert T. Fischer, Military History Project Director at Stout Field, assisting in writing book entitled *Indiana's Citizen Soldiers* published by the Adjutant General of Indiana. Indianapolis, 1980; Major Brewer was awarded the Silver Star for this action.

(23) *Ogawa, Record of the 3rd Battalion,* p. 38;
39th Infantry History, p. 644.

(24) Pfc. Townsend was awarded the Silver Star for this action.

(25) 152nd Infantry journal.

(26) Nagayoshi Detachment, Operation Order #73, 2100 7 February;
39th Infantry History, p. 646.

(27) 151st Infantry AAR, p. 4;
152nd Infantry journal, 1145.

(28) Memo Ransohoff to Monteith, 1800-07 February 1945.

(29) Regimental Biographies, 149th Infantry.

(30) MacArthur, General Douglas, *Reminiscences,* p. 204.

(31) Chase, Major General William C., *Front Line General,* p. 96.

(32) *Ibid.,* p. 99.

(33) *Ibid.,* p. 10.

(34) *Ibid.,* p. 64.

(35) *Ibid.,* p. 65.

AMERICAN CANNONADE
(8 FEBRUARY)

Determined to keep pressure on the Japanese MLR, General Easley planned an all-out assault for 8 February. 38th Division Field Order #12, signed by General Chase, outlined the overall plan.

The 151st Infantry, with the 603rd Tank Company attached, would pass through the 152nd Infantry at 0800 and press the attack eastward on Highway 7. From right to left along the front, the 2nd Battalion 151st would relieve Major Mangold's 3rd Battalion 152nd and be responsible south of the road. North of the road, the 1st Battalion 151st Infantry would relieve the 2nd Battalion 152nd. 1st Battalion 152nd would provide left flank security for the two 151st battalions and patrol north and east to the Santa Rita River. 2nd and 3rd Battalions 152nd would become the division reserve after their relief by the 151st. Division Artillery would place preparatory fires in front of the leading infantry units for 1 ½ hours (0630-0800) prior to the attack.

3rd Battalion 151st, from its present position along the Santa Rita River south of the Highway 7 bridge, would "attack north along Santa Rita River, destroy enemy vicinity Santa Rita River bridge, and continue attack to east along Hwy 7 . . . Effect junction with 149th Inf." Regarding the junction, the order repeated the instructions: "1st Bn 149th Inf and 3rd Bn 151st Inf gain contact as early as possible by every means available."[1]

The Japanese, of course, had observed the flanking move of 3/151 on 7 February to their left and rear, but Major Ogawa did not consider this force a threat. He was confident that Mount Shinshu and Mount Fumetsu, high above the Santa Rita River, would prove to be impervious to any attack mounted from the river.

After a nightlong harassment by Japanese infiltrators and mortar and artillery fire, American troops on the front lines gladly welcomed daylight and the scheduled artillery barrage. This 38th Division Artillery bombardment was by far the largest to precede any attack during the battle. It seemed that the high command was determined to atone in one day for all the frustrations since 31 January, many of which were blamed on inadequate artillery support. The largest previous barrage preceding an attack had been 2,105 rounds on 6 February with the average for the other days of February numbering 535 rounds (no rounds were fired in preparation for the attack on 2 February).

During what turned into a three-hour concentration, Division Artillery's 6 battalions (72 guns) plastered the front line positions on the Japanese MLR and rear areas with 16,919 rounds, roughly one-third the total expended during the entire battle. Artillery observers and front line commanders saturated with metal every known or suspected enemy machine gun, mortar or artillery position, ammunition dump and head-quarters area. So far ranging was the artillery that 3rd Battalion 151st south of the bridge over the Santa Rita reported at 0650 that the rounds were falling uncomfortably close.[2]

The records do not divulge the reasoning behind the decision to give massive artillery support on this date. Since General Hall would not give it to General Jones and General Chase was not on the scene when the decision was made, we must conjecture that General Easley persuaded Hall. It is also probable that Colonel Paddock, a man known to have a deep concern for his troops and the commander of the men who would make the attack, had a strong voice. As usual, General Chase was at the right place at the right time to reap the benefits of this wisdom.

To the Japanese, the bombardment must have seemed endless. Major Ogawa recalled in his memoirs written nearly 40 years later that the barrage started at 0530 *after* an all-night shelling. He estimated its dura-tion as five hours and its intensity as 50,000 rounds, augmented by the fire from three cruisers in Subic Bay. He wrote that 5,000 shells fell on his artillery position near the hairpin during a 30-minute span. Both 105-mm pieces were damaged, but after repair, continued to fire.[3]

In the artillery fire that smothered Mount Shinshu, a 155-mm round blew the log and dirt cover from Sergeant Hijikata's firing trench. Superior Private Hiroshi Yabuwaki and Pfc. Yasuroku Asaha, who had been posted as sentries, were killed instantly. Hijikata, a survivor who returned to Japan, described Yabuwaki as "flat as a pancake" with his abdomen gouged out.[4]

When Sergeant Nagai returned to duty, he had found his own previous foxhole destroyed. He had readily accepted Engineer 2nd Lieutenant Akio Nakamura's offer to share a three-man cave. Not used to wearing a helmet because of his wound, Nagai had been caught in the open with Lieutenant Shinfune when the early morning bombardment started. "We were lying flat on the ground. I heard a voice calling. I turned my head and saw my faithful friend Superior Private Yonekazu

Namura of the Morinaka Squad bringing a helmet for me. He had come through the bombardment!"[5]

The 39th Regimental Gun Platoon (75-mm) at Mount Shinshu tried to return fire, but American artillery killed three men and seriously wounded Squad Leader Corporal Matsui and three gunners. The position received a near direct hit, but the survivors quickly recovered and continued firing. The blanket of artillery found the battalion 70-mm gun position between Fumetsu and Ichinose. Despite a direct hit, the log and dirt roof held, although a gunner was killed by a flying shell fragment.[6]

By coincidence, 8 February was the Japanese Declaration of War Day. First established on 1 September 1939 to commemorate the beginning of World War II in Europe, the date was changed in 1942 to 8 January to honor Japanese accomplishments in the Pacific Ocean War.

On the eighth of each month, Japanese civilians were to think about the hardships and suffering on the battlefield and forget about their own private lives. This was a day of thrift—no smoking, no drinking, restaurants and places of entertainment closed—have a simple meal, go to Shinto temple and pray. Major Ogawa, deep in his headquarters cave at Mount Fumetsu, observed the sacrificial day by respectfully reading aloud the Emperor's Declaration of War during the three-hour bombardment. He ended the reading by exhorting his men to fight to the finish.[7]

✦   ✦   ✦

Little has been said of the 38th Division Artillery, which by its presence or absence markedly determined the progress at ZigZag Pass. The artillery was emplaced in the dry rice paddies north of Olongapo and could easily cover the fronts of the 151st and 152nd attacking east and the 149th attacking west. It was composed of the 138th, 139th and 163rd Battalions of 105-mm howitzers and the 150th Battalion of 155-mm howitzers. Each battalion had three batteries of four guns each. The three 105-mm battalions generally supported respectively the 149th, 151st and 152nd Regiments, and the 155-mm battalion supported all three.

38th Division Artillery also controlled two battalions of the 24th Division: the 63rd of 105-mm guns, which originally supported the 34th Infantry in the Zambales Operation and had been part of the 34th RCT; and the 11th of 155-mm howitzers loaned to XI Corps to substitute for the 150th, which was enroute from Oro Bay when the Zambales Operation began. The battalions were tied together by position area survey with targets in the pass so that the thunder of all 72 guns could be brought down immediately on one point at one time, if needed.[8]

Of the XI Corps Artillery, the 155-mm rifles of the 983rd F.A. Battalion were used sparingly. Because of a lack of ammunition, the 8-

inch howitzers of the 544th F.A. Battalion, mentioned in the Eighth Army's AAR, were not used in ZigZag Pass.[9]

Brigadier General William Spence commanded the 38th Division Artillery. The 51-year-old Georgian had served brilliantly as a young officer in World War I. A graduate of West Point in 1916, he organized and trained a battery of the 18th F.A. that became part of the 3rd Division in France in April 1918. After serving in the Aisne-Marne operation with this unit, he commanded the 2nd Battalion 150th F.A. of the 42nd "Rainbow" Division in the St. Mihiel and Meuse-Argonne offensives. In World War II, he organized and commanded the 93rd Division Artillery, which arrived in the Pacific in January 1944. He assumed command of the 38th Division Artillery in November 1944.[10]

The journals of the three 38th Division infantry regiments and their battalions showed a marked change on 8 February. The 38th Division staff had prepared a 1:10,000 scale map based on the reports of ground and aerial observers and aerial photographs, which had become available on 3 February. Units could now report their locations in the same all-numbers co-ordinate system used by Corps and Division instead of the letter-number system they had been using. The map was a vast improvement over the 1:50,000 maps with which the troops had been struggling.

The new map pinpointed the known and suspected locations of enemy mortars, machine guns, anti-tank guns and ammo-supply dumps. It showed with a reasonable degree of accuracy the hills and ridges the Japanese had chosen for their defensive positions. Now all American units had a better sense of the Japanese defensive scheme and were using the same co-ordinate system to designate their locations.[11]

💣   💣   💣

Sleep was difficult for the 151st Infantry encamped along Highway 7 during the night of 7-8 February. Besides being "keyed up" for the impending attack, artillery fire was continuous all night. The 1st Battalion 151st was aroused at 0400 and a hot breakfast served to all at 0500. By 0630, the battalion was on the march in the order of B, C, Hqs, D and A Companies, in column on either side of the road.

Frequent pauses to permit the evacuation of casualties from front to rear and movement of supplies from rear to front made the going slow. At about 0730, the battalion moved off the road in single file onto a trail leading to the 2nd Battalion 152nd CP on the reverse slope of Mount Hissho. Nearly denuded by constant shelling, the hill was now a barren plateau.

Major Stewart's plan of attack for his 1st Battalion called for B and C Companies to cross the hill abreast, with A Company following 200 yards behind C Company. Stewart attached a platoon of D Company's heavy machine guns to each of the two leading rifle companies. The rest of D Company and Headquarters Company brought up the rear.[12]

While the artillery preparation was in full sway, guides from the 152nd Infantry led the 1st and 2nd Battalions 151st to their positions on the Line of Departure (LD), the eastern slope of Mount Hissho. Major Stewart and Colonel Mottern, respectively commanders of the 1st and 2nd Battalions 151st, received their copies of Field Order #12 on their way to the LD. Information concerning the enemy was meager, only that "they are out there and plenty." Colonel Mottern was further handicapped because his E Company was still enroute to Luzon from Oro Bay, New Guinea, and two platoons of G Company had not returned from a patrol to eliminate snipers north of the Division CP.

To the men of the 152nd on the front lines and to the 151st relieving them, it was inconceivable that the Japanese had any fight left in them after the pounding they had received. When the artillery fire lifted at 0800, as originally scheduled, relief of the 152nd by the 151st had not been fully effected. At once the enemy brought down heavy mortar fire on the LD. Thirty-Eighth Division Artillery resumed its bombardment.[13]

B and C Companies 151st reached the Line of Departure on Mount Hissho in the midst of this heavy and accurate Japanese mortar barrage. Both the 1st Battalion 151st and 2nd Battalion 152nd were in the open atop the hill as the Japanese mortars began to cover the area systematically. The battalions suffered moderate to heavy casualties before American counter battery fire silenced the enemy. But the damage had been done. Forty-five minutes elapsed while medics treated and evacuated the casualties. Considerable intermingling and confusion in both battalions was the natural result from the barrage.[14]

True to his sobriquet—"front line general"—General Chase arrived at the 151st Infantry CP at 0845, perhaps to determine the cause of the delay. Chase was like a breath of fresh air. With a natural bubbly personality, he was confident, upbeat, with an enthusiasm that permeated the division. Sergeant Keller of D Company 152nd summed up the feeling: "With General Jones and Colonel Stillwell we had to stop and investigate every time we were fired on. When we got General Chase we just went!"[15]

Finally the 1st and 2nd Battalions 151st were in place; but when they moved out at 0900, they received the usual withering machine gun and rifle fire from the entire ridgeline on both sides of the road. A draw leading to the northern end of Mount Ege was a mass of scattered bamboo left in a complex tangle by American artillery and mortars.[16]

After relieving 3rd Battalion 152nd, Colonel Mottern advanced F Company against the still strong positions on Ichinose Heights. When G Company's two platoons returned from their patrols north of the Division CP, he sent that company to the right into sniper-infested foliage guarding well-concealed emplacements. To the men of G Company, it must have seemed as if the bombardment had not taken place. The Japanese riflemen were still in front in their accustomed positions protecting the Morimoto and Morinaka machine guns.[17]

The machine gunners of the Ueno and Ogaki Squads kept up a rapid tattoo all morning. After the cover over the trench he had repaired the night before was destroyed, Sergeant Ueno jumped out of his trench and held his heavy machine gun on his knees while firing at F Company's men approaching.[18]

At 1305, F Company reported that it had lost almost all of one platoon and requested tanks and flamethrowers. Tanks mauled the machine gun nests, despite the threat of suicide attackers, until one tank exhausted its ammunition. Believing the position was reduced, another section of tanks moved to place fire on the bamboo-strewn draw. The platoon of tanks withdrew after Corporal Mano's 70-mm gun crew disabled one tank.[19]

Both Sergeants Ueno and Ogaki were killed in this tank fusillade, but their men and the suicide tank attackers continued the fight. At 1440, 2nd Battalion 151st called for ambulances and blood plasma, pleas indicative of its hard battle. Company G reached the foot of the southern slope of Ege, but could not wrest this left anchor of the Japanese line from Lieutenant Shinfune's well dug-in and determined troops.[20]

💣 💣 💣

North of the road, 1st Battalion 151st advanced but 300 yards for the day. Major Stewart's men started from the Hissho ridge to which 2/152nd had pulled back before its relief to avoid the preparatory artillery barrage. Stewart's objective was to occupy all of Mount Minami. The fighting was fierce, and 1st Battalion made little progress toward reducing this rock-solid redoubt.[21]

Shortly after crossing the Line of Departure, the terrain became so rough that 1st Battalion's attack unraveled into a movement by column of rifle companies. C Company maintained the lead; next B Company; A Company brought up the rear. The men had to be especially wary of booby traps the Japanese had left along the trail.

Major Stewart and the Battalion S-3 marched with the head of C Company most of the day. There was little communication with Captain Stephen M. Walker commanding A Company in the rear. To Captain

Walker, it seemed that the leading elements were meeting only sporadic resistance at the front. To him, the attack was a succession of short movements forward and frequent halts while C Company cleaned out pockets of the enemy.[22]

General Easley visited the 151st CP at 1340. He decided to call for an air strike to burn out suspected ammo dumps at the hairpin and mortar sites back of the Japanese MLR that were not crushed during the three-hour artillery barrage. Front line battalions marked their positions with colored smoke. At 1500, the 309th Bomb Wing dropped seven napalm bombs (one in back of Mount Kita), starting three fires in the area.[23]

From the air, Captain Ransohoff reported ammo dumps hit, causing numerous explosions and flames, which were still burning when he left the scene at 1740. The strike had no immediate effect on the front line fighting. 1st and 2nd Battalions 151st resumed their attacks at 1525, but were met with the same familiar refrain: "heavy machine gun fire." Sergeant Iga's machine gun even joined in from 700 yards away on Mount Shinshu. By 1600, neither battalion had reached a point where it could dig in without being pinned down by Japanese fire. Colonel Paddock ordered both to pull back to the initial LD.[24]

Major Stewart ordered his companies to dig a battalion perimeter for the night. Stewart chose an open spot on a forward slope for the perimeter, hardly large enough for a battalion in Captain Walker's opinion. In the tightly organized perimeter, each rifle company was responsible for a third of the area. Each man had brought a K-ration with him for supper.

As Walker crouched with one squad leader and his assistant squad leader concerning some detail of organizing the perimeter, a Japanese light machine gun fired a burst of six or seven rounds. The burst killed the assistant squad leader instantly, placed three bullets in the squad leader's chest, but left Walker untouched. After first aid, men from his squad dug a hole to protect the badly wounded squad leader until he could be evacuated the next morning. He subsequently recovered.

The Japanese moved around the perimeter all night, throwing grenades, but doing little damage. Fortunately, the battalion's grenades were collected before darkness and redistributed to the men in the outer foxholes on the perimeter. This move served a double purpose. Men on the perimeter could retaliate against the Japanese, and men on the inside would not make unwise tosses.[25]

The gains made by the 151st during the day may seem insignificant, but another important piece of real estate had been seized from the enemy. 3rd Battalion 152nd had driven a wedge into the defense at

Ichinose Heights on 7 February. 2nd Battalion 151st's constant pressure at the same point on 8 February finally overcame the few die-hard defenders and secured this northern portion of the twin-domed Mount Ege ridge. The Ichinose Anti-tank Company for practical purposes ceased to exist; Lieutenant Kato reported the Ueno and Ogaki HMG Squads "destroyed."

The greatest loss to the Japanese was another incomparable and irreplaceable fighter—1st Lieutenant Masanobu Miyazaki, the 10th Company commander. A death bullet found him bravely leading his company in resisting the 1st Battalion 151st attack on Mount Minami. His willingness to assume any responsibility regardless of danger, personal bravery under fire, and leadership ability were an inspiration to all. Ogawa wrote that, "he exemplified the ideal of the military spirit."[26]

✦   ✦   ✦

1st Battalion 152nd on the 151st's left could show greater gains for the day despite an inauspicious start. At 1145, while waiting for the 151st's attack to develop, a Japanese artillery barrage caught Colonel Cornwell's men in the open and caused several casualties.

Undaunted, the battalion moved out at 1245 in a column of companies with A Company leading. Its path carried the battalion toward the

Peace Memorial at top of the "2" erected in 1980's by Kazanobu Miyazaki, brother of Masanobu Miyazaki, killed 8 February; Ichinose Heights is in the background

rugged defenses of steep Mount Kita, organized by Major Ogawa to combat flank attacks against his stronger positions nearer the road. The air strike held up the 1st Battalion at 1350, and Cornwell did not resume his march until 1600.

Surprisingly, there was practically no opposition. All three rifle companies dug in on this dominating height for the night. The 10th Company had occupied Kita in force previously, but Major Ogawa had shifted most of Lieutenant Miyazaki's defenders south to meet the more immediate threat along the road.[27]

Only a few 10th Company men protecting the two 90-mm mortars in rear of Mount Kita, commanded by Master Sergeant Fujimoto, were defending Kita. After expending all his ammunition on the 1st Battalion 152nd, Fujimoto rendered the mortars inoperable and buried them to prevent their falling into enemy hands.

Sergeant Hijikata on Mount Shinshu covered Fujimoto's withdrawal. He opened fire on 1st Battalion men moving down the hillside against Fujimoto's rear guard and claimed several Americans fell from his accurate fire. The rear guard survivors eventually made their way back to Mount Fumetsu.[28]

Miraculously, Hijikata's heavy machine gun was still operating, despite the Americans' nearly constant artillery barrages since early morning. "When we disassembled the gun for cleaning at the end of the day, only the aiming sight had been broken," Hijikata wrote later. "I went to the Battalion Headquarters cave to report my casualties and the damaged gun. Major Ogawa and Lieutenant Kato were there. After I completed my report, Lieutenant Kato said, 'You have had a rough day, haven't you?' I nodded, and he handed me a bottle of whiskey. I brought it back to the gun position, and my squad finished it off that evening."[29]

By occupying Mount Kita, 1st Battalion 152nd had outflanked the seemingly impenetrable Japanese position at Minami. Colonel Cornwell telephoned to the rear for 500 hand grenades and machine gun, BAR, M-1, and .45-caliber ammunition in case the enemy tried to knock him off this key objective during the night. 1st Battalion patrols had roamed northward to the Santa Rita River and found no opposition.[30]

During the 1st Battalion 152nd's advance, Sergeant Ancelet of D Company again showed his prowess with explosives. He and members of his mortar platoon reported demolishing five pillboxes, nine supply dumps and two high caliber guns. Constant danger from booby traps and ammunition dump explosions always accompanied those charged with cleaning up enemy positions that had been overrun. This was the first inkling of the considerable Japanese stores and equipment that would be captured after each successful attack.[31]

❧ ❧ ❧

Colonel Funkhouser's 3rd Battalion 151st, dug-in along the river about 500 yards south of the Santa Rita River bridge, did not advance appreciably during the day for reasons not readily apparent. The battalion's missions given in Field Order #12 were to attack north along the river, destroy the enemy in the vicinity of the bridge, continue the attack eastward along Highway 7, and effect a junction with the 149th Infantry. The sequence of reports during the day regarding the battalion's movements makes interesting reading.

At 1105, an artillery liaison officer from the 139th F.A. reported that the lead elements of the 3rd Battalion were pinned down by machine gun fire just east of the river and south of the bridge. At 1220, Colonel Paddock reported to his regimental command post by radio that the 3rd Battalion "was held down by machine gun firing from position near bridge." Colonel Monteith, XI Corps G-3, reported at 1400 that artillery fire had "successfully silenced" this enemy fire.

At 1257, Colonel Funkhouser reported that the bridge was "blown and badly damaged," that he was advancing east, but had not made contact with the 149th Infantry. At 1350, Captain Ransohoff reported from the air that he could not locate elements of the 3rd Battalion that had reportedly reached the Santa Rita River bridge. At 1735, Colonel Funkhouser radioed Colonel Paddock that an I Company combat patrol had reported reaching a point at 1230 that we know now would have placed the patrol directly south of the Nakayama Battalion's defensive position. About an hour later, Captain Ransohoff observed the lead elements of the 149th under sniper fire not more than 1,000 yards northeast of the patrol's position at 1230. The patrol returned to the company perimeter by 1730.[32]

Colonel Funkhouser had ostensibly accomplished his first mission by capturing the bridge, but had failed to accomplish his second and more important mission of making contact with the 149th Infantry. The second mission, on the surface, does not appear to have been hazardous or difficult. The air strike would not have been a deterrent. The strike was set to fall 1,000 yards north of the bridge and north of Highway 7. Each company marked its position with colored smoke grenades for identification during the air strike. The 3/151 received special instructions by radio to identify its element nearest the target area.

Funkhouser could not very well follow his orders and attack east on Highway 7. Beyond the bridge, the road begins a sharp, twisting ascent to the high ground of the East Pass. Two-thirds of the 5th Company occupied this height and could have put up a stout defense.

Unaware of the Nakayama Battalion's location, Funkhouser may have been hesitant to send only a small patrol to make contact with the 149th. However, he could have sent I Company in its entirety on the southerly route taken by its patrol to reach the 149th Infantry. No reason is apparent why I Company could not have bypassed the enemy, and by working south and east, have reached the 149th.

The opportunity was missed. The Nakayama Battalion introduced a new element into the battle in the east the next day, giving Funkhouser little chance to make contact. It is difficult to understand why Funkhouser, who was apparently in direct radio contact with his own regiment, if not the 149th as well, could not explain his options and obtain more positive direction.

At 1735, Captain Ransohoff observed that Funkhouser's men were occupying the same "slit trenches" of the previous night. He reported no sign of 3rd Battalion troops on Highway 7 as he said he had expected. Company L dug a separate perimeter 700 yards east of the river south of the road about 1,400 yards west of the Nakayama Battalion. At the end of the day, Division attached 3rd Battalion 151st to the 149th Infantry in an effort to effect a better co-ordination for the expected link-up the next day.[33]

♦ ♦ ♦

In contrast to 3/151st, the 149th made good progress, despite determined opposition from the Nakayama Battalion. Major Nakayama had constructed his defensive line about 1,200 yards west of Balsic. His positions were dug into rough ground along a ridgeline with hills closely abutting Highway 7 like the convergence of Mount Minami and Mount Ege in the West Pass.

Most of the approximately 300 men comprising the battalion were Air Force personnel who had flown and serviced 25 fighter/reconnaissance planes out of the San Marcelino Airfield. After the Mindoro airfields became operational for the Americans in December 1944, 22 of the planes had been destroyed in less than a month. The remaining three were flown to Saigon.

On 10 January, the day after the Lingayen landings, General Yamashita ordered the airmen to join his Shobu Group at Baguio. Colonel Nagayoshi had their orders changed, placing them under his command. Apparently not telling the airmen beforehand about the change in orders, Nagayoshi commandeered the group as they marched through his lines along Highway 7 and made them a part of his North Garrison Unit. On 23

January, Nagayoshi placed Major Takao Nakayama, who had joined the 39th Infantry in Manila, in command of the airmen with the mission of stopping any American force advancing from Dinalupihan.

In addition to the 265 men from San Marcelino, Nakayama also had under his command a platoon of the Manila Bay Special Attack Force. He organized his command into three companies of approximately 100 men each. He positioned two companies on his main line and used his remaining company as a reserve. Major Nakayama was an experienced infantry officer and considered an excellent commander by the airmen.

The provisional battalion commander was fortunate in having as commander of his First Company an experienced infantry officer, 1st Lieutenant Yuichiro Nagata, communications officer of the 15th Air Force Unit. Nagata had been in the same class at the Military Academy in Tokyo as Kiyotaka Kato, the 3rd Battalion 39th Infantry Machine Gun Company commander, but had later joined the Air Force.

According to Lieutenant Nagata, only about 50 of the airmen turned infantrymen possessed rifles. The remainder were armed only with hand grenades. It was vital to their survival that they retrieve the weapons of any Americans they killed.

For heavier armament, Colonel Nagayoshi allotted Major Nakayama the platoon of either two or three tanks of 1st Lieutenant Keuichi Araki and one 50-mm mortar/grenade launcher from the 39th Regiment. The versatile airmen had adapted five machine guns from their planes for infantry use.[34]

Company G, the point of the leading 2nd Battalion 149th Infantry, moved out cautiously at 0700 from Balsic along Highway 7, gradually ascending into ZigZag Pass. At 0800, machine gun fire from a cave north of the road pinned down the lead platoon. Colonel Skelton ordered G Company to destroy the enemy position and left the company under command of the trailing 1st Battalion. 2nd Battalion moved on with F Company at the point. Using white phosphorous and demolition hand grenades, G Company overcame the Japanese in the cave at about noon without casualties.[35]

In the meantime, F Company had run into a strong machine gun pillbox position at 1030. This hornet's nest held up the 2nd Battalion until 1315. Captain Ransohoff observed late in the afternoon that F Company's leading elements were now slightly forward of the spot a patrol had penetrated the previous day. The captain counted eight men being borne to the rear on stretchers, indicative of the hard fighting during the day. 2nd Battalion alone reported 35 casualties, including two lieutenants and six sergeants. Company F was the hardest hit, numbering 12 killed among a total of 26 casualties. In its first brush with the Nakayama Battalion the 149th suffered its largest daily casualty figure during the campaign. The regiment reported killing 30 of the enemy during the day.[36]

Unlike the Americans, who were using tanks daily to try to smash through the pass, Colonel Nagayoshi reasoned that his tanks from the 2nd Tank Division could be used to better advantage in the less rugged terrain to the east. The tanks, with their five-man crews, were the standard 1937 vintage medium Type 97 of Japanese tank regiments. They weighed 16 tons and carried a 47-mm gun and two 7.7-mm (.30-caliber) machine guns, one firing to the front and the other to the rear. Their armor was inferior to the American M-4 Sherman's and greatly inferior to most German and Russian tanks. In Bataan's rough and inhospitable terrain, the tanks could not exploit their 24-mph speed and 130-mile range.

Major Nakayama had planned to counterattack the strung out Americans on his front with his tanks at the first opportunity. At 2030, he launched two tanks and a company of riflemen to destroy the lead American company in perimeter west of Balsic. The Japanese force came close enough to see and fire on the lead company's foxholes, but there was never any danger of a breakthrough. Colonel Dishman, the 2nd Battalion commander, brought down heavy artillery fire on the suspected location of the tanks and called on the 138th F.A. Battalion to harass the intruders the rest of the night.[37]

From the beginning of the ZigZag operation, the Americans had found that locating the Japanese defensive positions was one of their greatest problems. Observation and identification of worthwhile targets for the artillery had taxed all commanders. Cleared areas were very scarce in the pass and then only on hilltops. Artillery forward observers on the ground could see only a few yards.

Therefore, air observation was used to the maximum extent to direct artillery fire. Artillery observation planes roamed the skies from before dawn until dusk and many times after dark. Lieutenant Colonel Joseph H. Hodges, Jr., CO of the 11th F.A. Battalion, was a veteran of all the 24th Division's campaigns. This was the only time he had seen observation planes sent up at night to adjust artillery fire.[38]

The light, single engine L-5 and Piper Cub observation planes utilized the dry rice paddies northeast of Olongapo for landing fields. The fields were behind the area where the 155-mm howitzers of the 11th F.A. Battalion were emplaced in a dry streambed. As they cruised the battle-field in the 65-80 mph range, the planes were in constant danger of being hit by Japanese machine gunners.[39]

On 3 February, Major Ogawa stationed six machine guns in an anti-aircraft zone in the area south of Highway 7 between the battalion 70-mm guns and the Jukaki-dai. Sergeant Hijikata claimed the artillery observation planes steered clear of this area until Ichinose Heights fell on 7 February.[40]

One observation plane had already been lost, but not due to enemy fire. On 5 February, a plane of the 150th F.A. Battalion flew across its battery front and was destroyed by a 155-mm round fired by one of the "Long Toms" deep in the rear.[41]

In mid-morning 8 February, 1st Lieutenant Hollister G. DeMotts, one of the artillery observation plane pilots, received a letter from his wife at mail call at the 11th F.A. Battalion CP. Talking with 1st Lieutenant Edwin A. Ellinghausen, B Battery commander, DeMotts mentioned something in the letter his wife had written about his son. DeMotts then told Ellinghausen that he must leave to fly a mission.[42]

The mission turned out to be adjusting fire for the 138th F.A. Battalion. After bracketing a target at about 1230, DeMotts radioed "fire for effect." That was the last message received from DeMotts.

Major Cogswell of the 38th Division Artillery immediately went aloft and located the plane in a wooded area 800 yards north of Highway 7 about 1,000 yards west of the 149th Infantry's leading elements. The plane had apparently made a crash landing in a small clearing. There was no evidence of fire, but the nose and one wing appeared to be damaged. Nothing could be seen of DeMotts.[43]

1st Lieutenant Willis L. Chilcote of St. Louis, MO, commanding C Battery 11th F.A., sent a patrol on 9 February that was successful in finding the plane and recovering DeMotts's body. From reports of ground observation of the plane, Chilcote deduced the circumstances regarding the crash.

The plane was not severely damaged. DeMotts had not reported mechanical problems and was within gliding range of American lines. Chilcote concluded that ground fire had forced the plane down. "There were many bullet holes in the plane and cockpit that were of a horizontal path. In addition, there were holes of a vertical path." It appeared to Chilcote that DeMotts "was hit in the air, managed to land the plane without extensive damage, but died from enemy rifle fire while on the ground."[44]

✦　　✦　　✦

Meanwhile, the Japanese were contemplating their future, which must have preyed on their minds constantly. When darkness came, Lieutenant Nakamura, Sergeant Nagai, as spokesman, and Pfc. Oshita fried dry bread with palm oil in their cave on Mount Ege. "The taste of the bread was delicious. We sat in a circle in the cave and smoked my last Imperial gift cigarettes. We were buried deep in thought anticipating what tomorrow would bring."[45]

Chapter 16
NOTES

(1) 38th Division Field Order #12 08-0830 February 1945 par. 3.e.

(2) 1st Battalion 152nd Infantry journal reported barrage started at 0600. The 151st Infantry attack did not start until 0900. 151st Infantry AAR reported "artillery preparation was continuous from 0600 to 0900," p. 4;
38th Division Artillery Unit History (ZigZag Pass phase), M-7 Operation, Luzon, 16 January-30 June 1945. Department of the Army, The Adjutant General's Office, Washington, D.C. (Summarized in Appendix C of this volume.)

(3) Ogawa, Major Hironori, *Record of the 3rd Battalion, 39th Infantry Regiment in the "Big Asia War,"* p. 40.

(4) *How the Kato Company Fought: The Record of the 3rd Machine Gun Company 39th Infantry Regiment*, Tamotsu Nagai, Editor, 1990, p. 209.

(5) *Ibid.,* p. 218.

(6) *History of the 39th Infantry Regiment,* edited and published by the 39th Infantry Association, p. 647.

(7) Ogawa, *Record of the 3rd Battalion,* p. 40;
39th Infantry History, p. 647.

(8) 38th Division Artillery Report (Appendix C).

(9) After Action Report (AAR) of the Commanding General Eighth Army on the Nasugbu and Bataan Operations Mike 6 and Mike 7. Property of the Office of the Chief of Military History, Section VIII, Subic Bay Operations, p. 98.

(10) Regimental histories and biographies of World War II leaders of 38th Division units. 38th Division files National Records Center, College Park, MD.

(11) Author used a copy of this map in the preparation of this volume.

(12) Walker, Major Stephen M., *The Operations of Company A, 151st Infantry in the Attack Through ZigZag Pass 8-11 February 1945,* Advanced Infantry Officers Course, 1949-50, p. 13.

(13) 151st Infantry AAR, p. 4.

(14) Walker, *The Operations of Company A,* p. 14.

(15) Keller interview by author, 27 July 1990.

(16) 151st Infantry AAR, p. 4.

(17) *Ibid.,* p. 5.

(18) Kato Company History, p. 187.

(19) 151st Infantry AAR, p. 5.

(20) *Ibid.*;
151st Infantry journal;
Kato Company History, p. 43.

(21) XI Corps G-3 Periodic Report #11, 1800-08 February 1945.

(22) Walker, *The Operations of Company A*, p. 14.

(23) 151st Infantry journal.

(24) 151st Infantry AAR, p. 5;
Kato Company History, p. 205;
Memo Ransohoff to Monteith Report of Air Observation 8
February 1945.

(25) Walker, *The Operations of Company A*, p. 15-16.

(26) Kato Company History, 43;
Ogawa, *Record of the 3rd Battalion*, p. 41.

(27) 1st Battalion 152nd Infantry journal.

(28) Ogawa, *Record of the 3rd Battalion*, 41;
39th Infantry History, p. 647;
Kato Company History, p. 209.

(29) Kato Company History, p. 210.

(30) 1st Battalion 152nd Infantry journal.

(31) Hq 38th Division, General Order #6, 4 March 1945, Award of
Silver Star Medal to Sergeant Ancelet.

(32) 1105—Report by 38th Division G-2—Summary Report of
Morning's Activities;
1220—151st Infantry journal entry #58;
1400—Monteith memo to CG XI Corps;
1257—Message G-2 38th Division to G-2 XI Corps—1600;
1350—Memo Ransohoff to Monteith—Report of Air
Observation;
1735—151st Infantry journal entry #85;
1350—Memo Ransohoff to Monteith—Report of Air
Observation.

(33) 151st Infantry journal entries #65, 66, 94;
1735—Memo Ransohoff to Monteith—Report of Air
Observation.

(34) Letter, Nagata to author, 24 June 92;
The Sho Army Operations, Part 2: The Decisive Battle for Luzon.

Senshi Sosho Operations, Vol. 60, p. 262;
39th Infantry History, p. 621.

(35) 2nd Battalion 149th Infantry journal.
(36) *Ibid.*;
Memo Ransohoff to Monteith—Report of Air Observation.
(37) 2nd Battalion 149th Infantry journal.
(38) 38th Division Artillery Report (Appendix C);
Hodges letter to author, 15 October 1988.
(39) Letter of 1st Lieutenant Willis L. Chilcote, commanding C
Battery 11th F.A. to author, 29 November 1990.
(40) Kato Company History, p. 209.
(41) *YANK Magazine*, March 1945;
Chilcote letter to author, 18 October 1990.
(42) Ellinghausen letter to author, 19 October 1991.
(43) Message—G-2 38th Division to G-2 XI Corps, 1905-08 February.
(44) Chilcote letters to author, 18 October 1990 and 29 November
1990.
(45) Kato Company History, p. 220.

"KILL OR BE KILLED"

(9 FEBRUARY)

Front line units had sensed a slackening in Japanese mortar fire since the early morning artillery bombardment of 8 February, but this perspective changed that night. What 38th Division Headquarters termed an "extremely heavy mortar and artillery barrage" rained down on the 1st and 2nd Battalions of the 151st and the 1st Battalion of the 152nd the night of 8-9 February. To the frontline commanders, it seemed that the Japanese were purposely shifting their fire from one area to another to cause the Americans to disclose their positions. The Nipponese attempted to penetrate the perimeters of the 151st in several places (Mottern called them Banzai attacks), but to no avail. Any Japanese casualties the GIs inflicted were removed before dawn.[1]

Colonel Wilson, the 38th Division G-2, called this "sudden flare-up" at 2050 the "most extensive firefight yet experienced." The fight lasted nearly two hours. Colonel Wilson reported, "extremely heavy 120-mm and possibly some 150-mm artillery heard."[2] Colonel Nagayoshi had no 150-mm artillery. Despite the complete silence of the Japanese on the subject of 120-mm mortars, it is evident they were used extensively after Sergeant Fujimoto destroyed the two 90-mm mortars on 8 February. How else to explain the extremely heavy and widespread mortar fire that descended many times on the Americans during the battle and continued after 8 February?

A photograph in the 38th Division AAR shows a group of soldiers crowded around a captured 120-mm mortar with a notation that three others had been destroyed. The 1:10,000 map prepared by Division G-3 locates three of the mortars—one on Mount Minami, one near the Shinshu position and one on the hairpin side of the Santa Rita River north of the bridge. On 6 February, Corps Technical Intelligence had identified mortar fragments found in the vicinity of Familiar Peak as 120-mm.[3]

Veterans of the Kato HMG Company, when shown the photograph in the 38th Division AAR, thought the scene was posed and had nothing to do with ZigZag Pass. Major Ogawa in his memoirs and the 39th Infantry history make no mention of 120-mm mortars. However, they do describe in some detail the acquisition of other extra heavy weapons for the battle: two tanks, the two 90-mm mortars, two additional 37-mm anti-tank guns, and two 105-mm howitzers. It is one of the several mysteries of ZigZag Pass that the Japanese make no mention of 120-mm mortars in their memoirs of the battle.

At daybreak, three dazed Japanese soldiers wandered into the A Company 151st perimeter. They obviously thought they were in an area still controlled by their battalion. Zealous American riflemen, who rarely saw the enemy at night, were all too eager to dispatch three such tempting targets in daylight.[4]

Incredulously, there were no American casualties during the night. Division G-2 concluded that the "very ferocity of his [the Japanese] defense indicates he is resolved to make a determined last stand." This was nothing new. As one historian of the war in the Pacific so aptly observed: "Among the characteristics that [made] the Japanese a formidable opponent was his refusal to accept defeat even in a hopeless situation."[5]

In selecting his plan of attack for 9 February, General Chase had few alternatives except to continue the attack of the previous day. 1st Battalion 151st and 1st Battalion 152nd north of the road, and 2nd Battalion 151st and (as the attack developed) 2nd Battalion 152nd south would renew their frontal assaults on the main Japanese line. North of the road 1st Battalion 151st was to consolidate its hold on the western slope of Mount Minami and then strike eastward to secure the remainder of Minami. 1st Battalion 152nd's objective was the northern portion of the Shinshu position.

To the south, 2nd Battalion 151st would attempt to occupy the remainder of Mount Ege and then press on toward Mount Fumetsu. The primary objective of 3/151st was to make physical contact with the 149th Infantry. Although maintaining good radio communications, the two were still 1,500 yards apart. Division, urged by Corps, was pressing Colonel Paddock and Colonel Skelton to make physical contact. 3rd Battalion 151st was to make an all-out effort to shake hands with the 149th this day.[6]

Company E 151st Infantry had still not reached the battlefield. General Chase, therefore, ordered Colonel McIntosh to alert one battalion from the 152nd to reinforce the attack on the right. McIntosh chose Colonel Rice's 2nd Battalion.[7]

Following a much lighter artillery preparation (408 rounds) than the day before, the 151st attacked at 0900. Colonel Mottern's 2nd Battalion south of the road met immediate heavy machine gun fire from the Morimoto and Morinaka machine guns defending Mount Ege. Two more heavy machine guns supporting the enemy's 70-mm gun between Fumetsu and Ichinose Heights helped stop the battalion in its tracks.

Mottern had planned to use flamethrowers on the Japanese bunkers protecting the machine guns, but discovered early in the day that the flamethrowers did not work. He made an urgent call for more while F and G Companies, using grenades, tried to advance against Sergeant Morimoto's machine gun. The flamethrowers never did arrive. By 0945, 2nd Battalion 151st was in desperate straits. Both companies cowered under heavy Japanese automatic fire. The men were firing wildly. 1st Battalion 151st across the road was even reporting that Mottern's men were firing into them. It was time for the reinforcements from the left.[8]

McIntosh initially sent a rifle platoon (the third) from G/152nd, reinforced with a light machine gun and 60-mm mortar, to help 2nd Battalion 151st. Colonel Paddock also sent a platoon of tanks to help reduce the opposition facing Mottern.[9]

These measures had little effect. 2nd Lieutenant Yoneji Yanase, leader of the battalion 70-mm gun platoon, had devised a scheme to deal with the tanks. He felled a tree across the road at the eastern end of Mount Minami, and Pfc. Senji Fujihara volunteered to lead a three-man team to destroy the lead tank. One of the volunteers was Pfc. Masahiro Kawanaka from Sergeant Iga's heavy machine gun squad.

Fujihara's team dug in carefully along the road and camouflaged their positions expertly. By pre-arranged signal, Japanese machine gun fire pinned down the rifle squads protecting the tanks. Division G-2 described the action: "One man with explosives [probably Fujihara] threw same into track of tank, which exploded, wrecking the tank, setting the tank on fire, and blowing up ammunition." Kawanaka was killed by the blast of a tank shell. The damaged tank effectively blocked the road for the rest of the day. After dark, soldiers of the Yanase Platoon emptied the tank of everything of value.[10]

At 1117, Mottern said he was receiving "terrific mortar fire" and requested that the 2nd Battalion Anti-tank Platoon be sent forward immediately to serve as infantry. The enemy was dug into deep tunnels. Mottern's men were using pole charges and grenades, but the tenacious defenders kept up a steady fire.[11]

Anticipating that additional help would soon be needed, Colonel McIntosh had already started the remainder of G Company 152nd to the right and followed with F Company and 2nd Battalion Headquarters. The timely arrival of these companies negated the need for the anti-tank platoon. Showing a spirit of co-operation so necessary to insure success, the two battalion commanders, Rice and Mottern, from different regiments, devised a tactical plan on the spot.

Company F 152nd would attack beyond Ichinose Heights toward forbidding, as yet untried, Mount Fumetsu. In the meantime, G Company 152nd would attack south along the Ege ridge. Company G 151st would continue its move started the previous day around Mount Ege's southern end.

Captain Summers's F/151st, severely punished by constant enemy rifle and mortar fire the last two days, was reduced to one rifle platoon and would remain on Ichinose Heights in reserve. One platoon of G/151st would clean out the persistent Japanese riflemen in the valley to the right rear who were making life miserable for truck drivers trying to reach the forward areas with supplies.[12]

The plan of the two battalion commanders slowly started to show results. Despite fanatic opposition that Division G-2 called "incredibly stubborn," the two G Companies finally occupied much of Mount Ege and dug in together for the night. Company F 152nd, unable to proceed in its sector because of a nearly impenetrable stand of artillery-shredded bamboo, returned to the original perimeter on Ichinose to dig in with F/151st.[13]

Sergeant Tarao Nishioka, newly appointed chief of a heavy machine gun squad helping to defend the battalion 70-mm gun in front of Mount Fumetsu, described the action and his frustrations: "An artillery bombardment started early in the morning. Since an observation plane directed it, it never missed the target. We couldn't fire at all, because if we fire one shot, they fire 300 shots, which never miss the target."

On one occasion when American fire lifted, Nishioka raised his head to look outside his bunker. He could see the enemy infantry advancing. All the Japanese guns in his area started firing at once. Nishioka was elated for a moment to see enemy soldiers falling or seeking cover from his fire. But soon another heavy bombardment dispelled the euphoria. Nishioka said this kind of fighting was repeated many times a day.[14]

An observation plane flew low and communicated with the leading American elements by megaphone. Sergeant Nagai was startled by the loud voices coming from an airplane. When the plane finished circling, a heavy bombardment immediately followed. Nagai said, "I hated those observation planes worse than the P-47s."[15]

Nakamura, Oshita and Nagai sat tight in Nakamura's cave during the bombardments. "We covered our ears with our thumbs and our eyes with the palms of our hands." A shell exploded on top of the cave and showered them with dirt. Nagai saw a scarlet beam of light at the moment of impact. But the logs covered with 40 centimeters (16 inches) of earth held. If the round had landed near the entrance, it would probably have exploded 10 kilograms (22 lbs.) of gunpowder, providing the trio with an honorable death on the battlefield.

Nagai remembered, "The sound of small arms fire comes closer. We hear the hissing sounds of flamethrowers and grenades before the explosions. Any moment we expect the enemy to burst into our cave, but another bombardment starts. The hissing sounds pass us by. We wonder why the enemy doesn't enter our cave. They know the locations of our heavy machine guns, so we know they will be back."

After the Americans had returned to their perimeters for the night, the three dazed Japanese came out of the cave at sundown to inspect the damage. They found an American corpse, probably an officer, "deeply sunburned with short cut hair" with a pistol in a holster at his waist and his hand still holding a carbine. Nagai removed his pistol, first aid kit and a magnetic compass. Oshita took his carbine, wristwatch, binoculars and shoes. Other soldiers envied the pair's good fortune. They started to comb through places where the Americans had fought to try to find guns and hand grenades.[16]

Although the 38th Division officially claimed that Mount Ege had been captured, Lieutenant Shinfune's 9th Company had not been destroyed and still occupied the southern portion. Warrant Officer Hitoshi Takao's platoon had suffered relatively little damage. The battle would now move eastward, but Shinfune's company, anchored by the Morinaka and Morimoto heavy machine guns, was still capable of offensive action.

Sergeant Nagai was the new leader of the Morinaka gun, which had been originally sited on the southern portion of Mount Ege. Sergeant Morinaka had shown cowardice and irresponsibility in the face of the enemy and had lost the respect of his men. The other gun, that of Sergeant Morimoto and his crew, had moved to Mount Ege after Mount Koko was evacuated on 5 February.[17]

🔹 🔹 🔹

Progress was also slow north of Highway 7. 1st Battalion 151st had secured the western slope of Mount Minami on 8 February. Colonel Paddock assigned the complete occupation of Minami as the objective for the 1st Battalion on 9 February. Sergeant Shiro Takamura's six-man heavy machine gun squad, which had moved from Mount Koko the night of 5 February, would furnish the principal opposition. The last remnants of the 10th Company commanded by the one surviving officer, 2nd Lieutenant Ryuchi Koujitani, would support Takamura.[18]

Filipino carrying parties, escorted by the Battalion Ammunition and Pioneer Platoon, arrived at about 0730. They rather hastily dumped ten-in-one rations and five-gallon cans of water on the ground and then departed just as hastily. This particular ration was hardly applicable, because it was difficult to prepare with the enemy continually sniping at the battalion. But after a meal of sorts, 1st Battalion was ready to go.

In preparation for his attack, Major Stewart, the battalion commander, asked for and got 400 grenades, 4 cases of M-1 rifle ammunition and 2 cases of carbine ammo. Again, the rough ground, still thick with underbrush despite the artillery fire, dictated a movement of a column of companies. The order would be B, A, Hdq. and D. Stewart left C Company behind to organize the high ground occupied the night before and to keep the supply trail open.[19]

The attack had no sooner started at 0900 than the Japanese pinned down B Company with a scathing fire so intense that Stewart thought part of it was coming from 2nd Battalion 151st across the road.

After an American artillery and mortar barrage, 1/151st worked through a maze of caves and emplacements hidden by bamboo. B Company blew up an enemy ammo dump and, taking a small rise just short of the objective, was able to reduce Japanese firing from farther down the road. After knocking out three pillboxes, the battalion was ready to make its final assault. By 1600, the 1st Battalion was digging in on the eastern rise of Mount Minami. Occupation of this significant terrain feature finally insured American domination of the 900-yard section of relatively straight road east of the "2."[20]

With C Company absent, Stewart organized a better and more roomy battalion perimeter than the previous night. Captain Walker of A Company observed lights several hundred yards to the southeast. These probably came from activity around Major Ogawa's headquarters on the southern portion of Mount Fumetsu. Artillery fire would make the lights disappear for a while, but they were visible at intervals throughout the night.[21]

The Miyazaki 10th Company ceased to exist. Only three dazed survivors found their way back to Mount Fumetsu on 10 February. All the members of a squad of the Operations Company attached to the 10th Company were killed 8-10 February. A tank round killed Sergeant Takamura and two of his machine gunners instantly. The intrepid

Takamura Squad had braved and stubbornly resisted all attempts at dislodgement for three days.[22]

💣 💣 💣

On the extreme left, Colonel Cornwell's 1/152nd continued its success of the day before. At the end of 8 February, Cornwell, with his advance headquarters and three rifle companies, occupied prominent Mount Kita 700 yards north of Highway 7. By thus outflanking Mount Minami, Cornwell had made Major Stewart's 1/151st attack easier. Mount Kita also gave 1/152nd a good jumping off point for an attack 9 February toward the northern area of Mount Shinshu.

Mount Kita

Despite its exposed position, 1st Battalion 152nd suffered no casualties during the night of 8-9 February. By bringing his whole battalion to the top of Mount Kita, Cornwell had hoped to discourage the Japanese from assaulting him. However, Major Ogawa had decided to make one last bid to retain Mount Kita, the key to his front line, during the night of 8-9 February.

When Master Sergeant Yoshio Maeda of the 10th Company came to his headquarters after dark 8 February, Ogawa asked him to attack and recapture Mount Kita. Maeda returned to Kita at about 2200 with ten men and a stack of grenades, determined to avenge the death of company commander Miyazaki. The Japanese crawled back into the holes of their original defense and at daybreak gave Cornwell's troops a lively grenade fight until nearly noon 9 February.[23]

Cornwell assigned B Company the mission of clearing Maeda's grenadiers from the south side of the hill and C Company the north side. Using smoke grenades and demolition charges, B and C Companies blew several caves and finished "mopping up" Mount Kita by 1150. They killed all of Maeda's men in the process. Carrying parties, which had been ready to move at daybreak, could now bring forward rations, water and ammo.[24]

Enemy mortar fire became particularly heavy at about 1030, falling on Battalion Headquarters as well as the front lines. Sergeant Ancelet of D Company climbed a tall tree and through his binoculars observed a Japanese mortar man dropping rounds down the tube of his mortar. He located the position on the map, and artillery fire quickly dispersed the crew.[25]

At about this time, Cornwell received word of the 2nd Battalion 152nd's move south across the road to assist 2nd Battalion 151st. Colonel Rice's battalion, trailing Cornwell, had secured the ground in rear of 1st Battalion, prepared to help where needed, either north or south of the road.

With 2/152nd removed to the south, Colonel McIntosh ordered Cornwell to leave a holding force on Kita and push on 600 yards east across a rough, jungle-covered valley to the northern edge of the Shinshu position. The regimental commander told Cornwell to "use artillery to fullest extent."[26]

Utilizing a "rolling barrage" that sometimes fell as close as 100 yards in front, B Company, the only attacking company, fought its way to within 200 yards of its objective. This was the only time the 11th F.A. Battalion fired a rolling barrage in its five Pacific campaigns.[27]

Besieged on his right as well as frontally, Sergeant Iga, defending Shinshu, found it "very hard to fight against enemies that attack from front and sides day and night." He praised his gunner, Superior Private Mitsuo Kizu for his accurate and steady fire in the face of overwhelming odds. KIGEN-SETSU was coming and Iga hoped "our planes will come and help us." KIGEN-SETSU was a holiday established in 1872, observed each year on 11 February, commemorating the enthronement of the first emperor, Jinmu, in 660 B.C.[28]

Cornwell himself dug in with B Company, leaving A and C Companies to hold Mount Kita. After Captain Thomas, the B Company commander, and Lieutenant Ward of the 139th F.A. Battalion registered artillery and mortar fire on suspected enemy approaches, Cornwell and B Company dared the Japanese to attack their salient.[29]

Counterattack was the last thing on the minds of the Japanese on Shinshu. Since the heavy bombardment the day before, Shinshu looked like the jagged, pockmarked slope of a volcanic ash field, according to Sergeant Hijikata. Despite losing the aiming sight of his gun during the bombardment, Hijikata could still deliver heavy, although erratic, fire.

But the infantrymen of 1/152nd and their artillery observer located Hijikata's emplacement. Red smoke shells, quickly followed by a terrific artillery concentration, caved in the dirt and log roof over the firing trench. Fortunately, the squad had retired into its cave back of the firing trench. No one was injured.[30]

One benefit of B Company's bold move to Shinshu did not become evident until later. Lieutenant Shigeo Otani, commander of the two 105-mm artillery pieces, had been unable to fire during the day because of the heavy American artillery shelling. Both guns were damaged, and he had expended most of his ammunition. Now threatened by infantry, he buried his guns during the night.[31]

● ● ●

The horror of battle was beginning to tell on even the hardiest of Nippon's native sons. The constant pounding by mortars and artillery; the incessant din of exploding shells; the zing of bullets tearing the air overhead; tanks rumbling into position firing their ear-shattering blasts; the drone of the dreaded observation planes followed by earth crushing artillery shells; the constant fear that this breath may be the last; the compulsion to risk death to help comrades; the fear of being called a coward in the face of danger and of comrades not saying you died a heroic death—all this weighed heavily on the minds of the unfortunate Japanese of the 39th Infantry.

There was the ever-present knowledge that men armed with death-dealing weapons were coming for you with automatic guns that covered and enabled flamethrowers to pinpoint with searing heat and smoke the inner reaches of caves and bunkers. If the sudden detonation of a 500-pound bomb from above was not frightening enough, there was the companion of air strikes—napalm's sea of flame—which destroyed everything within reach.

Only at night could the Japanese move. On the evening of 10 February, heavy machine gun squad leader Tarao Nishioka received an order from Battalion Headquarters to move to the battalion 70-mm gun position and "defend the position to the death." In a stream of consciousness, Nishioka recorded his thoughts. "This is serious order. No way to go home alive. Fight to death in defense. We must die in place where we are. Only question is when do we die?

"Get a little sleep. Up while still dark. We can't move at all after dawn. I push my men to move out. But we do not reach position before dawn. Airplanes arrive. Bombardment starts. Only individual movement now by leaps and bounds. The position is close—move, move! We finally make the trench. Then the fight starts."[32]

It was disheartening and morale shattering to see positions the men had worked on for weeks crushed and uprooted by the shrieking artillery and the silent mortar shells. Explosions accompanied by concussions and strong winds mowed down the dark woods, opened up the jungle and exposed carefully camouflaged bunkers.

And destruction of positions always meant mutilated and torn bodies. Those not buried right away were stinking, decomposed, sometimes with arms swollen as large as a live man's thigh.[33]

The omnipresent artillery observation planes made cooking impossible. It was hard to prevent "smoke from leaking out into the jungle." A wisp of smoke was an aiming point for a bombardment. It seemed as if a microphone attached to a loudspeaker had been set up at the Water Place so that the enemy could hear when any Japanese approached to fill his canteen. After the battle, Japanese returning to their old positions looking for food were guided by an unburied friendly body left at the Water Place.[34]

Near constant bombardments made the soldiers nervous and emotionally disordered. The necessity of holing up in the caves to avoid being killed by explosions made them feel like animals with no chance to escape. The sounds of the bombings and the engines and the crash of artillery, in the words of Sergeant Nagai, "started to lean on us. We all became neurotic, not only because of the overwhelming power of the sounds, but also because of the psychological pressure on us."[35]

Napalm was the most terrifying weapon of all. It came as a complete surprise; the Japanese had never heard of it. As Sergeant Nagai described his first encounter with napalm, "They dropped a thing like a drum can. When it hit the ground and exploded, suddenly it became a sea of fire . . . the whole area enveloped in flames . . . it was really unbearable."[36]

The term *napalm* was derived from its composition of the aluminum salts of *na*phthalenic and *palm*itic acids. It was a powder used to thicken gasoline to produce "jellied gasoline" for use in bombs. In ZigZag Pass, it was delivered in 165-gallon wing tanks, each fitted with an igniter. The

P-47s would jettison one of their two wing tanks as they flew low in successive passes over the target.[37]

💣   💣   💣

Meanwhile, east of the Santa Rita River, Colonel Funkhouser started moving 3rd Battalion Headquarters and K Companies 151st forward at 0800 toward I Company and, farther east, L Company. These latter two companies also moved out at 0800, their primary mission to link up with the 149th Infantry. At this time, L Company's perimeter was approximately 1,500 yards west of the lead elements of the 149th.

Colonel Skelton's twin tasks for the day were obvious. He assigned 2nd Battalion 149th the mission of eliminating the tanks near the road and 1st Battalion of making contact with 3/151st by a wide sweep south of the road. However, Major Nakayama decided that 9 February was not going to be a good day for the American forces to his front and rear to make physical contact.[38]

After a preliminary artillery preparation, 2nd Battalion 149th stepped out with E Company north of Highway 7 and G Company south. The two companies had hardly started when Major Nakayama's men opened fire with all the weapons available to them. The tanks were protected by machine guns and riflemen and would prove to be much more effective in the daytime than they had been the night before.

Colonel Dishman, the 2nd Battalion commander, immediately brought down artillery fire, which had practically no effect. Bazookas, too, were useless against the tanks. The foliage was so thick that the rockets were detonated or thrown off target by leaves and branches before reaching the tanks. The 81-mm mortars were also ineffective. The tankers merely changed their position upon hearing the dull sounds of the mortars firing.

The tanks were of great concern to Colonel Skelton. He reported, ". . . believe there are five tanks, but they move frequently and bazookas are ineffective." Some of the bazooka rounds were duds, and five known direct hits failed to stop the tanks. Skelton felt it was essential that he have anti-tank guns in order to move west, but the regiment's 57-mm anti-tank guns were still at Division Headquarters at Olongapo. They had been too heavy and cumbersome for the 149th to transport over the trail to Dinalupihan.[39]

The artillerymen's aim improved in the afternoon. With an amazing bit of shooting, the 138th F.A. Battalion reported at 1640 that it had set fire to two tanks with direct hits. The 38th Division AAR reported one direct hit at a range of 9,000 yards. Lieutenant Brinson, C Company 149th Infantry Exec, reported that artillery fire knocked out one tank, and a "lucky round" from an 81-mm mortar knocked out another. The 38th Division Artillery history makes no mention of the incident.[40]

The 149th received 16 casualties for the day and reported killing 42 Japanese to 38th Division G-2. The 1st Battalion's lone action accounted for five, and the 2nd Battalion, the remainder. In its blocking role in Dinalupihan and Orani, 3rd Battalion 149th accounted for none of the Japanese dead.[41]

The 1st Battalion 149th's attempts to join 3/151st were unsuccessful. Colonel Bonnycastle assigned the mission to C Company, whose commander ordered a platoon-size patrol to accomplish the task. The patrol had not gone far when the lead squad became engaged in a firefight with five of Major Nakayama's men. After killing all of them, the squad leader searched the bodies. The documents he found proved to be worthless.[42]

Company L 151st, advancing toward the patrol, made little progress, probably because of the fierce action with the tanks and the necessity of having to pull back when artillery fire was called in. It was just as well. Soon after mid-day, Colonel Funkhouser received orders canceling his flanking mission and instructing him to return to the main action between the horseshoe and the hairpin.

* * *

While F and G Companies 152nd were moving into their attack positions against Fumetsu and Ege, Colonel Paddock had decided to reinforce the assault on the Japanese MLR. Colonel Funkhouser was contributing little toward the overall effort. Therefore, at 1118 Paddock requested through Division G-3 that General Chase detach the 3rd Battalion from the 149th and return it to 151st regimental control. Permission was finally gained at 1300. Paddock ordered 3rd Battalion 151st to march west, keeping south of the road, and move into position to help 2nd Battalion 151st.[43]

Funkhouser promptly acknowledged receipt of the order and reported his lead elements to be 2,200 yards east of the Santa Rita River and 200 yards south of the road (if true, this position was 200 yards south of the point where the tanks had blocked the 149th Infantry earlier in the day). He said he could not reach the 2nd Battalion 151st until late the next day. He had been unable to retrieve the rations that had been dropped at 0900. He repeated his plea for more rations.[44]

Paddock shot back this impatient reply, "I am not satisfied with the progress of your battalion. Get moving and move fast!" He also ordered Funkhouser to report his position every 30 minutes.[45]

The weary troops of 3rd Battalion plodded slowly back over ground that by now was all too familiar. By the time of the first report, they had covered only 400 yards. The delay may have been caused by L Company looking for the three men it reported MIA and being reluctant to leave without them. At 1800, the battalion occupied its original bivouac at the river with L Company still 700 yards east of the river.[46]

Thus ended General Easley's attempt to throw a cordon around the southern flank of the Japanese forces. 3rd Battalion's initial flank march 7 February had revealed the lack of Japanese defenses south of Highway 7, but the battalion had accomplished little since. Another bold march of 2,500-3,000 yards would have reached the 149th Infantry. Even patrol contact would have been acceptable. Inexplicably, Colonel Funkhouser had not accomplished his primary mission nor had he attempted to interrupt Japanese communications along Highway 7.

Major Ogawa was well aware from the start of Colonel Funkhouser's sally to the east. What appeared to the Americans as a serious breach of the enemy lines did not annoy the Japanese commander at all. Seeming to divine Funkhouser's indecision after his initial daring, Ogawa made no attempt to disturb the 3rd Battalion 151st. He was confident this new American threat would not endanger his well-entrenched troops. He was also well aware of the disastrous attempt of the Sakura Company to dislodge A Company 34th from its isolated position on 3-4 February. Major Nakayama seemed similarly unconcerned about the presence of 3/151st on his flank and rear.

The records do not reveal the reasons for Funkhouser's hesitation and timidity. At one time, he reported heavy resistance at the Santa Rita River Bridge, but during the rest of the three-day saga, the records are silent regarding enemy contact. His initial orders may have been vague when he started his march on 7 February, but no one could question his primary mission as specified in Field Order #12 of 8 February: he was to "gain contact as early as possible by every means available" with the 149th Infantry (see page 215).

If contact with the 149th could not be made, it is not implausible to expect some aggressive action by a battalion perched on the enemy's flank in a position to attack either of its two wings. Field Order #12 also ordered Funkhouser to "attack north along Santa Rita River, destroy enemy vicinity Santa Rita River bridge and continue attack to east along Highway 7." Nothing in the records suggests that the 3rd Battalion made the attack or made any effort to patrol and learn more about the enemy's dispositions.

On the other hand, the order to attack along Highway 7 east of the bridge was ill advised. Highway 7 climbs steeply from the river to the East Pass, which was defended by 2/3 of the 5th Company 39th Infantry. To order an isolated battalion to attack an enemy of unknown strength on higher ground without prior reconnaissance is unreasonable and unconscionable.

Lack of supplies, as evidenced by the number of messages regarding them, was a problem for Funkhouser, but troops from early historical times have carried three days' rations. Captain Ransohoff reported the battalion digging in near the river the evening of 8 February in the same foxholes occupied the night before, so there would have been no difficulty locating the battalion for supply airdrops. (The 149th Infantry at Dinalupihan was supplied daily by air-drops during the entire battle.)

It would appear that General Easley's initial plans on 7 February and General Chase's subsequent Field Order #12 the following day were conflicting and confusing to Colonel Funkhouser. His original mission was two-fold: (1) to reach the bridge and (2) make patrol contact with the 149th Infantry. General Chase's Field Order #12 inserted a new element into Funkhouser's thinking. He was to destroy the enemy at the bridge, attack eastward along Highway 7 and effect a junction with the 149th. It is not surprising that Funkhouser, faced with these inconsistent orders, had nothing to show for his work on 9 February. If General Chase had permitted Funkhouser to continue his original mission unimpeded, the 3rd Battalion might well have made contact with the 149th on either 8 or 9 February.

🔸　🔸　🔸

There was consternation in Lieutenant Nakamura's cave on Mount Ege near sunset. Since the enemy knew there were heavy machine guns in the area, Sergeant Nagai was certain the Americans would be back. He feared tomorrow's attack would be much more severe and more thorough. "It will be tomorrow that I find out if I live or die," he mused.

Nagai looked for the squad leader of the machine gun defending in that area and found him in his cave. The night before, Nagai had pointed out a possible enemy approach route that should be defended, but the squad leader had not manned his gun at all on 9 February.

Nagai implored him to fire his gun the next day to give protection as well as inspiration to his men. The squad leader responded, "I don't feel good. I will stay in the cave. If the enemy comes, I will kill myself with a grenade." Nagai pleaded with him. "If you are prepared to die, do it firing your gun. This is not the time to be thinking about your health; it is a time to kill or be killed."[47]

Nagai and the others could not bear this shameful scene. The gun in question was #10334, the most revered gun in the Kato HMG Company. On 26 April 1938, Superior Private Toshio Tsuda had fired the gun bravely in China until fatally shot in the head. It was incomprehensible that a Japanese warrior would prefer suicide in a cave to the glory of firing his gun to the end.[48]

Chapter 17
NOTES

(1) 38th Division G-2 Report #12, 1800-09 February 1945; 151st Infantry AAR, p. 5.

(2) Phone message, G-2 38th Division to G-2 XI Corps, 2145-08 February 1945.

(3) XI Corps G-2 Report #9, 1800-06 February 1945.

(4) Walker, Major Stephen M., *The Operations of Company A 151st Infantry in the Attack Through ZigZag Pass*, Advanced Infantry Officers Course, 1949-1950, The Infantry School, Fort Benning, GA, p. 16.

(5) 38th Division G-2 Report #12, 1800-09 February 1945; Miller, John, Jr., *The United States Army in World War II, Cartwheel: The Reduction of Rabaul,* p. 351.

(6) 151st Infantry AAR, p. 5; Message G-3 38th Division to G-3 XI Corps, Journal entry #13, 0910-09 February 1945.

(7) 151st Infantry AAR, p. 5.

(8) 151st Infantry journal.

(9) 151st Infantry journal.

(10) G-2 38th Division summary at 2140 (reported by 152nd Infantry); *How the Kato Company Fought: The Record of the 3rd Machine Gun Company 39th Infantry Regiment*, Tamotsu Nagai, Editor, 1990, p. 43, p. 205.

(11) 151st Infantry journal.

(12) 38th Division G-3 journal; 151st Infantry AAR, p. 5; 152nd Infantry journal.

(13) Teletype G-2 38th Division to G-2 XI Corps 1835-09 February 1945; 151st Infantry journal.

(14) Kato Company History, p. 197-198.

(15) *Ibid.,* p. 220.

(16) *Ibid.,* p. 221-222.

(17) Ogawa, Major Hironori, *Record of the 3rd Battalion, 39th Infantry Regiment in the "Big Asia War,"* p. 43, p. 45;
Kato Company History, p. 193, p. 195;
History of the 39th Infantry Regiment, edited and published by the 39th Infantry Association, p. 648.

(18) 151st Infantry AAR, p. 6;
Kato Company History, p. 43;
Ogawa, *Record of the 3rd Battalion,* p. 42.

(19) 151st Infantry journal;
Walker, p. 16.

(20) 151st Infantry journal.

(21) Walker, p. 17.

(22) Kato Company History, p. 43;
Ogawa, *Record of the 3rd Battalion,* p. 42;
39th Infantry History, p. 647.

(23) Ogawa, *Record of the 3rd Battalion,* p. 42;
39th Infantry History, p. 648.

(24) 1st Battalion 152nd Infantry journal.

(25) Sergeant Ancelet was awarded the Silver Star for this action and his actions on 7-8 February defusing booby traps and destroying ammunition dumps.

(26) 1st Battalion 152nd Infantry journal, 1345.

(27) Chilcote, 1st Lieutenant Willis L., letter to author, 18 October 1990.

(28) Kato Company History, p. 206.

(29) 1st Battalion 152nd Infantry journal.

(30) Kato Company History, p. 210.

(31) *39th Infantry History,* p. 648.

(32) Kato Company History, p. 198.

(33) Kato Company History, p. 215, p. 212.

(34) *Ibid.,* p. 220.

(35) *Ibid.*

(36) *Ibid.,* p. 219-220.

(37) Polmar, Norman and Allen, Thomas B., *World War II, America at War, 1941-1945,* p. 572-573.

(38) 151st Infantry journal, entries #5, #16.

(39) 38th Division G-3 journal, 0315-10 February 1945.

(40) 38th Division G-2 report #12, 1800-09 February 1945;
G-3 message, 38th Division journal entry #30;
38th Infantry Division Historical Report, M-7 Operation (AAR);

Brinson, Captain Arthur, Cavalry monograph: *The Battle of ZigZag Pass*, delivered at the Armored School, Fort Knox, K., 5 May 48, p. 10. At the time of the battle Brinson was C Company 149th Infantry Exec;
38th Division Artillery Unit History, M-7 Operation, Luzon, 16 January-30 June 1945. Department of the Army, the Adjutant General's Office,Washington, D.C.

(41)   38th Division G-2 to XI Corps G-2 telephone message, 09-1820 February 1945;
2nd Battalion 149th Infantry journal.

(42)   Brinson, p. 10.

(43)   38th Division G-3 Report #48, 09-1800 February 1945;
151st Infantry journal.

(44)   151st Infantry journal, 1325.

(45)   *Ibid.,* 1445.

(46)   *Ibid.,* 1800.

(47)   Kato Company History, p. 223.

(48)   *Ibid.*

WELCOME SUPERIOR PRIVATE MATSUYAKI

(10 FEBRUARY)

The 38th Division had made significant gains on 9 February by storming the middle of the Japanese main position in ZigZag Pass. With the occupation of the Kita/Kasuga/Minami/Ege ridgeline, the perspective of the battle changed. The terrain advantage now favored the attackers. To the American front, the Japanese defensive belt continued in depth with successive lower elevations until reaching the Shinshu/Fumetsu ridge, which crowded the highway as the road approached the hairpin. From there, Highway 7 descended abruptly through the hairpin to the Santa Rita River. East of the river, the terrain rose to the rugged, steep, jungle-covered hill mass of the East Pass.

There was no need for a change in orders for this day. Everyone in the 151st and 152nd regiments knew that the next two objectives would be Mount Shinshu and Mount Fumetsu. The 149th's mission was obvious too: surmount the barrier of the Japanese tanks and drive westward to the Santa Rita River.

The lineup for the assault against the new Japanese MLR follows: from left to right, Colonel Cornwell's 1st Battalion 152nd Infantry would clean up the northern portion of Shinshu and attempt to drive past the hairpin. Colonel Stewart's 1st Battalion 151st Infantry would assault and secure the remainder of Mount Shinshu. These two battalions would maneuver north of the road. Colonel Mottern's still under-strength 2nd Battalion 151st and Colonel Rice's 2nd Battalion 152nd would combine to assault Mount Fumetsu south of the road. With battalions from both regiments on both sides of the road, General Chase placed troops north of the road under command of Colonel McIntosh and those south of the road under Colonel Paddock.

The 3rd Battalion 152nd was to patrol in the rear areas, and 3rd Battalion 151st, returning from its attempt to reach the 149th Infantry, would travel from the Santa Rita River to the horseshoe. An air strike of approximately 90 minutes duration would be placed on the Nakayama Battalion's lines between the 149th Infantry and the Santa Rita River.[1]

Japanese forces bypassed in the relentless American attack eastward were still active, but not a threat. Lieutenant Shinfune's 9th Company and two HMG Squads (Morimoto and Morinaka) held the southern portion of Mount Ege. These troops, now isolated from the main battle, would make only occasional harassing forays against the American right flank and rear.[2]

Colonel Paddock organized Companies F and G 151st and G 152nd south of the road into assault detachments "to clean out and demolish tunnels as they advanced." The assault detachments contained riflemen with grenades, a rifleman with a flamethrower and an engineer specialist in explosives to seal the caves.[3]

Before the companies south of the road could even start their assaults, they had to overcome positions still active on Mount Ege. An emplacement within a few yards of the perimeter of the two G Companies revived and started giving trouble. Two assault teams reduced it on the second attempt. Investigation revealed an elaborate cave containing 25 enemy dead. Members of one team actually climbed on top of the 9th Company command bunker, but 1st Sergeant Shinichi Nishiguchi, aided by the Morimoto and Morinaka Squads, drove them off.[4]

The plateau between Ege and Fumetsu, a jumble of small hillocks and ridges, looked like a no-man's-land, but was full of bunkers, caves and foxholes with concealed apertures from which the enemy could still discharge a deadly fire. The companies would consume the entire day confronting these installations.

Taking a suspected strongpoint did not signal the end of opposition in that particular sector. Caves, underground tunnels and trenches honey-combed the entire area from the horseshoe to the hairpin. The GIs could occupy a ridge or knoll, but the Japanese might still control the draws between the ridges. Every pillbox, every cave, every hole had to be sealed as the troops advanced because the enemy would stay in a hole for days and harass the supply lines.[5]

As part of the Kato Company history, Sergeant Nagai describes this day as starting as usual with the annoying sound of a surveillance plane flying over the Japanese positions looking for the telltale signs of smoke from cooking fires. At times the planes, always in direct communication with men on the ground, stall their engines and fly very low, almost touching the treetops.

Far down in the valley below Mount Ege, the roar of engines of tanks and trucks is mingled with the thunder of the artillery, the scream of shells overhead and the deafening explosions that always follow. The boom of the guns reminds Nagai of the drums at festivals back home. Ground fire joins the chorus. "We wait for the enemy foot soldiers to show up. We wait for the mortars to open up. That will be a sign the enemy is approaching."[6]

Lieutenant Shinfune's 9th Company had no anti-tank mines that worked. Instead, the men felled trees and carefully positioned them with great effort to block the road. Much to the surprise and chagrin of the Japanese, the Americans easily remove the obstacles with a winch attached to the front of a truck and pull the huge tree trunks aside. Nagai sums it up: "It is quite a simple job for them. We can only watch their actions and have no chance to attack."[7]

At about noon, the bombardment and shooting slows down, then stops. It is lunchtime. The Americans have done their morning chores; now the Japanese can do theirs: climb out of their trenches, stretch, do exercises, relieve themselves. There is no guarantee of total safety, but at this time of day, they do not feel the enemy is likely to attack.

Soon, the afternoon shooting starts. The mortars are back. Engineer Lieutenant Nakamura, one of Sergeant Nagai's foxhole mates, counts 75 rounds in one minute. Suddenly, Nagai sees smoke creeping up from the valley in front of them (the Americans were using a smoke screen that was not reported in the 38th Division records). Nagai sees enemy helmets through the smoke and starts firing the American pistol he picked up the day before. But the Americans concentrate on bigger game—the heavy machine guns.

The Morimoto machine gun suddenly stops firing. Flames engulf the area. An American assault team holds higher ground and can fire down on its targets. The flamethrower fire-stream incinerates trees, bushes—everything in its path. Superior Private Tsuneo Kita and Pfc. Minoru Jinno are burned to death. Pfc. Hiroshi Konishi tries to escape to another trench, but is shot in the back of the head.

The Morinaka Squad is not spared. Nagai, Nakamura and Oshita, a sapper, still share the same foxhole. The cover on their hole catches fire. Oshita gets out of the hole and Nagai crawls into a communications trench. Nakamura has already left to get help from the Shinfune Company. Because of the smoke, the Americans do not notice Nagai and Oshita. Mortar shells descend. Nagai recalls, "Then comes a red flash. The roar of an explosion and blast hit me. I cover my ears and close my eyes. Dirt and sand fall over me. The blast keeps hitting my back. I am ready to be killed by the shells and keep thinking, 'Maybe this one, maybe the next one.'" By lying in the ditch, he is saved. Oshita and Nakamura also weather the attack.

In late afternoon, the Americans take off their shirts and start digging in near the Morinaka machine gun's bunker. Lieutenant Shinfune arrives with reinforcements, and the medic, Ishii, immediately goes to work on the wounded. Shinfune decides to attack with grenade launchers while the Americans are digging their foxholes. He abandons his attack when the first shot explodes in the treetops and showers the attackers with fragments. Nagai thinks that Lieutenant Shinfune should simply move the launcher to another location to avoid the trees. He thinks the company commander should lead his men in a grenade attack supported by light machine guns he has brought with him. Instead, Shinfune leads his men down the ridge to the left to get some water, then retires for the day. Thoroughly disgusted with the Shinfune 9th Company, Sergeant Nagai begins thinking how he can retrieve the Morinaka heavy machine gun from the bunker.[8]

Colonels Mottern of the 151st and Rice of the 152nd devised a two-pronged assault on the two hills of Fumetsu. Company G 152nd, with F Company 152nd following, would move toward the northern edge of the hill abutting the road. Both companies would destroy enemy emplacements as they advanced. Company G 151st, now reinforced and covered by the weapons platoon of F/ 151st, would go for the southern hill. Tanks would not be used, possibly because of the disastrous results of the previous day.[9]

It was providential that the two battalion commanders planned this attack carefully. They, of course, had no way of knowing that Fumetsu, as the rallying point for the 3rd Battalion 39th Infantry's last stand, had been fortified with special attention. The logical approaches up the draws were overgrown with young bamboo. S-2 151st reported that young bamboo laced with barbed wire filled one draw and part way up its hill (Japanese survivors of the battle swear they had no barbed wire available, but the evidence in this case in favor of barbed wire seems overwhelming).

The defenders also placed sharpened bamboo poles at an angle of about 70 degrees six to seven yards in front of the five heavy machine guns protecting Fumetsu. Tunnels and trenches provided rapid movement from one position to another along the entire hillside.[10]

The attack bogged down an hour after its start. Accompanying his own G Company leading the assault, Colonel Rice was hit by mortar fire, not severely, but seriously enough to cause his evacuation from ZigZag

Pass. Major Byus, the Battalion Executive Officer, temporarily replaced Rice. This was the second advancement in nine days for Byus. The former F Company commander had been named Battalion Exec and promoted to Major on 1 February. Now he was battalion commander. Colonel McIntosh named Captain McCown, the H Company commander, the new 2nd Battalion Exec.[11]

Colonel Mottern asked Colonel Paddock for Cannon Company to come forward at once with its 105-mm SPMs to help get the attack going again. Captain Messer, Cannon Company commander, sited his guns on the eastern slope of Mount Minami ready to fire 500 yards across the road directly into the Fumetsu fortress. But this firepower was not used. With artillery blasting the hill, the two G Companies reached the edge of Major Ogawa's last stand bastion and dug in for the night.[12]

Meanwhile, north of the road, Major Stewart called his company commanders to the 1st Battalion 151st's CP on Mount Minami at daybreak to plan the attack. The objective for the day was the oval-shaped defensive area of Shinshu, defending with Fumetsu the turn of the road into the hairpin. Studded with machine guns and reinforced with survivors of the attacks on the MLR, Shinshu would be a tough nut to crack.

The Shinshu defenders were well aware that only a miracle could save them. "It was the eve of the holiday of KIGEN-SETSU; therefore, every soldier believed a miracle would happen tomorrow," Sergeant Iga philosophized. "It was the only way for us to survive the battle."[13]

Major Stewart's orders constituted the first definite plan the 1st Battalion Company commanders had received since entering the battle on 8 February. Company A on the left would attack cross-country 200-300 yards off the road and approach the hill from the northwest. 1st Battalion 152nd to the north would provide left flank protection.

On the right, B Company was to move along the north side of Highway 7 and strike at the hill from the south and southwest. Company C was to constitute the reserve. The C Company commander was to bring his troops forward from the company's position on the rear slope of Mount Minami to the battalion perimeter on the forward slope. Here, the battalion CP furnished Colonel Stewart good observation of Shinshu.

Captain Walker, the A Company commander, called his platoon leaders together and outlined his plan. The company would march in a column of platoons in the order 2nd, 1st, Company Headquarters, 3rd and 4th (weapons platoon). Walker attached a light machine gun from the weapons platoon to each of the 1st and 2nd platoons.

By keeping to the left in the shelter of a narrow draw, it appeared that the company could reach dense woods near the northern slope of Shinshu without being detected by the Japanese. From these woods, 2nd Platoon on the right and 1st Platoon on the left would begin their assaults. The company command group and the 3rd and 4th Platoons behind would follow the 2nd Platoon. Walker urged his troops to conserve water. Though it was not yet 0730, it was already hot. The day would be a scorcher! Sufficient food and water apparently had not been brought forward for the assault troops.

Company A moved out promptly at 0800 in a generally northeast direction to take advantage of the protection afforded by the draw. Visibility was limited to a few yards, making orientation very difficult. Artillery fire on the objective reduced Japanese resistance to occasional inaccurate rifle fire and machine gun bursts. At 0900, hampered only by this sporadic fire, the company reached the relative safety of the woods. The expected Japanese mortar barrage did not materialize.

Captain Walker gathered the leaders of the assault platoons around him at the base of a large tree to plan the assault. Walker observed a soldier at port arms a few feet from the tree and called to him with the idea of using him as a messenger. But Platoon Sergeant Boothe cried, "Captain, that's a Jap!" Boothe calmly shot the intruder, who was a Jap, before he could interrupt the meeting. There were actually numerous Nipponese riflemen wandering about the woods, hidden by the dense foliage.

Shots rang out from time to time in the woods. In the space of a half-hour, three SCR 536 radio (walkie-talkie) operators in the 2nd Platoon were wounded and removed to the rear. The enemy was very discerning in picking targets. Radio operators were a high priority, not only because they controlled communications, but also because American officers were usually close by.

Walker determined by observation from the woods that a finger of the draw the company had followed led to the objective from the northwest. He ordered the 2nd Platoon to follow this draw and the 1st Platoon to move through the woods on the left of the 2nd. The company command group would follow the 2nd Platoon with the 3rd and 4th Platoons behind in that order.

It was unbearably hot when the company moved out again for the final approach to the objective. There were signs that the shortage of food and water was beginning to take its toll. No one had fallen out, but many were panting at the least exertion and using the slightest halt as an excuse to drop to the ground.

The 2nd Platoon's path led almost immediately into a long, narrow, neck-high Japanese trench running in a southeast direction toward the objective. With a BAR at the ready, 1st Lieutenant Wesley E. Cooke led his platoon into the trench. The platoon passed several small tunnels bored back from the main trench on either side. The leading elements fired into each tunnel as they passed and tossed in a phosphorous grenade even though they saw no enemy. At about 1030, Cooke and his men climbed out of the trench about 50 yards from the crest of the hilltop objective.

Lieutenant Ogata's remaining 11th Company riflemen, who had withdrawn to Mount Shinshu from Mount Koko the night of 5 February, and Sergeant Iga's machine gun immediately opened up on the exposed Americans. In the ensuing firefight, the Japanese infantrymen confused the Hoosiers by darting through trenches and caves to numerous firing positions on the slope. American artillery had so churned up the hill that it was more difficult than ever to spot enemy positions.[14]

It was proving to be another rough day for Sergeant Iga's squad. A bullet hit Superior Private Misao Yoshizu, Iga's gunner, in the mouth and came out his right cheek. Superior Private Hisaharu Tometa replaced him. "We carried Yoshizu with his bloody red face to the rear and treated him, but he died on the 13th," Iga wrote later.

When Superior Privates Ryuji Konai and Hiroshi Nakanishi went to the supply cave for more ammunition, Nakanishi's right leg was blown off above the knee. "He asked me several times to kill him with a grenade," Konai said, "but I treated him in the cave. He died at midnight from loss of blood."[15]

Captain Walker, forward with the 2nd Platoon, was out of touch with the rest of his company. He sent a runner to locate and establish contact with the 1st Platoon. A Japanese sharpshooter killed the runner en route. Walker judged he was too close to the enemy to call for artillery or 81-mm mortar support. Fortunately, a 60-mm mortar observer, who was also forward, made radio contact with the weapons platoon. Rounds from the light mortars were soon on the way.

The mortars buttoned up the enemy, and Walker was able to maneuver again. Several men from the 2nd Platoon, overcome by heat exhaustion, left for the rear or rested in sheltered areas to recuperate. Despite these losses, Cooke led the remainder of his platoon in short rushes to within 20 yards of the crest of Shinshu. The 1st Platoon was now back in contact with the company and was located a few yards to the left rear of the 2nd Platoon.[16]

The B Company attack had bogged down on the road short of the objective in the face of Japanese strength anchored by the Hijikata heavy machine gun. The battalion commander ordered C Company in reserve to come forward to aid B Company. He also attached two of D Company's heavy machine guns to C Company and ordered up 10,000 rounds of machine gun ammunition. A Japanese sniper shot and killed the C Company commander as he led his company forward.[17]

Company B's initial slow approach along the road had lulled Sergeant Hijikata's men into complacency. They were more concerned with getting their damaged gun ready to repel the enemy. A communications officer on the way to the regimental gun position stopped by their cave to report on the battle. He turned to leave but jumped back into the cave, shouting, "The enemy! They are here!" A nimble soldier of the Ogata 11th Company leaped out of the cave to fire, but was cut down immediately.

Hijikata thought his time had come. He was still having trouble getting his gun to fire. At that moment Hisaji Tometa of the Iga Squad stopped B Company's advance with several well-placed bursts.[18]

As daring as the A Company assault platoons had been in reaching their objective, Walker could not budge them to make the final assault. The heat and lack of water had so enervated the men that they could scarcely move. To sustain the momentum, Walker gathered five men from the 3rd Platoon and the company Communications Sergeant and slowly and laboriously moved south across the western slope of Shinshu to a fringe of trees in B Company's and Sergeant Hijikata's zone of action. 2nd Platoon's fire covered him. He sent back word for as many men as possible to join him in the growth of trees. By 1400, Walker still had only 12 men and one light machine gun to attack the Japanese position.

Walker's tough volunteers were ready and willing to fight, but even they were almost overcome by the searing, dusty heat on the barren top of Shinshu. Battalion asked Walker to mark his forward position. Walker tossed a red smoke grenade over the crest of the hill. As the red smoke unraveled upward, Lieutenant Ogata's 11th Company and Sergeant Hijikata's squad grazed the crest with extremely heavy rifle and machine gun fire. Ogata's men also launched light mortar rounds toward the trees hiding Walker's assault team, but overshot the mark. Most of the Japanese fire seemed to come from three machine gun positions just over the rise.

Walker's machine gunner delivered ineffective but harassing fire toward the Japanese. With this cover, Pfc. Robert Ballentyne and Pfc. Eugene DeGrandchamp volunteered to knock out the three machine guns. With three grenades each, they jumped up and raced over the crest. In a short time they returned, and Ballentyne said, "Got one, Captain." After resting a few moments, they made another sortie. This time DeGrandchamp returned alone and reported that Ballentyne had been killed.

DeGrandchamp said, however, that he knew the location of the two other guns and believed he could direct mortar fire on them. He made his way back about 200 yards to the company mortar position and directed fire on the supposed location of the Japanese guns. Before Walker could determine if the rounds had been effective, he received orders to return to the battalion perimeter. The company withdrew with difficulty along its attack route under cover of its 60-mm and D Company's 81-mm mortars, picking up stragglers as it returned.[19]

Japanese resistance along the road and a blazing sun proved too tough for B and C Companies to overcome. At 1350, B Company was forced to withdraw 150 yards because of heat exhaustion. The battalion commander recalled both companies to the battalion perimeter in late afternoon.

At 1100, Colonel Paddock had ordered Major Stewart, suffering from battle fatigue, to the rear. The Executive Officer, Major Paul R. Lemasters, immediately took command and guided the 1st Battalion for the rest of the day. Reporting that his advance troops were completely exhausted after fighting their way through a thicket of pillboxes, Lemasters succeeded in bringing up a hot meal for everyone in the battalion before dark.[20]

General Chase and Colonel Paddock visited the 1st Battalion 152nd CP atop Mount Kita early in the day to scan the terrain B Company had traversed and occupied the previous day in its attack toward Mount Shinshu. Colonel Cornwell had the situation well in hand. With only "slight harassment by enemy," the battalion had suffered no casualties during the night. Rations, water and ammo had already reached the front line soldiers. Cornwell was moving A Company up to join B Company and finish the attack on the northern end of Shinshu. This was the area where the Japanese artillery and regimental guns were thought to be emplaced.[21]

The two companies attacked the regimental gun position, situated in a cave, repeatedly with machine guns, flame-throwers and automatic rifles. The enemy fought back with only rifles and hand grenades. Suffering no casualties, the GIs killed six and wounded one Japanese and captured one of the 75-mm regimental guns.[22]

1st Battalion 152nd began "mopping up" its newly won area. Demolition squads from the 113th Engineers helped demolish the many log and dirt pillboxes bypassed in reaching the objective. By the end of the day, 1/152nd was digging in on the slope overlooking the hairpin.[23]

The rapid American advance had produced a prize sought since the campaign began. A lone Japanese soldier had survived a satchel charge explosion in one of the caves. B Company men pulled him from the hole, dazed but unhurt, as soon as they realized he was still alive. The 149th Infantry had captured several Formosan laborers, but this was the first Japanese soldier to surrender in the main battle area. Taking prisoners usually signaled that the end of a campaign was near.

Superior Private Yoshio Matsuyaki proved to be an intelligent, knowledgeable and cooperative prisoner. He was a member of the 6th Battery, 10th F.A. Regiment, 10th Division. Not until Matsuyaki was interrogated did the 38th Division learn that two 105-mm howitzers and 65 men constituted the only Japanese artillery in the pass. Only 100 rounds of ammunition were left for the guns, Matsuyaki said (he either did not know or did not report that the 105s had been disassembled and buried the night before). He had seen 15 tanks at Dinalupihan in January, but had not seen any in the pass.

Matsuyaki cried out for water and said he had had no food or water for three days. He said the detachment's food supply would probably last for another month. Rice went uncooked because the observation planes prevented building fires at night. He estimated that only 350 Japanese troops remained in the pass and that many were malaria-ridden.[24]

The interrogation was conducted under the supervision of Nisei 1st Lieutenant Yoshikazu Higashi. The fighting exploits of the Nisei in North Africa and Europe are well known, but the contributions of the Nisei in the Southwest Pacific Theater to the war effort, though not as combat soldiers, are equally noteworthy.

Hawaiian Nisei composed the 100th Battalion, which fought in North Africa and Italy until March 1944. After the 100th merged with the 442nd Regimental Combat Team of Nisei from Hawaii and the mainland internment camps, the 442nd fought with great distinction in the Italian campaign and in the Vosges Mountains in France. With 18,143 individual decorations and a concomitant number of casualties, the 442nd was probably the most decorated unit in United States military history.

Presently living in Carmel, CA, Higashi had joined the 38th Division in January 1945. He was placed in charge of a Prisoner of War Interrogation Team in the Division G-2 section composed of 11 Nisei plus 1 Caucasian officer. Besides interrogating prisoners, Nisei also translated captured Japanese documents, including battle plans, lists of Imperial Navy ships and Japanese secret codes. We have seen how valuable were the documents captured in Zigzag Pass in developing the Japanese order of battle, disclosing to front line troops the location and armament of the enemy, and revealing his background, training and morale.

The Nisei were second generation Japanese, born and educated in the United States. They were the sons of Issei, who had migrated from Japan to America and were incarcerated in internment camps in the western U.S. for the duration of the war. As American citizens, the Nisei were encouraged to volunteer for Army service, and 9,507 did despite the harsh and unreasonable treatment of their parents. Succeeding generations of Japanese Americans were known as Sansei and Yonsei, continuing the Japanese number correlation—*ichi, ni, san, yon*, et cetera—to name the generations.[25]

Japanese tanks continued to frustrate Colonel Skelton and the 149th Infantry. Skelton believed he had encountered five tanks on 9 February, but they moved frequently and his reports indicate that only three had been definitely counted. Before digging in, he had established tank traps with 2.36-inch bazookas near the road and constructed a tank barrier. Despite the report that two tanks had been destroyed on 9 February (see pages 243-244), the 149th radioed Division G-3 at 0809 on 10 February that two tanks had harassed the frontline troops during the night and at daybreak. Artillery had taken the tanks under fire.[26]

An air strike was to be delivered some time between 1000 and 1130 to blanket the Nakayama Battalion's positions. The last plane over would execute a slow roll to signal to the ground troops that the strike was over. Then Skelton was to "contain tanks and advance aggressively there-after."[27]

At 0840, Major Purlee, assistant division G-3, requested XI Corps to furnish anti-tank weapons for the 149th. Corps first replied that any AT guns furnished must come from the east, then advised at 0940 "that AT weapons could not be furnished from the east." Corps finally closed the subject at 1030 with this message: "No possibility supplying AT guns. Do utmost to fulfill mission with ammo at hand. Imperative division mission be completed today."

No reason was given why the AT guns could not be furnished, but the reasons are obvious. It was not practical to manhandle the heavy, bulky 57-mm AT guns overland by trail from Olongapo to Dinalupian. The C-47s supplying the 149th with airdrops could not transport the 38th Division's AT guns from San Marcelino because no airfields were serviceable at Dinalupihan. Helicopters had not come into general use in World War II for ferrying equipment by air. Corps may have requested XIV Corps to furnish AT guns or SPMs from the 40th Division to the east, but, if so, the reply must have been negative.

At 1027, the 149th reported through Division Artillery that a tank had moved back into the same vicinity as the tank that had held up the advance the day before. Skelton radioed that the tank, in defilade, barred any advance either north or south of the road. His men were using bazookas and 81-mm mortars, but could not contain "him" as he moved continuously. Skelton said he could hit the tank with an AT gun easily but knew of no other way to get "him." He repeated his request—in vain—for one or more AT guns.

The air strike at 1100 started six huge fires (five distinct fires north of the road reported by 2/149). A 138th F.A. liaison plane estimated the strike covered an area 350 yards by 200 yards, and that black smoke rose 6,000 feet. The P-47s dropped sixteen 500-pound HE bombs (8,000 pounds total) and 250 pounds (2,350 gallons) of napalm, and strafed 48,000 rounds of .50-caliber ammunition. The air strike was completed at 1110.

At 1120, the 2nd Battalion 149th moved forward to occupy the area covered by the air strike. Skelton reported that a battalion tank destroyer team was taking care of the tank. At 1225, Company E spotted three tanks and a command car. Colonel Dishman, the 2nd Battalion commander, attempted to place artillery fire on these targets, but apparently unsuccessfully. The 149th reported no further advance during the day. At 1700, the battalion withdrew into the previous night's perimeter.[28]

The 2nd Battalion 149th killed seven Japanese definitely during the day and suffered 4 KIA and 21 WIA of its own. The day's action was costly to the Kentuckians. Among the 2nd Battalion's 25 casualties were two officers and eight sergeants. All four companies got into the fight, and G Company (12 casualties) was the hardest hit. In summary, the 149th Infantry had a very frustrating and non-productive day.[29]

The exact number of tanks in the Nagayoshi Detachment will probably never be known. According to the 39th Infantry history, the Chief of Staff of the 2nd Tank Division left one platoon of two tanks with the detachment during his visit on 28 December 1944. The Table of Organization and Equipment for a Japanese tank regiment called for three medium tanks in each platoon. The tanks caused Colonel Skelton so much grief that at least three tanks must have been present.[30]

A sure way of knowing how many tanks Major Nakayama controlled would have been to count the number of tanks destroyed during the battle.

However, the 38th Division did not report this information in its AAR. Sightings of tanks by the 149th continued for several days after 10 February. Division G-3 reported two tanks destroyed on 11 February but not whether these were destroyed on that day or that was the number destroyed in the campaign by that date. On the same day, 2nd Battalion "encountered tank believed knocked out by air strike." On 12 February, Company F "sighted one tank" at 1035. On 13 February, 2nd Battalion was "held up by fire believed from tank." On 14 February, F Company spotted three tanks, one "burned and other two knocked out by TD" (tank destroyer; to be discussed later). This last sighting, if true, at least confirms that three tanks were present.[31]

✿　✿　✿

Major Ogawa was reaching the end of his resources that had been none too plentiful from the start. At nightfall, he ordered platoon commander Master Sergeant Masafumi Kanechika to move the remaining 75-mm regimental gun (Yoshida Squad) to Mount Fumetsu to defend against enemy tanks advancing along the road the next day. He placed Master Sergeant Fujimoto in command of the remainder of the Regimental Gun Company, which would serve as infantry. The company commander, 1st Lieutenant Yuasa, had been called to Detachment Headquarters to co-ordinate fire for the North Garrison Unit.[32]

Ogawa's headquarters area at Fumetsu was in shambles following the attack of the 2nd Battalions of the 151st and 152nd. Despite his hopeless situation, Ogawa was determined to refortify this last stand area during the night and continue to make the Americans pay for its reduction.

His two 70-mm guns had been destroyed, but their protection, the Togo and Onishi HMG Squads, was still intact. Ogawa pulled these squads back to Fumetsu. The Kubota HMG Squad, the one remaining 37-mm AT gun and the Yoshida 75-mm Regimental Gun Squad, along with the surviving infantrymen, would give him a reasonably formidable defense. He would need it. Contrary to their usual practice, the Americans did not return to their perimeters on Mount Ege for the night but dug in at their day's end location. After the destruction of their positions during the day, the Japanese had precious little time for repair to withstand the merciless attack they expected the next day.[33]

Colonel A. J. Hastings, the 38th Division Chief of Staff, was so elated by the day's progress that in early afternoon, he started planning for the next day's attack. He assigned the details to Colonel Paddock, who immediately requested permission to fly over the battlefield as an aid in his planning. With two planes and pilots already lost, General Chase was reluctant to risk losing his senior ground commander, but finally gave permission. After aerial observation and consultation with his battalion commanders, Paddock submitted his plans to Colonel Hastings at 1650. He would have another battalion to add weight to the attack on the main line on 11 February. Colonel Funkhouser's 3rd Battalion 151st had returned to the pass. The men had refreshed themselves in the Kalaklan stream near the sawmill and were ready to join the battle.[34]

Chapter 18
NOTES

(1) 38th Infantry Division Historical Report, M-7 Operation (AAR) p. 24, p. 27;
38th Division journal.

(2) *History of the 39th Infantry Regiment,* edited and published by the 39th Infantry Association, p. 650.

(3) 38th Division AAR, p. 27.

(4) 151st Infantry AAR, p. 6;
39th Infantry History, p. 650.

(5) 151st Infantry AAR, p. 6;
2nd Battalion 152nd Infantry S-2 journal.

(6) *How the Kato Company Fought: The Record of the 3rd Machine Gun Company 39th Infantry Regiment,* Tamotsu Nagai, Editor, 1990, p. 228.

(7) *Ibid.,* p. 229.

(8) *Ibid.,* p. 230-232.

(9) 151st Infantry journal.

(10) 151st Infantry S-2 journal, entry # 12, 1100.

(11) 152nd Infantry journal, 1300.

(12) 151st Infantry AAR, p. 6.

(13) Kato Company History, p. 206.

(14) Walker, Major Stephen *M., The Operations of Company A, 151st Infantry in the Attack Through ZigZag Pass,* Advanced Infantry Officers Course, The Infantry School, Fort Benning, Georgia, 1949-1950, p. 17-20.

(15) Kato Company History, p. 206.

(16) Walker, p. 20-21.

(17) 1st Battalion 151st Infantry journal, 0935;
Walker, p. 18.

(18) Kato Company History, p. 210.

(19) Walker, p. 21-23.

(20) 151st Infantry journal;
38th Division G-3 journal.

(21) 1st Battalion 152nd Infantry journal.

(22) *39th Infantry History,* p. 649;
Teletype G-2 38th Division to G-2 XI Corps, 1000.

(23) 1st Battalion 152nd Infantry journal.

(24) 38th Division G-2 Report # 14, 1800-11 February 1945.

(25) Higashi, Lieutenant Colonel (ret) Yoshikazu, letter to author, 8 May 1998;
Takaki, Ronald, *Strangers From a Different Shore,* p. 400-402.

(26) 38th Division G-3 journal.

(27) *Ibid.*

(28) *Ibid.;*
2nd Battalion 149th Infantry journal.

(29) 2nd Battalion 149th Infantry journal.

(30) *39th Infantry History,* p. 620;
Barker, A. J., *Japanese Army Handbook 1939-1945,* p. 127.

(31) 38th Division G-3 Periodic Report #50, 1800-11 February 1945;
2nd Battalion 149th Infantry journal, 11, 12, 13, 14 February 1945.

(32) *39th Infantry History,* p. 649;
Ogawa, Major Hironori, *Record of the 3rd Battalion, 39th Infantry Regiment in the "Big Asia War,"* p. 43.

(33) Kato Company History, p. 199;
38th Division G-3 journal.

(34) 151st Infantry journal.

FURTHER CHANGES IN COMMAND

(11 FEBRUARY)

After the pounding they had taken the past three days, the Japanese could muster only feeble fireworks for the night of 10-11 February. No mortar or rifle fire. "Lots of grenades were thrown," 1st Battalion 151st reported to the Regimental S-2. Sensing a definite reduction in Japanese firepower, the Americans were eager to attack on 11 February.[1]

Colonel Paddock's plan, formulated the day before, continued to divide the western battlefield into two halves with Highway 7 being the dividing line. North of the road, 1st Battalion 151st, with Major Lemasters in command, would continue its attack of 10 February. On the extreme left, the 1st Battalion 152nd had ranged 800 yards north the day before, leaving a gap between the 1st/152nd and the 1st/151st. Colonel McIntosh inserted his relatively fresh 3rd Battalion, under Major Mangold, into the breach on the left of 1/151st. These two battalions would attempt to move forward through the Shinshu defenses to the hairpin. The 1st Battalion 152nd would continue to patrol to the north and also help destroy the numerous pillboxes, trenches and spider holes in rear of the two attacking battalions.

South of the road, 3rd Battalion 151st would pass through Colonel Mottern's 2nd Battalion 151st on the right and attack abreast with 2nd Battalion 152nd on the left. The mission south of the road was similar to the one in the north: clear out enemy positions in the Fumetsu area and move to the Santa Rita River. To give better co-ordination, the plan preserved the command arrangement started on 10 February for Colonel McIntosh, commander of the 152nd, to direct the troops north of the road and for Colonel Paddock, commander of the 151st, to give direction south of the road.[2] Despite the preparations the day before, Colonel Paddock's carefully laid plans for the attack on 11 February went awry at the start on the extreme right.

When it was time for the assaulting troops to move out at 0900 following the daily preparatory artillery barrage, there were disconcerting reports from Colonel Funkhouser's 3rd Battalion 151st. The battalion was slow in taking its position in the attack and had difficulty in getting organized. 1st Battalion 151st north of the road had already begun its attack. This was too much for Colonel Paddock. Obviously exasperated by Colonel Funkhouser's performance the last three days, he relieved Funkhouser on the spot and named Major Robert King, the Battalion Executive Officer, the new commander of 3/151st.[3]

Since the dawn of KIGEN-SETSU on 11 February, Major Ogawa's men had waited for their deliverance by Japanese planes, but instead, another relentless American assault began. First reports from the lead elements south of the road were encouraging. Resistance was not too heavy; the Hoosiers were receiving some rifle fire, but not much mortar fire.[4]

The opposition came from Fumetsu where most of the survivors from the MLR had gravitated. Colonel Hastings thought the resistance was negligible, but Colonel Thompson, 151st Exec, assured him the Japanese were far from through. At about that time, what the 151st journal called an "Arty shell . . . Enemy round" landed in a foxhole, killing four men of K Company, ample proof that it was still dangerous at the front.[5]

2nd Battalion 152nd found only light opposition on the western slope of the northern hill of Mount Fumetsu. But Fumetsu was a large area. Major Byus had no hint of the prize he had acquired and made no special effort to search for Major Ogawa's headquarters. The battalion spent most of the day finishing the tedious work of finding and destroying caves and entrenchments. He ordered his rifle companies to dig in in place for the night rather than give up the ground they had won.[6]

Even for Colonel Mottern's embattled 2/151st, the war did not stop after its relief by the 3rd Battalion. While reorganizing behind a hill 250 yards back of the front lines, the enemy fired on the battalion from within the hill. Mottern called to the rear once more for engineer demolition crews. A hastily formed engineer/infantry team destroyed two pillboxes that had escaped detection by the assault detachments scouring the area the previous day.[7]

Moreover, as 2nd Battalion 151st was leaving ZigZag Pass forever, one of the best-timed arrivals of the war was taking place. Captain King (no relation to the 3rd Battalion commander), Commanding Officer of E Company 151st, reported for duty to Colonel Thompson at 1240. The company had docked at Olongapo at 2015 the night before, at the end of its long voyage from New Guinea, and marched to the pass this morning.

How many times could Mottern have used this near full complement of six officers and 182 enlisted men during his battalion's hard fighting the last three days?[8]

✐   ✐   ✐

North of the road, 3rd Battalion 152nd on the left and 1st Battalion 151st on the right targeted Mount Shinshu, defended tenaciously by Sergeant Iga's and Sergeant Hijikata's heavy machine guns and supporting infantry. Major Lemasters's plan for 1/151 was the same as Stewart's the day before. Company A would assault the same objective from the north and west and B Company would move along the road and attack Shinshu from the southwest. The 603rd Tank Company and the 113th Engineers would support the 1st Battalion.

After a breakfast of coffee and sandwiches left over from the night before, A Company moved out at 0800 single file in a column of platoons. Captain Walker planned to follow the same route to the objective that had proved so successful on 10 February. This time, he made sure each man had a full canteen of water. Some men even carried two full canteens. The heat exhaustion returnees gave the company an effective strength of approximately 100 men.

At 0930, A Company reached the woods northwest of Mount Shinshu. Captain Walker planned to assault with two platoons abreast as before. He substituted the 3rd Platoon on the left in place of the 1st Platoon because the 1st was critically short of leaders. Lieutenant Wesley Cooke's 2nd Platoon on the right would again bear the brunt of the action.

Walker set up his 60-mm mortars about 300 yards northwest of the objective. At about 1000, with artillery and 81-mm mortar fire smothering the objective knoll on Shinshu, the 3rd on the left and 2nd Platoons of A Company began their assault from the woods.

When the 2nd Platoon came within 100 yards of the crest, with the 3rd Platoon still in the woods, the forward artillery observer with the company lifted his fire. Walker kept the "extremely accurate" 81-mm mortar fire coming until it started to cause casualties in the 2nd Platoon as the men crept to within 30 yards of the top.[9]

When the mortar barrage finally lifted, Sergeant Iga and his supporting infantry poured an intense fire into the 2nd Platoon. The gunner was Superior Private Hisaharu Tometa, who had replaced the wounded Yoshizu the day before. Firing steadily with a hot hand most of the morning, Tometa moved out of his trench to look for the enemy when the Americans disappeared briefly from his sights. Bravely he gained the ridgeline, toting his machine gun with him. As he was returning to his trench, he fell from a shot by a 3rd Platoon rifleman hidden in the woods.

Bleeding from his back and chest, Tometa died a moment later from a second shot in the chest.[10]

Walker sensed that the Japanese had reinforced the hill since the previous night. This observation was probably correct. A defending force will usually reinforce an area under attack one day if the attackers then withdraw to their original starting point for the night. All too often the battalions of the 38th Division returned to their original positions after a successful attack and gave the enemy time to recuperate and re-entrench during the night.

The Japanese placed heavy fire from light mortars and rifle grenades on the 2nd Platoon trying to take cover in various shallow depressions below the crest. Walker estimated that 100 mortar shells dropped in 15 minutes, only half of which detonated. Dud rifle grenades struck several men. Lieutenant Cooke, as well as the 3rd Platoon leader, became casualties. Company A pulled back and reorganized under cover of 60-mm and 81-mm mortar fire.

Lieutenant Lloyd G. Clark, B Company 113th Engineers, arrived at about 1300 and began the systematic destruction of the caves and pillboxes overrun by A Company but not destroyed during the advance. Ammunition and supplies continued to burn and explode throughout the day. This work by the engineers restricted the movement of the remaining Japanese and enabled the Americans to move about with greater freedom.

A section of two tanks appeared at 1400 and joined the company to support the attack. The tanks stopped in a depression about 200 yards northwest of the objective. The external telephones at the rear of the tanks were not working. Only with the greatest difficulty could Walker induce the section leader to unbutton his tank long enough for Walker to give him his plan of action.

The plan was for the two tanks to charge to the top of the hill and destroy any Japanese positions in sight or pointed out by the infantry. The 2nd Platoon, now reduced to ten men, would accompany the section leader's tank and the 3rd Platoon would escort the other tank. The section leader promised to relay these instructions by radio to the second tank.

Almost immediately, the section leader started toward the objective with the 2nd Platoon hurriedly trying to catch up and provide security. The second tank started to its left and brought its 75-mm cannon to bear on a squad of the 1st Platoon cowering in a deep depression. Walker and others furiously pounded on the hull with rifle butts until the tank commander opened a slit long enough to learn he was about to fire on friendly troops. Obviously embarrassed, the tank reversed its field and lumbered off toward the battalion perimeter. Shortly thereafter, the section leader, evidently realizing that his other tank was missing, turned in the same direction and bid a hasty retreat.[11]

The enemy version was different. The Japanese felt it was the quick-witted action of machine gun squad leader Sergeant Hijikata, who fired smoke shells that temporarily blinded the Americans and caused the tanks to withdraw.[12]

The performance of the 603rd Tank Company in ZigZag Pass is debatable. At times, the tankers performed creditably. At other times, they did not perform so well. Their very presence instilled fear and lowered the morale of the Japanese. The tanks put the fear of God in the Iga Squad this day. "We didn't have any weapons to fight tanks," Superior Private Ryuji Konai moaned. "Even if we struggled with all our might, there seemed no way to escape [when the tanks appeared]."[13]

On 4 February, at the "2" with E Company 34th, tanks helped make the first serious dent in Major Ogawa's main line. They were instrumental in the reduction of Mount Minami and other key positions. At other times, they drew enemy fire and thus located hostile weapons. But on 11 February, they were of no help to A Company 151st in its attack on Mount Shinshu.

General Hall had a low opinion of the tankers. In December 1949, Hall wrote of his frustrations to Captain Walker. Hall complained that the tanks "in the ZigZag fight" did us little or no good. "They could have been of much help, but no one seemed to be able to make them fight." Hall admitted he couldn't get them to fight. He mentioned one instance of mapping out a possible route off the road for a tank commander after the latter said that he might get blown up if he followed the road. "I don't think he ever tried it," Hall concluded the story in disgust.[14]

At 1600, deserted by the tanks and with B Company again bogged down on his right, Captain Walker started digging his perimeter for the night. He chose an area in defilade about 75 yards northwest of the objective. He did not consider this a good spot, but he was determined not to withdraw to the battalion area a second night.

Company A had hardly started digging when Colonel McIntosh, commander of the troops north of the road, ordered the company back to its battalion perimeter. The 151st Infantry had been notified at 1352 that it would be pulled out of the pass for another mission. With mortar and machine gun fire buttoning up Shinshu, A Company withdrew, as on the previous day, along the same trail. The 1st Battalion 151st moved in a column of companies to a safe portion of Highway 7 and boarded trucks for Olongapo. For the first time in almost five days, the battalion could bathe and have a decent meal.

Company A suffered 43 casualties during its four days in the pass plus numerous heat exhaustion cases. Among its casualties were two of its three officers, the first sergeant, the supply sergeant, two platoon sergeants, two staff sergeants and several squad leaders and assistant squad leaders. None of these men were among the heat exhaustion cases. Company strength for its new mission was one officer (Captain Walker) and 80 enlisted men.[15]

Major Stewart, 1st Battalion commander, received orders at 1200-11 February promoting him to Lieutenant Colonel effective 31 January 1945. Characteristically, Stewart had reported to the regimental CP ready for duty earlier in the morning, but Colonel Thompson had ordered him to return to the rear for additional rest.[16]

By the end of the day, Major Mangold's 3rd Battalion 152nd had occupied the ridge northwest of the hairpin curve in the highway. Companies K and L joined perimeters on a hill next to the road while I Company dug in on a hill 150 yards to the north. Colonel McIntosh moved his own 1st Battalion into the space vacated by 1st Battalion 151st. During the night, the men of Company K tossed hand grenades down the slope into a group of chattering and shouting Japanese perhaps preparing for a counterattack.[17]

☙   ☙   ☙

With the main battle now shifted to the Shinshu/Fumetsu area, all was quiet in the western end of the horseshoe/hairpin sector of the battlefield. Still in charge of the Morinaka HMG Squad at Mount Ege, Sergeant Nagai started the day on outpost duty with squad member Hisakazu Kobayashi. No guns or mortars were firing on Mount Ege; the American fire now centered on Mount Shinshu and Mount Fumetsu. Most of the 151st and 152nd Infantry had bypassed Nagai's position and moved on to the east. Neither the 151st nor the 152nd ever did occupy the southern portion of Mount Ege. Lieutenant Shinfune and nearly half his company survived the battle.

The first order of the day was to retrieve the Morinaka machine gun from the bunker where the Americans began digging in the previous day. Returning to the position soon after daybreak, Nagai and Kobayashi observed a group of about 20 Americans (probably an assault team) in column with a flamethrower in the middle, scouts with "tommy" guns in front, and riflemen in the rear. They were moving away from the area where Nagai knew the gun had been located. When the Americans were out of sight, the two Japanese rushed to the bunker, picked up the machine gun and manhandled it back to their position. A quick check determined that the gun was still functioning properly.

There was a huge tree at a corner of the communications trench that connected several positions on Mount Ege. The tree was a real giant with massive roots straining in all directions. Lieutenant Koyama with seven men, including Sergeant Nagai, decided to build a new position around the giant tree. With the Morimoto and Morinaka machine guns as anchors on opposite sides of the tree, they created a circular position with two-man foxholes connected by trenches. The roots of the gigantic tree were so large, the men bored holes through them for observation and for firing their rifles.

Nagai and Kobayashi returned to the position the Americans had abandoned earlier in the morning. They brought back quite a haul of useful items: a bazooka and two shells they later presented to battalion headquarters; a machete, a necessity for moving through the jungle; a wire cutter which could be wielded with one hand, smaller than the Japanese two-handed version, with a grip covered with rubber to prevent an electric shock; a poncho that could be used in inclement weather, or snapped to another to erect a tent (Nagai considered the American poncho greatly superior to Japanese army rainwear and owed his later good health to this piece of equipment); an emergency medical kit containing tincture of iodine, sulfa drug, bandages and quinine; mosquito repellant; and a wristwatch type compass. All of these items, taken for granted by the American soldier, were apparently either not standard issue in the Japanese army or in short supply.[18]

✦   ✦   ✦

To summarize the day's activities, the 38th Division was moving cautiously this late in the campaign to avoid unnecessary casualties. The 151st and 152nd regiments did not attack Mounts Shinshu and Fumetsu frontally, but made gains on the flanks, setting the stage for a more substantial advance the next day. Removal of the 151st Infantry in early afternoon for another operation disrupted plans for the rest of 11 February.

In the east, the 149th Infantry reported that the air strike at 0915 was "very effective." Yet, two battalions striking abreast along the road gained only 300 yards for the day. "Heavy sniper fire" was the only opposition the 38th Division reported holding up the 149th. Company E sent a patrol forward to neutralize the snipers; three hours later, after using 60-mm mortars on the snipers and machine gun nests, the company captured two machine guns and one rifle.

38th Division credited the 149th with destroying two tanks and capturing two truckloads of ammunition and a large CP installation, besides the two machine guns. It is not clear whether the two tanks were the tanks previously destroyed or were two additional tanks destroyed. Despite caution and the limited opposition, the division still lost 12 KIA and 26 WIA on both fronts during this day. The relatively low casualties on 11 February can be directly attributed to the costly, bloody fighting of the previous four days in the West Pass.[19]

In its first combat, the 151st Infantry had performed admirably during its four days in the pass. In one 24-hour period, 2nd Battalion 151st alone placed 135 tons of metal on enemy positions, burning out four each 60-mm and 81-mm mortar tubes in the process. Although only two rifle companies of the 2nd Battalion were in action, two officers were killed and five were wounded during the battle. The Battalion Exec, the H Company commander and one other officer were relieved because of emotional instability, and another officer was relieved for inefficiency.

The 151st suffered casualties of 34 KIA, 202 WIA, and 1 MIA for a total of 237 during its four days in the pass. Twenty men were reported injured, which may have been another way of designating psychoneurotic cases.[20]

💣　💣　💣

Soon after the change in command of the 38th Division, General Hall was satisfied that General Chase could break the Japanese hold on the horseshoe-hairpin area. Hall and his staff had used the last three days to plan the next operations that would complete the original XI Corps mission of liberating the remainder of the Bataan Peninsula and capturing the islands guarding the entrance to Manila harbor.

XI Corps plans called for landing one Regimental Combat Team at Mariveles on the southern tip of the peninsula with the mission of linking with another RCT driving down the east coast road. Immediately following the occupation of Mariveles, one reinforced infantry battalion would land on Corregidor to augment the main assault force, the independent airborne 503rd Parachute Infantry.

The 151st Infantry, designated the South Force, commanded by General Chase, had been selected for the landing at Mariveles. General Krueger had moved the 1st RCT of the 6th Division from I Corps on his left flank as reinforcement for XI Corps to constitute the East Force under command of General Spence, the 38th Division Artillery commander. The 3rd Battalion 34th Infantry, which had seen little action in ZigZag Pass, reinforced by A Company, would make the amphibious assault on Corregidor. But that is another story.[21]

💣　💣　💣

The reader will recall that XI Corps was operating under a directive from Sixth Army: Field Order #46 dated 30 January (see page 73). Field Order #46 also outlined broad objectives for I and XIV Corps. The key phrase in the instructions to I Corps, operating on Sixth Army's left flank, was "capture San Jose." General Yamashita, commander of all Japanese forces on Luzon, considered this town, strategically located at the junction of Highways 3 and 5, vital to his future operations. All through January he had stockpiled ammunition and other supplies from Manila at San Jose awaiting transportation north on Route 5 to the main positions of his Shobu Group in northern Luzon. He also wanted to hold San Jose open to enable the 105th Division from the Shimbu Group to move up Route 5 and join his forces.

San Jose itself was not occupied by the Japanese, but defended by eight surrounding strongpoints. The most important of these was Munoz, eight miles southwest of San Jose. One company of the 20th Infantry 6th Division had been repulsed at Munoz on 30 January, and Major General Edwin D. Patrick, 6th Division commander, realized the defenses were stronger than originally perceived.

The main I Corps attack, as directed by Field Order #46, began on 1 February with the 20th Infantry's mission the capture of Munoz. Attacking across flat, open ground under a broiling tropical sun, the 20th made only slight gains against the enemy firmly entrenched in the rubble of Munoz. After two days of fruitless attacks, General Patrick lost patience with the 20th Infantry, which he felt had also been slow in a previous engagement, and relieved its commander, Colonel Washington M. Ives. Now on 11 February, Colonel Ives arrived at the 152nd Infantry CP as the new Commanding Officer of the regiment.[22]

The officers of the 152nd were justifiably mystified by General Krueger's change in the command. Colonel McIntosh had taken over troops in the heat of battle that General Hall felt were dispirited and lacked the will to fight. In nine days he had welded them into a confident, hard-hitting regiment. There were also cries of understandable resentment in a National Guard unit when a regular Army officer, especially a West Pointer,[23] replaces one of their own. The officers could not help comparing the relief of their own Colonel Stillwell with the relief of Colonel Ives. A typical comment: "Colonel Stillwell was sacked—period—but Colonel Ives was given a second chance."

"Mackey" Ives had earned his spurs in peacetime and combat. Munoz had been defended by 2,000 tough, seasoned troops supported by 55-60 immobile, well dug-in tanks, a battery of 105-mm howitzers and several 47-mm anti-tank guns. Eventually, most of the 6th Division became engaged. A bombing and strafing attack with napalm by 50 planes plus an all-out bombardment by division and corps artillery had been planned for 7 February to break the stalemate at Munoz.

The bombardment became unnecessary when the Japanese defenders were annihilated in their attempted escape from Munoz the night of 6-7 February. However, the delay at Munoz had made the defense of San Jose successful. By 4 February, the stockpile of supplies at San Jose had started northward, and most of the 105th Division had slipped through the town to join Yamashita.[24]

General Patrick later admitted to his artillery commander, General Charles E. Hurdis, who became division commander 14 March when Patrick was mortally wounded, that he had been wrong about Ives. "In light of the Japanese strength ultimately discovered there [Munoz], Colonel Ives's relief was regrettable and unjustifiable," Patrick confided to his successor.[25]

General Chase was delighted to receive Ives and commented that the 152nd was "well-commanded."[26]

Chapter 19
NOTES

(1) 151st Infantry S-2 journal, 0720-11 February 1945.
(2) 151st Infantry journal, 1650-10 February 1945;
     38th Division AAR, p. 27.
(3) 151st Infantry journal, 0907;
     151st Infantry AAR, p. 7.
(4) 151st Infantry journal, 1000-1010.
(5) *Ibid.,* 1220.
(6) 152nd Infantry journal, 1725.
(7) 151st Infantry AAR, p. 6.
(8) 151st Infantry journal entry #37.
(9) Walker, Major Stephen M., *The Operations of Company A 151st Infantry in the Attack Through ZigZag Pass, 8-11 February 1945,* Advanced Infantry Officers Course 1949-1950, The Infantry School, Fort Benning, Georgia. p. 23-24.
(10) *How the Kato Company Fought: The Record of the 3rd Machine Gun Company 39th Infantry Regiment*, Tamotsu Nagai, Editor, 1990, p. 207.
(11) Walker, p. 24-26.
(12) Kato Company History, p. 211.
(13) *Ibid.,* p. 207.
(14) Walker, p. 30-31.
(15) *Ibid.,* p. 24-27.
(16) 151st Infantry journal, 1000, 1200.
(17) Schoonover, Major James F., *The Operations of the 3rd Battalion 152nd Infantry in Zig Zag Pass, Luzon, 29 Jan.-14 Feb. 1945,* Advanced Infantry Officers Course, 1947-1948, p. 14.
(18) Kato Company History, p. 195, p. 237-238, p. 240-243.
(19) 38th Division G-3 Periodic Report #50, 1800-11 February 1945; 2nd Battalion 149th Infantry journal.
(20) 151st Infantry AAR, p. 6-7.
(21) Smith, Robert Ross, *Triumph in the Philippines*, p. 331.
(22) *Ibid.,* p. 190-194;
     Avengers of Bataan, 38th Infantry Division Historical Report M-7

Operation, Note to text made by Major Kenneth W. Brewer, Executive Officer, 3rd Battalion 152nd Infantry, p. 27.

(23) Washington Mackey Ives earned his nickname "Mugger" at West Point (Class of 1924) as a 5'8"-175 lb. present day equivalent cornerback. He was the same "quiet, simple, sincere, unpretentious" helpmate to others at graduation, at retirement in 1954, and in 1970 when he died from a heart attack on the Fort Sam Houston golf course at age 67. The Florida native was 42 years old at the time of the battle. West Point Assembly, June 1974.

(24) Smith, *Triumph*, p. 198-200.

(25) *Ibid.,* Note p. 195.

(26) *Ibid.,* Note p. 399 quoted from Chase comments on 3 December 1956.

20

"PLEASE NOT TO WORRY ABOUT THE EMPEROR"
(12 FEBRUARY)

It was far safer on the American front lines the night of 11-12 February than in the rear areas. Major Ogawa had organized demolition patrols (perhaps some of Lieutenant Oda's men who had signed a death petition in blood) to harass the enemy. The primary targets were artillery pieces, supply dumps and vehicles.

Especially marked for destruction were the hated artillery liaison planes that made movement almost impossible and discouraged cooking at any time. Constantly hovering over the battlefield, they detected the slightest movement in the daytime or faintest light at night and then brought down instant, accurate artillery fire.

Ogawa's marauders, knowing the ground and trails well, easily bypassed the front line perimeters and stealthily moved against their targets in the rear.

At about half an hour before midnight, an undetermined number of Japanese hit the Cub Strip situated on the dry rice paddies northeast of Olongapo. The infiltrators destroyed two liaison planes of the 983rd F.A. Battalion with phosphorous grenades, then set afire a small ammo dump with picric acid and dynamite. They wounded one American with a hand grenade before melting into the darkness.

At 0320, a second group struck, burning two XI Corps planes and wounding another guard. The group also attacked an 11th F.A. Battalion position nearby. One of the two infiltrators killed by the alert artillerymen had explosives strapped to his back.[1]

There had been previous raids on the planes at San Marcelino Airstrip and against the Olongapo dam that controlled the town's water supply, but this night's work was by far the enemy's most ambitious and successful venture.

With the formation of the East and West Forces, General Easley, as on 7 February, was the senior officer present in the pass and, therefore, commander of the remaining American forces. His alternatives, however, were much simplified compared with the dilemma he had faced five days earlier. His primary objective now was to compress the Japanese into an ever-smaller space between the vise of his 152nd Regiment attacking from the west and the 149th still 2,500 yards to the east. He approved Colonel McIntosh's orders for the day for the 152nd to attack on a regimental front.

North of the road, 3rd Battalion on the left would occupy the hairpin curve, then advance along Highway 7 toward the bridge; 1st Battalion on the right would attack along Highway 7 until the road began the hairpin turn, then clear Mount Shinshu of any remaining Japanese. South of the road, 2nd Battalion would move past Fumetsu cross-country to Highway 7 at a point about 500 yards south of the hairpin. The 149th would continue its push west, 2nd Battalion north of the road, 1st Battalion south.[2]

Early on the morning of 12 February, Major Ogawa ordered 25-30 men of the Regimental Gun Company, who had no gun to serve, to move across the road from Mount Fumetsu and help in the defense of Mount Shinshu. These men would fight as infantry and reinforce Lieutenant Ogata's 11th Company survivors. 2nd Lieutenant Takeshi Sasaki, the only remaining officer of the 11th Company, had been badly wounded, so Master Sergeant Fujimoto of the gun company assumed command of the first line of Shinshu's defenses.[3]

Anticipating the most resistance, Colonel Cornwell's 1st Battalion, accompanied by tanks, jumped off at 0800 following a 30-minute artillery barrage. Company B was on the forward slope of an unconquered knoll in the Shinshu area by 0830 after knocking out one of the 11th Company light machine guns.[4]

Sensing that the Japanese were cracking, the 1st and 3rd Battalions of the 152nd Infantry moved with purpose against Fujimoto's makeshift defense supported by the heavy machine guns of Sergeant Iga and Sergeant Hijikata. Fighting mainly with only rifles and grenades, the diehard defenders turned the enemy back three times, but finally succumbed to overwhelming numbers. The Americans killed many of the remaining 11th Company riflemen and destroyed three of its light machine guns. Five soldiers of the Regimental Gun Company were killed and five more wounded.[5]

A hand grenade war ensued for the third consecutive day. The Americans stood on higher ground and gradually bored in. The strain was beginning to tell on Sergeant Iga. "Enemy occupied the ridge line in front, then approached our cave from the right side and back. We defended our position among the many dead and wounded in our trenches. It is a wonder we survived half a month against an enemy ten times our number with mastery of the air. Our situation became worse every day."[6]

Sergeant Kyujiro Iga, Section Leader 3rd Battalion Machine Gun Company 39th Infantry, 1944

. . . and in 1991

When the American attack started, the Hijikata Squad's heavy machine gun was still serviceable. However, lacking a sight, the gun's accuracy was not reliable. Ammunition was so low that the 11th Company men gathered cartridges from dead soldiers and set them in the metal firing boards for the machine guns. "Finally," Hijikata admitted, "our gun was broken beyond repair and could fire no more. The enemy was so near that we could hear them talking. We did not want them to know how few our numbers really were. We moved around the trenches shouting so as to deceive them."[7]

When Japanese fire from Fumetsu held up B Company, the Hoosiers fired tracers to identify the active pillboxes, which the tankers readily destroyed with their 75-mm guns. The remaining Japanese 75-mm regimental gun, using an improved German-made armor piercing shell, immobilized one tank with a direct hit. Ogawa had ordered the gun moved from Shinshu to Fumetsu the night before for just that purpose. Highway 7, which the tanks used almost exclusively, could be covered better from Fumetsu than from Shinshu. Master Sergeant Masafumi Kanechika died heroically while scoring the direct hit on the American tank. An American shell damaged the regimental gun, killing three of the crew and wounding one. The remaining gunners got the gun operating again and continued firing until their ammunition was exhausted.[8]

Colonel Cornwell found enough opposition west of the hairpin to occupy 1st Battalion for the remainder of the day. As usual, roving Japanese riflemen made life in the open chancy. One killed 1st Lieutenant Cork, the Battalion S-2, late in the afternoon.[9]

* * *

2nd Battalion moved against Fumetsu at 0900. Four Japanese heavy machine gun squads put up a lively scrap all morning. After being bombarded by a tank, newly appointed squad leader Matsuo Masuda moved his gun to the battalion headquarters cave position. With Pfc. Isao Kawanishi he started firing at about 30 U.S. soldiers as they came over a ridgeline about 200 meters distant.

A flamethrower team on his left and about ten Americans ten meters to his right rear attacked him immediately. "I was hit by a hand grenade fragment and fell back into the cave. I got out of the cave on the back side and escaped a certain death," Masuda remembered. Kawanishi also escaped during this brush with the enemy only to be killed on Mount Koko later in the month while on patrol looking for food.[10]

The GIs damaged the squads of Corporal Sanji Onishi and new squad leader Torao Nishioka severely. Onishi and two of his men were apparently killed simultaneously when a tank round found their emplacement; two of Nishioka's men were shot in the head. Lieutenant Kato, himself, had to take over one machine gun squad to ward off the persistent Americans. He reported that the inside of the battalion headquarters position "was a terrible mess."[11]

A tank scored a direct hit on Sergeant Masao Togo's squad. Superior Private Fusataro Hirayama died instantly. Sergeant Togo lost his right eye and the round shattered his right shoulder. The same shell wounded superior Private Shizuo Hanaoka. All three were buried by debris under the fallen dirt and log roof over their position, but Togo lived to tell the tale.[12]

Warrant Officer Kazuichi Ishihara, commander of the 3rd Heavy Machine Gun Platoon, sent Superior Private Kaichi Akiyama forward to gain information about the progress of the battle. A member of one of the suicide squads, who fought tanks, Akiyama thought the battle was going worse than the day before. He reached the forward positions by crawling through a communications trench mostly caved in from artillery fire.

During a lull, Akiyama stumbled across a grisly scene at the Onishi heavy machine gun position. Strewn around the destroyed gun were the bodies of Onishi, Superior Private Susumu Hashimoto with the right upper part of his body mangled, and Superior Private Yujiro Aida disintegrated by a tank shell. "When I returned to my position," Akiyama wrote later, "my hole had been obliterated by tank fire. If I had not been sent forward to scout, I would have been killed by the tank bombardment."[13]

By noon, the Japanese were no longer contesting the 2nd Battalion's advance. Major Byus bypassed Fumetsu and started cross-country for Highway 7 south of the hairpin. By 1350, Byus had moved to a position on the road only 300 yards shy of the Santa Rita River bridge.[14]

* * *

Major Mangold left L Company behind to help 1st Battalion clear its trouble spots. Following mortar and artillery preparations, the 3rd Battalion moved through the Shinshu defensive position with I and K Companies abreast, K on the right. The companies then advanced along the road 400 yards south of the hairpin, but were stopped by mortar fire. The enemy could still interdict much of the road between the hairpin and the bridge with 120-mm mortars firing from the East Pass. By 1400, most of the enemy positions west of the river had been silenced. Colonel Ives ordered Mangold to send a strong patrol to seize and hold the bridge and its environs.[15]

The three battalions had accomplished an enormous amount of work during the day. At a price of 16 KIA and 90 WIA, the 152nd reported killing 110 Japanese, still appearing to be well fed and well equipped with both personal and military items. The regiment destroyed nine ammunition dumps in abandoned caves, finding 20,000 rounds of .30 caliber, 400 cases of 75-mm artillery ammunition, several hundred hand grenades and a knee (50-mm) and 90-mm mortar ammunition cache so heavily booby-trapped as to preclude inventory. These reports are inconsistent with numerous Japanese comments on the scarcity of ammunition. Perhaps distribution from the ammunition dumps to individual units was at fault.[16]

One prize was a 120-mm mortar with ammunition captured intact. Besides rice and ammunition dumps, 3rd Battalion found large caches of clothing and new flame-throwers. One pillbox "yielded a finely tailored horse gas mask."[17]

Colonel Wilson, Division G-2, summed up the day's activities: "The density and elaborateness of the enemy installations . . . indicate the importance of this area to the enemy defensive plan. Defenses range from literally uncountable simple trenches to complex connecting tunnels, vaults and pillboxes. Stubborn resistance continues amid this entrenched maze . . . the increasingly disorganized appearance of the overrun positions indicates that the enemy withdrawal has become hasty and confused."[18]

By the end of the day, neither battalion had been able to reach the bridge. 1st Battalion 152nd dug in on the north side of Highway 7 along the southern base of Shinshu; 2nd Battalion on the road in the Santa Rita River valley about 300 yards west of the bridge; and 3rd Battalion on the road south of the hairpin about 400 yards behind 2nd Battalion.

On the grassland of Lieutenant Otani's former 105-mm artillery position, American soldiers, stripped to the waist, were constructing new 81-mm mortar positions under bright lights. Searchlights were sweeping the road.[19]

✦   ✦   ✦

At the eastern end of the battlefield, the 149th Infantry showed greater progress on 12 February than on any of the last three days, possibly due to a bit of luck the day before. A patrol of C Company had come across the five dead of the Nakayama Battalion killed by the company's platoon-size patrol of 9 February that had attempted to reach 3rd Battalion 151st. The company commander, leading the patrol, had the bodies searched again, and this time a map was found sewn in the lining of one of the enemy uniforms. The map showed a detailed plan of Major Nakayama's defenses and proved to be of considerable help in reducing the remaining strongpoints east of the Santa Rita River.[20]

Helped the second day in a row by an air strike, the 149th gained 500 yards 12 February. Formidable enemy positions that withstood artillery and mortar fire until 1030 held up the 1st Battalion south of the road. The Kentuckians attacked the positions with BARs, grenades and rifles and killed 60 of the Japanese airmen at a cost of only one casualty to the battalion.[21]

Colonel Dishman's 2nd Battalion north of the road moved out at 0900 behind an artillery barrage that destroyed an oil dump and Japanese command car. The artillery observer first reported the enemy running from the artillery fire. After the next round he joked, "They aren't running now!"

At 1400, the 2nd Battalion encountered a strongly fortified position 400 yards north of the highway in dense undergrowth. After pulling back for artillery fire to knock out this resistance, Colonel Dishman withdrew his battalion to the previous night's perimeter when the artillery proved to be ineffective. 2nd Battalion killed 28 Japanese during the day, but suffered 11 casualties of its own. The 3 killed were all in E Company, as were the 4 men killed 11 February in this relatively hard hit company.[22]

It was evident to Major Ogawa early on 12 February that the enemy would soon pass through his positions on Mount Fumetsu and get into the Santa Rita River valley in his rear. Surrounded on all sides, he knew it would be only a matter of time until the Americans systematically destroyed all of his men. He reported to Colonel Nagayoshi—what he had dreaded ever since the campaign began—that he was being overwhelmed and now was the time to begin the pre-arranged withdrawal and conduct guerrilla warfare. At 1200, he issued his last order in ZigZag Pass:

North Garrison Unit • 1200 Noon • 12 February • Fumetsu-zan
"Order for North Defense Force"
1. You are familiar with the enemy situation.
2. North Garrison Unit, carrying wounded who can make the journey, breaks through the enemy lines and sallies forth to Kosaku-yama.
3. Each unit starts movement after sunset, assembles at Battalion Headquarters [Mount Fumetsu] by 2000. Battalion Adjutant will direct order of march.
4. Shinfune 9th Company moves directly to Kosaku-yama from Ege-zan, provides right flank protection for main body. Time of departure for Kosaku-yama: 2200. Main body leaves three squads as rear guard so that enemy will not become aware of our intentions. Rear guard will withdraw before dawn and join main group.
5. Details of departure will be announced later.
6. I will be at Battalion Command Post at Fumetsu-zan.
7. Special instructions:
   A. Carry as much food and ammunition as possible.
   B. Destroy all equipment that might be of use to the enemy.
   C. Burn all documents.
   D. Veterinarians destroy horses.
   E. Communications Platoon cease operations at 2000, remove and carry all operational radios.
                                                            —Major Ogawa

Wire communications on Fumetsu were in shambles and definitely out to Lieutenant Shinfune on Mount Ege. A runner must have passed the order to units without radios.[23]

By the strangest of coincidences, a voice from the outside came in loud and clear before the communications platoon signed off at 2000. The 39th Infantry Communications Company at Mount Kongo had worked diligently, trying to communicate daily with each headquarters to which the Detachment had been assigned: Manila Defense Force, the 2nd Tank Division, the Kembu Group. Nothing had been heard from any of these forces since the start of the battle at the West Pass. The operators had been pounding their keys day and night. As if by a miracle, the 2nd Tank Division responded to a signal. Nagayoshi learned of the general battle situation on Luzon and about the capture of Manila by the Americans; but most importantly, he was able to report the brave stand his troops had made along Highway 7 to prevent the Americans on his front from reaching Manila, as well as his decision to begin guerrilla warfare.[24]

At 1800, Ogawa sent this message to Colonel Nagayoshi:

1. North Defense Force will sally forth at 2200 tonight to Kosaku-yama. Presently we have strength of 80 men.
2. All survivors will assemble at Santa Rita-yama and prepare for guerrilla warfare.
3. All men are ready to die an honorable death.
4. If you do not hear from us in two weeks, consider us dead.
5. "Long live the Emperor and his empire!

Nagayoshi replied immediately:

1. I agree with your plan.
2 Please not to worry about the Emperor and his empire.
3 I pray for your safe passage and ultimate victory.[25]

At dusk, Major Ogawa called a meeting of his remaining officers, platoon leaders and squad leaders to tell them the plans for vacating their positions that night. Then came emotional scenes as soldiers, who had built, defended and lived in their caves and trenches for nearly two months, were now asked to abandon them.

They were forced to make agonizing decisions regarding the wounded. Which could stand the march or be helped to walk and which had to be left behind to fight to the finish or commit suicide? They begged Superior Private Takao Ogiuchi of the Takamura HMG Squad to join the column, but Ogiuchi refused because of his poor condition. He stayed, caring for Ohmae of the engineers until the latter died. An explosion at Mount Fumetsu on 13 February killed Ogiuchi. Five other wounded machine gunners and many badly wounded soldiers from other companies were to die in similar fashion on Shinshu or Fumetsu on 13 February.[26]

Sergeant Hijikata bade farewell to an old friend. "Our heavy machine gun, which could no longer fire, was just a lump of steel. The gun barrel had been burned and changed color. It looked like a dead soldier who had fought bravely and had many scars on his body. There is a difference between human flesh and cold steel, but we felt the battered gun had a soul. 'You've done a great job. Thank you for your excellent service,' we said. We disassembled the gun and buried it in the cave with due ceremony. 'Soul of heavy machine gun sleep in peace forever,' we prayed. I could not stop the flow of tears."[27]

The night of 12-13 February was the first of the campaign devoid of Japanese harassing activity. The reason, of course, was that Ogawa's men were withdrawing from the pass. After assembling at the 3rd Battalion Headquarters on Mount Fumetsu, 80 survivors, led by the regimental gun company of 20 men, marched 1,200 yards south to the base of Mount Kosaku, the highest point on the battlefield. Arriving just before dawn, they waited for Lieutenant Shinfune's 9th Company to join them.

Despite being slowed by the wounded, Ogawa's men made good time against no opposition. Ogawa had visualized an unusually difficult withdrawal through the American lines that he had expected would surround Mount Fumetsu. However, 2nd and 3rd Battalions 152nd had dug in east of Fumetsu in the Santa Rita River valley, and the 1st Battalion was encamped in the Shinshu area north of the road.[28]

Fortunately, Lieutenant (jg) Chusaku Ito's naval company, guarding the East Pass, skirted around the 2nd Battalion 152nd's position on Highway 7 and was able to join Ogawa that night. The battalion commander sent a runner to inform Lieutenant Shinfune of the withdrawal. He feared the runner had been killed when the 9th Company was nowhere to be found at Mount Kosaku early on 13 February.[29]

Lieutenant Shinfune had received the message to withdraw and had his troops ready to march at 2200 on 12 February. Sergeant Nagai continued to have nothing but contempt for Lieutenant Shinfune and the 9th Company men for the way they treated attached troops like the machine gunners and the engineers. He blamed Shinfune, the officer in charge in the Mount Ege sector, for not communicating to him the purpose of the sortie and the destination. When he packed his belongings, Nagai could not find his rucksack and his writing materials he had left in the 9th Company headquarters cave when he was wounded. He could only conclude that some of the 9th Company men had stolen them. They had also hoarded grenades, which could have been used in defense and saved lives the last five days. They never distributed enough provisions to troops attached to the company.[30]

Only one of the two heavy machine guns on Mount Ege could be carried during the withdrawal. Lieutenant Koyama, the leader of the 1st Platoon of the machine gun company, decided to carry the Morimoto gun. The men disassembled the Morinaka gun, wrapped the parts in pieces of canvas and buried them by the side of the huge tree. They also buried any items not needed for immediate use, such as gas masks. They could always find the giant tree again if they wanted to retrieve any of the items. Then they disassembled the Morimoto gun completely, wrapped the pieces in cloth or blanket and distributed the pieces among themselves. They could carry only so much ammunition: 1 box of 600 rounds and several bullet boards of 30 rounds each.[31]

The survivors tried to soundproof everything so as not to give their presence away in the jungle. They taped the handles of cooking vessels filled with rice or wrapped them with cloth. They wrapped cloths and ropes around their shoes to prevent slipping. Each man wrapped cloth around each of the seven grenades he carried. If he carried a sword, he wrapped it in cloth if the scabbard was missing. Gas mask bags were handy for carrying extra food.[32]

Finally, the band of about 40 strong moved down the rugged slope of Mount Ege toward Mount Kosaku. Lieutenant Shinfune's men led the way, followed by Lieutenant Koyama's machine gunners and the engineers. It was an inky black night; it was so that dark Sergeant Nagai couldn't see his finger when he touched his nose. Each man could see only the glowing, phosphorescent leaf mold smeared on the back of the man in front of him. The shadowy forms looked like so many fireflies in the darkness, making it difficult to know which one to follow. Glowing human forms were the only moving creatures in the area. Some men maintained contact by tying strings around their waists. Each man depended solely on the radiating human figure ahead and the string to guide him through the jungle that night.[33]

Chapter 20
NOTES

(1) 38th Division G-2 Periodic Report #15, 1800-12 February 1945.
(2) 152nd Infantry journal;
     XI Corps G-3 Periodic Report #15, 2000-12 February 1945.
(3) *History of the 39th Infantry Regiment,* edited and published by
     the 39th Infantry Association, p. 663.
(4) 152nd Infantry journal.
(5) *39th Infantry History,* p. 663.
(6) *How the Kato Company Fought: The Record of the 3rd Machine
     Gun Company 39th Infantry Regiment,* Tamotsu Nagai, Editor,
     1990, p. 208.
(7) *Ibid.,* p. 212.
(8) *39th Infantry History,* p. 650-652;
     38th Division G-2 Periodic Report #15, 1800-12 February 1945,
     reported two tanks destroyed.
(9) 1st Battalion 152nd Infantry journal, 1710.
(10) Kato Company History, p. 197.
(11) *Ibid.,* p. 198-199.
(12) *Ibid.,* p. 200.
(13) *Ibid.,* p. 203.
(14) 152nd Infantry journal.
(15) Schoonover, Major James F., *The Operations of the 3rd Battalion
     152nd Infantry in Zig Zag Pass, Luzon, 29 Jan.-14 Feb. 1945,*
     Advanced Infantry Officers Course, 1947-1948, p. 14;
     152nd Infantry journal.
(16) 152nd Infantry journal;
     38th Division G-2 Periodic Report #15, 1800-12 February 1945.
(17) 38th Division G-2 Periodic Report #15, 1800;
     Schoonover, *The Operations of the 3rd Battalion 152nd Infantry,*
     p. 15.
(18) 38th Division G-2 Periodic Report #15, 1800.
(19) 152nd Infantry journal;
     Kato Company History, p. 208.
(20) Brinson, Captain Arthur, Cavalry monograph: *The Battle of
     ZigZag Pass,* delivered at the Armored School, Fort Knox, KY, 5

May 48, p. 10. At the time of the battle Brinson was C Company 149th Infantry Exec;

(21) 38th Division AAR, p. 28.

(22) 2nd Battalion 149th Infantry journal, 0900.

(23) Ogawa, Major Hironori, *Record of the 3rd Battalion, 39th Infantry Regiment in the "Big Asia War,"* p. 45-46;
       39th Infantry History, p. 662.

(24) *39th Infantry History,* p. 664.

(25) Ogawa, p. 46;
       39th Infantry History, p. 662.

(26) Ogawa, p. 45;
       Kato Company History, p. 192.

(27) Kato Company, history, p. 212.

(28) Ogawa, p. 47;
       39th Infantry History, p. 664;
       152nd Infantry journal.

(29) Ogawa, p. 47;
       39th Infantry History, p. 664.

(30) Kato Company History, p. 244-245.

(31) *Ibid.,* p. 244-245.

(32) *Ibid.,* p. 245.

(33) *Ibid.,* p. 246.

21

"MOP-UP"

(13–15 FEBRUARY)

"If there is another war, I recommend that the military and the correspondents, and everyone else concerned, drop the phrase 'mopping up' from their vocabularies. It is not a good enough phrase to die for."

—Lieutenant General Robert L. Eichelberger[1]

With the enemy disintegrating rapidly, physical contact between the 149th and 152nd regiments was essential. Japanese opposition seemed to be concentrated north of the road, so a link-up route through that area was not considered. Advancing along Highway 7 was risky because of ambushes and mines. Since engineers were still removing mines from the road between the hairpin and the bridge over the Santa Rita River, the road east of the bridge was probably mined also. Moving south of the road along trails that had been previously reconnoitered was obviously the best route to effect the union.[2]

Besides effecting a link-up of his two regiments, General Easley's other mission for 13 February was to "mop up" the remaining Japanese positions. The battalions of the 152nd would continue along their previous day's paths, squeezing the enemy into a still smaller space. 1st Battalion 152nd had been "pinched out" by the 2nd and 3rd Battalions, but still had patrolling and much work to do in the rear areas checking and rechecking to see if any pillboxes, tunnels or caves had been overlooked and not destroyed. 3rd Battalion 152nd would attack north of the road, cross the river and seize the high ground east of the river. Concurrent with this attack, 2nd Battalion would attack along the road and send patrols south of the road to make contact with the 149th.[3]

Major Mangold, the 3rd Battalion commander, who would make the main effort of the day, decided to bombard his objective with high explosive and white phosphorus 81-mm mortar fire and cross the river while the enemy was pinned down and blinded by the smoke. Company L on the left and K on the right had no trouble crossing the river, but were slowed by the steep climb to the objective—the East Pass.[4]

Enemy contact was limited initially to rifle fire, but resistance increased from the 5th Company as the 152nd advanced closer to the Nagayoshi Detachment Battle Command Post at the East Pass.

The 5th Company had established a line known as the Bandai-zan (everlasting) position in the East Pass on 2 February as right flank security for the Command Post. Although the company was well dug in north of Highway 7 in defilade, one of its caves dug into a hillside had received a freak hit by a 105-mm round on 4 February. Of seven men in the cave, five were killed and one was wounded. Only Superior Private Atsumi Takakura emerged unscathed.[5]

Superior Private Atsumi Takakura,
5th Company 39th Infantry

Takakura in 1993

The Bandai-zan had been "smelled out" by American observation planes on 11 February and given an "unbelievably heavy bombardment by artillery and planes" on that day and on 12 February. "The thick jungle became naked. The bursting of shells was deafening. Huge trees fell with a tremendous roar and the pungent smell of phosphorous was everywhere. It was a picture of hell." Now reduced to only 41 men and its morale shattered by the rapid advance of the Americans, the 5th Company could no longer offer determined resistance.[6]

K and L Companies halted frequently while patrols fanned out to silence sporadic rifle fire. Finally, L Company had to halt to contain the Japanese in the Bandai-zan area. K Company moved on to the objective at the next hairpin turn of Highway 7 about 500 yards east of the Santa Rita River.

After their steep climb late in the afternoon, the men of K Company were completely exhausted. While they were digging their positions for the night, two Japanese machine gun squads surprised the unaware company and swept the area from a position just outside the perimeter. With his men now digging furiously, Lieutenant Kimberlin, the company commander, fully recovered from wounds received earlier in the battle, grabbed a BAR and slipped into the thick undergrowth. A sergeant armed with an automatic carbine joined him. They succeeded in outflanking the machine guns and in killing all 12 members of the two crews.[7]

With their chief support gone, the isolated survivors of the Bandai-zan position faded into the jungle, but continued to snipe at the Americans for three days. At midnight on the dark night of 16 February, the depleted 5th Company marched single file by compass through the jungle and reached Detachment Headquarters at Mount Kongo at dawn the next day.[8]

The long awaited—but now fully expected—announcement by radio of a junction of the two regiments came at 1120. Patrols from A Company 149th and G Company 152nd met near the hill that L Company 151st had occupied the night of 8-9 February. At 1230, the 113th Engineers started building a Bailey Bridge south of the old bridge over the Santa Rita River. 2nd Battalion 152nd and 1st Battalion 149th made wire contact in the afternoon, finally and permanently joining the 149th with the 152nd and Division Headquarters. At sundown, Colonel Patton, XI Corps G-2, announced that all organized resistance had ceased west of the Santa Rita River and south of Highway 7.

The first reports of abandoned equipment revealed the extent of the Japanese disintegration. Rifles, machine guns, field pieces, ammunition and rations littered the battlefield. An officer of the 152nd recalled the reaction of Colonel Ives, his new commanding officer. "Area is dirty—needs cleaning up!" "Yes, sir," was the reply, "We'll clean it up."[9]

Signs of chaos were everywhere. XI Corps G-2 noted that the trenches encountered 13 February were shallow and apparently hastily constructed. Numerous battle flags and sabers were captured, indications of increasing disorganization. Contradicting the previous reports of the scarcity of supplies, the Japanese left burning a dump containing one ton of rice and in other dumps gas masks, trousers, rope, harness and ammunition. Colonel Wilson, 38th Division G-2, concluded that their hasty departure "seems certainly an act of desperation rather than one indicating orderly withdrawal or intended return."[10]

None of the XI Corps or 38th Division reports gives any hint that G-2 suspected that the enemy had withdrawn. The supposition seemed to be that any survivors were still hidden in caves in the area or may have straggled away from the battlefield individually. So stealthily had Major Ogawa organized his withdrawal that G-2 did not even suggest that any

Japanese had escaped. Furthermore, extensive patrolling by both the 152nd and 149th on 14 February drew only a few scattered rifle shots but no contact with live Japanese.[11]

On 12 February, infantrymen of the 152nd had found "one bound Nagayoshi Detachment Operations Order dated from 14 December 1944 to 29 January 1945 belonging to the 9th Company 3rd Battalion 39th Infantry." The order revealed the complete Order of Battle of the Japanese forces on Bataan. Even though the order noted the 39th Regimental Headquarters in the listing of units of the North Garrison Unit, the headquarters was never found and destroyed.[12]

According to Superior Private Atsumi Takakura, 1st Platoon 5th Company, the headquarters at Mount Kongo was located approximately 1.5 kilometers (1,600 yards) north-northwest of the East Pass. The daily messenger's two hour walk between the two locations sometimes stretched to four or five hours when shelling was heaviest.[13]

Among the seven patrols the 152nd Infantry scheduled for 14 February to scour the immediate area for surviving Japanese, the regimental I and R Platoon was to patrol 1,800 yards north of Highway 7. This turned out to be the last chance for the Americans to find the Japanese headquarters. Apparently, no further 152nd patrols searched that far north.[14]

It seems incredible that in two weeks of battle, with constant air surveillance of the battlefield by reconnaissance planes directing artillery fire and P-47s bombing certain areas, telltale signs of human activity around the headquarters would not be noticed. Only troops with the highest degree of training and discipline could have kept their presence secret during the two weeks of the battle and three additional weeks until Nagayoshi's headquarters group, nearly out of food, "struck its tents" on 9 March and marched south.[15]

The 38th Division estimated killing 359 Japanese in the 24-hour period ending at 1800 on 13 February—280 by the 152nd, 79 by the 149th—and capturing 3 Formosan prisoners. The number killed estimated by the 152nd seems to be grossly in error considering that most of the enemy in its area had withdrawn the night of 12 February. The 152nd suffered 7 of its own killed and 31 wounded; 2nd Battalion 149th had 2 KIA and 8 WIA.[16]

Major Ogawa's force rested all the day of 13 February in the jungle at the base of Mount Kosaku searching and waiting for Lieutenant Shinfune. They could hear heavy firing in the battle area they had vacated the night before. Superior Private Akiyama, the only survivor of the

Onishi HMG Squad, changed Sergeant Togo's temporary bandage and washed his mangled shoulder to avoid infection. Togo had been slow to leave Mount Fumetsu, not catching the column until the first break. Lacking one eye, he had still managed to keep up with the column in the darkness.[17]

Even a deliberately slow pace did not prevent men of the Shinfune group from stumbling, falling and hurting themselves. They suppressed their groans; they were under strict orders not to make any noise. The hard, metal part of the machine gun each Kato man carried danced around on his back, digging into his flesh, causing more bother than the rifle he carried. The pace quickened at daylight when it became easier to see through the jungle gloom. Canteens were empty, and the men cut bamboo stalks and drank the water between the nodes. The water had a foul smell and a taste to match, but it was better than nothing.[18]

Their path led across communication wires laid by the Americans along the hillside. The insulating material covering the wires burned very well. The men cut the wires and stripped off the covering material to substitute for cooking fuel.[19]

At about noon, Shinfune's group came to a large field, posted sentries and took a much-needed nap. After resuming the march, they made contact with Major Ogawa's group miraculously, quite by accident, at about 1600. Having fought and been isolated at Mount Ege, Shinfune's group did not know the fate of the rest of the battalion. There was rejoicing to see friends still alive, but sorrow and anger to learn of other comrades' deaths. Each man made special inquiries about the fate of those with whom he had joined the regiment.

Sergeant Nagai was appalled by the condition of Sergeant Masao Togo. Bandages covered half his face; his right arm, with upper arm in a splint, rested in a sling. He pitifully explained his condition to Nagai. "I was hit by a tank gun. I can't move my right arm. My shoulder and arm have multiple fractures. My right eyeball is gone. I was buried in my shelter and barely made it here." He removed the bandage from his face. His right eye was just a socket without an eyeball. Nagai moaned to himself, "He cannot even be treated for his wound. If he is in pain, he does not show it." Togo's luck did not improve. Guerrillas shot him in the head on 1 March three kilometers east of Mount Santa Rita.[20]

Two members of Togo's squad, Shizuo Hanaoka and Jutaro Nakano, had been in the same bunker with Togo. They had crawled out just before the tank round hit. They had cuts on their bodies, but they were laughing because they could not call these cuts real wounds.

Chikara Goto also wore his right arm in a sling. The same tank round that killed his squad leader, Misao Kanazawa, on 4 February and another squad member, Toshi Inoue, had wounded him. Goto said, "I am the only one left from the Kanazawa Squad. I don't know if my arm will be all right. I don't want to die, but the Army doctor says he can only treat officers." Nagai recalled that this was correct. Only medics treated enlisted men.

Broad-shouldered Kazuhito Ishihara walked by. "My squad leader, Sergeant Ueno, was killed. Kiyoshi Ikuta and myself are the only ones left in the squad. All the others were killed by flame-throwers."

Most had a similar tale of woe. Fast-talking, but serious, Kiyomi Nakamura remembered 9 February when the same tank round killed his squad leader, Shiro Takamura, and two other squad members. "Yoshimi Yabushita and I are the only survivors of the Takamura Squad."

The meticulous Toshio Nagai of the Ohgaki Squad, who had a habit of bending his head to the right when he saluted, said, "We have been going through some rough times. Hatsuzo Hirose, Shigeo Adachi and I are the only ones left. Ohgaki was hit by the tanks on 8 February." This was the squad that manned the Water's Edge Position on 30 January.

Although they had taken a hammering on Mount Shinshu, its defenders, Sergeant Iga and Sergeant Hijikata, were in relatively good spirits. Both squads had three men left.

Someone told Sergeant Nagai to report to Major Ogawa and keep him company. Nagai found him alone without his usual one or two aides nearby. Nagai told him some anecdotes, which seemed to raise his spirits. Nagai remembered the battalion adjutant, Lieutenant Tasuke Fukunaga, who was usually with Ogawa, as a powerful leader in the days at Chiamussu, Manchuria. Now he was unstable, walking aimlessly back and forth during the rest period. Nagai learned later that Fukunaga was quite ill at the time.[21]

When darkness came, Major Ogawa's expanded column of about 120 men resumed its halting, agonizing night march. Lieutenant Koyama of the machine gun company and Lieutenant Nakamura of the engineers led the way. The objective would be Mount Santa Rita, another beacon on a dark night, 2,000 yards to the southeast. Mindful of his battalion's vulnerability if discovered by the Americans, Ogawa pushed on despite the obvious fatigue and deteriorating health of his men. "It was beyond description to say how hard it was," he wrote later.[22]

💣 💣 💣

14 February: Regardless of active Japanese demolition patrols that destroyed three 57-mm anti-tank guns and a truck in the division headquarters area the night of 13 February, GIs on the front lines considered the battle all but over. General Easley had only one objective in mind for 14 February. The 152nd and the 149th were to close and end the battle of ZigZag Pass.[23]

The companies of the 1st Battalion 152nd had a leisurely hot breakfast, and we can assume that the other companies in the regiment followed suit. East of the river and north of the highway, the 3rd Battalion 152nd continued its march to the east. Companies E and F 152nd south of the road were attached to the 3rd Battalion for operational control.

North of the road, Company K proceeded with caution through the thick jungle to avoid a firefight with the 149th. At 1130, after meeting only minor resistance, the company made contact with a patrol from F Company 149th Infantry approximately 300 yards north of the highway and 1,200 yards east of the river. At 1220, the two battalion commanders, Colonel Dishman 2/149th and Major Mangold 3/152nd, met, symbolically ending the battle. At 1330, for the first time in three years, American traffic could move freely along Highway 7 from Olongapo to Dinalupihan.[24]

Then began the inevitable assignment of the companies of the 152nd for special details—patrolling, setting up roadblocks, and guarding bridges, hospitals and other vital installations. Although the journal entries indicate a mild day of combat, the 152nd still reported casualties of six KIA and eight WIA.[25]

⚫ ⚫ ⚫

In the 149th's sector, 2nd Battalion pulled back into a draw south of the road at 0700 and let its supporting artillery thoroughly soak its planned area of advance against the Nakayama Battalion. This barrage of high explosive and white phosphorous shells, which burned undergrowth and uncovered several emplacements, was the largest in support of the 149th during the entire battle.

Colonel Dishman's men advanced rapidly against sporadic rifle and machine gun fire. Company G on the right had one TD (tank destroyer) attached and Company F on the left had two TDs. This is the first and only mention in the records of tank destroyers being used in the battle. They may have been the M-10 Wolverine with open top turret on an M-4 Sherman tank chassis carrying a 76-mm gun. Colonel Skelton probably obtained them from the 40th Division. It will be recalled that elements of the division had arrived in Dinalupihan on 3 February (see page 143) ahead of the 149th.[26]

In its rapid push west, 2nd Battalion reported destroying 75 vehicles of all types, but salvaging and putting back into service three 2 1/2 ton trucks. One of the TDs attached to F Company was knocked out of action and forced to withdraw. Of the 122 Japanese that Division Headquarters claimed were killed this day, 2nd Battalion 149th estimated that it killed 100 and itself suffered 1 KIA and 2 WIA.[27]

🖤   🖤   🖤

Daybreak of 14 February found Ogawa's men still some distance from Mount Santa Rita. They could hear shelling, explosions and engines, but the scouts discovered no immediate presence of the enemy. The drinking water was gone. The men cut more bamboo, but could never satisfy their thirst. Ogawa left the slow-moving main body and pressed on through the jungle with Lieutenant Kato to the base of the mountain to find a suitable camp.[28]

🖤   🖤   🖤

15 February: XI Corps declared 15 February as the day the campaign officially ended, but it would be hard to convince men of the 2nd Battalion 149th. Continuing their bloody work against the Nakayama Battalion, they spent most of the day blowing up three ammo dumps and sealing 40 to 50 caves with explosives. "These caves contained many enemy personnel, proved by loud screams which could be heard when WP and fragmentation grenades were thrown in." One wounded Japanese, who obviously could not escape, was captured by 2nd Battalion Aid Station personnel and carried to Regiment by the Battalion S-2, Lieutenant Luke.[29]

The Americans had tried to avoid this senseless killing. Surrender leaflets had been dropped as early as 1 February, and on 8 and 9 February, 35,000 descended in the vicinity of the Santa Rita River Bridge. Following an air strike 11 February, 5,000 more were dropped—but to no avail.[30]

The three day "mop-up" had cost the 38th Division known casualties of 16 KIA and 50 WIA (casualties of 1st Battalion 149th Infantry are unknown). In the sector of the 152nd, men, who could now be called true combat veterans, mourned their dead and began the routine of garrison duty. Casualties of 1st Battalion 152nd alone during the two-week battle totaled 303: 3 officers and 37 EM KIA and 10 officers and 253 EM WIA.

The regiment continued its assigned missions of guard duty and patrolling, but started to "shape up" its appearance. Men were to shave and clean up, latrines were to be kept sanitary, areas were to be well policed, arms and equipment would be cleaned, and "all enemy dead in the vicinity are to be buried by natives today." Garrison duty also had its advantages—arrival of the first packages from home since the troops left Leyte.[31]

🖜 🖜 🖜

After marching all night, Major Ogawa's men finally arrived on the west side of Mount Santa Rita at the headwaters of the river by the same name. The water was clear, but still had to be purified before Ogawa would allow his men to quench their uncontrollable thirst. Walking at night had worsened the condition of the wounded. The immediate concern was food; only one day's ration remained. Scouting parties were organized to return to the battlefield and retrieve caches of food.[32]

Meanwhile, on the battlefield, one irreconcilable Japanese soldier wanted the war to go on. At 1115, in the 1st Battalion 152nd area, he threw ". . . a grenade from a cave S of hairpin turn near Bn area . . ." at Private Groteguth of B Company. The patrol Lieutenant Keller dispatched to check the area could not find the miscreant.[33]

Chapter 21

NOTES

(1) Eichelberger, General Robert L., *Our Jungle Road to Tokyo*, p. 182.

(2) 152nd Infantry journal;
XI Corps G-3 Periodic Report #17, 2000-14 February 1945.

(3) 152nd Infantry journal.

(4) Schoonover, Major James F., *The Operations of the 3rd Battalion 152nd Infantry in Zig Zag Pass, Luzon, 29 Jan.-14 Feb. 1945*, Advanced Infantry Officers Course, 1947-1948, p. 15.

(5) Takakura, Superior Private Atsumi, interview by author, 20 October 1993.

(6) *History of the 39th Infantry Regiment,* edited and published by the 39th Infantry Association, p. 652.

(7) Schoonover, *The Operations of the 3rd Battalion 152nd Infantry,* p. 15.

(8) *39th Infantry History,* p. 652.

(9) 38th Division G-2 Report #16, 1800-13 February 1945;
XI Corps G-3 Periodic Report #16, 2000-13 February 1945;
Brewer, Major Kenneth W., interview by author, 27 July 1990.

(10) XI Corps G-2 Report No. 16, 1800-13 February 1945;
38th Division G-2 Periodic Report No. 16, 1800-13 February 1945.

(11) Message 152nd Infantry S-2 to XI Corps G-2, 0010-14 February 1945 (showing areas to be patrolled).

(12) XI Corps G-2 Report #17, 1800-14 February 1945.

(13) Takakura, Superior Private Atsumi, 1st Platoon 5th Company, letter to author, 10 April 1998.

(14) 152nd Infantry journal, 0905-14 February 1945.

(15) *39th Infantry History,* p. 666.

(16) 38th Division G-2 Periodic Report #16, 1800-13 February 1945;
152nd Infantry journal;
2nd Battalion 149th Infantry journal.

(17) *39th Infantry History,* p. 668;
How the Kato Company Fought: The Record of the 3rd Machine

Gun Company 39th Infantry Regiment, Tamotsu Nagai, Editor, 1990, p. 204.

(18) Kato Company History, p. 247-248.

(19) *Ibid.,* p. 249.

(20) *Ibid.,* p. 53, 250.

(21) *Ibid.,* p. 250-254.

(22) *Ibid.,* p. 254;

39th Infantry History, p. 668;

Ogawa, Major Hironori, *Record of the 3rd Battalion, 39th Infantry Regiment in the "Big Asia War,"* p. 49.

(23) XI Corps G-2 Report #17, 1800-14 February 1945.

(24) Schoonover, *The Operations of the 3rd Battalion 152nd Infantry,* p. 16;

1st Battalion 152nd Infantry journal;

2nd Battalion 149th Infantry journal;

152nd Infantry journal;

38th Division AAR, p. 28.

(25) 152nd Infantry journal.

(26) 2nd Battalion 149th Infantry journal;

Polmar and Allen, *America at War 1941-1945*, p. 792.

(27) 2nd Battalion 149th Infantry journal, 0930-14 February 1945;

38th Division G-3 Periodic Report #53, 1800-14 February 1945.

(28) *39th Infantry History,* 668;

Kato Company History, p. 254.

(29) 2nd Battalion 149th Infantry journal, 15 February 1945.

(30) XI Corps G-2 Report #12, 1800-09 February 1945;

38th Division G-2 Periodic Report #14, 1800-11 February 1945.

(31) 152nd Infantry journal;

2nd Battalion 149th Infantry journal;

1st Battalion 152nd Infantry journals, 14 and 15 February 1945.

(32) Kato Company History, p. 254-255.

(33) 1st Battalion 152nd Infantry journal, 1115-15 February 1945.

AFTERMATH

On 15 February, Major Ogawa established a temporary camp on the right bank of the Santa Rita River at the base of Mount Santa Rita. The rear guard, left at the old positions on Mount Fumetsu to disguise the move, arrived to increase the size of his force to about 200. Here, the wounded, many having been given only first aid, received their first medical treatment by a physician. It had been impractical for the two battalion doctors, 1st Lieutenant Soto Nomura and Lieutenant Jiro Asaue, to give proper medical care to any except the wounded officers over the widespread battlefield. Food was the most urgent problem; there was only a one-day supply on hand.[1]

Ogawa sent patrols back into the battle zone to look for food in caches the Americans might not have discovered. His Battalion Executive Officer, 1st Lieutenant Hiroshi Okeguchi, with 2nd Lieutenant Nakamura's Engineers Platoon, infiltrated the Mount Fumetsu positions the night of 16 February. The men found rice left at the old battalion headquarters.[2]

Sergeant Nagai returned with food from Mount Ege after sorties the nights of 16 and 17 February. Although successful also on the night of 19 February, his patrol narrowly escaped destruction when Americans still dug-in on Ichinose Heights brought it under fire. Ogawa sent two squads by different routes south to establish contact with Major Yamamoto's 2nd Battalion 39th Infantry at Mount Natib and bring back food.[3]

Other sorties for food gathering were not as successful. Lieutenant Yuasa of the Regimental Gun Company scouted toward Dinalupihan on 18 February, but lost a Sergeant Nakano of his company in the attempt. On another foray toward Dinalupihan on 28 February, Sergeant Yoshikazu Maeda was killed along with three other members of the Gun Company. Sergeant Iga led the last food collection party to the battlefield, losing two men of a six-man patrol at Mount Koko also on 28 February.[4]

The 150 survivors of the Nakayama Battalion turned north after the withdrawal, and, following their original orders, attempted to unite with General Yamashita. American forces were in complete control of all areas between Bataan and Baguio. As might be expected, most of the survivors were killed along the way or died from disease. Only 15, including Major Nakayama, eventually returned to Japan.[5]

Colonel Nagayoshi had given orders for the detachment to conduct guerrilla warfare if forced to withdraw from ZigZag Pass. His plan was for the North Garrison Unit to unite with the Central Garrison Unit near Mount Natib in central Bataan. From there, the Japanese would harass American and Filipino forces on the east coast of Bataan where the detachment had landed in December 1944.

After receiving provisions from central Bataan transported laboriously across the mountains by carrying parties of Major Yamamoto's 2nd Battalion, Major Ogawa broke camp at Mount Santa Rita on 3 March and headed for Mount Natib to join the Yamamoto Battalion. Ogawa eventually selected as his permanent campsite an area in the eastern foothills of Mount Natib on the Orani River, which flowed eastward into Manila Bay. In this area, the battalion was able to supply itself with food and begin guerrilla warfare.[6]

The rapid occupation by American forces of Highway 7 east of the Santa Rita River on 13 February had stranded the Nagayoshi Detachment Headquarters group at Mount Kongo. The Ogawa Battalion reached Mount Santa Rita on 14 February, but it was impossible for Detachment Headquarters to join them. American vehicles were constantly patrolling the highway, and blocking positions had been established at critical points. It seems incredible, though, that 152nd Infantry patrols did not find the headquarters group at Mount Kongo and that the regiment did not attack this considerable force of at least 100 men.

On 24 February, Captain Takeshi Okamoto, the Regimental Adjutant, ordered 2nd Lieutenant Sadao Itahashi of the 5th Company to find a weak point in the enemy lines along Route 7. Itahashi took five men for the unsuccessful attempt; he and Pfc. Kumata were shot and killed. After several days, Colonel Nagayoshi ordered Lieutenant Yamamoto, 5th Company commander, to scout for an escape route. The latter reported that any movement was impossible during the daylight hours, but that it was practicable to try to slip through at night.[7]

Colonel Nagayoshi selected the night of 9 March for his detachment headquarters group to sally forth and join his 2nd and 3rd Battalions at Mount Natib. With the 5th Company leading, followed by Regimental Headquarters and the Operations Company, the Detachment crossed Highway 7 safely. However, the 152nd attacked the rear guard, the Operations Company. The company commander, 1st Lieutenant Kazuichi Nishiyama, was killed in the ensuing firefight.

Cutting its own path, the detachment picked its way slowly through the jungle. Nagayoshi finally reached the area in the eastern foothills of Mount Natib on 20 March where the 2nd and 3rd Battalions had established base camp. Again, there was much rejoicing among men who had news of departed friends and many combat stories to tell. The morale of the 2nd Battalion men "rose" as they had not seen the regimental colors for a long time.[8]

The Nagayoshi Detachment made a brave stand on Mount Natib against elements of the 1st Infantry 6th Division, the 149th Infantry and Filipino guerrillas. These forces built a road with bulldozers through the jungle to establish a base of supplies closer to the Japanese. Supported by artillery and airpower, they slowly drove the detachment deeper into the mountains. Facing starvation and constantly harassed by the guerrillas, most of Nagayoshi's troops died from disease, malnutrition or guerrilla action. That the detachment did not disintegrate under the constant pressure of battle, disease and hunger is a tribute to the superb leadership of its officers and the fortitude and discipline of its men.[9]

✦   ✦   ✦

At noon on 15 August, the entire fleet of the Allied Forces in Subic Bay and Manila Bay sounded their whistles. Liaison planes dropped flyers, and a soft, feminine voice from a loudspeaker on one of the planes encouraged Japanese soldiers to come out of the mountains and surrender. The speaker was a Filipino girl who was the secretary/interpreter of the mayor of Dinalupihan. Printed in Japanese on the flyers was an Imperial decree to the soldiers announcing that Japan had surrendered unconditionally and to end the fighting.

Soldiers of the 39th Infantry who came back from foraging for food east of Mount Natib that day reported that they were not fired on and that the outside world seemed more peaceful. Major Kashiwagi, who was in temporary command because of Colonel Nagayoshi's illness, organized a negotiating group, headed by Lieutenant Kato, to make contact with the Americans. Not willing to surrender unless the war was indeed over, Kashiwagi instructed Kato to ask the Americans to let him listen to a radio broadcast from Japan and to request a U.S. newspaper that would confirm the termination of the war. If the war was really over, Kato was to arrange for a place and time where Kashiwagi could surrender officially for the Nagayoshi Detachment.

Kato thought that a higher rank would strengthen his negotiating position. He put another star (that he took from another officer's uniform) on his collar to promote himself to captain. 2nd Lieutenant Koyama similarly promoted himself to 1st Lieutenant. Koyama was an Osaka

Kiyotaka Kato in 1993, following cerebral hemorrhage in 1990

University graduate in Foreign Languages and would interpret. The seven-man patrol spruced up their uniforms, shaved and polished their firearms with Vaseline. They even received extra rations of rice to make them look more healthy and energetic. Carrying a Japanese flag and a white flag, the group marched down the mountain to Orani on 17 August.

Walking in broad daylight on a road bordered by spacious fields was a sensational feeling. For a long time, the Japanese had emerged only at night, like nocturnal animals, looking for food.

As they neared the village of Orani, the villagers screamed, "You must be surrendering!" Pointing at the flags, Kato told them, "We are not surrendering; we come to negotiate with the U.S. Army."

Several Americans approached with guns. Kato saw a captain with an MP armband and extended his hand. The officer, though surprised, shook hands. When asked if he knew Japan had surrendered, Kato responded that he had learned from the flyer that the war had been suspended, but that he did not know whether it was an unconditional surrender.

It was a tense moment, but gradually the strained atmosphere eased. The Americans showed Kato a newspaper, which convinced him of the surrender. Kato's feelings were mixed. The news of losing the war and terminating the fighting was "a big shock" to him. At the same time, the sense of relief to the survivors, now in complete isolation from the main

Japanese Army, to be free of their desperate and miserable conditions, was totally gratifying.

Kato was impressed with the captain, whom he found to be "a quiet, friendly person." After setting an official meeting date of 22 August, the Japanese started to leave. Fearful that Filipino bandits would attack his captives during their journey, the captain offered to provide guards for the return trip. Kato declined the offer and led his men back to their mountain hideaway without incident. On the way back, they noticed many caribou and chickens along the road. They laughed at their mindset of always looking for food, which had been their main preoccupation since leaving ZigZag Pass.[10]

On 21 August, Major Kashiwagi with 12 soldiers, each armed with a gun and three hand grenades, headed down the mountain. If the meeting went awry, they reasoned, they could still kill at least 30 Americans. After spending the night in the foothills, they arrived at the meeting place in Orani at 1600 hours. The captain of an American cannon company, who was the officer in charge of security for eastern Bataan, met them.

Kashiwagi also had to be convinced that the surrender was unconditional. The U.S. commander explained the terms of the surrender in detail and had the Japanese listen to a radio broadcast from Japan. The men of the Nagayoshi Detachment were speechless. Major Kashiwagi finally pulled himself together and shook hands with the U.S. captain, saying, "The war is over. The enemies of yesterday are friends today." As one of the three Nisei present translated his words, the Americans relaxed and cheered.

With darkness approaching, Kashiwagi asked if they could stay overnight. The captain took the major to the American camp in Balanga for supper after which they watched a movie together. Kashiwagi shared a room with the U.S. commander that night. He was not stripped of his gun or sword. The Americans' friendly attitude made a lasting impression on the Japanese.

The Cannon Company commander provided a jeep, two trucks and a 20-man guard team led by a 2nd lieutenant to aid Kashiwagi in communicating with his small detachments located in various parts of Mount Natib. On 26 August, the Americans escorted Kashiwagi's group back to their camp on Mount Natib, carrying as much food as possible.[11]

There was still the matter of receiving surrender orders from 14th Area Army Headquarters. As the end of August approached, Colonel Nagayoshi, who had recovered from his illness, began to think that his detachment had been considered dead and was not included in the 14th Area Army orders to surrender. On 31 August, in response to Nagayoshi's

Major Takenori Kashiwagi *(left)*, Executive Officer, and 1st Lieutenant
Kiyotaka Kato *(right)*, Machine Gun Company Commander, 39th Infantry,
with Major Kenneth W. Brewer *(center)*, Executive Officer, 3rd Battalion
152nd Infantry, in Balanga at time of surrender, 3 September 1945

inquiry, the American authorities confirmed that 14th Area Army had
issued the order to surrender and that General Yamashita's forces were
gathering in Manila. Nagayoshi finally made the decision to surrender.
His small and pitifully emaciated command prepared to leave the mountain on 3 September.[12]

Nagayoshi paid special attention to discipline to maintain the dignity
of the Japanese Army. Soldiers cleaned and polished their weapons,
including the machine guns, and buried the weapons that were in poor
condition. They cut their hair, shaved, washed their clothes and mended
holes and tears. A mere shell of 280 of an original force of nearly 4000
made their way down the mountain for the last time and finally surrendered in Orani and Balanga on 4 September 1945.[13]

The Nagayoshi Detachment was imprisoned at Cabantuan, 50 miles
north of Manila. The Americans treated the POWs strictly by the rules of
the Geneva Convention. Officers were not required to perform manual
labor; therefore, they received smaller portions of food. A ration of 1,000
calories a day was barely enough for subsistence. There was no cigarette
ration. Officers lay in their bunks much of the day with empty stomachs.
Because enlisted men had their work details and were better fed, their
physical recovery was much faster.[14]

Repatriation to Japan depended on shipping and investigations for war crimes. No member of the detachment was accused of war crimes, nor was any soldier in the 1st Battalion 39th Infantry fighting with the Shobu Group. The soldiers could not understand the system of repatriation of the Japanese armed forces. Colonel Nagayoshi left Manila for home on 3 November; Sergeant Iga, on the other hand, remained imprisoned in Manila for a year after the surrender. When repatriation time came, prisoners were transported in open trucks to the docks at Manila. Filipino civilians cursed and stoned them as they cruised through the city. Their only protection came from covering themselves with their blankets.[15]

Major Kashiwagi had asked the Nisei interpreters at the meeting on 22 August about the regimental flag that the officers had secretly brought with them for return to Japan. The Nisei told him they saw no difficulty in keeping the standard after the surrender. The U.S. Army said they had no interest in regimental colors.[16]

However, several days after internment, it became evident that the U.S. Army was indeed interested in regimental colors. The three highest-ranking officers in the regiment after Nagayoshi—Majors Kashiwagi, Ogawa and Yamamoto—hastily formed a plan to prevent their flag from falling into American hands.

The three majors cut the crest at the top of the pole into three pieces and distributed the pieces among themselves. While being moved to another location, they dropped the pieces into a river. Major Kashiwagi wrapped the blood stained portion of the flag, a small portion of the fringes, and a small section of the pole (5 centimeters) in the purple silk cloth that encased the flag. He kept this package in his stomach band. The two battalion commanders, Ogawa and Yamamoto, kept portions of the fringe and another small section of the pole (5 centimeters long) and pledged their lives to bring them home. They stripped lacquer off the remainder of the pole to disguise it as a cane for Colonel Nagayoshi, who was suffering from rheumatism.

The rest of the fringes were cut into several pieces and wrapped in paper with the lacquer. While Nagayoshi washed the next morning in an area where there were facilities to heat water, the three majors burned the paper with the fringes and lacquer. Only then could Nagayoshi and his officers breathe a sigh of relief that they had not surrendered their standard.[17]

When they returned home, the three majors prevailed upon a Buddhist nunnery in Himeji to accept and keep the smuggled pieces. Two nuns agreed to hide the pieces, even though the American Army of

Occupation was conducting searches for concealed weapons. The nuns justified their action by reasoning that a Buddhist temple, which was not supposed to shelter an army flag, could keep the remnants of this flag because there was no longer an army. Since there was no army, flags were meaningless. They considered the 39th standard as a symbol memorializing those who had died for the flag. Spirits of the dead must be kept in a temple, so the nuns would keep the flag with its spirits.

The secret must have leaked out. One day American MPs stopped by the nunnery and said they had to search the temple because the temple was harboring something related to the Japanese Army. A Buddhist priestess explained to them that certainly the nunnery contained many things related to the old army, but what was kept in the temple was related to the dead. If the MPs insisted on investigating the dead, she would open the gate. But they must have a search warrant signed by a proper authority and have a Christian priest with them. The Buddhist priestess emphasized that this was a humble temple, but it was a holy site; it should not be invaded by blood-stained soldiers! The MPs came back several times, but she was steadfast. The MPs had no proof and could not forcibly conduct their search. They finally gave up.

Major Kashiwagi kept the portion of the flag he had brought back, including the blood stained section, at his home in Kyushu until he joined the Self Defense Army. In 1959, some 15 former members of the regiment gathered in Tokyo for a memorial service. Kashiwagi's portion of the flag was framed and kept in the archives of the Self Defense Agency. Finally in 1965, all the pieces were put together, and the "blood stained flag" now resides in the archives of the Himeji Self Defense Force.[18]

The "blood-stained standard"

✦ ✦ ✦

What of the Americans? The 34th RCT and the 38th Division soon parted company after the battle and went their separate ways to new adventures in other Philippine campaigns. The 34th rejoined the 24th Division and fought for 75 days as part of X Corps in the conquest of eastern Mindanao. Remaining under XI Corps control, elements of the

38th Division cleaned up the remaining islands guarding Manila Bay after the Corregidor operation and fought on the slopes of Mount Pinatubo. The division concluded its combat east of Manila, helping to subdue the Shimbu Group in the Wawa Dam area.[19]

ZigZag Pass became an unpleasant memory, temporarily forgotten during the excitement of subsequent campaigns, the elation at the end of the war, the occupation of Japan and finally the return home. Only later would come the recriminations that would persist through the years: General Jones against General Hall, the 34th Infantry against the 38th Division for its delay in responding to calls for artillery support, the 38th Division against the 34th Infantry for pulling out of the fight prematurely, and the 152nd Infantry against a "system" that would permit the removal of a beloved and effective regimental commander and replacement by one not its own.

In close proximity to the Subic Bay Naval Base, the battlefield gradually became a congested area of residences, stores, roads and small businesses. The Japanese survivors began to return annually to ZigZag Pass in the 1970s to locate caves and positions they remembered and to erect memorials. At significant sites, they honored their dead comrades with offerings of food and drink brought from Japan and left for the Filipinos. The recurring theme in these ceremonies: "The sacrifice of those who died enabled those still living to return and honor their memory."

Not until 1991 did the first American return to join in the annual Japanese pilgrimages. There was no animosity. After bows and handshakes, the former enemies became fast friends like veterans of the same outfit returning for a reunion. Each side was interested in the other's account of the battle. In place of the 1945 axiom "kill or be killed," now there was peace and a deep sense of camaraderie and kinship.

Chapter 22
NOTES

(1) *History of the 39th Infantry Regiment,* edited and published by the 39th Infantry Association, p. 668.

(2) *Ibid.*

(3) *How the Kato Company Fought: The Record of the 3rd Machine Gun Company 39th Infantry Regiment*, Tamotsu Nagai, Editor, 1990, p. 255;
39th Infantry History, p. 668.

(4) *39th Infantry History,* p. 668;
Kato Company History, p. 53.

(5) Nagata, 1st Lt Yuichiro, letter to author, 24 June 1992.

(6) *39th Infantry History,* p. 669.

(7) *Ibid.,* p. 665.

(8) *Ibid.,* p. 666, 673.

(9) Smith, Robert Ross, *Triumph in the Philippines*, p. 334;
39th Infantry History, p. 675-679.

(10) *39th Infantry History,* p. 704-707.

(11) *Ibid.,* p. 709.

(12) *Ibid.*

(13) *Ibid.,* p. 710.

(14) *Ibid.,* p. 712.

(15) *Ibid.*

(16) *Ibid.,* p. 709.

(17) *Ibid.,* p. 723-724.

(18) *Ibid.,* p. 774.

(19) Smith, *Triumph*, Chapter XIX—Manila Bay: Minor Operations, Chapter XXII—The Seizure of Wawa and Ipo Dams, Chapter XXXII—The Conquest of Eastern Mindanao.

ANALYSIS

The grenade "attack" on Private Groteguth B Company 152nd Infantry on 15 February was typical of the Japanese soldiers' offensive spirit throughout the battle. They had resolutely carried the fight to the Americans from the start and disputed every foot of ground with fanatic zeal and determination. Woefully outnumbered, never flinching, they had fought nobly and honorably with limited resources against overwhelming odds, knowing there was no chance for relief or reinforcement.

During the Battle of ZigZag Pass, the North Garrison Unit had bewildered one American regiment (the 34th) and compelled it to retire; had held off another regiment (the 149th less one battalion) in the east with a makeshift, under-strength, largely garrison battalion; and, before succumbing in the west, a lone regular army battalion had given two other American regiments (the 151st and 152nd) all the fighting they wanted. There had been no panic or headlong retreat; the Japanese had the good sense to withdraw when the situation became hopeless.

In essence, two reinforced Japanese battalions had resisted an American corps of 4 regiments of infantry (3,000 men each), 7 battalions of artillery, a company of at least 6 tanks, and 16 P-47 planes. Major Schoonover, the 152nd Infantry S-4 (supply), reported from 38th Division records that the planes dropped 243 tons of bombs and 193,050 gallons of napalm and strafed with 1,728,000 rounds of .50-caliber ammunition. The Japanese had prolonged an operation the American commanding general expected to be over in 8 days into an 18-day ordeal.[1]

In addition to the obvious American advantage of complete mastery of the air, a simple chart will illustrate the enormous superiority in heavy weapons available to the Americans during the battle:

WEAPON	JAPANESE	AMERICAN
HMG (.30-caliber)	12	96
Heavy Mortar	8	72
	(6-120-mm; 2-90-mm)*	(81-mm)
Tanks	3 (47-mm)	6 (75-mm)

WEAPON	JAPANESE	AMERICAN
Anti-tank guns	4 (37-mm)	18 (57-mm)**
Artillery (70-mm)	2	0
Artillery (75-mm)	2	24 (SPM)
Artillery (105-mm)	2	48 (Howitzer)
Artillery (155-mm)	0	24 (Howitzer)
		4 (Long Tom Rifles)

It is difficult to determine the number and caliber of the mortars the Japanese used during the battle. Major Ogawa wrote many years later that he had two 100-mm mortars in the pass. Since there was no Japanese 100-mm mortar, we will assume these were 90-mm. The Americans reported finding six 120-mm mortars, although these are not mentioned in the Japanese records.

**Based on Table of Organization and Equipment, but probably not used. The numbers for American heavy machine guns and heavy mortars are based on the Table of Organization and Equipment for four infantry regiments, only three of which were in action at any given time. Only two of the 149th's three battalions faced the enemy during the battle.[2]*

In all the pages of military history, there are few better examples of a small force (the 3rd Battalion 39th Infantry) skillfully resisting a larger force far superior in numbers and armament. In choice of terrain for defense, construction of defensive positions from natural surroundings, disposition and use of weapons, leadership and bravery, the 3rd Battalion 39th Infantry has few peers.

Ironically, its one major battle in ZigZag Pass was almost anti-climactic when compared with its vicissitudes in reaching the battlefield and in its suffering and hardships following the battle. The saga of the Nagayoshi Detachment could well be studied by military historians as the model for an isolated regiment acting independently in the face of great adversity.

Little criticism can be leveled against Japanese tactics. Perhaps the only flaw was locating two 37-mm anti-tank guns at the Water's Edge Position. Sited to fire into the harbor, these guns were useless against an enemy attack in the rear by land and would have been just as useless against destroyers and cruisers, if the landing had been made at Olongapo instead of San Antonio. If used at all at the Water's Edge Position, a better location would have been on Mount Todai to cover parts of Highway 7 or the bridge into Olongapo. The overall best use of the 37-mm anti-tank guns would have been to use all four in the pass against tanks and infantry.

Were the Japanese successful? Yes. Their mission was to delay and inflict casualties on the American forces. They succeeded beyond their wildest dreams. The best estimate of American casualties is 1,400, including about 250 killed.[3]

But the Japanese soldiers' tenacious efforts in ZigZag Pass also delayed, if only for a few days, the opening of Manila Bay to shipping. Most of the equipment and supplies for the American forces fighting around Manila and in northern Luzon came across the beaches at Lingayen Gulf and then by truck to the various fronts. As long as Manila Bay remained closed to shipping (and it could not be opened until Bataan and Corregidor had fallen), the Americans were handicapped by long supply lines. Bataan and Corregidor could not be captured until the road between Olongapo and Dinalupihan was opened. The Nagayoshi Detachment's stubborn defense of this road slowed the American timetable for opening Manila Bay and establishing a more permanent base for supplying American troops fighting on Luzon.

✦   ✦   ✦

The XI Corps accomplished its missions successfully in the Zambales Operation, but at a price higher than expected and at a pace slower than anticipated. The Americans achieved all their objectives and made a vital contribution toward completing the recapture of the Philippines.

But the operation had not gone well. It lacked the dash and workman-like efficiency that characterized most American campaigns at this stage of the war. There were noticeable flaws in command, staff work and coordination between units. What went wrong? Many of the deficiencies have been discussed as they occurred, but a general critique is in order.

The first flaw to appear was the breakdown in intelligence as to the nature of the terrain and the enemy. General Hall seemed to have an unshakable, pre-conceived notion that Japanese opposition in Zambales and northern Bataan was not going to be a factor and could be brushed aside easily. Even though he knew the area from his visit 13 years earlier, he seemed to ignore the serious obstacle that the steep, jungled hillsides in ZigZag Pass would present to attacking troops. He did not seem to realize that the defense would naturally concentrate along the road where he chose to attack. He thought he could barrel right through the pass on Highway 7 with minimum artillery support, not waiting until his troops had time to fan out, discover trails and become familiar with the area. Good judgment and good staff work might have anticipated these conditions and prepared for them in advance. General Hall's lack of appreciation for the terrain is all the more puzzling because of his previous visit described in Chapter 4 (page 48).

Part of General Hall's complacency regarding terrain might have stemmed from a lack of detailed, large-scale maps. Without such maps, his knowledge of the ground he was asking his troops to capture was inadequate. Robert Ross Smith accurately described "the state of mapping of the [Philippine] islands . . . nothing short of lamentable."[4] ZigZag Pass does not look formidable on the 1:50,000 scale maps General Hall and all units except the 149th and 152nd Regiments used. Subic Bay had been under United States control since the turn of the century. The American plan for withdrawing into Bataan in 1941-42 depended on holding ZigZag Pass until all troops had passed through the Dinalupihan-Layac Junction bottleneck. It seems incomprehensible that terrain studies of the area had not been made and more detailed maps had not been produced before the war. If such were available in 1945, they evidently were not accessible to XI Corps or to Eighth Army, which staged the Zambales Operation. Eighth Army engineers reported receiving 279,350 maps airlifted from Hollandia for distribution to the units involved in the Zambales Operation. It is amazing that none of these maps gave a detailed picture of ZigZag Pass.

Despite the short time available for planning the Zambales Operation, the 91st Photo Reconnaissance Wing had flown 22 missions before the landing 29 January and had distributed 33,000 prints of 1:25,000 scale photo maps to Eighth Army and XI Corps. Unfortunately, none of these maps covered the ZigZag Pass area. No aerial photographs of ZigZag Pass were available to frontline troops until 4 February after the battle had begun. If they had been available during the planning stage, photomaps of 1:25,000 scale of the battle area might have alerted General Hall to the potential dangers in ZigZag Pass.[5]

General MacArthur had a ready and reasonable answer to the question of maps. His Chief of Staff, Lieutenant General Richard K. Sutherland, wrote to General Krueger, "The Philippines campaign, and the New Guinea campaign before it, were planned with a full realization of the inadequacy and unreliability of existing maps of the operational areas." He went on to say, "In each operation where insufficient time was allowed for compilation of adequate maps from aerial photography, there have been tactical advantages in early attack, which have outweighed the unsatisfactory mapping situation."[6]

✸　　✸　　✸

XI Corps grossly underestimated the number and quality of the Japanese troops defending the pass. The tough and well-trained 39th Infantry and elements of the 10th Division Artillery and Engineers had slipped into Bataan undetected by aerial reconnaissance and reported in only a general way by Philippine guerrillas. The air attack on the 2nd and

3rd Battalion landing site near Limay 16 December 1944 was apparently not reported or the significance of the Japanese landing not realized.

The XI Corps staff also underestimated the ability of the Japanese to turn the inherent defensive features of the ZigZag terrain into a veritable fortress within six weeks. These defenses were so strong that the attacking troops assumed the Japanese had spent the last three years building them! It is a tribute to Japanese skill in construction and camouflage that the fortifications were not observed and bombed prior to the start of the Zambales Operation. American air power had been established on Mindoro shortly after the 15 December 1944 landing and at Lingayen Gulf after the landing 9 January 1945. Daily reconnaissance and bombing missions were commonplace over Bataan for at least a month prior to the XI Corps landing 29 January—but apparently not over ZigZag Pass.

As to Japanese numerical strength, General Hall and his staff did not heed the guerrilla Colonel Merrill's estimate, made *after* the XI Corps landing, of possibly as many as 5,000 Japanese in the pass compared with the 900 XI Corps expected. It would seem that following such a report (even though it proved to be exaggerated), prudence would dictate caution. The initial attacking force (a regiment) against the Japanese MLR should have been enlarged to allow for the possibility of stronger enemy opposition than anticipated.

An officer of the 152nd Infantry summed up the frustrations of the attacking troops: "It seems to me General Hall missed a lot between the grades of major and major general. Why wasn't he better prepared for the Battle of ZigZag Pass?"[7]

Just as General Hall did not have accurate knowledge of the Japanese in ZigZag Pass, he did not know or ignored the true nature of his own troops. In November 1944, Headquarters SWPA planned for XI Corps to assist Sixth Army's Lingayen landing with a later landing at Vigan 120 miles farther north on the west coast of Luzon. The composition of XI Corps was to be the 32nd Infantry Division and the independent 112th Cavalry RCT. However, MacArthur or Krueger changed the composition of the corps to the 38th Division and the 34th RCT. The Vigan operation was scrubbed, and instead, MacArthur ordered the reconstituted XI Corps to land at San Antonio.

The reason for the change in units is not apparent from the records. A good guess would be that General Krueger, as the senior ground commander on Luzon, wanted the 32nd Division and not the untried 38th Division as reserve in his drive to Manila and for later operations in northern Luzon. Ostensibly, the combat-tested 34th RCT replaced the 112th RCT to help compensate XI Corps for the loss of the veteran 32nd

Division. However, 40 percent of the personnel in the rifle companies of the 34th were fresh from basic training and were to meet their units for the first time aboard-ship bound for the battle zone.

Several command and staff changes had also lowered the combat efficiency of the 34th. Colonel Jenna, the commander, was battle-tested, but lacked the verve, drive and overall leadership qualities of the previous commander, Colonel Aubrey S. Newman, still recovering from his serious wound on Leyte. The 1st Battalion commander, Lieutenant Colonel Oglesby, former battalion S-3, was seeing his first combat in his new position. His predecessor, the incomparable Thomas J. "Jock" Clifford, had taken over the 19th Infantry. Major Snavely, 2nd Battalion commander and former battalion S-3, had replaced the apt and experienced James Pearsall, who was stateside on leave. Both Oglesby and Snavely were combat veterans, but were new to the vital position of battalion commander. There were also new faces on the battalion and regimental staffs. Jenna used his only experienced battalion commander, Colonel Postlethwait, sparingly during the battle.

In short, General Hall was commanding an untried division and an RCT attempting to assimilate many untried replacements. In fighting the battle, General Hall made no allowance for the state of training or experience of his troops—not a criticism—but perhaps a flaw in judgment by the corps commander.

Another intangible—divisiveness—perhaps never far beneath the surface in many military operations, seemed more prevalent in ZigZag Pass. When men completely unknown to each other like the commanders and staffs of XI Corps, the 38th Division and the 34th RCT are suddenly thrown together to accomplish a task, friction is likely to develop. The "this is the way we do it" syndrome emerges to stifle or at least impede teamwork. It takes time to build confidence in each other and for a spirit of camaraderie to evolve. There just wasn't time for the commanders and their staffs to overcome this human tendency "to do it my way" before the troops came face-to-face with a determined enemy in a life or death struggle.

In the field of tactics, General Hall, at least in the early stages of the campaign, seemed wedded to the rigid concept of a one-regiment attack. This method worked well at first against weak opposition as the 34th raced into Olongapo and the 152nd began its move against defenses General Hall believed to be an Outpost Line of Resistance. One regiment was totally inadequate once the attackers reached the horseshoe. Not until the 34th Infantry was fully bloodied was General Hall convinced that two regiments were necessary on the main line to break the Japanese grip on the horseshoe-hairpin area.

From the start, there was a curious neglect of the long ridge sloping into the "2" on the left of the American approach route along Highway 7. Curious, because an age-old infantry axiom says, "take the high ground first." We cannot blame General Hall entirely for this neglect.

General Jones, and, in turn, Colonel Stillwell and Colonel Jenna, failed to appreciate the value of this dominating ridge the Japanese called Mount Koko. Its true strength and importance came to light only after the 152nd and then the 34th tried in vain to assail the ridge from the horseshoe area after being halted on the road. Koko was reduced only after the 1st Battalion 152nd, in its patrolling to support the 34th on 3 February, found a way to the top and attacked from the west along the ridgeline.

An alteration of the original plan for 1 February might have produced different results. Let us assume that both the 152nd and the 34th had been ordered on 1 February to prepare for an attack with one regiment south, the other north of the road. It would not be unreasonable to expect that the regimental commanders, with only half instead of all the battlefield to consider, would take the high ground first in their areas—Mount Koko to the north and Mount Kosaku (Familiar Peak) to the south. All the key features of the battlefield can be seen from Koko; Kosaku is the highest point on the battlefield. The outcome might have been more favorable for General Hall had he attacked along the flanks at first, taking the high ground, and dominating the battlefield from the start. But, in the interests of speed, he chose to attack head-on along the highway, with costly and time-consuming results.

In Pacific operations of this size, four regiments of infantry were usually employed and rotated: three for maneuver and attack and one for reserve and guarding supply lines. With the 151st in reserve, Hall was content to permit first the 152nd and then the 34th to attack east separately and independently. After the 152nd had been so easily repulsed on 1-2 February, it would seem that reinforcement of the 152nd by the 34th was in order, rather than replacement as was actually the case.

Both these regiments were in position to begin the attack together on 1 February while the 149th was getting into position and starting its maneuver around the left flank. Why withhold the 34th when the 151st was serving adequately as a reserve and guard for communications? We can only speculate that the results would have been far different and more favorable for the Americans had Hall used two regiments to attack abreast in the pass at the outset.

Attacking with two regiments on either side of the road would have lessened the effects of another vexing problem—congestion caused by relieving one regiment with another. All troops at the front could be supplied using only the one road—Highway 7, a narrow, winding passage in need of serious repair. Normal transportation of ammunition, rations, medical supplies and evacuation of casualties clogged the road. Add two marching regiments on 3 February, one going forward, the other moving to the rear, and chaos resulted. The Japanese took full advantage of the chaos with a surprising artillery and mortar barrage when the 34th relieved the 152nd.

In an overall assessment of the battle, Major Mangold, commander of the 3rd Battalion 152nd Infantry, complained that for the first six days there were no boundaries designated, no objectives or zones of action specified. His only orders were to continue the attack to the front (east). It seemed to Mangold that "they (higher headquarters) were trying to break through the pass by brute strength alone, giving no attention to maneuver. They piled up three and four battalions along the road to await commitment when there was room for only one."[8]

Ironically, it was the pervading concept in General Jones's plan of 4 February (see Chapter 12, pages 160-161) that was finally used in subduing the Japanese. Jones advocated assigning definite objectives (he called them "centers of resistance") for battalions to seize and hold. He started 3 February by assigning Mount Koko to the 1st Battalion 152nd. The battalion's persistent attacks on 4-5 February led to Major Ogawa's withdrawal the night of 5 February. Later the battalions of the 151st and 152nd, singly or in concert, 8-11 February, gradually broke the Japanese centers of resistance on Kita, Kasuga, Minami, the northern half of Ege, Shinshu and Fumetsu.

Regarding employment of artillery, the reluctance to use it has been well documented. Certainly by 2 February the artillery was fully emplaced in the dry rice paddies northeast of Olongapo and prepared to bring down concentrated fire on any part of the battlefield. But with General Hall's scenario of a frontal attack with bare-bones artillery support determined at the outset, it was not until 8 February with General Chase in command that a massive artillery bombardment took place. This barrage did not lead to an immediate breakthrough, but did lead to significant advances over the next three days.

On 6 February, General Hall told General Jones to "get his patrols out and find out what he wanted to shoot at [with his artillery]." How differently the battle might have gone if the patrolling had been done on 1-2

February, as General Jones wished, followed by a massive bombardment and two-regiment attack on both sides of the road on 3 February. Instead, the frontal, pell-mell, one-regiment push along the highway dictated by Hall was the only expedient left to Jones in order to comply with the corps commander's insistence on speed.

In defense of General Hall, he may have been uncertain of his supply of artillery ammunition. The ammunition was originally unloaded on 29 January at San Antonio. When the campaign progressed much more rapidly than expected, six different supply points had to be established as the troops advanced. The shortage of transportation hampered the displacement forward. No acute shortages of ammunition are mentioned in the unit journals, although artillery ammunition was rationed for two or three days following the heavy expenditure on 8 February awaiting arrival of the first re-supply ship.[9]

In the use of that other form of artillery—air power—General Hall cannot be faulted. Although planes from Mindoro and Lingayen roamed the skies of the Bataan Peninsula at will during the ZigZag battle, General Hall did not call for their support. They were used only to bomb and strafe areas away from the battlefield devoid of friendly troops. Hall was content to wait until his engineers completed repair of San Marcelino Airfield on 5 February. Then bombs and napalm started falling on the Japanese in ZigZag Pass the next day. Air power from San Marcelino undoubtedly hastened the Japanese demise.

There were no reported American casualties from air support, a tribute to General Hall's wise decision not to call for close support missions to aid the attacking troops. Mishaps to infantrymen from friendly air in World War II occurred under the best conditions of infantry-air cooperation. There were enough miscarried actions in the ZigZag Pass battle without chancing the serious casualties and demoralizing effect of a mislaid bomb on front line troops.

One of the cardinal rules of warfare, expounded by many great captains, is: "One can never be too strong at the crucial point of attack." General Hall had four sources of firepower available at ZigZag Pass: infantry, artillery, tanks and air power. He probably utilized his available resources of tanks and air power to maximum advantage, but was slow to employ his personnel and artillery. However, he apparently overlooked another potential source of enormous firepower: naval gunfire.

There are many references in Japanese accounts of the battle of receiving gunfire from warships anchored in Subic Bay. The Japanese could observe warships in the bay and it was natural to conclude they were supporting the ground troops. Men of B Company 152nd Infantry even swear that a naval gunfire officer accompanied a patrol on Mount Koko on 3 February and actually directed a salvo at a Japanese position.[10]

The available American records refute this claim. None of the army records mentions naval gunfire at ZigZag Pass, but warships were definitely anchored in Subic Bay during the battle. Destroyer *Young* was anchored 1-13 February during all the critical days of the battle. Destroyer *Luce,* 3-4 February; destroyers *Picking* and *Wickes,* 2-4 February and 7-13 February; cruisers *Hopewell* and *Phoenix,* 7-13 February; and cruiser *Denver,* 9-13 February, were all in Subic Bay at these times. It is not inconceivable that General Hall could have called for and gotten naval support to augment his strength at his "crucial point of attack." However, an examination of these ships' logs for the dates listed above reveal some sporadic firing at suspected Japanese gunboats in the bay but no salvos into ZigZag Pass. The Japanese expected these ships to fire on them; why didn't they?[11]

The attack of the 7th Cavalry Regiment of the 1st Cavalry Division in an area southeast of Manila on 7-9 May 1945 shows what can be achieved with thorough reconnaissance and heavy air and artillery concentrations that were not present initially at ZigZag Pass.

The Japanese were well dug-in at Kapatalin Sawmill located in hilly, dense jungle terrain at a horseshoe-shaped bend on Route 455. The ground and defenses bore striking resemblance, except on a smaller scale, to the horseshoe in ZigZag Pass. Perhaps the 38th Division's experience at the ZigZag had been shared among the troops on Luzon and lessons had been learned. The 7th Cavalry did not attack until it had obtained a complete picture of the Japanese defenses from captured documents and patrol actions. Then napalm and artillery laid bare the terrain at the sawmill, air and artillery bombardments reduced the bulk of the defenses to rubble and four artillery battalions were in position to provide extremely close support for the attack.

The cavalry's attack on 7 May overran the defenses by mid-afternoon 9 May. The 7th Cavalry killed some 350 Japanese in the area from 7 through 9 May; almost all of the rest of the original 650 defenders of the sawmill area had been killed by the air and artillery bombardments. The 7th Cavalry lost 4 men killed and 17 wounded, and attached guerrillas lost 2 killed and 4 wounded.[12]

"Not every operation can go according to plan and expectation . . ."[13] Robert Ross Smith accurately summarized the Battle of ZigZag Pass. But the battle was not unique in this respect. It is this writer's opinion that any battle dissected as closely as this one will show that few battles "go according to plan and expectation." The "fog of war" is ever present and plays no favorites. The bravery and élan of the American GI and the ultimate weight of American matériel in ZigZag Pass overcame flaws in leadership and insured final American victory.

Chapter 23
NOTES

(1) Schoonover, Major James F., *The Operations of the 3rd Battalion 152nd Infantry in Zig Zag Pass, Luzon, 29 Jan.-14 Feb. 1945*, Advanced Infantry Officers Course, 1947-1948, p. 18-19

(2) Table of Organization and Equipment No. 7-11, War Department, Washington 25, D.C., 26 February 1944.

(3) Smith, Robert Ross, *Triumph in the Philippines*, p. 330. (See Appendix B: American Casualties.)

(4) *Ibid.,* p. 704.

(5) Report of the Commanding General Eighth Army on the Nasugbu and Bataan Operations, Office of the Chief of Military History, p. 94-95, p. 112;
Schoonover, *The Operations of the 3rd Battalion 152nd Infantry,* p. 8.

(6) Dod, Karl C., *The Corps of Engineers: The War Against Japan*, p. 608

(7) Brewer, Major Kenneth W., Exec Off 3rd Battalion 152nd Infantry, letter to author, 19 December 1990.

(8) Schoonover, *The Operations of the 3rd Battalion 152nd Infantry,* p. 18.

(9) Eighth Army AAR, p. 117.

(10) Interview by author with Robert S. Maraman, 1st Sergeant B Company 152nd Infantry, 27 July 1990.

(11) National Archives, Washington, D.C.

(12) Smith, *Triumph*, p. 418.

(13) *Ibid.,* p. 330.

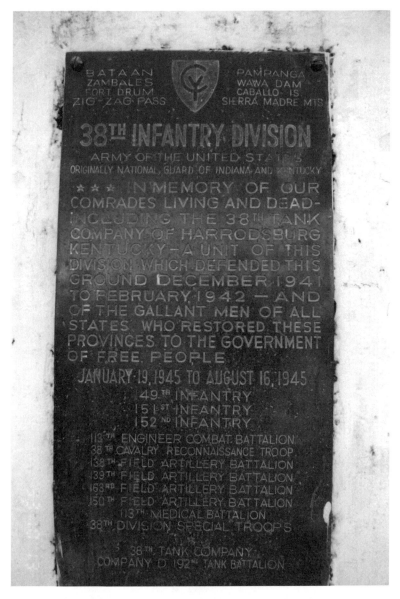

Plaque erected by 38th Division at Layac Junction

ABBREVIATIONS

AAA	Anti-Aircraft Artillery	GI	Government Issue (sometimes used as designation of soldiers in general)
AAR	After Action Report		
AKA	Attack Cargo Ship		
APA	Attack Transport	HE	High Explosive
APD	Fast Destroyer Transport	HMG	Heavy Machine Gun
		HQ	Headquarters
Arty	Artillery	IGH	Imperial General Headquarters
BAR	Browning Automatic Rifle		
		IJA	Imperial Japanese Army
Brig. Gen.	Brigadier General		
BLT	Battalion Landing Team	Inf.	Infantry
		Jg.	Junior Grade
Bn.	Battalion	KIA	Killed in Action
Cal	Caliber	LCVP	Landing Craft, Vehicles and Personnel
Capt.	Captain		
Comdr.	Commander		
CG	Commanding General	LD	Line of Departure
Co	Company	LMG	Light Machine Gun
CO	Commanding Officer	LST	Landing Ship, Tank
CP	Command Post	LSV	Japanese equivalent of American LST
Cpl.	Corporal		
C/S	Chief of Staff	Lt.	Lieutenant
Div	Division	M-1	Garand Rifle (standard armament for American infantryman)
EM	Enlisted Man or Men		
Exec	Executive Officer		
F.A.	Field Artillery		
FO	Forward Observer	Maj.	Major
F.O.	Field Order	Maj. Gen.	Major General
G-2	Intelligence Unit or Officer of Division and Higher	MG	Machine Gun
		MIA	Missing in Action
		MLR	Main Line of Resistance
G-3	Plans and Operations Unit or Officer of Division and Higher		
		M/Sgt.	Master Sergeant
		Mt	Mount
Gen.	General	NCO	Non-Commissioned Officer
GHQ	General Headquarters		

OCS	Officer Candidate School		Sgt.	Sergeant
			Sig	Signal
Off	Officer		SPM	Self-Propelled Mount
Pfc.	Private First Class		S/Sgt.	Staff Sergeant
Plat	Platoon		SWPA	Southwest Pacific Area
Prov	Provisional			
PSH	Portable Surgical Hospital		T/4	Technician Fourth Grade (equivalent of sergeant)
Pvt.	Private			
PW	Prisoner of War		T/5	Technician Fifth Grade (equivalent of corporal)
QM	Quartermaster			
RCT	Regimental Combat Team			
			TD	Tank Destroyer
Regt	Regiment		TO&E	Table of Organization and Equipment
Ret	Retired			
S-2	Intelligence Unit or Officer of Battalion or Regiment		T/Sgt.	Technical Sergeant (Platoon Sergeant)
			USMA	United States Military Academy
S-3	Plans and Operations Unit or Officer of Battalion or Regiment		WIA	Wounded in Action
			W.O.	Warrant Officer
			WP	White Phosphorous

APPENDIX A
ORDER of BATTLE

IMPERIAL JAPANESE ARMY

Nagayoshi Detachment:
Colonel Sanenobu Nagayoshi Commanding

North Garrison Unit
(Zig Zag Pass)

HQ 39th Infantry Regiment (Mt Kongo)
Major Takenori Kashiwagi (Exec)

2/3 5th Co. 2nd Battalion (HQ Guard)	*1st Lt. Tetsuo Yamamoto*
1st Platoon	*2nd Lt. Kazuo Yamana*
2nd Platoon	*2nd Lt. Sadao Itahashi*
Operations Company	*1st Lt. Kazuichi Nishiyama*
1st Platoon	*1st Lt. Akira Nakano*
2nd Platoon	*2nd Lt. Shoici Ohashi*

3rd Battalion (Mt Koko)
Major Hironori Ogawa

Headquarters Company	*1st Lt. Hiroshi Okeguchi (Exec)*
9th Company	*1st Lt. Yoshio Shinfune*
1st Platoon	*1st Lt. Kyokai Sunami*
2nd Platoon	*2nd Lt. Shozo Nakano*
3rd Platoon	*W.O. Hitoshi Takao*
10th Company	*1st Lt. Masanobu Miyazaki*
1st Platoon	*2nd Lt. Ryuchi Koujitani*
2nd Platoon	*2nd Lt. Yoshimitsu Shimizu**
3rd Platoon	*W.O. Taro Yamada*

11th Company	*1st Lt. Ukichi Ogata*
1st Platoon	*2nd Lt. Momoyo Jyohoji*
2nd Platoon	*2nd Lt. Takeshi Sasaki*
3rd Platoon	*W.O. Ichiro Sakai*

HMG Co (12-30-cal)
1st Lt. Kiyotaka Kato

1st Platoon	*2nd Lt. Akira Koyama*
2nd Platoon	*2nd Lt. Masanao Kobayashi**
3rd Platoon	*W.O. Kazuichi Ishihara*

Battalion Gun Platoon (2-70-mm)	*2nd Lt. Yoneji Yanase*
1/2 Regimental AT Company (2-37-mm)	*Captain Masaaki Ichinose*
2nd Platoon (2-37-mm)	*2nd Lt. Hiroshi Abe*
Chief Director	*W.O. Shigeru Uwane*
1/2 Regimental Heavy Weapons Company	*1st Lt. Katsutaro Yuasa*
Gun Platoon (2-75-mm)	*M/Sgt Masafumi Kanechika*
Mortar Platoon (2-90mm)	*M/Sgt Masatoshi Fujimoto*
Platoon Regimental Signal Company	*2nd Lt. Heiji Masai**
Platoon 6th Company 10th F.A. (2-105-mm)	*2nd Lt. Shigeo Otani*
Platoon 2nd Company 10th Engineers	*2nd Lt. Akio Nakamura*
6th Co. 2nd Provisional Inf. Bn. (Nouchi)	*1st Lt. Iwao Sakura*
Olongapo Navy Garrison	*Lt. (jg) Chusaku Ito*
Oda Platoon (Olongapo Engineers	
and shipyard workers)	*2nd Lt. _____ Oda*

1st Provisional Infantry Battalion
Major Takao Nakayama

Headquarters Company	
1st Company	*Capt. Yuichiro Nagata*
2nd Company	
Platoon 4th Company 10th Tank Regiment	*1st Lt. Keuichi Araki*

Central Garrison Unit
(7 kilometers NE of Bagac)

2nd Battalion
Major Shozo Yamamoto

Headquarters Company — *1st Lt. Keizaburo Maruo (Exec)*
  3rd Platoon 5th Company — *W.O. Tsutau Fujiki*
6th Company — *Capt. Koji Munemasa*
  1st Platoon — *2nd Lt. Shinichi Imoto*
  2nd Platoon — *2nd Lt. Seiitsu Ikuta**
  3rd Platoon — *W.O. Yuhei Ito*

2/3 HMG Company (8-30-cal) — *1st Lt. Goro Mukaida*
  1st Platoon — *1st Lt. Toshibumi Ayuzawa*
  3rd Platoon — *2nd Lt. Nobuyoshi Hidaka**
Battalion Gun Platoon (2-70-mm) — *1st Lt. Yoshito Tanaka*
1/2 Regiment AT Company (2-37-mm)
  1st Platoon — *1st Lt. Yasuo Hirano*
Platoon Regimental Gun Company
  (2-75-mm) — *1st Lt. Akira Kobayashi*
Platoon Regimental Signal Company — *Sergeant Sueichi Shimada*
Platoon 2nd Co 10th Engineers — *2nd Lt. _____ Kawazu*
2nd Company, 359th Independent
Infantry Battalion, 105th Division — *1st Lt. Yasuo Arai*

South Garrison Unit
(Mariveles-Cabcaben-Orion)

At Mariveles:

2nd Company (plus 1 MG Platoon) 1st Prov. Infantry Battalion (Ichinosawa)	*1st Lt. _____ Saisho*
Regiment Signal Company (less 2 Platoons)	_____
Platoon 2nd Company 10th Engineers	_____
Platoon 6th Company 10th F.A. (2-105mm)	*1st Lt. Motoyuki Nasu (Co. Cmdr.)*
3rd Platoon 7th Company 2nd Battalion	*W.O. Yoshinobu Matsubara*

(Above two units under command 31st Base Sector Cmdr)

At Orion:

2nd Platoon HMG Co. 2nd Bn. (4-30-cal)	*1st Lt. Isao Sugahara*
7th Company 2nd Battalion	*1st Lt. Shizuo Hashimoto*
1st Platoon	*2nd Lt. Shinichiro Takeda*
2nd Platoon	*2nd Lt. Kazuo Murakami**

Personnel (Approximate):

North Garrison Unit:	2111
Central Garrison Unit:	1124
South Garrison Unit:	658

Total: 3893

*Probational Officer. *"Promoted" to 2nd Lt. by author because there was no similar rank in the Army of the United States.*

ARMY OF THE UNITED STATES

(partial list)

XI CORPS:
Maj. Gen. Charles P. Hall Commanding

Chief of Staff	Brig. Gen. John A. Elmore
G-2 (Intelligence)	Col. John W. Patton
G-3 (Operations)	Col. Charles S. Monteith, Jr.

38th Infantry Division
Maj. Gen. Henry L. C. Jones Commanding
Maj. Gen. William C. Chase (7 February)

Assistant CO for Infantry	*Brig. Gen. Roy W. Easley*
Assistant CO for Artillery	*Brig. Gen. William Spence*
Chief of Staff	*Col. Albert J. Hastings*
G-2 (Intelligence)	*Col. Robert J. Wilson*
G-3 (Operations)	*Col. Alexander G. Kirby*

149th Infantry Regiment
Col. Winfred G. Skelton

Executive Officer	*Lt. Col. Elbert T. Mackey*
1st Battalion	*Lt. Col. Arthur C. Bonnycastle*
2nd Battalion	*Lt. Col. Silas B. Dishman*
3rd Battalion	

151st Infantry Regiment
Col. Ralf C. Paddock

Executive Officer	*Lt. Col. Norman L. Thompson*
1st Battalion	*Maj. Robert Stewart*
2nd Battalion	*Lt. Col. L. Robert Mottern*
3rd Battalion	*Lt. Col. William L. Funkhouser*
	Maj. Robert King (11 February)

152nd Infantry Regiment
Col. Robert L. Stillwell
Lt. Col. Jesse E. McIntosh (2 Feb.)
Col. Washington M. Ives (11 Feb.)

Executive Officer	*Lt. Col. Jesse E. McIntosh*
1st Battalion	*Lt. Col. Delbert D. Cornwell*
2nd Battalion	*Lt. Col. Charles H. Rice (WIA)*
	Major John Byus (10 Feb.)
3rd Battalion	*Major Harold B. Mangold*

38th Division Artillery
Brig. Gen. William Spence Commanding

138th F.A. Battalion (105-mm)	*Lt. Col. Walter Calvert*
139th F.A. Battalion (105-mm)	*Lt. Col. Carl DeBard*
163rd F.A. Battalion (105-mm)	*Lt. Col. Doyle C. Skelton*
150th F.A. Battalion (155-mm)	
11th F.A. Battalion (155-mm)	*Lt. Col. Joseph H. Hodges Jr.*
(24th Infantry Division)	
63rd F.A. Battalion (105-mm)	*Lt. Col. Thomas Long*
(24th Infantry Division)	

34th Regimental Combat Team
Col. William W. Jenna Commanding

34th Infantry Regiment	*Col. William W. Jenna*
Executive Officer	*Lt. Col. Chester A. Dahlen*
	(WIA 4 Feb)
1st Battalion	*Lt. Col. Charles E. Oglesby*
	(WIA 4 Feb)
	Maj. Carl O. Mann (4 Feb)
2nd Battalion	*Maj. Harry L. Snavely*
3rd Battalion	*Lt. Col. Edward M. Postlethwait*
63rd F.A. Battalion (105-mm)	*Lt. Col. Thomas Long*

APPENDIX B
AMERICAN CASUALTIES

A strange phenomenon of any battle is the considerable difference in killed and wounded compiled by the units involved. The Battle of ZigZag Pass is no exception. XI Corps, in its daily summaries, reported a total of 1,044 American casualties. The casualties reported separately by the four participating infantry regiments alone add up to 1,286. The total figure given in the official history is "about 1,400." This figure may be as accurate as any that can be found. The 1,286 figure includes only infantry casualties. If casualties of supporting units, which are not available now and were probably difficult to accumulate at the time, are added, the final total should be close to 1,400.

Since the large percentage of casualties occurs in the infantry, the care with which each of the regiments reported its casualties is crucial to obtaining an accurate figure. The 34th Infantry kept excellent records. In addition to the number of casualties reported in the journal, the regiment also listed casualties by name and company after each campaign after MIAs were accounted for. The regiment noted the hospital, clearing station or collecting company to which each wounded man was evacuated, so we can assume that no slightly wounded soldiers were included. The location of the cemetery and gravesites is given for those men KIA or mortally wounded.

In contrast, the 149th and 151st regimental records are scanty, and the 149th's are inconsistent. No regimental journal or After Action Report of the 149th could be found, and only the 2nd and 3rd Battalions kept daily logs. Since the 3rd Battalion was not engaged with the enemy, the only casualties that can be given for the regiment are those of the 2nd Battalion. But even these are at variance. For example, the 2nd Battalion 149th Infantry journal for 16 February 1945 contains these notations:

"*0830: Battalion departed perimeter and moved east on Highway 7 to the temporary cemetery.*

"*0900: A short service, led by Chaplain Daniel H. Frederick, including a three volley salute, held in the honor and memory of the 27*

men of the 2d Battalion, 1 arty liason [sic] pilot, & 1 man from the 1st
Battalion, 149th, who had died in the battle for ZigZag Pass."

The 2nd Battalion journal reports by name 32 men killed, 5 more than the 27 honored at the memorial service. No record of the total 1st Battalion casualties could be found.

Neither the 151st Infantry journal nor its S-2 journal reported casualties. The total 151st casualties are given in its After Action Report, but are not summarized day-by-day. The 152nd Infantry casualties are given in its journal, but are not broken down by battalion or company.

Several factors produce the discrepancies and inconsistencies cited above:

1. What is a casualty? Is a casualty anyone who sheds blood as a result of enemy action and, therefore, receives a Purple Heart, even though the wound is slight and the soldier immediately returns to the front? Or is a casualty one who passes through the battalion aid station to the regimental aid station and perhaps to the division clearing station or a hospital, thus missing some of the front line action? There seemed to be no consistent policy on this subject among the units engaged.

2. Time. A day was usually construed to mean the 24-hour period prior to 1800 of the day in question. There is no way of knowing on which day casualties that occurred in the afternoon were recorded. For example, casualties that occurred in the afternoon might not be recorded until after 1800, which would be counted in the next day's total. A battalion might record a casualty one day and its regiment might record the same casualty the next day resulting in a conflicting total of either day's casualties.

3. Missing In Action (MIA). If a soldier was unaccounted for at the end of a day's engagement, he was listed as MIA. In most cases, he would return to his unit later or be found dead. But casualty figures were usually reported only once—at the end of the day—and not corrected, if at all, until after the end of the campaign.

4. Pressure. Men in the heat of battle have much more on their minds than recording accurate casualty figures. The fact that most units, and certainly those in ZigZag Pass, made a conscientious effort to keep accurate records is highly commendable.

Daily Reports of Infantry Casualties

DATE	34TH	149TH	151ST	152ND	TOTAL
31 Jan	1-3-0[1]	0-1-0		3-5-1	4-9-1
1 Feb	0-2-0			14-43-1	14-45-1
2 Feb	1-6-0			5-26-0	6-32-0
3 Feb	4-39-8	0-1-0		4-26-1	8-66-9
4 Feb	41-131-6			0-22-0	41-153-6
5 Feb	21-58-0			9-33-0	30-91-0
6 Feb				10-19-0	10-19-0
7 Feb			(unknown)	17-110-2	17-110-2
8 Feb		18-20-0	(unknown)	4-22-0	22-42-0
9 Feb		4-21-0	(unknown)	8-15-0	12-36-0
10 Feb			(unknown)	5-35-0	5-35-0
11 Feb		4-9-0	(unknown)	3-23-0	7-32-0
12 Feb		3-8-0		16-90-1	19-98-1
13 Feb		2-8-0		7-31-0	9-39-0
14 Feb		1-2-0		6-8-0	7-10-0
15 Feb		0-1-0			0-1-0
Total	68-239-14	32-71-0		111-508-6	211-818-20
Total (including 151st Inf.)			34-202-1[2]		245-1020-21
Total by Regt.	321[3]	103	237	625	1286

[1] KIA-WIA-MIA

[2] Casualties of the 151st Infantry were not compiled each day, but totaled at the end of the campaign. Elements of the regiment were in action five days, but most of the casualties occurred on 8, 9 and 10 February.

[3] In its After Action Report, the 34th Infantry listed casualties of 61 KIA and 258 WIA (evacuated) totaling 319. To obtain the number of casualties for the 34th RCT, 3 KIA and 5 WIA of the 63rd F.A., and 2 KIA and 7 WIA of the 24th Medical Detachment should be added, for a total of 336.

APPENDIX C
TABULATION OF FIRING

38th Division Artillery
29 January-14 February 1945
(# of Rounds)

DATE	PREP[1]	I&H[2]	DF[3]	T/O[4]	TOTAL	GR.TOTAL
30 Jan						
105-mm		59			59	59
31 Jan						
105-mm		54			54	54
1 Feb						
105-mm	174			865	1,039	1,039
2 Feb						
105-mm		1511	123	410	2,044	
155-mm		163	27	235	425	2,469
3 Feb						
105-mm		239	211	297	747	
155-mm	142	71	106		319	1,066
4 Feb						
105-mm	589	296	11	1,244	2,140	
155-mm	150	100		314	564	2,704
5 Feb						
105-mm	255		804	877	1,936	
155-mm	248	220	430	559	1,457	3,393
6 Feb						
105-mm	2,105	234	219	1665	4,223	
155-mm		24		637	661	4,884
7 Feb						
105-mm	192	12	87	3,982	4,273	
155-mm	926	88	7		1,021	5,294

DATE	PREP[1]	I&H[2]	DF[3]	T/O[4]	TOTAL	GR.TOTAL
8 Feb						
105-mm	13,978		12	1466	15,456	
155-mm	2,941	104	63	65	3,173	18,629
9 Feb						
105-mm	292		552	841	1,685	
155-mm	116			98	214	1,899
10 Feb						
105-mm	232	932	674	802	2,640	
155-mm		138		105	243	2,883
11 Feb						
105-mm		109	778	199	1,086	
155-mm	154	368		299	821	1,907
12 Feb						
105-mm	987	188	102	204	1,481	
155-mm	413	155		390	958	2,439
13 Feb						
105-mm	139		40	465	644	
155-mm	269	58		248	575	1,219
14 Feb						
105-mm	240				240	240
TOTAL						
105-mm	19,183	3,634	3,613	13,317	39,747	
155-mm	5,359	1,489	633	2,950	10,431	
GRAND TOTAL	24,542	5,123	4,246	16,267		**50,178**

[1] Preparatory Fires prior to attack.
[2] Interdiction & Harassing Fires
[3] Defensive Fires
[4] Targets of Opportunity

105-mm F.A. Battalions—63rd (starting 5 Feb.), 138th, 139th, 163rd.
155-mm F.A. Battalions—11th, 150th (does not include 983rd, "long tom" rifle).

APPENDIX D
JAPANESE SOURCES

The untiring efforts of the late Dr. David E. Evans, professor of Japanese and Far Eastern History at the University of Richmond, led to the Japanese sources. Dr. Evans located the final residential address of Colonel Nagayoshi (d. 1984) and initiated a correspondence in behalf of the author with his widow, Takako Nagayoshi. Mrs. Nagayoshi showed the correspondence to Hiyotaka Kato, commander of the 3rd Battalion 39th Infantry Machine Gun Company, during an annual regimental reunion in Himeji. Mr. Kato wrote to the author and began a correspondence and chain of events that resulted in tours of the battlefield by the author with Japanese participants in the battle and acquisition of Japanese writings on the battle:

1. The 800-page *History of the Himeji 39th Infantry Regiment*. Edited and published by the 39th Infantry Association. 1983. Containing many photographs, the narrative covers the entire history of the regiment from its establishment in 1898 until its disbandment in 1945. The last 200 pages are devoted to the regiment's move south from Manchuria and combat in Bataan in World War II.

2. *Record of the 3rd Battalion 39th Infantry Regiment in the "Big Asia War."* Hironori Ogawa. 1984. Major Ogawa wrote the original version of his memoirs at Mount Natib during the regiment's guerrilla warfare (March-August 1945) and updated the manuscript after the American history of the battle was published in 1963. He describes his original dispositions, the tenacious defense by his troops and his reasons for shifting units during the battle.

3. *How the Kato Company Fought: The Record of the 3rd Machine Gun Company, 39th Infantry Regiment*. Tamotsu Nagai, Editor. 1990. This is a 400-page book of memoirs of the survivors of the company. The narrative is rich with personal experiences and characterized by minute record-keeping and scholarly attention to detail.

4. *The Sho Army Operations, part 2: The Decisive Battle for Luzon.* Japan Defense Agency. 1972. Only seven pages of this 700-page volume are devoted to ZigZag Pass, but they contain information about the Nagayoshi Detachment's dispositions on Bataan not given in any of the other publications.

5. Separate Monographs by participants:
    a. Masuda, Toshio, Machine gunner, 39th Infantry,
       A Soldier's Memories.
    b. Nagai, Tamotsu, 6 May 1994, *Chiamussu.*
    c. Nagai, Tamotsu, *The Battle at Taipei/Matsuyama Airport.*
    d. Yokoyama, Hasukazu, machine gunner, 39th Infantry,
       Memories of Chiamussu.

None of these publications mention the heroic and persistent defense by the airmen of the Nakayama Battalion in the East Pass. Mr. Nagai located one of the 15 survivors of the battalion, Yuichiro Nagata of Tokyo, a classmate of Hiyotaka Kato at the Military Academy. Nagata, a former commander of one of the companies of the Nakayama Battalion, provided the only account of the battalion's actions in the battle. By letter, he painfully, but graciously, "wrote what I did not want to recall" of his reminiscences of the fighting.

BIBLIOGRAPHY

Alden, John D. *U.S. Submarine Attacks During World War II*. Annapolis: Naval Institute Press, 1984.

Allen, Louis. *Burma: The Longest War 1941-1945*. New York: St. Martin's Press, 1984.

Anderson, Lt. Commander Gerald R. *Subic Bay From Magellan to Mt. Pinatubo*. Dagupan City, Luzon, Philippines: Lazar, 1991.

Barker, H. J. *Japanese Army Handbook 1939-1945*. New York: Hippocrene Books, Inc., 1979.

Belote, James H. and William M. *Corregidor: The Saga of a Fortress*. New York: Harper and Row, Publishers, 1967.

Bradley, General of the Army Omar N. *A Soldier's Story*. New York: Henry Holt and Company, 1951.

Brinson, Capt. Arthur. Cavalry Monograph: *The Battle of ZigZag Pass*, delivered at the Armored School, Fort Knox, KY, 5 May 1948.

Browne, Courtney. *Tojo: The Last Banzai*. New York: Holt, Rinehart and Winston, 1967.

Bruce, Robert. *The U.S. M-1 Garand Rifle*. Hampton, VA: Multi-Print, Inc., 1992.

Campbell, John D. and Harold P. Leinbaugh. *The Men of Company K*. New York: William Morrow and Company, Inc., 1985.

Cate, James Lea and Wesley Frank Craven. "The Pacific: Matterhorn to Nagasaki June 1944-August 1945." *The Army Air Forces in World War II*, Vol. V. Chicago: The University of Chicago Press, 1953.

Chase, Maj. General William C. *Front Line General*. Houston: Pacesetter Press, 1975.

Cook, Haruko Taya and Theodore F. *Japan at War: An Oral History*. New York: Thenen Press, 1992.

Coox, Alvin D. *Nomonhan: Japan Against Russia*. 2 Vols. Stanford, CA: Stanford University Press, 1985.

Daws, Gavan. *Prisoners of the Japanese: POWS of World War II in the Pacific*. New York: William Morrow and Company, Inc., 1994.

DeJesus, Ramon V. *Zambales*. Manila: Union Zambalena, 1990.

Dilley, Roy. *Japanese Army Uniforms and Equipment*. 1939-1945. London: Almark Publishing Co., 1970.

Dorn, Frank. *The Sino-Japanese War, 1937-41: From Marco Polo Bridge to Pearl Harbor*. New York: MacMillan Publishing Co., Inc., 1974.

Drea, Edward J. *MacArthur's Ultra: Codebreaking and the War Against Japan 1942-1945*. Lawrence, KS: University Press of Kansas, 1992.

_____ *Nomonhan: Japanese-Soviet Tactical Combat, 1939*. Leavenworth Papers No. 2, Combat Studies Institute, 1981.

Eichelberger, General Robert L. *Our Jungle Road to Tokyo*. New York: The Viking Press, 1950.

Evans, David C., Editor and Translator 2nd Edition. *The Japanese Navy in World War II*. Annapolis: Naval Institute Press, 1986.

Falk, Stanley L. *Bataan, the March of Death*. New York: W. W. Norton & Company, Inc., 1962.

_____ *Decision At Leyte*. New York: W. W. Norton & Company, Inc., 1966.

_____ *Seventy Days to Singapore*. New York: G. P. Putnam's Sons, 1976.

Fischer, Col. Robert T. *Indiana's Citizen Soldiers*, Military History Project. Indianapolis, 1980.

_____ *An Abbreviated History of the 38th Infantry Division at the 50th Anniversary of Activation in World War II*. Camp Shelby, MS, 21-22 June 1991.

Flanagan, Lt. General E. M., Jr. *Corregidor: The Rock Force Assault*. New York: Jove Books, 1989.

Forty, George. *M-4 Sherman*. Poole, New York, Sydney: Blandford Press, 1987.

Frank, Richard B. *Guadacanal*. New York: Random House, Inc., 1990.

Gunston, Bill. *An Illustrated Guide to German, Italian and Japanese Fighters of World War II*. New York: Arco Publishing, Inc., 1980.

_____ *An Illustrated Guide to Allied Fighters of World War II*. New York, Arco Publishers, Inc., 1981.

Halsey, Admiral of the Fleet William F. *Admiral Halsey's Story*. New York: McGraw-Hill Book Company, Inc., 1947.

Halstead, Murat. *The Story of the Philippines: The Eldorado of the Orient*. Chicago: Our Possessions Publishing Co., 1898.

Handbook on Japanese Military Forces. War Department Technical Manual TM-E 30-480. Washington: United States Government Printing Office, 1 Oct 1944.

Hayashi, Saburo. *Kogun: The Japanese Army in the Pacific War*. Quantico: The Marine Corps Association, 1959.

Headquarters, United States Army Japan. *Imperial Japanese Army in Manchuria 1894-1945*. Japanese Studies on Manchuria Vol. II., Foreign Histories Division, 1959.

Headquarters, Army Forces Far East, Japanese Monograph No. 77. *Preparations for Operations in Manchuria (Prior to 1943)*. Office of the Chief of Military History. Washington: Government Printing Office, 1954.

_____ Japanese Monograph No. 138. *Japanese Preparations for Operations in Manchuria January 1943-August 1945*. Office of the Chief of Military History. Washington: Government Printing Office, 1953.

Hogg, Ian V. *The Encyclopedia of Infantry Weapons in World War II*. New York: The Military Press, distributed by Crown Publishers Inc., 1977.

Hsiung, James C. and Steven I. Levine. *China's Bitter Victory: The War with Japan 1937-45*. Armonk, New York, London: M. E. Sharpe, Inc., 1992.

James, D. Clayton. *The Years of MacArthur*. 3 Vols. Boston: Houghton Mifflin Company, 1975.

Kenworthy, Lt. Col. Aubrey Saint. *The Tiger of Malaya: The Story of General Tomoyuki Yamashita and "Death March" General Masaharu Homma*. New York: Exposition Press, Inc., 1953.

Knox, Donald. *Death March: The Survivors of Bataan*. New York and London: Harcourt Brace Jovanovich, Publishers, 1981.

Kodansha. *Encyclopedia of Japan*. 1st Edition. Tokyo: Kodansha Ltd., 1983.

Krueger, General Walter, Jr. *From Down Under to Nippon: The Story of Sixth Army in World War II*. Washington: Combat Forces Press, 1953.

Luvass, Jay, Editor. *Dear Miss Em: General Eichelberger's War in the Pacific, 1942-1945*. Westport, CT: Greenwood Press, Inc., 1972.

MacArthur, General of the Army Douglas. *Reminiscences*. New York: McGraw-Hill Book Company, 1964.

_____ *Reports of General MacArthur, The Campaigns of MacArthur in the Pacific*, Reprint 1994, Vol. I.

_____ *Reports of General MacArthur, Japanese Operations in the Southwest Pacific Area*. Vol. II, Part II. Compiled from Japanese Demobilization Bureax Records.

MacDonald, Capt. Charles B. *Company Commander*. Washington: Infantry Journal Press, 1947.

Madej, W. Victor, Editor. *Japanese Armed Forces Order of Battle 1937-1945*. Vol. I. Allentown, PA: Game Marketing Company.

Manchester, William. *American Caesar: Douglas MacArthur 1880-1964*. Boston: Little Brown and Company, 1978.

Miyazaki, Kazunobu; Yoshikawa, Takehiko (Translator); Mann, B. David (Editor). *The Untold Story Behind the Battle of Bataan in 1945*. Translated and edited from *The History of the Himeji 39th Infantry Regiment 10th Division Imperial Japanese Army*, pages 592-686.

Montross, Lynn. *War Through the Ages*. New York: Harper and Brothers Publishers, 1960.

Morison, Rear Adm. Samuel Eliot. *History of United States Naval Operations in World War II*. Boston: Little, Brown and Company.

> Vol. III, *The Rising Sun in the Pacific, 1931-Apr 1942*. 1960
>
> Vol. VIII, *New Guinea and the Marianas, Mar 1944-Aug 1944*. 1960.
>
> Vol. XII, *Leyte, Jun 1944-Jan 1945*. 1958.
>
> Vol. XIII, *The Liberation of the Philippines: Luzon, Mindanao, the Visayas, Jun 1944-Jan 1945*. 1958.
>
> Vol. XIV, *Victory in the Pacific, 1945*. 1960.

Morrissey, Capt. George E., Surgeon 1st Battalion 34th Infantry. Diary.

Morton, Louis. *Military and Naval Preparations for the Defense of the Philippines During the War Scare of 1907*. Military Affairs. Summer 1949.

Nagai, Tamotsu, Editor. *How the Kato Company Fought: The Record of the 3rd Machine Company 39th Infantry Regiment*. 1990, p. 224.

O'Donnell, Michael J. and Sylvia, Stephen W. *Uniforms, Weapons and Equipment of the World War II GI*. Orange, VA: Moss Publications, 1982.

Polmar, Norman and Allen, Thomas B. *World War II America at War, 1941-1945*. New York: Random House, 1991.

Romulo, Carlos P. *My Brother Americans*. Garden City, NY: Doubleday, Doran and Company, Inc., 1945.

Schoonover, Maj. James F. *The Operations of the 3rd Battalion 152nd Infantry (38th Infantry Division) in ZigZag Pass, Luzon 29 January-14 February 1945*. Advanced Infantry Officers Course, 1947-1948, Fort Benning, GA. Monograph.

Smith, S. E., Editor. *The United States Navy in World War II*. New York: William Morrow & Company, Inc., 1966.

Stanley, Col. Roy M. II, USAF. *Prelude to Pearl Harbor*. New York: Charles Scribner's Sons, 1982.

Statements of Japanese Officials on World War II, Statement of Sanenobu Nagayoshi, 25 October 1948, General Headquarters Far East Command, p. 625.

Takaki, Ronald. *Strangers From a Different Shore: A History of Asian-Americans.* Boston, Toronto, London: Little, Brown and Company, 1989.

Taro Leaf, (24th Infantry Division Association Newsletter), Vol. 51, Issue #1, February 1997, p. 58.

Taylor, Lawrence. *A Trial of Generals: Homma, Yamashita, MacArthur.* South Bend, IN: Icarus Press, 1981.

Toland, John. *The Rising Sun.* New York: Random House, Inc., 1970.

United States Army in World War II. Washington: U. S. Government Printing Office.

The War in the Pacific

Appleman, Roy E., et al. *Okinawa: The Last Battle.* 1948

Cannon, M. Hamlin. *Leyte: The Return to the Philippines.* 1954.

Dod, Karl C. *The Corps of Engineers: The War Against Japan.* 1966.

Greenfield, Kent Robert, Palmer, Robert R., and Wiley, Bell I. *The Organization of Ground Combat Troops.* 1947.

Miller, John, Jr. *Guadacanal: The First Offensive.* 1949.

_____ *Cartwheel: The Reduction of Rabaul.* 1959

Milner, Samuel. *Victory in Papua.* 1957.

Morton, Louis. *The Fall of the Philippines.* 1953.

_____ *Strategy and Command: The First Two Years.* 1962.

Smith, Robert Ross. *The Approach to the Philippines.* 1953

_____ *Triumph in the Philippines.* 1963.

Valtin, Jean. *Children of Yesterday.* New York: The Reader's Press. 1946.

Villarin, Mariano. *We Remember Bataan and Corregidor: The Story of the American and Filipino Defenders of Bataan and Corregidor and Their Captivity.* Baltimore, MD: Gateway Press, Inc., 1990.

Walker, Stephen M. *The Operations of Company A, 151st Infantry in the Attack Through ZigZag Pass 8-11 February 1945.* Advanced Infantry Officers Course 1949-1950, Fort Benning, GA. Monograph.

Walters, Capt. Edward E. *The Operations of the 38th Infantry Division in the Landing at San Antonio-San Narciso Area and the Advance to Dinalupihan, 29 January-14 February 1945.* Advanced Infantry Officers Course, 1949-1950, Fort Benning, GA. Monograph.

Warner, Dennis and Peggy. *The Tide at Sunrise: A History of the Russo-Japanese War, 1904-1905.* New York: Charterhouse, 1974.

Whitman, Lt. Col. John W. *Bataan: Our Last Ditch, The Bataan Campaign, 1942*. New York: Hippocrene Books, 1990.

Wilson, Dick. *When Tigers Fight: The Story of the Sino-Japanese War 1937-1945*. New York: The Viking Press, 1982.

Wolfert, Ira. *American Guerrilla in the Philippines*. New York: Simon and Schuster, 1945.

INDEX

— A —

Abe, 2nd Lt Hiroshi: 60, 65-66, 68-70, 72

Adachi, Pfc Shigeo: 296

Adams, James L.: 68

Agaton, Crispina: 55

Aida, Sup Pvt Yujiro: 282

Aitape: 34-35

Akashi, 1st Lt: 176

Akiyama, Sup Pvt Kaichi: 282-283, 294

Allen, Pvt William F.: 68

American Forces

Armies

Sixth: 9, 31-35, 42, 55, 63, 73, 111, 152, 185, 188, 209, 275, 317

Eighth: 31-34, 41, 47, 59-60, 63, 111, 115, 217, 316

Battalions (Infantry)

1st 34th: 54-56, 65, 69, 71, 73, 98, 101, 108-109, 112, 115, 147-148, 150-151, 154-155, 159, 167-172, 174-175, 177-178, 191-192, 245, 274, 318

Secures trail junction on Highway 7, 31 January, 95-97

Attack on MLR at Mt Ege 3 February, 131-136, 139-140

Banzai attack on A Company, 140-141

Attack on MLR at Mt Ege 4 February, 149, 152-153

2nd 34th: 43, 49, 54-56, 65, 71, 101, 110, 115, 124, 142, 147-148, 161, 167-168, 174-175, 177-178, 183, 192, 199, 271, 318

Attack of E Company on MLR at "2" 4 February, 149-156

Attack of F and G Companies on MLR at Mt Koko 4 February, 156-159

HQ bombarded on 5 February, 169-172

3rd 34th: 55-56, 103, 115, 128, 131, 134, 142, 147-148, 153-154, 159, 168, 171, 175, 190, 192, 201, 274,

Skirmish at Lighthouse Point 30 January, 64-71

1st 149th: 36, 107-108, 119, 121, 131, 191-192, 202, 208, 215, 226, 280, 284, 293, 298

Attempts to establish contact with 3/151st 9 February, 243-244

2nd 149th: 101, 107, 177, 191, 202, 208, 273, 280, 284, 294

Attack against Nakayama Battalion 8 February, 225-227

Continuation of attack 9 February, 243-244

Continuation of attack 10 February, 261-263

Continuation of attack 14 February, 297-298

Continuation of attack 15 February, 298

3rd 149th: 36, 98, 101, 107, 177, 191, 244

1st 151st: 58, 199-200, 215, 233-235, 239, 251, 267-268

Movement into ZigZag Pass, 201-202

Attack on MLR at Mt Minami 8 February, 218-222

Continuation of attack 9 February, 237-238

Attack of A Company on Secondary Line at Mt Shinshu 10 February, 255-259

Continuation of A Company attack 11 February, 269-272

2nd 151st: 57, 63, 119-120, 199-201, 215, 221-223, 233-234, 238, 240, 244, 251-252, 254-255, 263, 267-269, 274

— B —

— C —

— Z —